I0828365

Paul's Letters

The Complete Portrait of the Messiah

Volume 6

Other volumes in The Complete Portrait of the Messiah series

Volume 1: *The Pentateuch*
Volume 2: *The Gospels*
Volume 3: *The Historical Books*
Volume 4: *Acts*
Volume 5: *The Wisdom Books*
Volume 6: *Paul's Letters*
Volume 7: *The Major Prophets*
Volume 8: *General Letters*
Volume 9: *The Minor Prophets*
Volume 10: *Revelation*

Also available from Time to Revive and Laura Kim Martin

reviveDAILY: A Devotional Journey from Genesis to Revelation, Year 1
reviveDAILY: A Devotional Journey from Genesis to Revelation, Year 2

Paul's Letters

The Complete Portrait of the Messiah

Volume 6

Kyle Lance Martin

Time to Revive and reviveSCHOOL

Richardson, Texas

Paul's Letters

Published in conjunction with Iron Stream Media, 100 Missionary Ridge, Birmingham, AL 35242.
IronStreamMedia.com

978-1-63204-105-0 (hardback)
978-1-63204-106-7 (eBook)

2 3 4 5—27 26 25 24

Dedication

Greetings friends and colaborers of the Lord Jesus Christ!

I am writing to you with an excitement that is beyond words. For I would like to dedicate this book to individuals like yourselves whose desire to grow closer to Jesus and go deeper in the Word of God brings such JOY to my heart. And my prayer for each one of you is that the Holy Spirit will reveal more of Himself to you in this in-depth time of studying the Word of God daily. Jesus said, "Blessed are those who hunger and thirst for righteousness, for they will be satisfied" (Matthew 5:6 NASB). So as you embark on this journey of studying each book of the Bible, may you experience a freshness and a fulfillment that can only come from the Spirit of God. You will have days that you won't want to wake up early and read. There will be moments when life throws you a situation that delays your personal devotional time with Him. But please press in and allow the Holy Spirit to strengthen your every step. This will allow you to exercise your faith muscles and walk out what you are learning in this. From my experience, obedience will bring education to life!

It will be quite a strenuous commitment, yet it's a part of an intentional strategy to equip the saints for His return. And your participation with reviveSCHOOL is a unique part of this preparation.

May the Lord receive all the glory, honor, and fame in this pursuit of righteousness.

Praying,
Dr. Kyle Lance Martin

Contents

WEEK 73

WEEK 74

WEEK 75

WEEK 76

WEEK 77

WEEK 78

WEEK 79

WEEK 80

WEEK 81

WEEK 82

reviveSCHOOL History and Introduction

In January of 2015, our ministry, Time to Revive, was invited from our home base in Richardson, Texas, to Goshen, Indiana, to help equip the local church to learn how to go out and share the gospel in their community. We called it reviveINDIANA. During this frigid first trip in January, our intention was to help facilitate a week of prayer and outreach as a form of training, which we hoped would lead to an intentional week of outreach later that year. Little did we know that God had other plans.

The week of prayer and outreach started with about 450 people from various churches in the community and, to our surprise, quickly swelled to over 3,000. And by the end of that first week, the Holy Spirit confirmed to a group of us, including local pastors, that the Time to Revive team should stay for 52 straight days! Imagine the phone calls we had to make to our spouses telling them we were going to stay a "little" longer.

Over the course of these seven weeks, the local church witnessed God move in mighty ways, and each person involved could tell you miraculous testimonies of how they witnessed, firsthand, how God was moving. The 52 days culminated on March 4 of that year where an estimated 10,000 people showed up to brave the cold temperatures and go out and share the love of Jesus Christ.

All the while, word of this was spreading throughout the state, and it led to the Time to Revive team being invited to seven different cities in Indiana over the course of the next seven months. We continued to witness the local body of believers in these various communities encouraged and equipped to continue to take out their faith and share with others. The gospel wasn't intended to stay only in the church building. Jesus commissioned each one of us to go and make disciples in our own Jerusalem, Judea, and Samaria and to the ends of the earth. Back in Goshen, the local body continued to go out regularly after those initial 52 days while keeping track of the days since that first amazing week. A couple of years later in 2017, the local believers invited our team to celebrate their 1,000th day of outreach in their community. It was during that time when a local man shared with us a dream he had, which led us to start a two-year Bible study in the community. Similar to the Apostle Paul as he taught 12 disciples in Ephesus to study the Word of God on a daily basis, Time to Revive's desire was to also provide in-depth teaching that would focus on where the Messiah is found in every book of the Bible from Genesis to Revelation. We knew this would deepen their commitment to sharing the gospel as well as deepen their relationship with the Lord and with those whom they were discipling.

> But when some became hardened and would not believe, slandering the Way in front of the crowd, he withdrew from them and met separately with the disciples, conducting discussions every day in the lecture hall of Tyrannus. —Acts 19:9

This local Bible study started with 12 men who signed up and committed to study the Word of God in a barn on a county road in Goshen, Indiana. And on January 1, 2018, we launched reviveSCHOOL with 54 men in this initial group. They studied the Scriptures daily, using the online resources, then gathered in the barn to discuss them in person. Each student studied the Bible daily using these resources:

- a Scripture reading plan to stay on track,
- a 29-minute teaching video (by Kyle Lance Martin, Indiana pastors, and TTR teachers),
- a devotion (written by Laura Kim Martin),
- reading guide questions to help facilitate discussion and critical thinking,
- lesson plans to summarize the daily teaching, and
- a painting of each book of the Bible by Mindi Oaten.

Upon the completion of the two-year study in the Word, Time to Revive celebrated over 200 students who had joined reviveSCHOOL with a graduation ceremony in January 2020. Plans were made for these individuals to take the Word and launch reviveSCHOOL groups not only in the United States but also throughout various nations. However, with worldwide travel restrictions due to the COVID-19 pandemic, this travel didn't happen. Thankfully, God had another plan, His plan was "above and beyond" all that Time to Revive could ask or think of (Ephesians 3:20–21).

With all the reviveSCHOOL materials already available online, the Holy Spirit spread the word to pastors and leaders of nations all throughout the world. Believers were hungry for biblically sound teaching and resources to grow closer to the Lord. As exemplified in Acts 19 with Paul and the disciples, and all the people of Asia, the Word of God through reviveSCHOOL truly spread—from a barn in Indiana to the nations.

> And this went on for two years, so that all the inhabitants of Asia, both Jews and Greeks, heard the message about the Lord. —Acts 19:10

By God's grace, reviveSCHOOL has become an outlet for individuals to gain fresh insight into the Messiah all throughout the Scriptures, as well as to develop an understanding of the role of Israel from a biblical perspective.
I am humbled and honored that you would select reviveSCHOOL for your learning. When we started with 12 guys in a Bible study, we had no idea that reviveSCHOOL would be as far reaching as it has become. Our team would delight in knowing that you are studying the Word of God and using the resources with reviveSCHOOL. We pray that through these resources you will grow closer to the Lord and that you are inspired to walk out the plans that God has for your life by exposing others to the love of Christ.

To God be the glory!
Dr. Kyle Lance Martin

For further information about how to sign up for this two-year study in the Word of God or if you would like to launch a reviveSCHOOL group in your community, state/province, or country, please go online to www.reviveSCHOOL.org.

How to Use this Bible Study Series

The *Complete Portrait of the Messiah* Bible study series contains multiple components for each lesson. These components work together to provide an in-depth study of how Jesus is revealed throughout the whole of Scripture. Below is a description of each component and how you can use each one to maximize your study experience.

Teaching Notes and Video Lessons
The teaching notes summarize the main points of each video lesson and include a QR code to access the video teaching. If you have access to the internet via your phone, you can scan the QR code to watch the video lesson.*

The Daily Word Devotional
Dig deeper into personal application for each lesson through *The Daily Word* devotional. This day-by-day devotional encourages you with thoughts for application and further Scripture readings.

Reading Guide Questions
These questions will guide you into a more detailed exploration of each lesson's content. Examine the concepts of the daily Scripture readings in more detail.

The Bible Art Collection
This Bible study series is augmented by a one-of-a-kind, especially inspired series of original artwork created by artist Mindi Oaten. These 66 acrylic paintings creatively depict the revelation of Christ in each book of the Bible. Viewing each of these original art pieces will inspire your understanding and further enrich your understanding of Jesus throughout all of the Scriptures. These can be found at https://www.mindioaten.com/pages/mindi-oaten-art-bible-art-collection or https://www.reviveschool.org/

About the Cover

Romans
"The Righteousness of God"

Artist Notes: Mindi Oaten

I wanted to have one piece in this series showing the cross, and it seemed Romans was the best book to do so. The primary theme of Romans is the good news, artistically summed up in one piece, showing God's plan of salvation through Christ on the cross, resulting in righteousness for all humankind, both Jew and Gentile.

Positioning of the elements was key for me. The bitten apple (sin and death) resting on the Torah (the old law) and the broken olive branch representing the Jewish people who did not receive Christ when He came to earth. The gift and butterfly, central and at the foot of the cross, are positioned so the red ribbon (the blood) could drop down and flow over it. The blood covers the sin and death, the old law. The Holy Spirit (feather, right side) enters when those who take the gift receive the blood sacrifice of Jesus over their lives. This is represented by the ribbon flowing from the gift, across the old law, and off the right side of the painting as the journey of life continues on.

The Cross

"If you confess with your mouth, 'Jesus is Lord,' and believe in your heart that God raised Him from the dead, you will be saved." (Romans 10:9)

This is the first book in which I painted the cross. I felt it was significant to show the cross in Romans because Paul's main message emphasizes what Jesus did for us on the cross, in that whoever believes He died for them and was resurrected on the third day will be saved. We have the basic gospel message in this painting.

White Cloth

"He was delivered up for our trespasses and raised for our justification." (Romans 4:25)

The cross is draped in white, representing the resurrection of Christ. White represents purity, a call to live a righteous and holy life.

Five Butterflies

"Do not be conformed to this age, but be transformed by the renewing of your mind, so that you may discern what is the good, pleasing, and perfect will of God." (Romans 12:2)

The butterflies are a symbol of the resurrection of Christ, and in Him, we are free to soar. The butterflies represent new life, eternal life, change, renewal of the mind, and new creation. Five represents the number for grace.

White Feather

"Therefore, no condemnation now exists for those in Christ Jesus, because the Spirit's law of life in Christ Jesus has set you free from the law of sin and of death. What the law could not do since it was limited by the flesh, God did. He condemned sin in the flesh by sending His own Son in flesh like ours under sin's domain, and as a sin offering, in order that the law's requirement would be accomplished in us who do not walk according to the flesh but according to the Spirit." (Romans 8:1–4)

The white feather represents the Holy Spirit that is given to us when we receive the gift, when we accept Christ as our Savior.

Torah

The Torah shown here represents the old law. As the scripture above states in verses 3–4, Christ came to fulfill the law through His death on the cross.

Bitten Apple

"For all have sinned and fall short of the glory of God." (Romans 3:23)

There's that bitten apple again! A symbol of sin that entered from the beginning. We all sin.

Gift and Red Ribbon

"For the wages of sin is death, but the gift of God is eternal life in Christ Jesus our Lord." (Romans 6:23)

This represents the gift of God by sending His only Son, Jesus, to die on the cross to save us. The red ribbon symbolizes Jesus' blood, the atonement for our sins. The blood drapes over the law, it fulfills the law. And again, in Romans 8:1–4 (above), Paul speaks of the gift of God by giving His only Son as the ultimate and final sin offering.

Garden Element–Olive Branches: Grafted into the Family of God

> Now if some of the branches were broken off, and you, though a wild olive branch, were grafted in among them and have come to share in the rich root of the cultivated olive tree, do not brag that you are better than those branches. But if you do brag—you do not sustain the root, but the root sustains you. Then you will say, "Branches were broken off so that I might be grafted in." True enough; they were broken off by unbelief, but you stand by faith. Do not be arrogant, but be afraid. For if God did not spare the natural branches, He will not spare you either. Therefore, consider God's kindness and severity: severity toward those who have fallen but God's kindness toward you—if you remain in His kindness. Otherwise you too will be cut off. And even they, if they do not remain in unbelief, will be grafted in, because God has the power to graft them in again. For if you were cut off from your native wild olive and against nature were grafted into a cultivated olive tree, how much more will these—the natural branches—be grafted into their own olive tree? (Romans 11:17–24)

The branches on the tree represent the Gentiles grafted in while the branch broken on the ground, to the left of the Torah, represents those who are broken off.

*In reviveSCHOOL, the theme name for Jesus in Romans is *Justifier*.

WEEK 70

Lesson 1: Romans 1

Justifier: The Power of the Gospel

Teaching Notes

Intro

Paul wrote over half of the 21 letters (epistles) in the New Testament. Today's lesson will include an overview of this new section, Paul's letters, an overview of Romans, and Romans 1 itself. Paul's letters would have been hand-delivered to the people of a region. Every letter had an audience and a theme. Paul wrote Romans to the believers in Rome and clearly identifies himself to them in this letter. Paul, initially known as Saul, was from the tribe of Benjamin. He was also a Roman citizen (Acts 16:37). He was born in Tarsus around the same time as Christ was born. Around AD 33–34, Paul was traveling on the road to Damascus to persecute Jewish believers of Jesus when he himself met Jesus. He immediately began to proclaim Jesus as the Son of God in the synagogues (Acts 9:20). Galatians 1:17–19 says Paul went to Arabia and then back to Damascus for three years before traveling to Jerusalem, where he met with Cephas and James (Jesus' brother).[1]

Paul disappeared for three years when he received a revelation from Christ (Galatians 1:11–12). Paul was responsible for the spread of Christianity throughout the Roman Empire. The book of Acts describes Paul's three missionary journeys—it is the timeline of his life after his conversion. All the epistles he wrote were the psalms (like David expressing his emotions) of those encounters. In the epistles, Paul either wrote back to those he had visited or he wrote ahead to those he wanted to visit. Second Corinthians 10:10 states Paul's "letters are weighty and powerful, but his physical presence is weak, and his public speaking is despicable." Paul found his strength, power, and source in the Lord (Philippians 4:13). Paul had discovered God's grace was sufficient for him (2 Corinthians 12:9–10). All of this enabled Paul to finish the race well (2 Timothy 4:7).[2]

Romans was written near the end of Paul's third missionary journey while he was ministering in Corinth (Romans 16:1, 23). Although Paul wanted to visit

[1] John MacArthur, *The MacArthur Bible Commentary* (Nashville: Thomas Nelson, 2005), 1499.

[2] MacArthur, 1499.

Rome, he went to Jerusalem (Romans 15:25). He did not make it to Rome until later, but he sent this letter through Phoebe (Romans 16:1). While in Jerusalem, Paul was beaten and arrested by the Romans. Even when they realized Paul wasn't guilty, they kept him in prison for two years (Acts 21). Paul appealed his case to Caesar, was put on a ship to Rome, but was shipwrecked on the journey. Once in Rome, he ministered for a time before being arrested again, and in AD 65–67, where church tradition says he was martyred (2 Timothy 4:6).[3]

Rome was the capital of the Roman Empire and by far was the most important city of that time. Founded in 753 BC, the city was not mentioned in Scripture at all until the New Testament. Rome was located along a river 15 miles from the sea. In Paul's day, it's estimated about one million people lived in Rome, many of them slaves. Church tradition maintains Paul was martyred during Nero's reign, outside of Rome along the Ostian Way. The church in Rome was probably started by those who had been in Jerusalem on Pentecost (Acts 2). Paul began his letter by saying he wanted to come to Rome but was prevented from doing so (Romans 1:13). Romans has much to study, and it can be intimidating. MacArthur says Paul's main purpose in writing Romans "was to teach the great truths of the gospel of grace to believers who had never received apostolic instruction."[4] Unlike some of the other epistles, Romans wasn't written in response to bad theology or because people were living ungodly lifestyles. It was Paul speaking with authority into the believers there in Rome to impart truth to them. Paul wrote to them for five reasons: to edify them (Romans 1:11), to preach the gospel (Romans 1:15), to get to know them so they could encourage him (Romans 1:12), so they could pray for him (Romans 15:30), and to help Paul continue to do ministry (Romans 15:28).[5]

As we have studied each book of the Bible, we've come up with one word or phrase we believe describes Christ in that book. Our word for the book of Romans is *Justifier* (Romans 4:23–25). Jesus literally became our answer, our *Justifier*, the One who came in our place so we could have life. You'll see this theme of *Deliverer* and *Justifier* in Jesus who puts us in right standing with God. When you think about the cross, begin to think about Jesus as the *Justifier*.

Teaching

Romans 1:1–7: Paul introduces himself as a servant of Christ, an apostle, and a preacher in the first four verses. Paul was "singled out for God's good news" (v. 1). Paul was also a missionary to the Gentiles; his whole call in life was to share with them the good news (v. 5).

---

[3] MacArthur, 1499.

[4] MacArthur, 1500.

[5] MacArthur, 1500.

Romans 1:8–15: According to Warren Wiersbe, Paul expressed his concern for them, was thankful for them (v. 8), prayed for them (vv. 9–10), loved them (vv. 11–12), was in debt to them (vv. 13–14), and was eager to visit them (v. 15).[6]

Romans 1:16–17: Paul was not ashamed of the gospel, so he carried it first to the Jew and then to the Gentile (v. 16). For in the gospel, "God's righteousness is revealed from faith to faith, just as it is written: The righteous will live by faith" (v. 17). There was nothing that would stop Paul from sharing what he believed; not persecution, not beatings, nor even shipwreck. Paul preached the message, but he knew that it was the power of God who did (and still does) the work. Paul was eager to preach the good news so the people could see how they could be delivered from their willful spiritual ignorance and evil self-indulgence and rescued from the wrath of God. Truly the gospel can set people free, but only the power of God can overcome mankind's sinful nature and give new life.[7] Wiersbe points out Paul had confidence in the gospel for these reasons: "The origin of the gospel: it is the gospel of Christ. . . . The operation of the gospel: it is the power of God. . . . The outcome of the gospel: it is the power of God unto salvation. . . . The outreach of the gospel: "to everyone that believeth."[8]

Paul's ministry was to the Jew first, and then to the Gentile. Christ's ministry was first to Israel, and through Israel, the gospel came to the world. This gospel is meant to go to everybody.

Closing

Spend time reading Romans 1. Don't rush through it, but give yourself time to really read and process. Can you imagine what would happen if we really got what Paul wrote and began to live it out? Our communities would be completely different. If we were completely unashamed of who we are in Christ, then people would either say, "Here comes that crazy person," or people's lives would be radically changed. Don't be ashamed of the gospel—you have nothing to lose. It's really God's power working through you into a person so they can receive salvation.

The Daily Word

Paul was eager to preach the good news in Rome. He excitedly anticipated proclaiming truth to first the Jew and then the Greeks. Why? He was eager because he wasn't ashamed of the gospel. Paul knew it was God's power, not his own

[6] Warren W. Wiersbe, *The Wiersbe Bible Commentary: New Testament* (Colorado Springs: David C. Cook, 2007), 411.

[7] Wiersbe, 412.

[8] Wiersbe, 412.

strength, that would bring salvation to those who believed. Therefore, Paul expected God to do great things through his ministry.

How often do you hear the words "Go share the gospel" and immediately get nervous? "Who? Me? Isn't that for the preachers and missionaries? Surely not me!" Dear child of God, *perhaps you need to rethink this.* Are you ashamed of the gospel? Are you relying on your own strength and power to share the good news? As a believer, *God's power works through you.* As you walk with Him and He leads you to share, guess what happens? Fear slips away, and His power shows up. So, stand up, open your mouth, and share the good news of Jesus Christ to those the Lord leads you to. He is at work in their lives already, preparing them for the gospel. You have nothing to lose and everything to gain in the power of God at work within you!

So I am eager to preach the good news to you also who are in Rome. For I am not ashamed of the gospel, because it is God's power for salvation to everyone who believes, first to the Jew, and also to the Greek. —Romans 1:15–16

Further Scripture: Acts 4:12; Galatians 6:14; 2 Timothy 1:8

Questions

1. Romans 1:1 refers to Paul as a bond-servant. What is a bond-servant and why do you think Paul referred to himself as one? Do you consider yourself as a bond-servant for Jesus Christ? Why or why not?
2. What do you think would have happened to the Gentiles if Paul had not been obedient to God when he had his "Damascus road" experience (Acts 9:3–9)? What if Ananias hadn't been obedient (Act 9:10–19)? Why do you think God chose Saul to take the gospel to the Gentiles?
3. In Romans 1:16, Paul said, "For I am not ashamed of the gospel." Can you say the same, and if so, do your actions show it?
4. What does Romans 1:20 mean? Would this be a good verse to use when someone professes to be an atheist? Do you "see" God in nature?
5. Romans 1:24, 26 says God gave them over to "the lusts of their hearts to impurity" and "degrading passions" amongst each other. Does this mean God gave them the desire to perform unnatural sexual acts with each other (Leviticus 18:22; Judges 17:6; 21:25; Romans 1:21; 1 Timothy 1:9–10; Jude 7)?
6. Name some other things that Romans mentions as the result of living an unrighteous life. Are there any that are "more wrong" than the others (Exodus 20:1–17; James 2:10)?
7. What did the Holy Spirit highlight to you in Romans 1 through the reading or the teaching?

WEEK 70

Lesson 2: Romans 2

Justifier: God's Righteous Judgment

Teaching Notes

Intro

Throughout the book of Romans, Paul tries to communicate to the believers in Rome how to determine if they were in right standing with God. The only way believers can do this is because they have been justified through Christ—the *Justifier*. Romans 4:25, one of the theme verses for the book says He—meaning Jesus—was "delivered up for our trespasses and raised for our justification." Jesus took everything on Himself and put it on the cross so we wouldn't have to. Through Jesus' death, burial, and resurrection, we have been justified.

Teaching

Romans 2:1–3: *Nelson's Commentary* breaks this chapter into three principles, which we will see today. In the first century, people thought they were free from God's wrath because they hadn't done the things listed in Romans 1:29–32. But Romans 2:1 says, "Therefore, any one of you who judges is without excuse." We might think, "I might not do those things, but I'm going to judge someone who is doing them." Jesus warned against this in Matthew 7:1–6.

Principle #1: God judges righteously.[1] Because God sets the standard, He is the only One who can judge. We didn't set the standard, and we do fall into these things (Romans 1:29–32). Warren Wiersbe said, "Certainly the Jews would applaud Paul's condemnation of the Gentiles in Romans 1:18–32. In fact, Jewish national and religious pride encouraged them to despise the 'Gentile dogs' and have nothing to do with them."[2] But Paul uses this judgmental attitude to prove the Jews were guilty because they were doing the

[1] Thomas L. Constable, *Expository Notes of Dr. Thomas Constable: Romans*, 50, https://planobiblechapel.org/tcon/notes/pdf/romans.pdf.

[2] Warren W. Wiersbe, *The Wiersbe Bible Commentary: New Testament* (Colorado Springs: David C. Cook, 2007), 414.

very things they condemned. The Jews "thought they were free from judgment because they were God's chosen people."[3]

Romans 2:4–11: As Warren Wiersbe said, "Instead of giving the Jews special treatment from God, the blessings they received from Him gave them greater responsibility to obey Him and glorify Him."[4] It's not God's judgment that leads people to repentance but His kindness and goodness. Exodus 34:6 says, "Yahweh is a compassionate and gracious God, slow to anger and rich in faithful love and truth." Everybody views God as a God of wrath who is ready to come down and hammer people because they've messed up. We think He's out to get us. But the reality is that it's the kindness of God that leads us to repentance. Since people are so thickheaded and/or spiritually religious, they're actually storing up wrath instead of repenting. God gave them (the Jews) time to repent, and they said, "No," simply because they were His chosen people.

Principle #2: God's judgment will deal with what every person really did.[5] The gospel went forth to the Jew and the Gentile in Romans 1—2. They chose to repent or not. Ultimately, God's judgment fell on both. "He will repay each one according to his works" (v. 6). God is going to judge us based on deeds, dealing with the consistent actions of a person's life. "For example, David committed some terrible sins, but the total emphasis of his life was obedience to God. Judas confessed his sin and supplied the money for buying a cemetery for strangers, yet the total emphasis of his life was disobedience and unbelief."[6] People either have the mentality to persist in doing good or the mentality of being self-seeking and disobeying. Does my life reflect my faith in Christ? If it does, then I'll be persistent in who I am. If not, then I'll clearly be self-seeking and disobedient. I will see some form of judgment for every single thing I've done. This could mean taking away rewards or receiving rewards; it could mean eternal life or wrath and condemnation. There is no favoritism to the Jew or to the Gentile. If you're not living according to the will of God, you will experience either affliction and distress (v. 9) or glory, honor, and peace (v. 10). True saving faith really results in obedience. Even though you might have an occasional fall (into sin), it doesn't take away your salvation. That's the key with David and Judas. David still had the faith and belief. Judas probably never had it. God shows no favoritism; He has equal justice for everybody.

---

[3] Wiersbe, 414.

[4] Wiersbe, 414.

[5] Constable, 51.

[6] Wiersbe, 415.

In reference to verse 6, A. M. Hunter said, "A man's destiny on Judgment Day will depend not on whether he has known God's will but on whether he has done it."[7] Here are a couple of perspectives on Romans 2:7: (1) If a person obeys God perfectly, he will receive eternal life; (2) eternal life is a free gift and a reward for good deeds; (3) Christians experience eternal life to the extent we do good deeds; (4) those self-righteous and unbelieving store up something that will come on them in the future, namely condemnation.[8] These are all thoughts. We know that salvation is based on faith alone and not works. When you have faith, you will walk it out.

Principle #3: God's judgment is He will treat everyone evenhandedly.[9]

Romans 2:12–16: Judgment will be the same for everyone whether they know the Law or not (v. 12). God will judge "what people have kept secret" (v. 16), meaning we can't hide anything from God. The lens of judgment is the gospel. The lens of judgment of everything we've done when God looks at us will be through the lens of Christ Jesus. Judgment is coming, but God has also given us an out—salvation through Christ Jesus.[10]

Romans 2:17–24: The term "Jew" is a religious term. The term "Israelite" is a national term. And the term "Hebrew" is a racial term. The mentality is that all three are the same. If the Jews really thought they were the light for the Gentiles (vv. 19–20), then they should obey the same things they taught others (vv. 21–24). Even though the Jews thought they were the light and the teachers, they were doing the same things the Gentiles were doing. Because they did this, "the name of God is blasphemed among the Gentiles" (v. 24; Isaiah 52:5). The Gentiles were not fooled by the Jews' activity. Neither group was exempt from God's judgment.

Romans 2:25–29: The law and circumcision does not determine who is safe from God's judgment (vv. 25–27). "A person is a Jew who is one inwardly, and circumcision is of the heart—by the Spirit, not the letter" (v. 29). It is not about what you do. It is all about how your heart has been changed. The Jewish mentality was to seek man's praises. But true heart change results in praise from God. Wiersbe said, "When you recall that the name 'Jew' comes from 'Judah,' which means 'praise,' this statement takes on new meaning."[11]

---

[7] A. M. Hunter, *The Epistle to the Romans,* Torch Bible Commentaries (London: SCM, 1955), 36.

[8] Constable, 53.

[9] Constable, 53.

[10] Constable, 56.

[11] Wiersbe, 415.

Closing

If God's going to come and judge righteously based on the truth, if He's going to judge every single one of us, if He's going to treat every one of us equally, then it must be about the heart as it says in verse 29, "a person is a Jew who is one inwardly, and circumcision is of the heart—by the Spirit, not the letter. That man's praise is not from men but from God." If you are remotely concerned about God's judgment, then get your heart right. Getting your heart right has nothing to do with going to church; it has everything to do with experiencing Jesus, who is the *Justifier*. Getting your heart right will take care of God's judgment. It's not performance-based. It has everything to do with radically changing your heart because that's what God looks at.

The Daily Word

God sent His Son Jesus into the world to save the world. God chose to do this knowing sin leads to death. He loves His people and desires to give them eternal life. Therefore, out of the riches of His kindness, restraint, and patience, God allows the opportunity for repentance to all people. Because all people sin, all people need a Savior.

If you are prone to judge others and point out their sin, *stop*. There's a good chance you have a few issues of your own and need God's mercy, love, and forgiveness just the same. Allow the Lord to deal with others. Allow the Lord's kindness to draw a person to repentance. *You are called to love others. You are called to discern when to speak truth in love.* You are not called to judge and criticize. By judging others, it's like taking matters into your own hands, trying to correct someone else's behavior. God is in control. He is working in ways you can't see to draw each person to repentance. Be kind and compassionate, rich in love, and full of mercy, just as Christ is to the church. Trust God loves and cares for each person even more than you do, pray without ceasing, and give it time.

Do you really think—anyone of you who judges those who do such things yet do the same—that you will escape God's judgment? Or do you despise the riches of His kindness, restraint, and patience, not recognizing that God's kindness is intended to lead you to repentance? —Romans 2:3–4

Further Scripture: John 3:17; Romans 2:1–2; James 4:11

Questions

1. What does Romans 2 say about judging others? Is it ever our job to judge the actions of others (Matthew 7:1–6; 1 Corinthians 5:12)?
2. Read Romans 2:7–11. Based on your reading, how do you explain why bad things happen to good (righteous) people (Genesis 3; 50:19–20; Matthew 5:45; Romans 5:3–5; James 1:2–4)?
3. According to Romans 2:14–15, does anyone, whether a believer or not, have any excuse to sin? Besides the law, what does God give us to convict us of sin (John 16:7–8)?
4. How does Romans 2:23–24 correlate with Ephesians 2:8–9? Because we are saved by grace, does this give us the right to blatantly sin (Romans 6:1–7)?
5. What did the Holy Spirit highlight to you in Romans 2 through the reading or the teaching?

WEEK 70

Lesson 3: Romans 3

Justifier: No Differences Between Jews and Gentiles

Teaching Notes

Intro

This week is a drastic move from the emotion and passion of Song of Songs to Paul's more theological discussion about how the gospel is meant for both the Jews and the Gentiles, and both will face judgment. There's so much in Romans 3. We'll focus mainly on the first eight verses. In this section, Paul addresses what people were already voicing about why the gospel was for Jew and Gentile alike.

Teaching

Romans 3:1–2: In verse 1, Paul asks what advantage Jews have through circumcision. Basically, he was addressing whether it even mattered that someone was a Jew—*What's the point or purpose of being a Jew?* Paul answered his own questions in verse 2—the benefits of being a Jew were "considerable in every way." First, the Jews were given God's spoken word (v. 2b). God gave the Jews supernatural messages—the entire Old Testament. According to Romans 9:4–5, the Jews were the Israelites—God's chosen people, the adopted children of God, the ones who entered into the covenant with God, the ones who had worshipped in God's presence in the temple, and the ones who shared in the lineage of the Messiah, who is over all things. The benefit of circumcision was because the Jews had been entrusted with all these gifts from God. The Jews were given God's Word to pass it down to us (Acts 7:38; Galatians 3:8; 2 Timothy 3:15; Hebrews 5:12; 1 Peter 4:11).

Romans 3:3–4: Paul's second question in verse 3 is—*Will Israel's unbelief or unfaithfulness cancel God's promises to them?* The question asks if God will change His promises because of their unfaithfulness. Dr. Tom Constable explains that as Paul was trying to determine when Israel's unfaithfulness began, he found only two who were present at Sinai when God gave Israel His law—Caleb and Joshua—who had remained faithful. Yet, "Still God brought the whole nation into Canaan as He had promised, though the unbelieving generation died in the wilderness."[1]

MacArthur writes, "If all mankind were to agree that God had been unfaithful to His promises, it would only prove that all are liars and God is true."[2] MacArthur further explains, "God will fulfill all the promises He made to the nation, even if individual Jews are not able to receive them because of their unbelief."[3] For Jews to receive God's promises, they must individually come to repentance and faith. In verse 4b, Paul recited Psalm 51:4 to give more evidence for God's righteousness and truthfulness: "Against You—You alone—I have sinned and done this evil in Your sight. So You are right when You pass sentence; You are blameless when You judge." God is not done with the Jews; He keeps His promises!

Romans 3:5–6: Paul asks his third question in verse 5—*If the Jews' unrighteousness reveals more of God's righteousness, is He unrighteous or just to inflict wrath? If my sin points to God's perfection, is it right for God to show His wrath against me?* If God condoned sin, He would have no righteous heirs for judgment (v. 5). How would God judge the world then? MacArthur explains this concept with this example: Picture "a jeweler who displays a diamond on black velvet to make the stone appear even more beautiful. He is simply paraphrasing the weak, unbiblical logic of his opponents—the product of their natural unregenerate minds."[4] MacArthur's point is our sin shows how holy God is, but that doesn't make it right to keep sinning just to make God look better.

Romans 3:7–8: Paul's fourth question is—*If my lie amplifies God's truth, why am I judged?* This question is similar to the third question. Paul's answer was, "No!" Their condemnation as sinners is deserved. Constable states, "Paul implied this objection is so absurd that it is not worth considering."[5] Why do we even have this lifestyle? Verses 9–20 begin to unpack this question.

---

[1] Thomas L. Constable, *Expository Notes of Dr. Thomas Constable: Romans*, 64, https://planobiblechapel.org/tcon/notes/pdf/romans.pdf.

[2] John MacArthur, *The MacArthur Bible Commentary* (Nashville: Thomas Nelson, 2005), 1512.

[3] MacArthur, 1512.

[4] MacArthur, 1512.

[5] Constable, 66.

Romans 3:9–20: Paul points out that the Gentiles are the same as the Jews—we're all under sin. This passage then explains how sinful and unrighteous we all are. MacArthur identified 14 indictments Paul lists in verses 10–18:[6]

1. No one is righteous (v. 10).
2. No one understands (v. 11).
3. No one seeks God (v. 11).
4. All have turned away from God (v. 12).
5. All have worked together to be unprofitable (v. 12).
6. No one does good (v. 12).
7. Their throat is an open tomb (v. 13).
8. They have all lied and been deceitful (v. 13).
9. Their mouths are full of snake venom (v. 13).
10. Their mouths are full of curses and bitterness (v. 14).
11. Their feet shed blood (v. 15).
12. Their ways create destruction and misery (v. 16).
13. They do not know the way of peace (v. 17).
14. They have no fear of God (v. 18).

Romans 3:21–31: Jew and Gentile, both are sinners. And God will judge them all. Wiersbe explains, "The whole world is guilty, Jews and Gentiles. The Jews stand condemned by the law of which they boast, and the Gentiles stand condemned on the basis of creation and conscience."[7] No one will be justified by the works of the Law, but by God's righteousness through faith in Jesus Christ. When we put our faith in Christ, there is no distinction between Jew and Gentile. God still has a plan for His people that is fulfilled through belief in Christ as Savior and Lord (vv. 21–22). Verse 23 sums it up, "For all have sinned and fall short of the glory of God." And they are justified through Christ Jesus (v. 24).

Closing

Christ is the *Justifier* who restores us to freedom in Him. Our freedom came at a great cost—Christ gave up His life to purchase that freedom for us. Through Christ, God has passed over the sins we've committed (v. 25). We have become righteous in God's eyes (v. 26), not through the law but through our faith in Christ. Jesus is the *Justifier*.

---

[6] MacArthur, 1513.

[7] Warren W. Wiersbe, *The Bible Exposition Commentary: New Testament* (Colorado Springs: David C. Cook, 1989), 522.

The Daily Word

Every person, both Jew and Gentile, has sinned. Everyone is unrighteous apart from God's grace in their lives. But thankfully, God has a plan for all His people. Every single person can be justified freely by God's grace through the redemption found in Christ Jesus. This means you can't boast about keeping the law. Also, you can't boast about your good works.

Jesus Christ died on the cross so you could be saved from death, the penalty for sin. Jesus died in your place. He is your justifier. Because everybody sins, *Jesus is everyone's justifier through faith.* Believe God has a plan for His people. And Jesus, as your justifier, is a part of God's ultimate, loving, gracious plan. In Jesus, you receive freedom, grace, and eternal life.

For all have sinned and fall short of the glory of God. They are justified freely by His grace through the redemption that is in Christ Jesus. —Romans 3:23–24

Further Scripture: Romans 3:21–22; 2 Corinthians 5:21; James 4:17

Questions

1. What was the advantage of the Jews having the Old Testament? (Deuteronomy 4:5–8; Galatians 3:8; 2 Timothy 3:15; 1 Peter 4:11)
2. Why is it foolish for believers to let on that a nonbeliever is a good person? According to verses 9–12, are Jews any better off than Gentiles? What does it say about our righteousness?
3. What does a biblical fear of God consist of? (Psalm 36:1; Proverbs 1:7; 9:10; 16:6; Acts 5:1–11)
4. Paul put together 14 Old Testament quotations that indict the character and conduct of all people. What are the 14 indictments? (Romans 3:10–18)
5. What is the good news God offers to everyone, Jew or Gentile, even though no one is good and all have sinned?
6. What did the Holy Spirit highlight to you in Romans 3 through the reading or the teaching?

Lesson 4: Romans 4

Justifier: Justification Through Faith

Teaching Notes

Intro

Here we are in Romans 4! When I first did radio, I taught through the book of Hebrews. I thought Hebrews was tough to teach, but that was because I hadn't taught through Romans. Romans was Paul's letter to a group of believers in Rome, whom he longed to be with. Unfortunately, Paul made it to Rome later as a prisoner. Tradition says the letter to the Romans was delivered by Phoebe. Remember at the very beginning of this letter, Paul expressed his desire that everyone would hear about the gospel and that the righteous would live by faith (Romans 1). Those words from Paul set up where we are going to go today.

Teaching

Romans 4:1–3: Paul writes about Abraham. Why was Abraham important enough for Paul to mention in this lesson? The Jews were given the Word of God and Abraham was mentioned in the Word of God. Wiersbe writes, "Abraham was justified by faith, not works (vv. 1–8)."[1] How can Abraham be justified by faith when Christ technically wasn't around? Because Abraham believed God's words; that was enough to justify him through faith.

You can understand this text when you understand the context of who Paul was writing to and what Abraham meant to them. Abraham was the physical ancestor of Israel (John 8:39). Abraham is also the father of "us all" (Romans 4:16). If Abraham was justified through his works, he would have had the right to brag. Constable wrote, "Abraham had no grounds for boasting 'before God,' because he received justification by faith, not 'by works.'"[2] If Abraham was justified because of his beliefs, what did he believe? Abraham believed he was going to be made into a great nation, that he was going to blessed, and that the prophetic

[1] Warren W. Wiersbe, *Wiersbe's Expository Outlines on the New Testament* (Colorado Springs: David C. Cook, 1992), 372.

[2] Thomas L. Constable, *Expository Notes of Dr. Thomas Constable: Romans*, 85, https://planobiblechapel.org/tcon/notes/pdf/romans.pdf.

promise would come to fruition (Genesis 12:1–4). He believed he was going to have a child who would lead to an innumerable number of decedents (Genesis 12:7; 15:4). To put it simply, he believed the word from the Lord. Constable wrote,

> Trust in God's promises is what constitutes faith, and what results in justification. The promises of God vary. These promises constitute the content of faith. The object of faith does not vary, however. It is always the person of God. For us, God's promise is that Jesus Christ died as our Substitute, and satisfied all of God's demands against sinners (3:24–25). Note God "credited" Abraham's faith "to him as righteousness" (v. 3). Faith itself is not righteousness. Faith is not meritorious in itself. It is only the vehicle by which God's righteousness reaches us. However, it is the only vehicle by which it reaches us.[3]

In verse 3, Paul writes, "Abraham believed God, and it was credited to him for righteousness." The word "credited" has also been translated as "accounted." John MacArthur writes, "Credited is used in both financial and legal settings. This word occurs nine times in chapter 4. It means to take something that belongs to someone and credit it to another's account. It is a one-sided transaction. Abraham did nothing to accumulate it. God simply credited it to him. God took his own righteousness and credited it to Abraham as if it were actually his."[4] The only way God was able to credit this righteousness to Abraham was because he believed.

Romans 4:4: Constable writes, "'Work' yields wages that the person working deserves or earns. 'Faith' receives a gift that the person believing does not deserve or earn."[5] There is nothing Abraham could have done to deserve righteousness; it was only given because he believed. Just to clarify where we are as a ministry, let's read Ephesians 2:8–9: "For you are saved by grace through faith, and this is not from yourselves; it is God's gift—not from works, so that no one can boast." You cannot earn salvation.

Romans 4:5–7: David also seems to be a common thread whom Paul liked to use. David also spoke about God crediting righteousness. David wrote about his blessing of forgiveness because he knew he did not deserve righteousness from God (Psalm 32:1–2).

---

[3] Constable, 86–87.

[4] John MacArthur, *The MacArthur Study Bible: NIV* (Nashville: Thomas Nelson, 2013), 1691.

[5] Constable, 87.

Romans 4:8: Sin does not cancel justification. Once you have experienced the forgiveness of Christ, of being justified by God, justification cannot be taken away. This is tricky because these words are coming from the Old Testament. In the Old Testament, those who believed in God were justified by faith in the Word of God. Today, we are justified through our faith that God sent His Son Jesus to die for us.

Romans 4:9–12: Wiersbe writes, "Abraham was justified by grace, not law."[6] All Abraham had heard from the Lord happened before his circumcision. So, a Jewish person cannot say, "Oh, his righteousness is because he kept the Law." He believed before he was circumcised. Paul knew the timeline. God knows what He is doing. Fourteen years after Abraham received and believed the word of the Lord, he was circumcised. Abraham's circumcision served as a seal. Abraham was the father of the believing Jews and the believing Gentiles (Galatians 3:29). Abraham was justified through grace.

Romans 4:13–15: It is impossible to keep the law perfectly; that's why you must receive righteousness through faith.

Romans 4:16–17: These verses summarize the previous verses (vv. 13–15). Constable writes, "God gave His promise, to make Abraham 'the father of many nations' (v. 13), unconditionally ('in accordance with grace')—after the patriarch stood justified. Abraham obtained the promise simply by believing it (i.e., 'by faith'), not by keeping the Law."[7]

Romans 4:18–22: Wiersbe writes, "Abraham was justified by resurrection power, not human effort (vv. 18–25)."[8] Abraham's faith did not waiver because of his circumstances, which brought glory to God. He fully believed God's promise. The more Abraham walked it out with God, the stronger his faith became.

Romans 4:23–25: My prayer is that we would start seeing this radical faith in the American church. MacArthur writes, "If Abraham was justified by faith, then all other people are justified on the same basis."[9]

---

[6] Wiersbe, 373.

[7] Constable, 93.

[8] Wiersbe, 374.

[9] John MacArthur, *The MacArthur Bible Commentary* (Nashville: Thomas Nelson, 2005), 1518.

Closing

Three terms are important to understand:

Justification	Past Tense	Saved immediately from sin's penalty
Sanctification	Present Tense	Saved progressively from power of sin.
Glorification	Future Tense	Saved ultimately from sin's presence.[10]

Today we talked about justification. In the Old Testament, justification came from faith and belief in God, pointing to the promise of salvation coming from Jesus. For us, justification comes through faith in the promise fulfilled in the death, burial, and resurrection of Jesus Christ.

The Daily Word

Abraham was considered righteous and received justification from sin because of His faith in God's promises. *Abraham believed.* Abraham believed God's words were true. He didn't work hard to earn righteousness—he received it through faith. Abraham did not waiver in unbelief at God's promise but was strengthened in his faith and gave glory to God. He did what God asked of him, fully convinced that what God had promised He was also able to perform.

There is no amount of human effort, good works, or keeping of the law that will result in righteousness. *You are saved by grace through faith.* Through believing. God grants you righteousness through faith as you receive Him and His promises. Stop striving. Stop attempting to earn right standing with God by following laws and rules. Just believe in God's promises by faith. Today, believe in what you can't see, and trust God and His promises.

This is why the promise is by faith, so that it may be according to grace, to guarantee it to all the descendants—not only to those who are of the law but also to those who are of Abraham's faith. He is the father of us all in God's sight. —Romans 4:16–17

Further Scripture: Genesis 12:2, 4; Romans 4:20–21; Ephesians 2:8–9

[10] *NIV: The Woman's Study Bible* (Nashville: Thomas Nelson, 2013), 1593.

Questions

1. How do verses like Romans 4:3–6 correlate with James 2:17–26?
2. How was Abraham justified before God? How are we justified before Him?
3. What was the argument from the Jews about circumcision? Why was circumcision given? (Romans 4:11)
4. How is God described in Romans 4:17? (Genesis 17:5; Hebrews 11:11–12)
5. Why did Abraham's faith grow stronger? Why did Jesus die? Why was He raised?
6. What did the Holy Spirit highlight to you in Romans 4 through the reading or the teaching?

Lesson 5: Romans 5

Justifier: Justified and Reconciled

Teaching Notes

Intro

We are continuing to work our way through the book of Romans, which is a fun book and very foundational to our faith in Jesus. We will process some things you've learned and make it practical.

Teaching

Romans 5:1–2: Romans 5 starts with "therefore," so we have to stop and think about how Romans 4 led to this "therefore" statement. Romans 4:3 states Abraham "believed God, and it was credited to him as righteousness." This is justification—we are justified in Jesus Christ (Romans 5:1). In Ephesians 2:8–9, Paul emphasizes we are saved through faith; salvation is a gift from God that cannot be earned. Faith is the critical step in salvation. "Without faith it is impossible to please God" (Hebrews 11:6).

When we think of how justice is enforced in our country, we often think of the court system. A case may be heard in a lower court, but if either party is unhappy with the ruling, they can appeal the case to a higher court. The appeals may continue all the way up to the US Supreme Court, but when the Supreme Court makes a ruling, it is final. One of the names for God is Judge, and He is the Supreme Judge of all the earth. God is love, but He is also just. He has to be just; because if He's not, then He's corrupt. The only way we can be justified is for someone to pay the price for our sins. The 1828 Webster's Dictionary defines justification as "an act of free grace by which God pardons the sinner and accepts him as righteous, on account of the atonement of Christ."[1] Jesus paid the price for our sins, so by faith, we receive the righteousness of Christ.

Romans 5 gives several benefits or blessings of being justified with God. First, we have peace with God (v. 1). This peace means there is no longer any enmity between us and God. Ephesians 2:13 explains those who were far away from

[1] Tim Kelley, "Spiritual Misalignments," One Place, https://www.oneplace.com/ministries/grace-thoughts/read/articles/spiritual-misalignments-8538.html.

God were brought near to Him through the blood of Christ. In fact, Jesus is our peace (Ephesians 2:14a). This peace means we are no longer enemies of God. Philippians 3:18 says, "Many live as enemies of the cross of Christ." James 4:4 says being friends with the world makes people enemies of God. Joshua said we have to choose this day whom we will serve (Joshua 24:15).

Second, by faith, we have access to God's grace (v. 2a). In Romans 1:16–17, Paul explains God's righteousness is revealed through faith and those who have received His righteousness will then live by faith. Those who are justified then choose to live by faith because they have access to the Father. But it's not enough to know we have access to God; we have to use it. We have to take a stand for our faith. We either live for Jesus or live for the world. Third, we also "rejoice in the hope of the glory of God" (v. 2b). Our hope is based on Jesus' promise that He is coming back and we will live with Him forever. The stand we must take is a temporary stand. It lasts only until this life is over, then we'll be with Jesus.

Romans 5:3–5: When Paul wrote this letter, he wrote to those who had to take a stand for Jesus when it resulted in persecution and suffering. If we take a stand, if we step out in faith, then we will be tested. If we walk with Jesus, there will be tribulation or suffering. But Paul told believers to rejoice even in affliction (v. 3). When we walk through suffering, it produces in us endurance (perseverance). When we persevere during hard times, it produces character and hope (v. 4). Our character is developed in hard times in ways that it would never develop in easy times. The more we experience Jesus in hard times, the more our faith becomes certain and our hope is solidified. This hope never disappoints because God's love has been poured into our hearts by the Holy Spirit (v. 5).

Romans 5:6–8: Paul emphasizes that while we were helpless sinners, Christ died for us. It's important to remember what God has done for us so we can minister to those who don't yet know Him. Paul suffered many things as a disciple of Christ. He was stoned, beaten, shipwrecked, and bitten by a viper. But he lived in reckless abandon to Christ because He knew God loved him and had a plan for his life. Faith and fear cannot coexist; faith gives us the ability to throw off fear. When tribulation comes, if you're walking in fear, you'll run. But if you're walking in faith, you'll persevere.

Romans 5:9–11: Since we have been justified by faith, we will be saved from His wrath (v. 9). But those who have not been saved by faith, those who are out of Christ, those who are enemies of God, will suffer God's wrath. But we have been "reconciled to God through the death of His Son" (v. 10).

What's our responsibility now that we know we have been saved? We can live our lives differently because we know Christ has done these things for us.

In 2 Corinthians 5:18, Paul said God "gave us the ministry of reconciliation." Everyone who has been reconciled to God has been given a ministry. We stand between God in heaven and people on earth. With Jesus as our Advocate, we are in the middle, making an appeal to man to be reconciled with God. When Jesus walked this earth, His goal was reconciliation—to reconcile the world back to God (2 Corinthians 5:19a). Jesus didn't impute their trespasses and condemn them; instead, He told them how to be saved. Everywhere He went, Jesus was the messenger and minister of reconciliation to a lost and dying world. Then He did the ultimate reconciliation—He died on the cross. Now He has handed this ministry of reconciliation to us. We, the body of Christ, have been given this ministry of reconciliation. We have been given a word—the gospel—which is the power of God to salvation for those who believe (Romans 1:16). We each have the responsibility to speak about Jesus. We are ambassadors for Christ to plead on Christ's behalf (2 Corinthians 5:20).

Closing

This is an amazing book about how to live for Jesus, about who we are and what our identity is. But don't just take this as knowledge. Let the knowledge transform you so that you can go out and share this with the people around you, and they can be reconciled back to God.

The Daily Word

People long for peace in their lives. They search for peace in every corner of the world. Why? Because God created you to long for something more than this world offers. However, nothing in this world will deliver the peace your soul longs for. You may be going through a crisis, persecution, or affliction, and as you walk through this hardship, you long for peace. *The Lord Jesus Christ is that peace your soul longs for.*

Jesus is your Prince of Peace. You find peace with God through faith in Jesus Christ. Yes, the Jesus who demonstrated His love for you while you were a sinner—that Jesus—is the peace of this world. When you search for peace, turn to Jesus in faith and receive His grace. He will be your peace—even in the midst of despair. As you walk through affliction, Jesus will grant endurance, grow your character, and give you hope. His love has been poured out for you. Give thanks to Him in all circumstances, and His peace that passes all understanding will guard your hearts. Let go of control and walk with Jesus. Remember, He is the peace your soul longs for.

Therefore, since we have been declared righteous by faith, we have peace with God through our Lord Jesus Christ. We have also obtained access through Him by faith into this grace in which we stand, and we rejoice in the hope of the glory of God. —Romans 5:1–2

Further Scripture: Isaiah 9:6; Romans 5:3–5; 2 Thessalonians 3:16

Questions

1. How are you justified before God? What is the result of being justified? (Ephesians 2:14)
2. What are some spiritual blessings that assure you that you cannot be lost after being justified? (Romans 5:1–11)
3. Is being justified an escape from the trials of life (John 16:33)? Can trials or suffering separate us from the love of God (Romans 8:35–39)? If you can't escape from trials, then what is the purpose for them? (James 1:2–4; 1 Peter 1:6–7)
4. Meditate on Romans 5:6–8 for a minute. What comes to your mind when you think about Jesus dying for you while you were still in your sins? How much more do you think He cares for those who are His children?
5. Compare Adam bringing death to Jesus bringing life in Romans 5:12–19. Compare law and grace in verses 20–21 (Romans 7:8–12; Galatians 3:19, 21–24).
6. What did the Holy Spirit highlight to you in Romans 5 through the reading or the teaching?

WEEK 71

Lesson 6: Romans 6

Justifier: Dead to Sin

Teaching Notes

Intro

While Paul had already visited most of the churches to whom he wrote, Paul had yet to visit the church in Rome when he wrote his letter to them. Paul used a lot of rhetorical Questions as he wrote Romans, probably as a teaching method to keep the Romans engaged. Chapter 6 begins with one of these rhetorical Questions, which sets up the main point of the chapter: *Christians are dead to sin.* This point follows the case which Paul makes in chapter 5 that Jesus dealt with our sin and justified us from our sin.

Warren Wiersbe notes three themes around which Paul organizes his argument in Romans 6:

- Know (6:1–10)
- Reckon (6:11)
- Yield (6:12–23)[1]

Teaching

Romans 6:11: This is the theme verse of chapter 6. Paul bluntly states that Christians are dead to sin. As a result, we have become alive to God.

Romans 6:1: The opening rhetorical question, "What shall we say then?" functions like the word "therefore." Paul built on his argument from the conclusion of chapter 5, "The law came along to multiply the trespass. But where sin multiplied, grace multiplied even more so that, just as sin reigned in death, so also grace will reign through righteousness, resulting in eternal life through Jesus Christ our Lord" (Romans 5:20–21). Some in the early church thought that since sin resulted in more grace that there was no reason to try to avoid sin. More sin would mean more grace and grace was a good thing.

[1] Warren W. Wiersbe, *The Wiersbe Bible Commentary: New Testament* (Colorado Springs: David C. Cook, 2007) 423–24.

Romans 6:2–5: Paul emphatically points out that Christ has made us dead to sin. As a result, Christians should no longer desire to live in sin. Paul begins verse 3 with the phrase, "Or are you unaware." This implies the Romans knew the truth that they were dead to sin conceptually but had failed to come to a full understanding. Freedom from sin came with the Romans' relationship with Jesus. The same glory of God that raised Jesus from the dead enabled them to walk in a new way of life because of their faith in Jesus. The word "glory" that Paul uses here is the same word John uses in John 11 when Jesus speaks with Martha after Lazarus' death: "Jesus said to her, 'Didn't I tell you that if you believed you would see the glory of God?'" (John 11:40) In the same way Martha saw God's glory when her brother was raised from the dead, God's glory was on display when the Romans were freed from the power of their sin through Jesus' atoning death on the cross. Just as their death to sin resembled Jesus' physical death on the cross, they were enabled to live a new kind of life because of Jesus' physical resurrection from the dead. Jesus said, "A thief comes only to steal and to kill and to destroy. I have come so that they may have life and have it in abundance" (John 10:10). The Romans' death to sin was meant to lead them to the abundant life that Jesus promised.

Romans 6:6–7: The power of sin over the Romans had been abolished through Jesus' work. Sinful actions no longer held any power over them. Ephesians says, "But that is not how you learned about the Messiah, assuming you heard about Him and were taught by Him, because the truth is in Jesus. You took off your former way of life, the old self that is corrupted by deceitful desires; you are being renewed in the spirit of your minds; you put on the new self, the one created according to God's likeness in righteousness and purity of the truth" (Ephesians 4:20–24).

Romans 6:8–11: Paul again points out the reality of Jesus' physical death and resurrection. This time, he emphasizes the fact that the resurrected Jesus will never experience death again. In the same way, the Romans should "consider yourselves dead to sin but alive to God in Christ Jesus" (v. 11). This was Wiersbe's "Reckon" section of the chapter.[2] The Romans had to consider themselves dead to sin in order to actually be dead to sin. They had to understand what Jesus had done for them and what that meant for them as His followers.

Romans 6:12–14: Having considered themselves dead to sin, the Romans now had to yield to the Lord.[3] They were to present themselves to the Lord for righ-

[2] Wiersbe, 424.

[3] Wiersbe, 424.

teous purposes. Their minds were not to be distracted by unrighteous things but to be devoted to the Lord. Their eyes were not meant to be distracted by things of the world but to be aware of what the Lord would have them to do.

Romans 6:15–23: Paul fully answered the rhetorical question with which he began the chapter. If the Romans chose to continue sinning, they would show themselves to be slaves to sin. If they fully surrendered to Christ, they would present themselves as slaves to righteousness. The fruit they received from unrighteousness were things they are now ashamed of. As they presented themselves as slaves to righteousness, they would receive sanctification and eternal life. There was no way sin would produce the fruit of God. Sin only produced death. God's gift of eternal life was only available through trusting Jesus and offering themselves as slaves to righteousness.

Closing

We know intellectually we are dead to sin, but Paul challenges us to really consider what it means for us to be dead to sin and alive in Christ. Then he challenges us to consider how we are yielded to Christ. How are we offering ourselves up to the Lord to be used for righteous purposes? How are we pursuing Christ as our master in order to pursue the abundant life He has promised?

The Daily Word

Everyone has sinned and fallen short of the glory of God. People live in bondage to a variety of sin: false gods and idols, addiction, pride, deception, and more. People live as slaves to sin. Just as a slave would obey a master, a slave to sin obeys whatever sin dictates. However, if you live as a slave to righteousness, then you will obey your master, Jesus Christ.

In Christ, you are set free and are no longer a slave to sin. In Christ, you are dead to sin and alive in Him, which leads to righteousness. Christ came to set you free from the bondage of sin. He has given you eternal life through grace, an unearned gift for you to receive. Stand firm. Don't give in to the yoke of slavery but renew your mind and your spirit in Christ. You are *alive* in Christ! You are *alive!*

So, you too consider yourselves dead to sin but alive to God in Christ Jesus. —Romans 6:11

Further Scripture: Romans 6:16–18, 23; Ephesians 4:20–24

Questions

1. According to Scripture, is it wise to continue to live in sin after receiving Jesus as Lord? How then are you to live (Galatians 2:19–20)?
2. Explain the symbolism of baptism. What does it speak to as a new believer? (Ezekiel 36:26, 2 Corinthians 5:17, Ephesians 4:24)
3. Why should you no longer be slaves of sin if you are in Christ? Are you walking in this truth today?
4. How do you prevent sin from reigning in your mortal body (Romans 12:1)? How are you to present yourself to God (Colossians 3:5, 1 Peter 2:24)? Read how David's sin in Psalm 51 affected his whole body.
5. What are the two unyielding truths in Romans 6:23? What does Scripture say eternal life is? (John 10:10, 17:3)
6. What did the Holy Spirit highlight to you in Romans 6 through the reading or the teaching?

WEEK 71

Lesson 7: Romans 7

Justifier: Living Free from Sin

Teaching Notes

Intro

Romans is a pivotal book in the New Testament as to who we are in Christ. Paul begins chapter 7 with the question of being under the dominion of the law even though believers were saved through Christ. There is an old Native American story about two dogs fighting to take control—a white dog and a black dog. When a man was asked which dog wins, he replied, "The one that gets fed. The one that doesn't get fed eventually dies from starvation." John 8 says Jesus set us free from sin, but our fleshly sin nature keeps trying to pull us back into sin. The dilemma is that since we still have a sin nature, we still sin. If we're not careful, we try to blame our sinfulness on that sin nature. But the Bible says we are dead to sin. My heart is, we are meant to live free from sin.

Teaching

Romans 7:1–6: Paul explored the issue of being under the law by using an example from marriage (vv. 1–2). Paul said a woman who was married was bound by law to her husband as long as he lived. If he died, she was then released from that covenant promise. If she married someone else before her husband died, then she became an adulteress (v. 3), because it was illegal to have two husbands. Therefore, the covenant was broken only by death. In the same way, believers have become dead to sin through the body of Jesus Christ (v. 4). That means we are in a covenant relationship with Christ so we can bear much fruit for Him (v. 5)—love, joy, peace, patience, kindness, goodness, faith, gentleness, self-control (Galatians 5:22–23). Before Christ, we operated freely in our sinful passions and "bore fruit of death" (v. 5). But now, we've been freed from that covenant with death (remember that the husband had to die for the wife to be free), as we became alive to Christ and now serve the Spirit. There was a death, and in this case, it's a continuous death to what we had been held captive—the Law (v. 6). The newness of the Spirit comes with that death.

Romans 7:7–12: Paul's next question was to ask, "Is the law sin?" (v. 7) Paul answers his own question, "Absolutely not!" Why? Because without the law, he would not have known what sin was. The law included the guardrails to keep us from falling off the cliff of sin, but they were also supposed to point us to Jesus—to His holiness and His righteousness. Jesus had to become the *Justifier* to move us beyond the law. Paul used the example of coveting as an example of being told the law. That death in the law came when sin deceived Paul and he realized he could not fulfill the law on his own (vv. 8–12). The law is holy.

Let's talk about this thing with the law by going to Galatians 2. The background of Galatians 2:15–21 is that Peter comes to Antioch and eats with Paul and the Gentile believers. But when certain Jewish "elites" come from Jerusalem, Peter pulls away from the Gentiles. He feared the Jews who lived according to a much stricter lifestyle, specifically, the act of circumcision. Paul calls Peter out on the hypocrisy. Paul pointed out they had both been justified by Christ, but Peter was trying to go back under the law and perform under its expectations. If we are not careful, we will actually try to rebuild the things that brought us into spiritual death in the first place. We'll try to do the right things and live by the right rules but lose focus on the One who is righteous.

Galatians 5:1 says, "Christ has liberated us to be free. Stand firm then and don't submit again to a yoke of slavery." We've been freed, so don't become entangled again. The "yoke of slavery" mentioned here is the law. John 15:4–5 records Jesus' instructions to "abide in Him," and He will abide in us. Without Christ, we can do nothing (v. 5b). But if we're not careful, we'll fall back into the trap of trying to uphold the law and legalism. If we could keep the law on our own, Jesus would not have had to die on the cross for us.

Romans 7:13–25: Paul then asked, "Did what is good cause my death?" (v. 13). Once again, he answered his own question, "Absolutely not!" It was the sin in his life that was producing his death. Paul explained that the law is spiritual and from God, but he is made of flesh and subject to sin (v. 14). Paul described the conflict this caused: "For I do not understand what I am doing, because I do not practice what I want to do, but I do what I hate. And if I do what I do not want to do, I agree with the law that is good" (vv. 15–16). The reality is we have the mind of Christ in us. Now if Paul did what he did not want to do, it was because of the sin that lived with him (v. 20). Paul cried out, "What a wretched man I am! Who will rescue me from this dying body?" (v. 24).

Closing

I have been in this place of being the wretched man who could not control the sin in his life. I want to walk with Jesus and show Him to my children at home.

I want to share Jesus at my workplace. How can I do this with sin in my life? Galatians 5:16–18 says, "I say then, walk by the Spirit and you will not carry out the desire of the flesh. For the flesh desires what is against the Spirit, and the Spirit desires what is against the flesh; these are opposed to each other, so that you don't do what you want. But it you are led by the Spirit, you are not under the law."

Galatians 5:19–21 lists the works of the flesh: "sexual immorality, moral impurity, promiscuity, idolatry, sorcery, hatreds, strife, jealousy, outbursts of anger, selfish ambitions, dissensions, factions, envy, drunkenness, carousing, and anything similar." But verses 22–23 list the fruit of the Spirit: "love, joy, peace, patience, kindness, goodness, faith, gentleness, self-control."

In Romans 7, we find we have a choice to make. Will we walk in the fruit of the Spirit? Or will we walk back under the law? Galatians 5:24–26 describes this process: "Now those who belong to Christ Jesus have crucified the flesh with its passions and desires. Since we live by the Spirit, we must also follow the Spirit. We must not become conceited, provoking one another, envying one another." We have the ability to live in the Spirit and have His fruit.

The Daily Word

When you receive Jesus as your Savior and confess with your mouth, He is Lord, you are a new creation. You were released from the law, from your old ways, and from sin. Christ liberated you and set you free. Stand firm in Jesus. Stand firm! Don't go back to the old ways when you were a slave to the law, striving to work for your salvation. Don't go back to your old sin patterns. Don't live in that bondage again. You have been set *free*. You belong to Christ.

But it's hard, right? You want to do good, but you struggle and feel like a failure. Remember, walking with Jesus is not about keeping the law and striving to do good and be better. *It's about walking with Jesus and living in His Spirit.* He calls you to abide in Him. Spend time with Him. Allow His love to fill you up, and as you abide in Him, not the things of this world, you will begin to bear fruit—the fruit of the Spirit. Apart from Him, you will struggle, unable to produce the fruit of the Spirit on your own. Apart from Him, you will strive to keep the law. But your striving is not the freedom He has called you to live in. He has released you from the law so you can live in freedom. Today, abide in Him and walk in the Spirit, not in your flesh.

Therefore, my brothers, you also were put to death in relation to the law through the crucified body of the Messiah, so that you may belong to another—to Him who was raised from the dead—that we may bear fruit for

God. . . . But now we have been released from the law, since we have died to what held us, so that we may serve in the new way of the Spirit and not in the old letter of the law. —Romans 7:4, 6

Further Scripture: John 15:4–5; Galatians 5:16–18, 22–23

Questions

1. What does Romans 7 say about a woman who is joined to another man after she has already been married? According to Scripture, how sacred is the covenant of marriage? (Genesis 2:24; Matthew 19:3–9; Ephesians 5:25–31)
2. How does earthly marriage compare to Jesus (the Bridegroom) and the church (His bride)? (Isaiah 62:5; Revelation 19:7)
3. According to Romans 7, what are we supposed to die to and why?
4. What does Romans 7 say about the law (Matthew 5:17–20)? Do you think the law can ever be a bad thing? Explain why you answered the way you did.
5. Do you ever feel the way Paul felt in verse 19? Is there any way you can be a "good' person? (Mark 10:18; Luke 18:19)
6. What two things wage war against each other within us? How can we be free from death? (John 3:16; 8:32; 14:6)
7. What did the Holy Spirit highlight to you in Romans 7 through the reading or the teaching?

WEEK 71

Lesson 8: Romans 8

Justifier: No Condemnation Through Christ

Teaching Notes

Intro

Many scholars suggest Romans 8 is the most beautiful chapter in the Bible. Why? First, there's no condemnation or judgment in the chapter. And it contrasts the law versus the Spirit. The chapter can be divided into four sections: (1) Freedom from Judgment—No Condemnation (vv. 1–4); (2) Freedom from Defeat—No Obligation (vv. 5–17); (3) Freedom from Discouragement—No Frustration (vv. 8–30); and (4) Freedom from Fear—No Separation (vv. 31–39).

Teaching

Romans 8:1–4: The word "condemnation" means to express strong disapproval about something or someone. But there is no strong disapproval for those who are in Christ Jesus, because the *Justifier* has removed the penalty (v. 1). Believers have been set free from any penalty for the sin in our lives (v. 2). The Spirit of Life has set us free. However, sometimes we are set free from things and we don't know how to act in that freedom. For example, in the movie *The Shawshank Redemption*, Morgan Freeman's character was set free from prison, but he didn't know how to act with that freedom because he was so bound to the laws that had ruled his life in prison.

The law was weakened by the flesh, and it no longer did what God intended it to do. The law was set up to guide us with lanes to run in and boundaries to stay within to keep us holy. We chose to ignore those boundaries, weakening the presence of the law in our lives. When I was younger, I was a ski instructor in a children's ski school. Sometimes the day on the slope with little ones was tough. We'd joke afterwards that it would be the perfect job if we didn't have the children. However, our whole purpose was to be there for them. Likewise, the law was given to us to help us, but we mess it up and weaken it.

The phrase "Who walk not according to the flesh" is not in some of the more reliable manuscripts. It's a tricky statement that tends to paint a picture of conditions to meet in order to have life in Christ—in order to live in the Spirit. We do not have to perform to meet Jesus. There is NO condemnation in Christ. God loves us. He has set us free, and He meets us where we are (Romans 5:8). We are free from judgment AND there is no condemnation. God is not sitting up there making lists about our sins and casting judgment down on His children.

Romans 8:5–17: As believers, we are all "in process"—the process of growing in Christ. In this section of verses, some scholars will start to set up the case for identifying those who are saved or not. Although this is true, we need to remember that all believers are "in process" and always growing in Christ, so keep that in mind.

Verse 5 divides believers into two groups—those with their minds on the things of the flesh and those with their minds on the things of the Spirit. I remember when I became a believer and I was still having thoughts in my head—thoughts that judged others, that were cynical, that were off-color. I wondered to myself why Christ had not taken all that from my life. I was a little defeated, wondering what I was doing wrong.

John 15:1–4 talks about pruning branches off a vine. Fruit grows from the support of the branches. Pruning those branches takes time; they do not grow overnight. We have a peach tree in our back yard. I hacked off a ton of branches, and we'll have to wait a year or so to see the branches fill out and fill in those I pruned. As the tree fills in, it fills in the way I want it to in order to produce the best fruit. (Galatians 5:22–24—fruit of the Spirit has to grow.)

Being in the Spirit is one of life and peace, while being in the flesh is hostility toward God (vv. 6–7). As I grew in my faith, I learned to set my mind on the things of Christ. I knew sin was dead to me, but it was like I had to retrain my brain and my body in the Spirit. Thoughts, jokes, feelings, and emotions would still creep into my brain, but since I knew that I was dead to sin and had life in Christ, I could cast them away. Over time, I kept winning those small battles, and I experienced freedom from defeat. I knew I could win those small battles and was not obligated to submit to those (Ephesians 5:7–10). If we do not have the Spirit of God within us, Christ does not belong to us (v. 9). Therefore, as believers, we are NOT in the flesh. With Christ, the life of the Spirit and His righteousness are in us.

The Spirit raised Jesus from the dead, and He lives within us, giving us life (v. 11). We are debtors then to the Spirit, not to the flesh (v. 12). We are not slaves to sin, and we owe it nothing. If we live by the flesh, we will die; but we can put to death the flesh by walking in the Spirit and live (v. 13). When we are led by the Spirit, adopted as sons of God (vv. 14–17), we walk out our lives as children of the Father—the child of One who wants to lead us by the Spirit into righteousness. We are to be those who lead our children and those around us. We lead them into a relationship with Christ; set an example of living by the Spirit;

share our own experiences and walk; teach them to do the same; and disciple them in trial and error.

Romans 8:18–30: The trials of this present age are transient (2 Corinthians 4:17–18)—they come and go (v. 18). We're all still waiting for the second coming of God's Son (v. 19). God is coming; He has a plan that sets even His creation free from its bondage to corruption (vv. 20–21). The whole of God's creation is groaning together, even mankind, waiting (v. 22–23). Wiersbe writes, "Today's groaning bondage will be exchanged for tomorrow's glorious liberty!"[1] God wants us to walk by the Spirt, so that we can walk out His plan as we prepare for His return (vv. 24–25). The Spirit helps us when we are weak and intercedes for us with groanings too deep for words (vv. 26–27). If we all submit to the lordship of Jesus in obedience, He will cause all to come together (v. 28). God calls us to be conformed in the image of Christ (v. 29). God is getting us ready to usher in Jesus' return (v. 30).

Romans 8:31–39: Paul gave us these powerful words in verse 31b: "If God is for us, who can be against us?" God has equipped us with everything we need, so that we can get ready for His return (v. 32).

Closing

God has a plan for His creation, for His people and for His return. We do not walk in condemnation or fear. We walk by the Spirit of God, to fulfill His purpose for us and His kingdom.

The Daily Word

The mind set on the Spirit of God brings life and peace, whereas a mind set on flesh brings death. Therefore, set your mind on the Spirit. Walk in the power of the Spirit. When afflictions and suffering come, as you walk in the Spirit, you will respond in the Spirit and not in your flesh. Even though you walk through pain, in the Spirit you will receive the fruits of peace and joy. You will walk in God's love for you. You will walk believing in God's faithfulness, allowing all things to work together for good for those who love God and are called according to His purpose. *This is walking in the Spirit.*

As believers, you live life in victory, not defeat! You are more than victorious through Christ who loves you and gave His life for you. As you walk in the

[1] Warren W. Wiersbe, *The Bible Exposition Commentary: Matthew–Galatians* (Colorado Springs: David C. Cook, 1989), 540.

Spirit, you walk believing nothing has the power to separate you from the love of God. *Nothing.* So do not live defeated. Live with your shoulders back, your eyes fixed ahead on Christ, and walk in the power of His Resurrection. You have victory in Christ. Walk in His peaceful, life-giving Spirit. Stand firm and remain in Christ's love.

No, in all these things we are more than victorious through Him who loved us. For I am persuaded that not even death or life, angels or rulers, things present or things to come, hostile powers, height or depth, or any other created thing will have the power to separate us from the love of God that is in Christ Jesus our Lord! —Romans 8:37–39

Further Scripture: Romans 8:5–6, 28; 1 Corinthians 15:57

Questions

1. Romans 8:1 speaks of condemnation. Have you ever found yourself being under condemnation? If so, have you released yourself? If not, take a few minutes to ask Jesus to remove that burden from you.
2. Romans 8:4 talks about not walking "according to the flesh, but according to the Spirit." What does "walking in the flesh" look like to you? What about walking in the Spirit?
3. Romans 8:18 states that suffering here is not "worthy" to be compared to the glory to come. Where else is this type of suffering mentioned (2 Corinthians 4:17; James 1:12; 1 Peter 5:10)?
4. How would you compare Romans 8:28 to Jeremiah 29:11? What are the differences and/or the similarities?
5. How does Romans 8:38–39 speak to your heart? Do you see your love with God like this? Why or why not?
6. What did the Holy Spirit highlight to you in Romans 8 through the reading or the teaching?

WEEK 71

Lesson 9: Romans 9

Justifier: God Fulfills His Promises

Teaching Notes

Intro

It has been a great week, and I am excited to teach through these next chapters in Romans. In Romans 9—11, Paul discusses the future of Israel. These chapters are all about how God still has a plan for the Israelites. Some people today will discredit that God still has a plan for Israel. The church has not replaced Israel. God still has a plan for Israel and for the Jewish people.

I am going to discuss all three chapters but will break down chapter 9. Warren Wiersbe identified three things that paint a picture of Romans 9—11: "The emphasis in Romans 9 is on Israel's past election, in Romans 10 on Israel's present rejection, and in Romans 11 on Israel's future restoration."[1] If you only focus on one of these chapters, you are going to miss the big picture.

At the end of Romans 8, it says God has a plan for believers. Nothing can separate God's people from His love. If that's true, you have to wonder about the Jewish people, who have rejected His Son. I want to walk through some characteristics of God to show you once God says something, He means it.

Teaching

Romans 9:1–3: First, we will talk about "God's faithfulness."[2] God is going to keep His promises. He means what He says. When the Holy Spirit is taking over, the conscience can be trusted. Paul communicated his feelings of sorrow and anguish; his deep pain. Paul was willing to go to hell if it would benefit or save his brothers. We know it's not possible, but Paul's heart is completely for the Lord and His people that he would give up everything for them.

Romans 9:4–5: Paul begins to describe all the promises to the Israelites. MacArthur breaks down the realities of the Israelites:

---

[1] Warren W. Wiersbe, *Wiersbe's Expository Outlines on the New Testament* (Colorado Springs: David C. Cook, 1992), 542.

[2] Wiersbe, 543.

- *Israelites*: "The descendants of Abraham through Jacob, whose name God changed to Israel (Genesis 32:28)."[3]
- *Adoption*: "Not in the sense of providing salvation to every person born a Jew, but sovereignly selecting an entire nation to receive His special calling, covenant, and blessing, and to serve as His witness nation (Exodus 4:22; 19:6; Isaiah 46:3–5; Hosea 11:1)."[4]
- *Glory*: "The glory cloud that pictured God's presence in the Old Testament was with the Israelites. His glory was supremely present in the Holy of Holies in both the tabernacle and the temple, which served as the throne room of Yahweh (Exodus 16:10; 24:16–17; 29:42–43; Leviticus 9:23–24)."[5]
- *Covenants*: "A covenant is a legally binding promise, agreement, or contract. Three times in the [New Testament], the word *covenants* is used in the plural (Galatians 4:24; Ephesians 2:12). All but one of God's covenants with man are eternal and unilateral—that is, God promised to accomplish something based on His own character and not on the response or actions of the promised beneficiary."[6] There were six covenants with man:

    1. Covenant with Noah (Genesis 9:8–17)
    2. Covenant with Abraham (Genesis 12:1–3)
    3. Covenant of law (Exodus 19—31; Deuteronomy 29—30)
    4. Covenant of priesthood (Numbers 25:10–13)
    5. Covenant of an eternal kingdom (2 Samuel 7:8–16)
    6. The new covenant (Jeremiah 31:31–34; Ezekiel 37:26; Hebrews 8:6–13)[7]

All but the Mosaic covenant are eternal and unilateral. Because of Israel's sin the Mosaic covenant was messed up, but it has been replaced by the new covenant (Hebrews 8:7–13).

---

[3] John MacArthur, *The MacArthur Bible Commentary* (Nashville: Thomas Nelson, 2005), 1535.

[4] MacArthur, 1535.

[5] MacArthur, 1535.

[6] MacArthur, 1535.

[7] MacArthur, 1535.

- *Service*: The temple service "refers to entire sacrificial and ceremonial system that God revealed to Moses (Exodus 29:43–46)."[8]
- *Promises*: "Probably this refers to the promised Messiah, who would come out of Israel, bringing eternal life and an eternal kingdom (Acts 2:39; 13:32–34; 26:6)."[9]

Romans 9:5: The Messiah was a physical descendant of the ancestor of the Jews. There are religions that claim Jesus is the son of God but not God; verse five clearly states Jesus is God over all. It does not get any clearer than that. Jesus is God in human flesh. Why do we celebrate and encourage Jews? Because the Messiah came from them.

Romans 9:6–8: The Word of God had not failed. Paul wrote, "For not all who are descendants of Israel are Israel." This is because Abraham had a child with his wife's maid Hagar, who carried his son Ishmael. But that was not God's plan. Thus, not all the descendants of Abraham are part of God's plan. MacArthur wrote, "Just as not all of Abraham's descendants belonged to the physical people of God—or national Israel—not all of those who are true children on Abraham through Isaac are the true spiritual people of God and enjoy the promises made to Abraham's spiritual children."[10]

Romans 9:9–13: God's promise went through Abraham to Isaac to Jacob. MacArthur wrote, "God's choice of Jacob resides solely in His sovereign plan, a perfect example of election unto salvation."[11]

Romans 9:14–18: These verses look at "God's Righteousness."[12] God determines who He will show mercy and compassion to.

Romans 9:19–29: These verses look at "God's justice."[13] All this is based on God's election. His righteousness and faithfulness. I know we are flying through this, but God patiently waited to demonstrate His wrath, make His power known, and put the riches of His glorious mercy on display. Then Paul uses verses from

[8] MacArthur, 1536.

[9] MacArthur, 1536.

[10] MacArthur, 1537.

[11] MacArthur, 1537.

[12] Wiersbe, 543.

[13] Wiersbe, 544.

the book of Hosea to show that God was going to pour out His love onto the Gentiles. However, this does not mean that God is done with the Jewish people.

Romans 9:30–33: These verses focus on "God's grace."[14] Israel stumbled over the Messiah. Because of Israel's rejection, you and I, the Gentiles have an opportunity for salvation.

Closing

The fact that the Jews stumbled over the Messiah, over the cross, does not negate the fact that in the past Israel had been elected. This is because it doesn't change who God is. He is faithful, righteous, and pours out His justice and grace. Because they stumbled, we have a chance to hear the gospel. Tomorrow we are going to unpack what that looks like for Jews and Gentiles.

The Daily Word

From the beginning, the Lord had a plan for the people of Israel—adoption by God, His presence with them, the covenants, the Law, the temple service, and the promises. The Lord has shown His faithfulness, justice, righteousness, and graciousness to the people of Israel. Even so, they stumbled over the stone, the living stone, Jesus. They missed Jesus as their Messiah. Consequently, they continue to live under the law and not in the grace the Lord had for them. Despite all that, God remains in control. God continues to pour out His mercy even when His people do not follow His will. He is in charge, and His character remains consistent—*He will fulfill His promises.*

God is working in ways beyond what you can see to display His greatness, both with Gentiles and Jews. What is the Lord doing through you today? Can you miss exactly what God wants to do? Perhaps, but by faith, believe in the God of mercy, love, justice, righteousness, and grace. His plan will come forth. As you walk with God, you can't mess up with Him. He has a patient love. He is with you and for you. Trust His plan will come forth.

And what if He did this to make known the riches of His glory on objects of mercy that He prepared beforehand for glory—on us, the ones He also called, not only from the Jews but also from the Gentiles? —Romans 9:23–24

Further Scripture: Romans 9:4, 32–33; 2 Peter 3:9

[14] Wiersbe, 545.

Questions

1. Romans 9:8 speaks about being children of God. What are the differences between children of the flesh verses children of God? What promise is being spoken? (Genesis 12:7; Galatians 3:16)
2. When you read Romans 9:17, do you think it means God placed Pharaoh in power just to harden his heart for God's people to be set free? (Exodus 4:21)
3. Why do you think God would lay a stumbling block in Romans 9:33 (Isaiah 8:14–15; 28:16)? Have you ever been tripped by a stumbling block? What did you do about it?
4. What did the Holy Spirit highlight to you in Romans 9 through the reading or the teachings?

WEEK 71

Lesson 10: Romans 10

Justifier: Why the Jews Rejected Jesus

Teaching Notes

Intro

We're in the study of Paul's letters he wrote to believers. Today we're on Romans 10. Paul wrote the believers in the church in Rome from Corinth, Greece. Paul made it to Rome, but only as a prisoner of the government. Paul wrote in this chapter specifically about the Israelites. Paul was a Roman citizen and he was a Jew. In chapter 9, we looked at how Israel was elected as God's chosen people because of God, not because of anything they had done. In chapter 10, we'll look at Israel's present rejection of God—rejecting Jesus as God's Son and as the Messiah. In chapter 11, we'll look at Israel's future restoration. Our word for Romans is *Justifier*. The Jews were waiting on the Messiah to come (Galatians 3:24). God chose them for that moment, and they said no to Him.

Warren Wiersbe outlines chapter 10 into three sections: "The Reasons for Their Rejection (10:1–13); The Remedy for Their Rejection (10:14–17); The Results of Their Rejection (10:18–21)."[1]

Teaching

Romans 10:1–13: What were the reasons the Jews rejected Christ? First, Wiersbe stresses that the Jews felt no need for salvation (v. 1).[2] Don't give up praying for those who do not know the Lord. Second, the Jews were passionate for God but they had no passion for learning more about God through knowledge (v. 2) (Galatians 3:24). Third, they were prideful and self-righteous (v. 3). Fourth, they misunderstood their own law (vv. 4–13). In verse 4, the word "end" means "fulfillment"[3] (Matthew 5:17; Romans 8:4).

[1] Warren W. Wiersbe, *Wiersbe's Expository Outlines on the New Testament* (Colorado Springs: David C. Cook, 1992), 546–48.

[2] Wiersbe, 546.

[3] John MacArthur, *The MacArthur Bible Commentary* (Nashville: Thomas Nelson, 2005), 1539.

Moses wrote that the one who lives by the law would be justified by them—that is, the works of the law (v. 5). However, righteousness comes from faith in Jesus as Savior and Lord (vv. 6–7), through proclaiming and believing that Jesus is the risen Lord (vv. 8–9). This confession saves us from feeling as though we have to perform, we have to measure up, we have to make it happen. Everyone who believes in Christ will be accepted (v. 10) because there's no distinction between Jew and Gentile, and our salvation is based on what He did (vv. 11–12). We have only to call upon His name (v. 13). Note that today, there is a very small percentage of Jews in Israel who are saying yes to Jesus.

Romans 10:14–17: What is the remedy for the Jews' rejection? Verse 14 asks how the Jews can call on Christ since they haven't believed in Him and they haven't heard about Him. Then, Paul asked, "How can they hear without a preacher?" Paul continued in verse 15 by asking how someone could preach to the Jews unless he was sent by God (v. 15a). "How beautiful are the feet of those who announce the gospel of good things" (Isaiah 52:7–10; Nahum 1:15). God sent Jonah as the messenger to Nineveh to preach salvation and peace. "All did not obey the gospel . . . Lord, who has believed our message?" (v. 16). Faith comes from what is heard, and what is heard is what is preached about Christ (v. 17). Maybe they had never heard the news of Christ.

Romans 10:18–21: What are the results of their rejection? The Jews had heard about Jesus because the news went out across the entire world (v. 18). Israel was guilty of rejecting Jesus, so the message went to the Gentiles (v. 19). The Jews will one day be angry and jealous over the Gentiles receiving Jesus. Isaiah stated he was found by those who weren't looking or asking for him (v. 20). These didn't even know there was something to look for. Meanwhile, God spreads His hands out to the disobedient and defiant Jews *all day long* (v. 21). He still yearns for all His people. Therefore, it's our responsibility to keep delivering the news of Christ.

Closing

Wiersbe shares four reasons the church must send out missionaries that he received from Dr. E. Meyers Harrison: "(1) *the command from above*—'go ye into all the world' (Mark 16:15); (2) *the cry from beneath*—'send him to my father's house' (Luke 16:27); (3) *the call from without*—'come over and help us' (Acts 16:9); and (4) *the constraint from within*—'the love of Christ constraineth us' (2 Corinthians 5:14)."[4] If you believe the love of Christ is inside you, it should compel you to go deliver the good news. You will get a word from above, from

---

[4] Warren W. Wiersbe, *The Bible Exposition Commentary: Matthew–Galatians* (Colorado Springs: David C. Cook, 1989), 548.

the word, from dreams and visions from outside your realm, but it really needs to come from within. Once you realize your Messiah is the *Justifier*, you can't stop telling others about Jesus.

The Daily Word

The message of the gospel is for all people. If you call upon the name of Jesus as Lord, you will be saved. However, the people of Israel rejected this message. They did not receive it. So, what now? They still need to hear the truth in a way that creates jealousy and, perhaps, even causes them to *become angry that they lack understanding.*

People need to hear the message of the gospel from your heart. Today, that's your job. You are to confess with your mouth, "Jesus is Lord," believing in your heart that God raised Him from the dead. How will people hear this truth unless your beautiful feet deliver it? How will they know the love of a Savior unless your life reflects His amazing, graceful love? Open your mouth and share this message. Share about the peace and freedom you found in Christ. Christ came for *all.* Pray for *all* to no longer reject the truth but receive God's love. May Christ's love compel you to share with someone today.

For there is no distinction between Jew and Greek, since the same Lord of all is rich to all who call on Him. For everyone who calls on the name of the Lord will be saved. —Romans 10:12–13

Further Scripture: Romans 10:8b–10, 14–15; 2 Corinthians 5:14

Questions

1. Paul explained that the Israelites had a zeal for God. But what was missing? (Romans 10:2)
2. In the New Living Translation (NLT), Romans 10:4 says, "For Christ has already accomplished the purpose for which the law was given. As a result, all who believe in Him are made right with God." In your own words, write the truths from this verse in a way someone unfamiliar with the Bible might understand it. (Galatians 3:24–25)
3. In Romans 10:8, Paul quotes from Deuteronomy 30:14: "That is, the word of faith that we proclaim." How is Romans 10:9–10 the explanation for this "word of faith"?
4. Describe what "confessing with your mouth Jesus as Lord" means, as though you were explaining it to a child.

5. Do you see a correlation between Romans 10:9–10 and Psalm 19:14? If so, explain it.
6. In Romans 10:18, Paul claimed all have heard the good news, quoting from Psalm 19:4. Read Psalm 19 and Romans 1:18–20 (Isaiah 52:10). Why do we need to go share the good news if it's already been proclaimed? (Isaiah 53:1; Mark 16:15; Romans 10:16; 2 Peter 3:9)
7. What did the Holy Spirit highlight to you in Romans 10 through the reading or the teaching?

WEEK 71

Lesson 11: Romans 11

Justifier: Israel's Rejection Not Total

Teaching Notes

Intro

The whole theme for Romans 9, 10, and 11 is Israel. Today, we will wrap up this section, which shows God is not done with Israel, His chosen people. Romans 9 talks about Israel's *past election* as God's people. Romans 10 talks about Israel's *present rejection* of God. In today's lesson, Romans 11 talks about Israel's *future restoration*. Despite everything, God is not done with Israel. As we read Romans 11, Warren Wiersbe says we cannot apply Romans 11 "to the church today because Paul is discussing a literal future for a literal nation."[1]

Over the years, people have been puzzled, confused, and perplexed with the country of Israel. The Roman government once called Israel "a nefarious sect." Historian Arnold Toynbee called the Israelites "a fossil civilization."[2] In the last two years, the United Nations took a vote and decided the Temple Mount never belonged to the Jewish people. Even in our day, people are still refuting the role of Israel. But the people in the church today need to realize our roots and heritage are in the Jewish people. In Romans 15:25–27, Paul took up a collection from the Gentiles, who had received the spiritual benefit of the Messiah, because they wanted to minister to the poor in Jerusalem. Christians are obligated to minister to the Jews rather than discredit them.

Teaching

Romans 11:1–4: Paul begins by talking about himself. If God had abandoned Israel, then what do we do with Paul who was an Israelite from the tribe of Benjamin? Then, in verses 2–10, Paul continues the argument based on the prophet Elijah. Verse 2 says God has not rejected His people. When Elijah pleaded with God against Israel, God said He had reserved 7,000 men for Himself who had not bowed down to Baal (vv. 2b–4). While these 7,000 men might not have been

[1] Warren W. Wiersbe, *The Wiersbe Bible Commentary: New Testament* (Colorado Springs: David C. Cook, 2007), 438.

[2] Wiersbe, 438.

a whole country, they were a remnant committed to God. In Romans 9:27, Paul quotes Isaiah, who said a remnant of Israel would be saved.

Romans 11:5–8: Paul then transitions to his time, when "a remnant chosen by grace" (v. 5), was chosen by God. The remnant within Israel found salvation (v. 7), while the rest were blinded and hardened. Paul refers to Isaiah 29:10 when he wrote, "God gave them a spirit of insensitivity, eyes that cannot see and ears that cannot hear, to this day." In Deuteronomy 29:4, Moses said God had not given Israel eyes to see and ears to hear.

Romans 11:9–10: Paul next quotes from David's word in Psalm 69:22–23. According to Wiersbe, Israel's blessings became a burden and a judgment. "Their spiritual blessings should have led them to Christ, but instead they became a snare that kept them from Christ."[3]

Romans 11:11–15: Because the Jewish people stumbled, salvation came to the Gentiles to make Israel jealous (v. 11). If the riches have come to the Gentiles, imagine what will happen when the fullness of the Jews takes place (v. 12). Paul was willing to magnify his ministry to the Gentiles so the Jews would become jealous so some of them could be saved (vv. 13–14). Their acceptance would bring life from the dead (v. 15). Just because we're in this period of the Gentiles, it doesn't mean God is done with His people Israel.

Romans 11:16–17: The first part of the dough offered up to God is a symbol so that the rest of the lump can also be holy (v. 16a). In the feast of firstfruits, the priest would offer up a sheaf as a symbol that the whole harvest was His. "If the root is holy, so are the branches" (v. 16b), was the same mentality. The roots represented everything else. As Wiersbe said, "When God accepts the part, He sanctifies the whole."[4] God accepted the founder of the nation—Abraham. Despite the sins of Isaac and Jacob, God still accepted the rest of Israel.[5] The branches that were broken off were the Jewish people who didn't believe (v. 17a). The Gentiles, represented by the wild olive branches, were then grafted into "the rich root of the cultivated olive tree" (v. 17b). Looking back at verse 16, the holy root was the patriarchs' calling, therefore all the branches are holy. The problem is some of those branches have broken off. The picture is this: many of the natural branches were broken off, resulting in more grafted branches than natural branches.[6]

[3] Wiersbe, 439.

[4] Wiersbe, 439.

[5] Wiersbe, 439.

[6] Wiersbe, 439–40.

Romans 11:18–24: Paul then warned the Gentiles not to brag that they were better than the Jews (v. 18). The Gentiles were told to be concerned about the broken branches. This means believers have a responsibility to care for these broken branches—the Jews. For if the Jews do not remain in unbelief, God will graft them in again (v. 23). God will keep His promises to the Jews (v. 24) because the root is still good.

Romans 11:25–27: "A partial hardening has come to Israel until the full number of Gentiles has come in" (v. 25). We don't know what that number is. We do know that we need to go to every country, tribe, tongue, and nation. The partial hardening means there will be a lot of broken natural branches until God says all the Gentiles that He has chosen have come to know the Lord. God's plan included a hardening among the Jews, so the Gentiles could become part of His kingdom. "In this way all Israel will be saved" (v. 26). Paul quotes Isaiah 59:20–21 to make this point. The *Liberator*—Jesus—will come from Zion and take away their sins (vv. 26b–27). God is going to keep His promise. All of Israel will be saved when the fullness of the Gentiles takes place.

Romans 11:28–32: "God's gracious gifts and calling are irrevocable" (v. 29). In Malachi 3:6 God says, "Because I, Yahweh, have not changed." God does not change! The disobedience of the Jews allowed the Gentiles to be saved by God's mercy, which in turn allows Jews who believe in Jesus to also be saved (vv. 30–31).

There is a partial hardening of the Jews until the fullness of the Gentiles takes place. Somewhere in this process, when they see Jesus the Messiah in our lives, they will begin to realize what they have done. Zechariah 12:10 says the Jews will look at the Messiah whom they pierced and weep bitterly for Him. At that moment, according to Matthew 23:39, they will say, "Blessed is he who comes in the name of the Lord" (NIV). When that happens, we will see Jesus for the Messiah will come back. Zechariah 14 tells us Jesus will put His feet on the Mount of Olives and split it in two when He comes back for His people.

Closing

Romans 9—11 show us God is not done with His own people, the Israelites.

The Daily Word

God is not done with His chosen people, the Jewish people. God will have mercy on all, both Gentiles and Jews. The Jewish people will come across the Cornerstone, Jesus, as the Gentiles make them jealous by portraying Christ's love. So there is a call for Gentiles—anyone who is not Jewish—*to live out their faith in a way that provokes the Jews to jealousy.* Allow them to see how amazing Jesus' grace and love is, how awesome His ways are, and the depth of His riches—both wisdom and knowledge. Today, live your life for Jesus in such a way the Jews will want to receive the Messiah as *their* Messiah.

There is more to consider regarding God's kindness. He has called His people to Himself; therefore, He is not done. May they see the one-and-only true Cornerstone, the Living Stone, Jesus, in their lives. For from Him and through Him and to Him are all things. *Live your life in Christ in a way that brings Him glory.* May Jesus' will be done until He returns.

I ask, then, have they stumbled in order to fall? Absolutely not! On the contrary, by their stumbling, salvation has come to the Gentiles to make Israel jealous. Now if their stumbling brings riches for the world, and their failure riches for the Gentiles, how much more will their full number bring! —Romans 11:11–12

Further Scripture: Zechariah 12:10; Matthew 23:37, 39; Romans 11:33, 36

Questions

1. Has God rejected His people, the Israelites (Romans 11:1, 15, 26–29)? Are we now God's chosen people? (Romans 2:29; 11:24–26)
2. What does Romans 11:11b mean by, "but by their [Israel's] transgression salvation has come to the Gentiles, to make them jealous? (Romans 11:14 15)
3. Gentiles are referred to as wild olive branches, and Jews as the cultivated olive branches. Who is the root of the olive tree? (Jeremiah 11:16–17; Hosea 14:4–6; Romans 11:16–18)
4. What caused the natural branches mentioned in Romans 11:21 to be cut off (Romans 11:17, 20, 23)? What did they not believe? (John 3:16–18; Romans 10:9–10)
5. Have you ever felt God owed you something (Job 41:11; Romans 11:35)? When reading Romans 11:36, do you wrestle with everything being from Him, through Him, and to Him? Why or why not?
6. What did the Holy Spirit highlight to you in Romans 11 through the reading or the teaching?

WEEK 71

Lesson 12: Romans 12

Justifier: A Living Sacrifice, the Body of Christ

Teaching Notes

Intro

Although Paul had never been to Rome, he wrote this letter to pour into those believers. In Romans 12—16, "Paul explains in great detail how believers are to practically live out the theological truths that come from Romans 1—11. God has graciously given believers so much that Paul exhorts them to respond in grateful obedience."[1] Can we obey what we know to be true? In this section, Paul walked them through the process of how they could get through life. When you walk out these truths, then Christ will be with you every step of the way.

Teaching

Romans 12:1: Wiersbe said the first two verses in this chapter address our relationship to God.[2] This applies to all believers, both men and women. The word "urge" can also be translated as "beseech," and means "to crawl alongside to help."[3] MacArthur said, "Under the Old Covenant, God accepted the sacrifices of dead animals. But because of Christ's ultimate sacrifice, the Old Testament sacrifices are no longer of any effect."[4] Now we present our bodies—not literally putting ourselves on an altar to die—but offering ourselves completely to the Lord. How do we do that? Living sacrifice means that it is ongoing—wherever I go, wherever I'm breathing, whatever I'm looking at or hearing, I'm giving everything to bring glory to Him without holding anything back. Scripture says that is holy and pleasing to the Lord. MacArthur continues, "Under God's control, the believers' yet-unredeemed body can and must be yielded to Him as an instrument of righteousness."[5] This is our "spiritual worship" (v 1).

---

[1] John MacArthur, *The MacArthur Bible Commentary* (Nashville: Thomas Nelson, 2005), 1544.

[2] Warren W. Wiersbe, *The Wiersbe Bible Commentary: New Testament* (Colorado Springs: David C. Cook, 2007), 441.

[3] MacArthur, 1544.

[4] MacArthur, 1545.

[5] MacArthur, 1545.

Romans 12:2: If we're going to be a living sacrifice to the Lord, then we can't be conformed to this age, this culture, or the customs of this time. Instead, we have to be transformed by the Word of God. We do this so when we come into an environment, we can discern what is good, pleasing, and the perfect will of God. The Word of God will renew your mind so when you come into an environment, the Holy Spirit will give you the gift of discernment so you can discern what you should be doing for the Lord. MacArthur said Paul's letter implied these believers were already being conformed to the Roman environment and were not being transformed by the renewing of their minds; Paul wanted them to stop giving into the values of the worldly age.[6] If people went into your house or into your car, would they see that you reflect the world or the Lord? The word "transform" means "metamorphosis" and "connotes a change in outward appearance."[7]

Romans 12:3–16: According to Wiersbe, because we have a relationship with the Lord, these verses address our relationship to other believers.[8] Verse 3 warns believers against elevating themselves above others. Jesus never did this, and neither should we. Instead, we should think sensibly about each other because each person can make a difference for the kingdom of God. This measure of faith is not saving faith, but according to MacArthur is "the correct proportion of the spiritual gift—or supernatural endowment and ability—the Holy Spirit gives each believer so he may fulfill his role in the body of Christ."[9] The measure of faith given to each believer may be different, but it is the amount needed to fulfill our role. Verses 4–5 describe the way believers work together as the body of Christ to fulfill God's purposes. Verses 6–8 describe the different gifts God has given to believers so each can contribute to the kingdom of God. MacArthur says prophecy could mean "speaking forth."[10]

Every believer has a unique role. We need people who can serve, who can teach, and who can give a prophetic word: 1 Corinthians 14:3 says people who prophesy "speaks to people for edification, encouragement, and consolation." Those three things are the guardrails for people who prophesy. The gift of exhortation calls others to obey and to follow God's truth. It may be used to warn or correct somebody regarding their sin. The gift of giving is not cheap, not tight, and does not give with stipulations or strings. When you give, you give with generosity and praise to the Lord. The gift of leading means "standing before."[11] Paul

[6] MacArthur, 1545.

[7] MacArthur, 1545.

[8] Wiersbe, 442.

[9] MacArthur, 1545.

[10] MacArthur, 1546.

[11] MacArthur, 1546.

called this the gift of administration to describe someone who guides or steers the ship. As MacArthur said, "In the New Testament, this word is used to describe leadership in the home and in the church."[12] Showing mercy means you actually care about people, and you do so cheerfully. We need all of these parts of the body of Christ. There is not one that is better than another.

Verse 9 points out we can't fake any of this. Verse 10 tells us to show love and honor to one another. Verse 11 tells us to serve the Lord diligently and to be fervent in spirit, or "'to boil in spirit.' This phrase suggests having plenty of heat to produce adequate, productive energy, but not so much heat that one goes out of control."[13] Verses 12–17 are talking about unity.

When you realize that in unity, we need each other, we realize there is not one part more important than another. The body of Christ needs all of these parts. The American church needs to embrace in humility that it's all about the Head—Jesus Christ.

Romans 12:17–21: Wiersbe says these verses describe our relationship to our enemies.[14]

Closing

Nelson's Commentary uses a funny phrase, "comparison-itis," to describe our tendency to compare ourselves with others. We do this when we think they are more valuable than us, when we think they are better than us, or we are better than them.[15] Instead of looking at others, the better question is to ask how God views us. When we do this, then no one else defines us—instead, God defines us. We are defined by renewing our minds in Christ and walking out the will of the Father. When we do that, we can express His gifts.

The Daily Word

God has been merciful to you through the death and resurrection of Jesus Christ. Because of Jesus, you are justified by faith. Just as you have received mercy from God, it is now your turn to pour mercy into others . . . not in your own strength but in the strength that comes from your daily worship of the Lord and the renewing of your mind. This means reading the Word, spending time in prayer,

[12] MacArthur, 1546.

[13] MacArthur, 1546.

[14] Wiersbe, 443.

[15] Earl D. Radmacher, Ronald B. Allen, and H. Wayne House, eds., *Nelson's New Illustrated Bible Commentary* (Nashville: Thomas Nelson, 1999), 1448.

thanking and praising the Lord. As the Holy Spirit works in you, your life will be transformed, giving you the strength to show the Lord's mercy to others.

Ask yourself and be honest: Are you renewing your mind daily in worship to the Lord? If you are worn out and weary, it may be time to pause and worship the Lord. Love the Lord with all you have. It's a daily living sacrifice. Then you are able to discern God's will. Through this discipline, you will be filled with His power and His Spirit to walk out the mercy and love He wants to pour out through you into His people. Then the world will know of His great love.

Therefore, brothers, by the mercies of God, I urge you to present your bodies as a living sacrifice, holy and pleasing to God; this is your spiritual worship. Do not be conformed to this age, but be transformed by the renewing of your mind, so that you may discern what is the good, pleasing, and perfect will of God. —Romans 12:1–2

Further Scripture: Romans 12:9–12; 1 Corinthians 6:19–20; Hebrews 13:15–16

Questions

1. In Romans 12:1, what does Paul mean when he said "to present your bodies as a living and holy sacrifice"? (1 Samuel 15:22; Psalm 40:6–8; Amos 5:21–24)
2. As Christians, how do we live in the world without conforming to it? How can we represent Christ with our actions? (John 4:7–9; 8:3–11; Luke 15:1–7)
3. According to Romans 12, what are some of the gifts God gives us? What gift(s) has God given you? How should you use your gifts to edify the church?
4. What does Romans 12 say about revenge and how to act toward your enemies? In your life, is this an easy thing to do?
5. Romans 12:18 says, "If possible, so far as it depends on you, be at peace with all men." What kind of peace can we have with Jesus as our Lord and Savior? (Isaiah 26:2–3; John 14:26–27; 1 Peter 3:9)
6. What did the Holy Spirit highlight to you in Romans 12 through the reading or the teaching?

WEEK 72

Lesson 13: Romans 13

Justifier: Our Relationship to Authorities; Putting on Christ

Teaching Notes

Intro

Our word for the book of Romans is *Justifier*. Jesus has justified our sins. Once we put our faith in Christ, we are justified. In Romans 12—16, we see how we can live out the theological foundational truths of Romans 1—11. In Romans 12, we talked about our relationship to God, to other believers, and to our enemies. In our relationship with God, we have the renewing of our minds that allows us to experience the will of God. In our relationship with other believers, we learned we aren't better than someone else and we can't think more highly of ourselves than someone else. All of us play an important part in the body of Christ. In our relationship with our enemies, we have to feed them, love them, bless them, pray for them, and take care of them. All of these are possible because of our relationship with Christ. According to Warren Wiersbe, the entire thirteenth chapter addresses our relationship to the state.[1] When Paul wrote this book, Nero was in power. Paul encouraged believers to submit to governing authorities. God put this in place: every believer is to be subject to the authorities.

Teaching

Romans 13:1: Believers must submit to governing authorities, for they have been instituted by God. Even when we don't like them or agree with them, we have to submit to them because God put them there. The question we have to ask is what does submission look like? The reality is submission is never easy. *Nelson's Commentary* said, "Human nature tends toward resistance and even rebellion, especially if the government is imposed, incompetent, and/or corrupt."[2] *Nelson's Commentary* offered four things to understand about submitting to authority.

[1] Warren W. Wiersbe, *The Wiersbe Bible Commentary: New Testament* (Colorado Springs: David C. Cook, 2007), 443.

[2] Earl D. Radmacher, Ronald B. Allen, and H. Wayne House, eds., *Nelson's New Illustrated Bible Commentary* (Nashville: Thomas Nelson, 1999), 1449.

First, we have to understand God is the ultimate authority.[3] The government as an institution has been established by God to serve His purposes. God raises up and takes away the leaders.

Romans 13:2: Those who resist authority are resisting God's command and will experience judgment (v. 2). According to *Nelson's Commentary*, the second thing we have to understand is "both followers and leaders are ultimately accountable to God."[4] *Nelson's Commentary* continues, "Submission to human authority reflects our submission to God's authority."[5]

Romans 13:3–4: Third, *Nelson's Commentary* states, "God uses government to carry out His good purposes on earth."[6] God designed it so the government could rule and regulate and help take care of people, not to dominate them. *Nelson's Commentary* continues, "Without question, some governments sometimes persecute those who do good."[7] Paul experienced that with Nero. But mainly, those who are criminal, and who do not obey the law are those who should fear the government. In other words, as long as we stay in the lanes, then we're fine. But when we do wrong, then we need to be afraid because the government, as God's avenger, will bring wrath on the one who does wrong (v. 4).

Romans 13:5: Fourth, *Nelson's Commentary* states, "Obedience is a matter of inner convictions as well as external law."[8] "Our motivation to obey must go beyond fear of punishment. As believers, we serve the highest of all authorities, God Himself . . . only when the government commands us to do what God prohibits can we disobey."[9] This goes back to Romans 12. Some of us conform to this world because we don't know what the Word of God says to discern what is right or wrong. If we don't know God's Word, then we just blend into the world.

Romans 13:6–7: For this reason, we have to pay our taxes because we believe the Word of God is true, because we believe these people are God's authorities, and because the Word of God says we're supposed to pay taxes. In addition to paying taxes and tolls to those whom we owe, we are commanded to show respect and honor to those we should respect and honor (v. 7).

---

[3] Radmacher et al., 1449.

[4] Radmacher et al., 1449.

[5] Radmacher et al., 1449.

[6] Radmacher et al., 1449.

[7] Radmacher et al., 1449.

[8] Radmacher et al., 1449.

[9] Radmacher et al., 1449.

Romans 13:8–10: These verses transition from obeying the government to loving others. "Love, therefore, is the fulfillment of the law" (v. 10). So, what is our relationship to the government and to the state? We love them.

Romans 13:11–14: We do this for Jesus' sake. We can't play games of hating people and not liking them and trying to cheat the system. Christ is coming back! Our salvation is nearer than when we first believed (v. 11). We can't play this game of being conformed to the world. We have to wake up and renew our minds. We have to ask God how we can show love. We don't have time to be mean to others, to be against our government, to be against our neighbors who vote differently from us. As believers, we have to get our act together. "But put on the Lord Jesus Christ" (v. 14). We are called to reflect Christ to this world. Don't make any plans to satisfy fleshly desires—don't be conformed to the world. Instead, we must put on Christ, put on truth, put on righteousness, put on peace, so we will reflect Christ. When we put on the Lord Jesus Christ, we have to do it when we're dealing with the government as well.

Closing

God is the ultimate authority. As followers and leaders, we are ultimately accountable to Him. God uses government to carry out His good purposes on earth. Ultimately, obedience is what matters. We have to be obedient to the Word of God wherever we're at. That means loving them (authorities) and looking like Jesus.

The Daily Word

As a believer, you serve God—the ultimate authority over all. And as a believer, you must submit to governing officials because God has instituted them. If you respect God as your authority, then you should respect governing officials. As you follow the Lord, you put on Jesus Christ. In doing so, you put on truth, peace, and righteousness, just like putting on clothing. When people see you, they should see the attributes of Christ. You display love to all people, even those placed as authority in government.

Love your governing officials. Pray for them. God desires for all to know His love. What if your role is to love like Jesus and look like Jesus as you interact with governing officials so they know the truth of the gospel through you? Don't let pride and fleshly desires get in the way. Trust God as your ultimate authority and humbly walk out the love of Christ. Be Jesus with skin on. Love others, love your neighbors, and love those in authority as governing officials. This is how the world will truly change—when they want to know the Jesus in you.

Everyone must submit to the governing authorities, for there is no authority except from God, and those that exist are instituted by God. —Romans 13:1

Further Scripture: Romans 13:7, 14; 1 Timothy 2:1–2

Questions

1. According to Romans 13, why should we respect governing authorities? How well do you think Christians do when it comes to being in subjection to governing authorities? Do you put your trust in politicians or God? Think about it.
2. Is it ever OK to disobey man's law? Why or why not? (Esther 3:2–4; Daniel 3:9–18; 6:11–13; Acts 4:18–20)
3. How can loving our "neighbor" keep us from breaking many of the commandments?
4. What or who is love? (Romans 13:10; 1 Corinthians 13:4–8; 1 John 4:8, 10, 18)
5. According to Romans 13:12, what day is near? (2 Peter 3:10–18)
6. What did the Holy Spirit highlight to you in Romans 13 through the reading or the teaching?

Lesson 14: Romans 14

Justifier: Love in Unity Without Judgment

Teaching Notes

Intro

The word that describes the Messiah (Jesus) in the book of Romans is *Justifier*, who has justified us before God. The context in chapter 14 is interacting with weak believers and with strong believers. Throughout this chapter, we'll see instructions to relate to "one another."

MacArthur describes the background of this chapter as having a threat to the unity of the church when "mature (strong) believers—both Jews and Gentiles—conflict with immature (weak) believers."[1] MacArthur goes on to explain this conflict:

> The strong Jewish believers understood their freedom in Christ and realized that the ceremonial requirements of the Mosaic Law were no longer binding. The mature Gentiles understood that idols are not gods and, therefore, that they could eat meat that had been offered to them. But in both cases, the weaker brothers' consciences were troubled, and they were even temped to violate their consciences (a bad thing to train oneself to do).[2]

MacArthur explains the issues the weaker believers were struggling with:

> The weak Jewish believer had difficulty abandoning the rites and prohibitions of the old covenant; he felt compelled to adhere to dietary laws, observe the Sabbath, and offer sacrifices in the temple. The weak Gentile believer had been steeped in pagan idolatry and its rituals; he felt that any contact with anything remotely related to his past,

[1] John MacArthur, *The MacArthur Bible Commentary* (Nashville: Thomas Nelson, 2005), 1550.

[2] MacArthur, 1550.

> including eating meat that had been offered to a pagan deity and then sold in the marketplace, tainted him with sin.[3]

This difference of understanding in faith was leading to conflict that could destroy the church's unity.

Teaching

Romans 14:1–12: Wiersbe summarizes these verses as, "Receive One Another."[4] Accept all, even those who are weaker in the faith, without arguing with them over issues not about salvation (v. 1). For example, Romans 12 provides information on the gifts of the Spirit, something that is misunderstood by weak or new believers and can often become something that divides a congregation when people are judged by having or not having gifts. The issue of food should not be a conflict, because believers are free to eat anything (v. 2). Those who have differing opinions should not judge each other, because God has accepted them both (v. 3). In fact, we should not criticize those who belong to the Master (v. 4). Some have different opinions about which day of the week is holy and should not be judged for that (v. 5). The day is observed to honor the Lord; the food is given by the Lord (v. 6). We live and die for the Lord, because we belong to the Lord (vv. 7–8).

Therefore, "Christ died and came to life for this: that He might rule over both the dead and the living" (v. 9). MacArthur explains it this way: "Christ died not only to free us from sin, but to enslave us to Himself (Romans 6:22); to establish Himself as Sovereign over the saints in His presence and those still on earth"[5] (Philippians 2:11; 1 Timothy 6:15; Revelation 17:14, 19:16). Verses 10–11 summarize Paul's teaching—Christ died for us all, so we have no reason or authority to criticize one another. Everyone will give praise and glory to God (Isaiah 45:23; 49:18; Philippians 2:10; Revelation 20:11–15). And we will all stand before the Lord to be judged (v. 12). Therefore, we are to receive one another.

Romans 14:13–23: Wiersbe summarizes this section as, "Edify One Another."[6] Verse 13 says do not criticize or put a stumbling block before one another (1 Corinthians 8:1). Paul restated that nothing is unclean in itself, but if someone thinks something is unclean, then it is unclean to him (vv. 14–16). This was given to Paul through divine revelation from Christ. In verse 17, Paul stresses his point—God's kingdom is about righteousness, not rules about what to eat or drink.

---

[3] MacArthur, 1551.

[4] Warren W. Wiersbe, *The Bible Exposition Commentary: Matthew–Galatians* (Colorado Springs: David C. Cook, 1989), 558.

[5] MacArthur, 1552.

[6] Wiersbe, 560.

We have been justified in Christ as citizens of God. We are to have "righteousness, peace, and joy in the Holy Spirit" (v. 17). Righteousness means to live holy lives (Ephesians 6:14). Peace means "loving tranquility, produced by the Spirit, that should characterize believers' relationships with God and each other (Galatians 5:22)."[7] MacArthur explains, "Joy in the Holy Spirit" is "another part of the Spirit's fruit, this describes an abiding attitude of praise and thanksgiving regardless or circumstances, which flows from one's confidence in God's sovereignty (Galatians 5:22; 1 Thessalonians 1:6)."[8] We are to focus on these fruits of the Spirit rather than what others are doing to be acceptable to God (v. 18). This removes the barriers between weak/immature believers and strong/mature believers who can function in unity and build up one another (v. 19). Don't cause others to stumble by what we do (vv. 20–21). Believers must not force their convictions on others but rather only share them with God (v. 22).

Closing

Wiersbe sums up this chapter with these words: "Believers may hold different convictions about many matters, but they must hold them in love."[9]

The Daily Word

The Lord calls you to receive one another. Just as you would receive a gift or accept a compliment, you are to receive one another. This requires you to love like Christ loves. Do not be judgmental. Do not argue about opinions when others are weaker in faith. Do not criticize. Do not be a stumbling block or a pitfall in your brother's way. That's a lot of "don'ts." However, as a follower of Christ in the kingdom of God, you are called to righteousness, peace, and joy in the Holy Spirit. Therefore, as you walk in the power of the Holy Spirit, you will bear these fruits demonstrating Christ's love.

Righteousness, peace, and joy create unity and promote encouragement. God's not asking you to play umpire or referee in the kingdom of God. God alone holds authority and judgment. He simply asks you to bear His fruit of the Spirit, which will result as you abide in Him and His love. Today, don't get bogged down by all the differences in the body of Christ. Seek to love and receive one another. Then the peace, joy, and righteousness you desire will abound through the power of the Holy Spirit!

[7] MacArthur, 1552.

[8] MacArthur, 1552.

[9] Wiersbe, 561.

For the kingdom of God is not eating and drinking, but righteousness, peace, and joy in the Holy Spirit. Whoever serves Christ in this way is acceptable to God and approved by men. So then, we must pursue what promotes peace and what builds up one another. —Romans 14:17–19

Further Scripture: Romans 14:1, 13; Colossians 3:14

Questions

1. Paul instructed us in Romans 14:1–3 not to pass judgment on one another on disputable matters. What are disputable matters? Do you think there is still this tendency today among believers and churches?
2. Read Romans 14:9. What does it mean that Christ might be Lord of both the dead and the living? (Philippians 2:8–11)
3. Paul instructed the Romans not to judge one another; instead, they were to do what (Romans 14:13)? How does what Paul said correlate with Romans 16:17?
4. According to Romans 14:14, Paul was convinced nothing is unclean in itself. What types of things was he referring to? (Romans 14:20–21)
5. What does Romans 14:17 say the kingdom of God consists of? Do you think we, as part of the kingdom, put a major focus on minor things, and as a result, we miss obeying Romans 14:19? If so, how can we change this pattern?
6. The same verbiage used in Romans 14:18 (acceptable or pleasing to God) is used in Romans 12:1. Explain how they are connected.
7. What did the Holy Spirit highlight to you in Romans 14 through the reading or the teaching?

WEEK 72

Lesson 15: Romans 15

Justifier: The Jerusalem Collection

Teaching Notes

Intro

Romans 14 contains a series of "one another's." Believers were commanded to edify, encourage, and build up "one another." Romans 15 will exhort believers to "please one another."

Teaching

Romans 15:1–4: When we think about serving others, we tend to think about doing things that we don't really want to do: the dishes, cutting the grass, picking up around the house, etc. But what would it look like for us to serve others in spiritual matters? John Macarthur pointed out that the word translated "to bear" in this passage is the same word used to describe carrying a pitcher of water (Mark 14:13), carrying a person (Acts 21:35), and of figuratively bearing an obligation (Acts 15:10).[1] Paul's exhortation to the Romans was for them to do whatever they could to help ease the burden of their brothers and sisters in Christ. Burden bearing could have been as simple as helping perform a mundane task, sharing a word of encouragement, or anything that put pleasing someone else before themselves.

Jesus was the ultimate demonstration of serving others before Himself. But the Romans could also find encouragement to care for one another in this way throughout Scripture. The Romans were to take the focus off themselves, including the things they did day-to-day that would normally distract them from caring for others, and place their attention on the needs, wants, and desires of others.

Romans 15:8–13: Wiersbe notes this section of Romans elaborated on Jesus' ministry to the Gentiles.[2] Jesus served the Jewish people so that Gentiles might also come to faith in Him. Both people groups were included in the work of Christ.

[1] John MacArthur, *The MacArthur Bible Commentary* (Nashville: Thomas Nelson, 2005), 1553.

[2] Warren W. Wiersbe, *The Wiersbe Bible Commentary: New Testament* (Colorado Springs: David C. Cook, 2007), 448.

Romans 15:14–24: Wiersbe notes a transition from Jesus' ministry to the Gentiles, to Paul's ministry to the Gentiles.[3] Paul's aim in ministry was simply to share the gospel of Christ with as many people as possible. Not only that, Paul's desire was to take the gospel to places where no one had ever heard of Jesus. Paul had never visited the believers in Rome. He had always been prevented either through his work in other places or unforeseen circumstances. However, he now planned to visit Rome as he traveled to share the gospel in Spain.

Romans 15:25–29: Paul's ministry was to the Gentiles, but Wiersbe points out that the Gentiles were to then minister to the Jews.[4] As Paul wrote his letter to the Romans, he was travelling to Jerusalem with a gift to the Jewish believers there, from the Gentile believers in Macedonia and Achaia. Why would the believers in Macedonia and Achaia want to make a contribution to the believers in Jerusalem? Why would Paul, the missionary to the Gentiles, even care about taking a gift from Gentile believers to believers in Jerusalem? Because the believers in Macedonia and Achaia were "indebted to them" (v. 27). The Gentiles were now part of the same spiritual family as the believers in Jerusalem. They had shared in the spiritual benefits of the Jews, namely salvation in Christ, so now they shared their material goods with the Jewish believers in Jerusalem.

Romans 15:30–33: Paul requested prayers for his deliverance from the "unbelievers in Judea" who may prevent him from delivering the churches' gifts to the saints in Jerusalem. He also asked for the Romans to pray that his plans to visit them might finally be fulfilled.

The Jerusalem Collection: A financial gift was collected from various churches in Greece and Asia Minor and sent to the impoverished mother church in Jerusalem under the leadership of Paul. This gift let the mother church in Jerusalem know they played a significant role in Paul's ministry to the Gentiles throughout the world. Paul understood the value of the Gentile church investing back into Israel both financially and spiritually. Paul had three motives for taking up this collection:[5]

1. *Help for the poor.* Paul wanted to help poor Christians in Jerusalem as a demonstration of the love of God that the Gentiles found in Christ. Paul also wrote about the collection to the Corinthian church: "I am not saying

---

[3] Wiersbe, 448.

[4] Wiersbe, 449.

[5] Scot McKnight, "Collection for the Saints," in Gerald F. Hawthorne, Ralph P. Martin, and Daniel G. Reid, eds. *Dictionary of Paul and His Letters* (Downers Grove, IL: IVP, 1993), 143–47.

this as a command. Rather, by means of the diligence of others, I am testing the genuineness of your love." (2 Corinthians 8:8) "For the ministry of this service is not only supplying the needs of the saints, but is also overflowing in many acts of thanksgiving to God. They will glorify God for your obedience to the confession of the gospel of Christ, and for your generosity in sharing with them and with others through the proof provided by this service. And they will have deep affection for you in their prayers on your behalf because of the surpassing grace of God in you. Thanks be to God for His indescribable gift" (2 Corinthians 9:12–15).

2. *Unity of the church.* Paul was eager to demonstrate to the church in Jerusalem that even though the Gentiles believers didn't observe the Law, there was only one gospel, one Lord, and, as a result, only one church.
3. *To stir up jealousy.* While Paul was called to share the gospel with the Gentiles, he maintained a passion to see his Jewish brethren come to faith in Christ after being provoked to jealousy over what the Gentiles experienced.

Closing

Paul's work in taking up the collection for Jerusalem runs all through the second half of Acts and through many of his letters. In 2 Corinthians, Paul boasts about the Corinthians' generosity in giving to this collection. If you have a desire to sow back into Jerusalem as the source of our spiritual blessing, don't hesitate to do so.

The Daily Word

What is hope? Hope is a desire or expectation for a certain thing to happen: "I hope you get better." "I hope surgery goes well." "I hope you get the job." It is the God of hope who fills you with all joy and peace as you believe in Him. If you are hoping for something, remain in the Lord, rest in Him, and abide in His love for you. Wait and trust the Lord. In Christ, you will have peace and joy while hoping. The Lord promises you will actually overflow with hope through the power of the Holy Spirit. Picture a kitchen sink overflowing with water and spilling all over a floor. That's how much hope the Holy Spirit will give you!

As you hope for unity in the body of Christ, walk in the power of the Holy Spirit. As you hope in the Lord for His future for your life, walk in the power of the Holy Spirit. Paul's travel plans were often altered even though he strongly desired and hoped to go to Rome. But God had another plan for him to travel to Jerusalem where He used Paul in a mighty way to serve the saints. When you focus on the hope found in Christ, you have peace and joy whatever the outcome may be, because you are aligned with God's will. Today, place your hope in the Lord alone!

Now may the God of hope fill you with all joy and peace as you believe in Him so that you may overflow with hope by the power of the Holy Spirit. —Romans 15:13

Further Scripture: Psalm 33:20–22; Romans 15:22–25; Hebrews 10:23

Questions

1. In Romans 15:2, Paul writes, "We should help others do what is right and build them up in the Lord." How could we put this command into practice? Has someone built you up in the Lord? How so?
2. How does Romans 15:12 point to Jesus? What did Isaiah mean by a "root of Jesse"? (Isaiah 11:1–5)
3. What did Paul mean in Romans 15:20? How would you explain Romans 15:21 to someone?
4. What did the Holy Spirit highlight to you in Romans 15 through the reading or the teaching?

WEEK 72

Lesson 16: Romans 16

Justifier: Paul's Final Greetings

Teaching Notes

Intro

Romans is truly about the gospel. It's about the Apostle Paul delivering a word to the church in Rome explaining how to practically live out what they knew to be true. In Romans 16, Paul mentions all the people who played an important part in his life. This chapter is like the conclusion—the list of credits at the end of a show or movie.

Teaching

Romans 16:1–2: Paul commended Phoebe to the Romans, entrusting her to deliver the letter to the believers there. She was truly the deliverer of the good news to the Roman church. Paul urged them to welcome her and assist her "in a way worthy of his people" (v. 2). In other words, make sure she has a place to stay, food, and fellowship with other believers. Can you imagine—Phoebe held one of the 66 books of the Bible, and she probably had no clue!

Romans 16:3–16: Paul sent greetings to Priscilla and Aquila, his coworkers who had risked their lives for him. He expressed thankfulness from both himself and the Gentile churches (v. 4). Paul urged the Romans to greet the church that met in their home (v. 5a), including Epaenetus, the first one in Asia to convert to Christ (v. 5b). Paul added greetings to Mary (v. 6), and fellow countrymen and prisoners Andronicus and Junia (v. 7). He greeted Ampliatus (v. 8), Urbanus and Stachys (v. 9), Apelles and the household of Aristobulus (v. 10), Herodion and the household of Narcissus (v. 11), Tryphaena, Tryphosa, Persis (v. 12), Rufus and his mother (v. 13), Asyncritus, Phlegon, Hermes, Patrobas, Hermas (v. 14), Philologus, Julius, Nereus and his sister, and Olympas (v. 15). Paul honored these people as hard workers who had done much in the ministry of Christ. As the one who established these churches, Paul sent their greetings to the believers in Rome (v. 16).

Romans 16:17–18: Paul told them to watch for and avoid those who caused "dissension and obstacles contrary to the doctrine" they had learned (v. 17). Be careful of them, because they don't serve Christ, but are in it for themselves (v. 18). They talk in ways that sound good; but be careful, because they aren't legitimate.

Romans 16:19–20: Paul consistently uses the phrase, "the grace of our Lord Jesus be with you," in his benedictions (1 Corinthians 16:23; 2 Corinthians 13:13; Galatians 6:18; Ephesians 6:24; Philippians 4:23; Colossians 4:18; 1 Thessalonians 5:28; 2 Thessalonians 3:18; 1 Timothy 6:21; 2 Timothy 4:22; Titus 3:15; Philemon 15:25).

Romans 16:21–24: These were the people Paul poured into, but at the same time he wasn't alone. Timothy was Paul's coworker; Lucius, Jason, and Sosipater were his fellow countrymen (v. 21). Tertius, who wrote the letter, was Paul's secretary (v. 22). Gaius hosted Paul and the church; Erastus handled the money, and Quartus was probably one of Paul's converts. This is the group who said hello to the remnant of believers in the church at Rome.

Romans 16:25–27: MacArthur describes "the mystery kept silent for long ages" (v. 25) as "the mystery that God would provide salvation for the Gentiles as well as the Jews."[1] It was something hidden in former times but was now made known.

This was a group of people that the Apostle Paul had gotten to know somewhere in his journey, whom he knew would be in Rome when his letter arrived. This provides the biblical basis for a ministry model that Kyle believes is from the Lord. When you look at the life of Jesus, there was a population of about 12,000 to 15,000 around the Sea of Galilee. Jesus poured into 12 people in that population (which aligns with Kyle's story about receiving a word in Ashville, NC on how to reach a city based on the formula: the square root of one percent of the population). At the time Paul wrote to Rome, there were about one million people in the city. When you take the square root of one percent of that number, Paul needed to pour into about 100 people in the city of Rome. While Paul didn't list 100 names in this chapter, if you add in the number of people in the home churches or in the households' names, you have to wonder if that added up to about 100 people.

Here's Paul's approach, which he learned from Christ: Paul knew he had to pour into the people. An effective ministry isn't just preaching to the masses; it's pouring into the people who will carry on the work of the Lord. The key is discipling people. This was what Paul did. Barnabas poured into Paul and John Mark.

---

[1] John MacArthur, *The MacArthur Bible Commentary* (Nashville: Thomas Nelson, 2005), 1560.

At the same time, Paul poured into Priscilla and Aquila. Acts 18:24–28 states Priscilla and Aquila poured into Apollos. Then Apollos took the gospel to Achaia. Paul poured into Titus and Timothy. In 2 Timothy 2:2, Paul told Timothy to share the gospel with "faithful men who will be able to teach others also." The end goal is that the remnant sustains itself and through discipleship can continue to carry the gospel. Instead of worrying about pouring into crowds of people, we need to worry about pouring into the person right in front of us. We have to pour into the remnant right in front of us so they can do the same. Remember Barnabas had to overcome his fear of pouring into Saul, who became Paul. Paul was a man who literally changed the world, yet nobody ever says Barnabas' name. But if Barnabas hadn't been obedient to the Lord by putting his hands on Paul and praying for him, who knows if others would have ever heard about the Lord. The people listed in this chapter were the people Paul poured into because Barnabas first poured into Paul.

Closing

When we find people who are willing to share the gospel message with others, we have to continue to pour into them. Why do we do this? Because our lives have been changed by the *Justifier*. In the book of Romans, Jesus serves as the Savior who justifies our sins. He has justified us by dying on the cross. That's the message the remnant embraces. When you embrace this incredible picture of salvation, you can tell everybody—one person at a time.

The Daily Word

Paul greeted many of the Roman Christians that he encountered along his journey while delivering the gospel. He poured into these specific people and spent time in their homes. Paul shared the good news with them so they could take the gospel even farther. Paul discipled all these people and invested in their lives.

You are called to do that same thing—to invest in the people around you with the message of the gospel. When you do, those people can carry the gospel to those around them, and the cycle continues. That was how Jesus did ministry and how Paul modeled Jesus' ministry by delivering the gospel truth that transforms lives. The question remains: What does your list of names look like? *Who are you pouring into with the message of Jesus' grace?* Perhaps your children, your grandchildren, your neighbors, or coworkers? You will impact lives when you love people like Jesus and share about His grace in your life. It's not a complicated program or conference; *it's simply loving people according to the gospel of Jesus Christ.* Today, go and love.

Give my greetings to Prisca and Aquila, my coworkers in Christ Jesus, who risked their own necks for my life. Not only do I thank them, but so do all the Gentile churches. Greet also the church that meets in their home. Greet my dear friend Epaenetus, who is the first convert to Christ from Asia. Greet Mary, who has worked very hard for you. —Romans 16:3–6

Further Scripture: Romans 16:19–20, 25; 2 Timothy 2:2

Questions

1. In Romans 16:17–18, Paul warns that people who caused division should be avoided. Have you known someone who caused division? How so? Did you avoid them? Did they divide many?
2. How would you explain what Paul tried to say in Romans 16:19? Why would this be important? (Psalm 19:7; 1 Corinthians 15:33; 2Timothy 3:15)
3. In most of Romans 16, Paul sent greetings to a list of people. In your opinion, was there a specific reason for this or was Paul just saying hello?
4. What did the Holy Spirit highlight to you in Romans 16 through the reading or the teaching?

WEEK 72

Lesson 17: 1 Corinthians 1

The Last Adam: Bringing Glory to God

Teaching Notes

Intro

Today, we start the first lesson in 1 Corinthians and our seventeenth lesson in the Pauline epistles. Corinthians is divided into two letters and was named after the city of Corinth, Greece. Mindi's painting for Corinthians is another diptych—two paintings put together that tell the complete story. The nine hands in the first painting represent the nine corporate gifts of the Holy Spirit that can only be obtained through love. The veil from the second painting is seen at the top of the first painting and represents the Holy Spirit covering all of us in the body of Christ. Our phrase for the Messiah in 1 Corinthians (from 1 Corinthians 15:45) is *The Last Adam*. The first Adam brought sin on humanity; *The Last Adam* would take on that sin as His own for humanity.

MacArthur explains, "With the exception of personal epistles addressed to Timothy, Titus, and Philemon, all of Paul's letters indicate the name of the city where the church addressed existed."[1] Paul claimed authorship in verses 1 and 13 (1 Corinthians 3:4–6; 4:15). Paul wrote the letter from Ephesus in the last half of AD 55 during his third missionary journey (1 Corinthians 16:21). Paul planned to stay in Ephesus for three years, leaving at Pentecost in the spring, and then moving on to Corinth.

The city of Corinth was located 45 miles south of Athens on the Isthmus of Corinth, a narrow strip of land that connected Peloponnese to the mainland of Greece. That means the city of Corinth actually had two seaports—the Saronic Gulf on the east side and the Gulf of Corinth on the west. This was a major and dangerous sailing route. Ships took a short-cut across the isthmus by using large logs to roll the ships across the land, saving time and evading the danger, making the city of Corinth an important trade city. Corinth hosted the Isthmian games, an athletic contest of that period (the other was the Olympic games). MacArthur notes, "Even by the pagan standards of its own culture, Corinth became

[1] John MacArthur, *The MacArthur Bible Commentary* (Nashville: Thomas Nelson, 2005), 1561.

so morally corrupt that its very name became synonymous with debauchery and moral depravity. To 'corinthianize' came to represent gross immorality and drunken debauchery."[2] Paul described this immorality in Romans 1:18–32.

Paul founded the church in Corinth on his second missionary journey (Acts 18:1). Paul first ministered in the synagogue, where he met Jewish believers, Priscilla and Aquila. Silas and Timothy later joined him there in ministry. Although most of the Jews rejected Paul's message of Christ, Crispus, the leader of the synagogue, his family, and others, accepted it and followed Paul into the new church (Acts 18:5–8). Paul remained in Corinth for a year and a half before he was charged by Jewish leaders before the Roman tribunal for religious crimes. Paul's charges were dismissed because he had not broken any civil laws. He left Corinth shortly afterward for Ephesus and then to Israel, taking Priscilla and Aquila with him.[3] The church in Corinth had become divided and worldly. Paul addressed those issues in this letter.

Teaching

1 Corinthians 1:1–9: Wiersbe summarizes verses 1–9 as "Called to Be Holy."[4] Paul began with identifying himself and Sosthenes, a leader of the synagogue (v. 1). After the Roman tribunal dismissed the charges against Paul, the Jews who had brought those charges beat up Sosthenes in front of the tribunal judge (Acts 18:17). Paul addressed the letter to all in Corinth who called upon Jesus as Lord (v. 2). Constable explains that verse 3 sums up Paul's whole theological outlook.[5] Paul gave thanks to God for the church in Corinth (v. 4) and pointed out that their lives had been enriched with the gifts from God of speech and knowledge (v. 5). Paul promised that the church would not lack any of the nine spiritual gifts while they waited on Jesus' return (vv. 6–7). As we wait on Jesus' return, He will give us whatever spiritual gifts we need at that time to do His work. Paul promised that Jesus would strengthen the church, and even though we still sin, we will be without accusation because of Christ (v. 8). Paul then reminded the church that God was faithful (v. 9).

In verse 8, Paul used the phrase, "the day of our Lord Jesus Christ." *The New Scofield Reference Bible* explains that the phrase refers to the period of time after the rapture. It can also be found in Scripture as "'the day of the Lord Jesus' (1 Corinthians 5:5; 2 Corinthians 1:14), 'the day of Jesus Christ' (Philippians 1:6),

---

[2] MacArthur, 1561–62.

[3] MacArthur, 1562.

[4] Warren W. Wiersbe, *The Bible Exposition Commentary: Matthew–Galatians* (Colorado Springs: David C. Cook, 1989), 568.

[5] Constable, 84.

and 'the day of Christ' (Philippians 1:10; 2:16)."[6] Where does the rapture take place in all of this? When the rapture actually takes place doesn't matter, because we'll be ready since we're eagerly awaiting His return.

1 Corinthians 1:10–25: Wiersbe summarizes verses 10–25 as "Called into Fellowship."[7] Paul encouraged the church to have no divisions but to be united (v. 10). Paul had heard about the rivalry among the members, especially as to whom they followed—Paul, Apollos, Cephas (Peter), or Christ (vv. 11–12). Paul reminded them Jesus had died for them, and they had been baptized in His name alone (v. 13). In fact, Paul had only physically baptized Crispus and Gaius and the household of Stephanas (vv. 14–16). Jesus alone is the priority. Instead, Christ sent Paul to evangelize with the message of His death on the cross (v. 17). The message of the cross is foolishness for those who are perishing; God's power is given to us who are saved (v. 18). That foolishness is our human attempt to tell the story of Christ (vv. 19–22). The message of the crucified Christ was a stumbling block for the Jews and seen as foolishness by the Gentiles (v. 23). Yet God's power and wisdom are given to all who are called, because He is greater than human power and wisdom (v. 25).

D. A. Carson wrote: "What would you think if a woman came to work wearing earrings stamped with an image of the mushroom cloud of the atomic bomb dropped over Hiroshima? . . . What would you think of a church building adorned with a fresco of the massed graves at Auschwitz? . . . The same sort of shocking horror was associated with cross and crucifixion in the first century."[8] Gordon Fee wrote:

> "It is hard for those in the christianized West, where the cross for almost nineteen centuries has been the primary symbol of faith, to appreciate how utterly mad the message of a God who got himself crucified by his enemies must have seemed to the first-century Greek or Roman. But it is precisely the depth of this scandal and folly that we *must* appreciate if we are to understand both why the Corinthians were moving away from it toward wisdom and why it was well over a century before the cross appears among Christians as a symbol of their faith."[9]

---

[6] The New Scofield Reference Bible, ed. E. Schuyler English, et al. (New York: Oxford University Press, 1967), 1233.

[7] Wiersbe, 569.

[8] D. A. Carson, *The Cross and Christian Ministry* (Grand Rapids: Baker Book House, and Leicester, England: Intervarsity, 1993), 12.

[9] Gordon D. Fee, *The First Epistle to the Corinthians*, New International Commentary on the New Testament (Grand Rapids: Eerdmans, 1987), 76.

Closing

Wiersbe summarizes verses 26–31 as "Called to Glorify God."[10] God calls the weak, the foolish, the insignificant, and the despised in the world to bring glory to Him. These will not boast of their own achievements but will boast only of the Lord (vv. 26–31). We, too, are called to bring all glory to Him.

The Daily Word

Do you ever wonder if you are adequate to serve the Lord? Do you ever wonder what you are called to? Perhaps you wonder if God is even faithful in your life? When Paul addressed the church in Corinth, those who were sanctified in Christ, he knew the church was divided, and different views were surfacing. Therefore, Paul spoke these truths to the believers: *Christ is confirmed among you. You do not lack any spiritual gift as you rest in the Lord. God will strengthen you. It is OK to feel weak, because Christ will strengthen you daily to be blameless, fully forgiven from Jesus. God is faithful. Period. No questions. You are called by God into fellowship, into relationship, into friendship with Jesus Christ.*

What are you called to today? To walk with the Lord. To love Him. To seek to know Him. When you remember these truths that Paul reminded the Romans of, guess what? It's not about you anymore. Instead, it's all about the Lord and His justifying, sanctifying, redeeming power, and grace in your life. So, boast in the Lord and His faithfulness. Don't question yourself any longer. You are saved, and you have His power at work in your life.

In this way, the testimony about Christ was confirmed among you, so that you do not lack any spiritual gift as you eagerly wait for the revelation of our Lord Jesus Christ. He will also strengthen you to the end, so that you will be blameless in the day of our Lord Jesus Christ. God is faithful; you were called by Him into fellowship with His Son, Jesus Christ our Lord. —1 Corinthians 1:6–9

Further Scripture: 1 Corinthians 1:30–31; 2 Thessalonians 3:3; 2 Timothy 2:13

Questions

1. Who was the audience of 1 (and 2) Corinthians? Why did Paul write this letter?
2. Who are called to be saints? Biblically, what is a saint and how do you live as one? (Ephesians 4:1, 4; Colossians 3:15–17; 1 Timothy 6:12; Hebrews 10:10)

[10] Wiersbe, 581.

3. What were some of the issues with the church that Paul addressed in this chapter? How is the church responding to these issues today?
4. What was the difference in how the Jews viewed Jesus and how the Gentiles viewed Him? What did the Jews request, and what did the Gentiles seek?
5. Even though sin was evident in the Corinthian church, how did Paul remind them about who they were? What did Paul tell them that they had in Christ?
6. What did the Holy Spirit highlight to you in 1 Corinthians 1 through the reading or the teaching?

WEEK 72

Lesson 18: 1 Corinthians 2

The Last Adam: God's Hidden Wisdom

Teaching Notes

Intro

As we reviewed yesterday, Corinthians is divided into two books and was written by Paul to the church in Corinth, Greece. Paul's actual time of ministry in Corinth is recorded in Acts 18. His letters were in response to his ministry there, and what he heard about the church after he left. While ministering, Paul obeyed Christ's commission to preach the gospel.

Wiersbe points out the parallel between Christ's commission and Paul's ministry. Christ's commission from Matthew 28:18–20 includes: go therefore (v. 18), make disciples (v. 18), baptize them (v. 19), and teach them (v. 20). Paul's ministry in Corinth from Acts 18 included: he went to Corinth (v. 1); he preached in the synagogue, and many heard, believed and were baptized (v. 8); he stayed with them for 18 months, making disciples and teaching them (v. 11).[1]

Paul fulfilled the commands of Christ's Commission. Did you know the statistics today are high for believers who have never shared their faith, never led someone to faith, and never baptized anyone? Paul walked out Christ's commands and commission obediently.

Teaching

1 Corinthians 2:1–16: Paul explained he had come originally, not because he was a brilliant speaker, but to share the message of Jesus Christ with them (vv. 1–2). Paul acknowledged he came in weakness and fear, but his words had been a demonstration of power by the Holy Spirit, not himself (vv. 3–4). Therefore, the faith of believers should be based on God's power alone, rather than anything Paul did (v. 5).

These verses may be one of the best evangelism lessons in the Bible. Paul acknowledged he was not a gifted speaker, and he was afraid to the point of trembling, and yet God gave Paul the power to share His message effectively.

[1] Warren W. Wiersbe, *Wiersbe's Expository Outlines on the New Testament* (Colorado Springs: David C. Cook, 1989), 573.

Jean Boonstra outlines the five excuses Moses gave God for why he couldn't do what God asked in Exodus 3—4 (and notes they all could have been used by Paul as well): (1) He wasn't good enough (3:11); (2) he didn't know enough to do it (3:13); (3) he didn't think people would believe what he said (4:1); (4) he was a terrible speaker (4:10); and (5) he wasn't qualified (4:13).[2] However, God demonstrated His power through both men.

Paul went on to explain God sent him to speak to the mature, genuine believers about the mysteries in God's wisdom (vv. 6–7). MacArthur explains verse 7 with these words: "[Mystery] does not refer to something puzzling, but to truth known to God before time, that He has kept secret until the appropriate time for Him to reveal it."[3]

Warren Wiersbe points out five characteristics of this wisdom that God has kept for the appropriate time:

1. It comes directly from God, not man (v. 7).
2. It has been hidden, waiting for God's timing (v. 7).
3. It involves God's ordained timing (v. 7).
4. It results in glory for God's people (v. 7).
5. It remains hidden from the unsaved world, and they were willing to crucify Jesus because they didn't get it (v. 8).[4]

In verse 9, God prepared His wisdom for those who love Him (Isaiah 64:4; 65:17). That wisdom continues to apply to believers' lives today. The Holy Spirit searches all mankind and reveals God's wisdom to us. Wiersbe notes four characteristics of the Holy Spirit (vv. 10–13):

- The Spirit indwells us as believers.
- The Spirit constantly searches the depths of God's wisdom and reveals it to us.
- The Spirit constantly teaches us God's wisdom and truth.
- The Spirit guides us in the process of maturing spiritually.[5]

On the other hand, unbelievers do not welcome God's Spirit—they see it as foolishness (v. 14). The unbeliever can be understood as "a natural," who lives in

---

[2] Jean Boonstra, "Moses' Five Excuses," Voice of Prophecy, April 18, 2014, https://www.voiceofprophecy.com/articles/blog/moses-five-excuses.

[3] John MacArthur, *The MacArthur Bible Commentary* (Nashville: Thomas Nelson, 2005), 1568.

[4] Wiersbe, 574–75.

[5] Wiersbe, 575–76.

nature without God, while the believer can be understood as "spiritual," who is open to the Holy Spirit.[6] (vv. 14–15)

Closing

In 1 Corinthians 3:1, a third type of person is added to "natural" and "spiritual"—the "carnal" man, who is a baby in faith because he will not let the Spirit work in his life.[7] Believers can know what is in the Lord's mind because we have the mind of Christ, and we mature as we study God's Word and listen to His Spirit's guidance.

The Daily Word

As a follower of Jesus Christ, you have the mind of Christ. You have the power of the Holy Spirit within you. As the Spirit dwells within you, He searches you, teaches you, and matures you so you may understand what has been feely given to you by God.

You may feel like a failure. You may feel weak, fearful, and tremble. You may not be a good speaker with lots of wisdom. However, your faith is not based on man's wisdom and strength but on God's power. You are a child of God, and you are able to do more than you can even imagine because God's power is alive within you. Paul shared the gospel in his weakness, in fear, in trembling, and while feeling inadequate. But he didn't let that stop him. He went in the power of Spirit. So today, step out in faith and trust that still, small voice that says, "You can do this." *You have the mind of Christ—full of His strength, power, and wisdom.* Walk it out in faith and believe this powerful truth for your life.

I came to you in weakness, in fear, and in much trembling. My speech and my proclamation were not with persuasive words of wisdom but with a powerful demonstration by the Spirit, so that your faith might not be based on men's wisdom but on God's power. —1 Corinthians 2:3–5

Further Scripture: Exodus 4:10–12; 1 Corinthians 2:13, 16

Questions

1. What seems to be Paul's qualifications for evangelism in 1 Corinthians 2:1–5?
2. What was the center of Paul's message to the Corinthians (Galatians 6:14)? Are you seeing this focus in the church today? Why or why not?

---

[6] Wiersbe, 577.

[7] Earl D. Radmacher, Ronald B. Allen, and H. Wayne House, eds., *Nelson's New Illustrated Bible Commentary* (Nashville: Thomas Nelson, 1999), 1463.

3. God's character includes being glorious (1 Corinthians 2:8). What other titles reflect God's glory? (Psalm 24:7–10; Acts 7:2; Ephesians 1:17; 1 Peter 4:14; 2 Peter 1:17)
4. Compare what Scripture says about God's wisdom versus man's wisdom. (1 Corinthians 1:18–30; 2:6–7, 13–14; 3:18–19)
5. Why can't the natural man receive the things of the Spirit of God? Who can receive these things? What does it mean to have the mind of Christ? (Romans 11:33–36)
6. What did the Holy Spirit highlight to you in 1 Corinthians 2 through the reading or the teaching?

WEEK 72

Lesson 19: 1 Corinthians 3

The Last Adam: The Problem of Spiritual Immaturity

Teaching Notes

Intro

MacArthur begins his commentary on 1 Corinthians 3 this way: "The cause of problems in the church was more than external, worldly influence. It was also internal carnality. The pressures of the world were combined with the weakness of the flesh."[1] Corinth was the center for travelers to come from all over the known world, going to and from Rome, Athens, and Ephesus. With all that was going on in the city around them, the Corinthian church was beginning to cave to the immorality that was prevalent there.

Wiersbe describes two groups from chapter 2—unbelievers who do not welcome God's Spirit and can be understood as the "natural," because they prefer to live in nature without God, and believers who can be understood as the "spiritual," because they are open to the Holy Spirit[2] (vv. 14–15). These two are divided as the unsaved and the saved.

Wiersbe points out another division covered in chapter 3—believers who are mature or immature. The mature are "spiritual" while the immature are "carnal" or living in the flesh.[3] Based on these divisions, Wiersbe breaks the chapter down into 3 sections: The Family, the Field, and the Temple.

Teaching

1 Corinthians 3:1–4: Wiersbe describes this section as "The Family—Maturity."[4] Paul pointed out he couldn't speak to the Corinthians as spiritual people because they were babies in Christ . . . they had a carnal mentality (v. 1). MacArthur points out the babies in the faith "had no excuse for not being mature, since Paul

[1] John MacArthur, *The MacArthur Bible Commentary* (Nashville: Thomas Nelson, 2005), 1569.

[2] Warren W. Wiersbe, *The Bible Exposition Commentary: Matthew–Galatians* (Colorado Springs: David C. Cook, 1989), 577.

[3] Wiersbe, 577.

[4] Wiersbe, 577.

implied that he should have been able to write to them as mature, in light of all he had taught them."[5]

Paul said he had given them milk instead of solid food because they weren't ready spiritually—they were still fleshly and were living like unbelievers with envy, strife, and selfishness (vv. 2–3). Milk was "not a reference to certain doctrines, but to the more easily digestible truths of doctrine that were given to new believers," while solid food included "the deeper features of the doctrines of Scripture."[6] That doesn't mean the truths are different, only that the teachings could go deeper into those truths (Hebrews 5:11–14). Therefore, choosing one leading disciple over another is a sign of being unspiritual (v. 4). Maturity comes not from the pastor or the leader but from Christ through the Holy Spirit.

1 Corinthians 3:5–9a: Wiersbe describes this section as "The Field—Quantity."[7] Paul pointed out he and Apollos were servants doing what God had called each of them to do, and each had been given different roles to fill (vv. 5–7). God gave the growth and received the glory. Further, God calls each of us to work together as coworkers "as one in purpose" in God's field (vv. 8–9a). Wiersbe points out there is "diversity in ministry," "unity in purpose," and "humility of spirit."[8]

1 Corinthians 3:9b–23: Wiersbe describes this section as "The Temple—Quality."[9] Believers are also God's building, built upon the foundation that Christ created (vv. 9b–11). The temple is built with the best—what is most valuable and what cannot be destroyed (vv. 12–13). No one should boast about what men do but instead realize everything comes from God (vv. 21–23).

Closing

So you belong to Christ and Christ belongs to God. It is a powerful picture that Paul paints. He tells the Corinthian church he wants to see growth, maturity, quantity of fruit and quality in the family, the field, and the temple.

The Daily Word

Just as Paul planted and Apollos watered, you have a role to play—displaying Christ's joy, peace, and righteousness in His kingdom. Remain responsible to your role. Don't worry about what others are doing. Rather, use the gifts the Lord

[5] MacArthur, 1569.

[6] MacArthur, 1569.

[7] Wiersbe, 578.

[8] Wiersbe, 579.

[9] Wiersbe, 579.

has given you. Open your eyes to see what God sees and how the roles all work together for the same purpose—to give glory to the Lord.

If you catch yourself glorifying man or even boasting in yourself, then stop, humble yourself in the sight of the Lord, release your prideful thoughts, and give praise and honor to the Lord. As you faithfully carry out your role, you may feel frustrated at times as you plant seeds of the gospel but do not see immediate growth. Remember, it's God who gives you power, God who gives you grace, and God who gives you wisdom. Ultimately, God gives the growth. *The kingdom belongs to God, and through Him it will grow.* Today, give thanks for your role, and let God focus on the growth!

What then is Apollos? And what is Paul? They are servants through whom you believed, and each has the role the Lord has given. I planted, Apollos watered, but God gave the growth. So then neither the one who plants nor the one who waters is anything, but only God who gives the growth. —1 Corinthians 3:5–7

Further Scripture: Matthew 6:33; Luke 6:20; 1 Corinthians 3:21–23

Questions

1. When Paul addressed the Corinthians as infants in Christ, what were the symptoms of their immaturity? (1 Corinthians 3:1–4)
2. In 1 Corinthians 3:9, Paul called the Corinthians God's field and God's building. What do you think he meant by this? What does a farmer expect to get from his field (Matthew 13:8)? What does a builder expect to get by building a structure? (1 Peter 2:4–5)
3. Paul wrote in 1 Corinthians 3:10–17 about the building for which Jesus laid the foundation. Do you think this building could be the local church as opposed to the individual Christian life? (Ephesians 2:19–22)
4. What are the qualities of gold, silver, and precious stones (1 Corinthians 3:12)? What about the qualities of wood, hay, and straw? What effect does fire have on each of these materials? What do you think these materials represent? (Proverbs 3:13–15a; 1 Corinthians 1:30; 2 Timothy 2:15–21)
5. Throughout 1 Corinthians 1—3, Paul talked a lot about the wisdom of this world versus the wisdom of God and having no means to boast. How does 1 Corinthians 3:21–23 remove not only any basis for boasting but also all competition between believers? (John 17:22–23)
6. What did the Holy Spirit highlight to you in 1 Corinthians 3 through the reading or the teaching?

WEEK 73

Lesson 20: 1 Corinthians 4

The Last Adam: Keys to Spiritual Fathering

Teaching Notes

Intro

Yesterday we learned that Paul was concerned about the divisions taking place within the Corinthian church. Today we continue in chapter 4 with Paul's teachings on those divisions. We're going to approach this chapter through looking at the 9 keys for being spiritual fathers and spiritual mothers.

Teaching

1. Spiritual fathers/mothers serve faithfully (1 Corinthians 4:1–2). We should be seen as servants of Christ.
2. Spiritual fathers/mothers are accountable to the Lord (1 Corinthians 4:3–5). We are not held accountable by anyone but God. The Lord is the one who evaluates us.
3. Spiritual fathers/mothers pour out sacrificially and release authority (1 Corinthians 4:6–8). Both Paul, Apollos, and Peter/Cephas had time with the Corinthians. All three of them poured into the church. We cannot compare one to another.
4. Spiritual fathers/mothers launch others off their shoulders. Their ceiling is the next generation's floor (1 Corinthians 4:8)! We want our children to go far beyond what we can accomplish for Christ.
5. Spiritual fathers/mothers exhibit both confidence and humility (1 Corinthians 4:9–13). Paul's confidence was in who God called him to be; his humility was in his willingness to take a back seat.
6. Spiritual fathers/mothers demonstrate foolish faith (1 Corinthians 4:10). Walking in faith in tough times can make a believer look foolish to those who are unbelievers.
7. Spiritual fathers/mothers model . . . teachers teach (1 Corinthians 4:14–16). God is raising up the fathers and the mothers to champion the next generation to be who they are meant to be in Christ—to model godly faith.

8. Spiritual fathers/mothers reproduce spiritual fathers/mothers (1 Corinthians 4:17). Timothy was a product of Paul's mentoring.
9. Spiritual fathers/mothers discipline lovingly and firmly (1 Corinthians 4:18–21). Spiritual fathers/mothers are not afraid to discipline in love (Hebrews 12:7–13).

Closing

Malachi 4:6 summarizes this whole chapter: "And he will turn the hearts of fathers to their children and the hearts of children to their fathers." May we be spiritual fathers and mothers as we raise the next generation.

Lord, raise up the fathers and mothers.
Lord, raise up teachable sons and daughters.

As we will see in 1 Corinthians 5, there was a little trouble with some "kids" submitting to their "fathers'" wishes.

The Daily Word

Like the Apostle Paul, live as a fool for Christ. What does that mean? It means your life may not make sense to those looking in from the outside. It means others may judge and evaluate you, but you know the real evaluation only comes from the Lord. Being a fool for Christ may look like weakness, but you know you are strong in Him. It may look like you are dishonored, but you are a distinguished, royal priesthood before the Lord. You may be persecuted and knocked down, but you endure the pain, just like Jesus. Even though what is seen may be deteriorating, the Lord looks at what is unseen. For what is seen is temporary, and what is unseen is producing a weight of glory.

Look around you. Look for someone who is a fool for Christ. Someone who doesn't live to please man but rather *lives to please the Lord in confident humility.* When you find that person, seek to imitate them as they imitate Christ. You will find ultimate fulfillment and peace when you live as Christ lived and love as Christ loves. Today, step out as a fool . . . a fool for Christ.

We are fools for Christ, but you are wise in Christ. We are weak, but you are strong! You are distinguished, but we are dishonored! —1 Corinthians 4:10

Further Scripture: 1 Corinthians 4:15–16; 2 Corinthians 4:16–18; Ephesians 5:1–2

Questions

1. Paul described himself and the other leaders of the church as "stewards of the mysteries of God." What is the definition of a steward in this context? Is this a highly elevated position?
2. According to 1 Corinthians 4:5, who is responsible to bring to light things hidden and reveal the motives of a man's heart?
3. In 1 Corinthians 4:6, what do you think Paul meant by telling the Corinthians not to go beyond what was written?
4. Read 1 Corinthians 4:7. Explain what point Paul was making to the believers at Corinth. (John 3:27, 30)
5. What do you suppose Paul meant in 1 Corinthians 4:15, when he said they had many instructors (tutors or guides) in Christ, but they did not have many fathers? Who is your "spiritual father/mother"?
6. What did the Holy Spirit highlight to you in 1 Corinthians 4 through the reading or the teaching?

WEEK 73

Lesson 21: 1 Corinthians 5

The Last Adam: Get the Leaven Out of the Mix!

Teaching Notes

Intro

We've looked at chapter 4 and the sin that had entered the Corinthian church, despite the fact that they had been mentored by several spiritual fathers. After teaching this lesson, I prayed for the people that are pouring into us as spiritual fathers and mothers, and I prayed we would be able to have humble hearts to receive what we need to hear—both encouragement and rebuke.

As Kyle taught earlier, there are five major sections in 1 Corinthians:

- Divisions in the church (1 Corinthians 1—4)
- Sexual immorality (1 Corinthians 5—7)
- Issues with food (1 Corinthians 8—10)
- Church etiquette (1 Corinthians 11—14)
- The resurrection of Jesus Christ (1 Corinthians 15)

Chapter 16 includes Paul's instructions on collecting funds for the saints, his travel plans and a final encouragement.

A brief history of Corinth includes:

- Corinth was destroyed by the Romans in 146 BC.
- It was re-founded by Julius Caesar in 44 BC.
- The city was located between two ports, and ships were rolled on large logs across the isthmus that connected Corinth and the Peloponnesian peninsular to the Greek mainland. It had become an important city for travelers and transport.
- It was made the capitol of the Achaean Province in 27 BC under Augustus Caesar.
- The church of Corinth was founded in Acts 18 with Paul, Priscilla, Aquilla, and even the help of Apollos.
- The book of 1 Corinthians was a letter to the "saints," believers who weren't lacking in spiritual gifts but were pretty immature spiritually.
- Paul was trying to minister into some of the issues within the young church.

Teaching

1 Corinthians 5:1–2: Verse 1 is a bit strange. Paul pointed out a stepmom and a stepson who were engaged in sexual immorality together . . . at a level not even to which the pagan Gentiles would stoop (v. 1). Note Paul's comment that it had been widely reported! There were some crazy things going on in Corinth at the time, even though it was nothing really new for Greco-Roman culture. The city of Corinth had become a hub of the Roman world. Verse 2 is confusing. Paul added that the saints in Corinth were puffed up with pride over this immorality rather than filled with grief. What could possibly have made the church prideful about those actions? Paul stated the immoral couple should have been removed from the church (v. 2b). Possibly the church didn't understand the spiritual immaturity of its actions and thought it was showing grace and acceptance to them. Haven't we made a lot of allowances today in trying to show God's love without discipline? Haven't we allowed things that should be black and white become gray areas in the church? The Apostle Paul would say we have to remain obedient to the Word of God.

1 Corinthians 5:3–5: The spiritual authority of mentors/fathers/overseers who speak into our lives should still carry weight even when they are not physically present. Our posture should be that of an openness to receive wisdom, correction, and training (v. 3). Paul told the church to gather, in the name of Jesus, and to turn the guilty ones over to Satan "for the destruction of the flesh" (v. 5). Even Paul's name was being drug through the mud in this case . . . as well as the witness of the church (vv. 4–5). As difficult as this is, sometimes we have to turn people over to the enemy to have their flesh consume them in order to wake them up. God did that to Israel in the Old Testament repeatedly.

1 Corinthians 5:6–8: Paul questioned what exactly the church had been boasting about. Were they perhaps just not open to the rebuke? Paul explained that a little old yeast can ruin a whole batch of bread dough (v. 6). The church needed to clean out the old yeast (the sexual immorality) so the bread could be good. Leaven rises quickly, so they needed to deal with the sin before the sin permeated the new dough (v. 7). Today, we've made peace with a long list of sexual sins—living together before marriage, pornography, fornication, adultery, divorce, homosexuality. We've made so many allowances in sexual freedoms.

Jesus is our Passover, so we rip out the yeast of malice and evil. We are called to be unleavened bread (v. 8). The recipe is very simple: the flour of Christ, the oil of the Spirit, the water of God's Word of truth, the salt of sincerity (legitimately, earnestly, and eagerly pursing the Lord).

1 Corinthians 5:9–13: Paul did not want the church to associate with sexually immoral people (v. 9). It was paramount for the early church to deal with these things (Revelation 2:6). Paul made it clear there is a difference in associating with immoral folks in the outside world; we must in order to share Christ, but not live immorally. Paul was specifically talking about those living a lifestyle of immorality who still call themselves a believer or "a brother" (vv. 10–11).

Paul reminded them they were not to judge those outside the church, but only those inside. Judging those outside the church is the responsibility of God (vv. 12–13). Judgment begins with the household of God. But we are to love, address, and correct those inside the church (Galatians 6:1; 1 Peter 4:17).

Closing

Joshua 7 tells of sin in the Israelites. Achan, one of the soldiers, ignored God's command to take nothing after a victory, and instead took things for himself that were set aside for God. In the next battle, the entire army of Israel was defeated because of Achan's hidden sin. The next morning, Joshua worked through the tribes of Israel to determine Achan's guilt. Achan and his entire family were executed and covered with rocks.

Aren't we glad we have the New Testament to guide us? We are to leave the outside work of judgment to the Lord because we have enough issues to deal with inside. Deuteronomy 17:7 says, "You must purge the evil from you," meaning inside the church.

The Daily Word

If you knew something would contaminate your favorite refreshing beverage, you would stay away from it so you could enjoy the pure, intended taste. Who wants to drink iced tea with a little dish soap? Yuck! The Christian life is similar. The Lord advocates for you to flee from certain things: sexual immorality, malice, and evil. These things contaminate the purity of your walk with the Lord.

Christ intends for your life with Him to be filled with sincerity and truth. He desires for you to love Him passionately, fervently, and earnestly, while focusing on the truth of His Word. When you dabble with sexual temptation and sin, when you look at others with envy, or when you entertain thoughts of malice, *you contaminate your walk with the Lord.* The Lord longs for you to walk sincerely with Him so you can fully receive all He has for you. God is a God of love, grace, and mercy. Today, as temptations arise, ask yourself: "Do I want to contaminate this cup of iced tea?" Choose to stay strong, stand firm, and remain pure for Jesus. He promises He will give you strength as you walk by the Spirit.

Therefore, let us observe the feast, not with old yeast or with the yeast of malice and evil but with the unleavened bread of sincerity and truth. —1 Corinthians 5:8

Further Scripture: 1 Corinthians 5:1–2; Galatians 5:16; 2 Timothy 2:21–22

Questions

1. What made the sin in this chapter so egregious (1 Corinthians 6:18–20)? What was the sin?
2. How was the church in Corinth rationalizing or minimalizing this sin? How is the church rationalizing sin today?
3. What did Paul suggest should be done as far as discipline for this person in sin? How well do you think the church does today with disciplining in love? What is supposed to be the purpose of church discipline? (2 Corinthians 7:7–10; 1 Timothy 1:20)
4. What did the image of yeast convey in 1 Corinthians 5:6–13 (Exodus 12; John 1:29; 1 Peter 1:18–25)? What is leaven a picture of?
5. What did Paul write about judging or condemning those outside of the church? Since the one being disciplined was a church member, did this discipline, done on the authority of Jesus, work (2 Corinthians 2:1–11)? What is the difference between judging those outside of the church and those who call on Jesus as Lord?
6. What did the Holy Spirit highlight to you in 1 Corinthians 5 through the reading or the teaching?

Lesson 22: 1 Corinthians 6

The Last Adam: Permissible but Not Beneficial

Teaching Notes

Intro

Chapters 1—4 dealt with divisions in the church. Chapters 5—7 deal with an overarching theme of sex. The Corinthian church had issues in how they handled their sexual relationships. In today's chapter, Paul dealt with some lawsuits among believers and then moved back into the overarching theme.

Remember, Paul wrote the letter to the Corinthians because the Corinthian church was having lots of problems. Their primary problem was they were functioning as babes in Christ. They combined the spiritual truths of Christ they learned from Paul with worldly, carnal desires and philosophies. Those outside the church could no longer tell what the Corinthian church believed because their conduct had become so worldly. Our phrase for Corinthians is *The Last Adam*, "So it is written: 'The first man Adam became a living being'; the last Adam became a life-giving Spirit" (1 Corinthians 15:45). Paul was surprised he was still having to write the Corinthians about these kinds of carnal, fleshly issues.

Teaching

1 Corinthians 6:1–8: Wiersbe observed that Paul commanded the Corinthian church to "Consider lost sinners."[1] The Corinthian church developed a habit of taking their civil disagreements before the secular courts. Paul admonished them to settle their disagreements with one another within the church. John MacArthur noted, "Suing another believer in a secular law court was a daring act of disobedience because of its implications related to all sin—the displeasure of God."[2] Believers who ran to nonbelievers to help them settle disagreements within the church showed their immaturity in their faith. Wiersbe pointed out, "Over 200,000 civil suits were filed in the federal courts in one recent twelve-month

[1] Warren W. Wiersbe, *The Bible Exposition Commentary: Matthew–Galatians* (Colorado Springs: David C. Cook, 1989), 587.

[2] John MacArthur, *The MacArthur Bible Commentary* (Nashville: Thomas Nelson, 2005), 1574.

period. Nearly 1 million lawyers . . . are handling them. In one year, more than 12 million suits were filed in the state courts."[3]

Paul pointed out that Christians were going to help Christ judge the world in the millennial kingdom, but the Corinthian church was unable to handle relatively minor disputes amongst themselves. "The one who is victorious and keeps My works to the end: I will give him authority over the nations—and he will shepherd them with an iron scepter; he will shatter them like pottery—just as I have received this from My Father" (Revelation 2:26–27). "The victor: I will give him the right to sit with Me on My throne, just as I also won the victory and sat down with My Father on His throne" (Revelation 3:21).

Further, Paul told the Corinthians that believers would be a part of judging angels. "Then I saw the beast, the kings of the earth, and their armies gathered together to wage war against the rider on the horse and against His army" (Revelation 19:19). Those who believe in Christ will take part in ruling over the angels that have fallen.

Paul challenged believers that it would be better for them to tolerate injustice or be cheated by another believer than to take these disputes before secular authorities (vv. 7–8). These types of disputes served to defame the name of Jesus before unbelievers and made it more unlikely they would become believers.

1 Corinthians 6:9–20: Wiersbe pointed out Paul's exhortation to "Consider the Lord."[4] Paul listed actions of people who will not "inherit God's kingdom" (vv. 9–10). While Christians may sometimes perform these actions, MacArthur noted, "People who are characterized by these iniquities are not saved. While believers can and do commit these sins, they do not characterize them as an unbroken life pattern . . . True believers who do sin resent that sin and seek to gain victory over it."[5] We will all have our moments of sin. No person is perfect. This list outlined the behaviors of the natural man. They described the lifestyle of a person who was not saved. It is not possible to combine the lifestyle of the natural man and the spiritual man. The Corinthian church tried to keep their old lifestyle and combine it with Christ. Many believers are doing the same thing. We don't want to give up anything that feels good, but we want to add Jesus to the mix. Paul pointed out that once we experience Christ we are "washed," "sanctified," and "justified." Believers are now different. The behaviors outlined in 9–10 are used to describe the unsaved, but if you are saved, this should no longer be part of your lifestyle.

---

[3] Wiersbe, 587.

[4] Wiersbe, 587.

[5] MacArthur, 1575.

While Paul noted, "Everything is permissible for me," the Corinthians were encouraged to "not be brought under the control of anything" (v. 12). "For you were called to be free, brothers; only don't use this freedom as an opportunity for the flesh, but serve one another through love" (Galatians 5:13).

Closing

Nelson's Commentary listed five suggestions to free us from the tyranny of things that may be permissible but not helpful:[6]

1. "Determine your limits."
2. "Let time go by before making decisions and commitments."
3. "Pay attention to agreement or disagreement with your spouse and/or a close friend or associate."
4. "To manage the commitment you are taking on, what are [you] willing to give up?"
5. "Commit to giving away as well as taking on."

Christians have a lot of freedom in Christ, but that freedom is not an excuse to live a life characterized by sin. We were bought with a price. Our question is not, "What is permissible?" but should be "What will build the kingdom?"

The Daily Word

As a believer, you were washed, sanctified, and justified in the name of the Lord Jesus Christ by the Spirit of God. You have freedom and peace in Christ. The Lord longs for you to walk in wisdom and truth through the power of His Holy Spirit. He equips you, He empowers you, and He strengthens you as you renew your mind in Him every day.

You have been given freedom through Christ. This does not mean you are free to choose a lifestyle of sin. Freedom in Christ does not give you permission to live in your flesh. Instead, you are to walk in the Spirit. So slow down. Think before you act. Think before you speak. Consider others and seek counsel. Focus on the Lord. Serve one another in love. Let some time pass before deciding to give in to a fleshly temptation such as sexual immorality, idolatry, adultery, greediness, or drunkenness. Think things through before you quickly give in. Then you will enjoy walking fully in the Lord's righteousness and grow in the kingdom of God.

---

[6] Earl D. Radmacher, Ronald B. Allen, and H. Wayne House, eds., *Nelson's New Illustrated Bible Commentary* (Nashville: Thomas Nelson, 1999), 1468.

And some of you used to be like this. But you were washed, you were sanctified, you were justified in the name of the Lord Jesus Christ and by the Spirit of our God. "Everything is permissible for me," but not everything is helpful. "Everything is permissible for me," but I will not be brought under the control of anything. —1 Corinthians 6:11–12

Further Scripture: Romans 6:1–2; 1 Corinthians 6:9–10; Galatians 5:13

Questions

1. First Corinthians 6:1–11 speaks on lawsuits against each other. Why do you think this topic warranted a place in the Bible? Does our society follow these rules on lawsuits? Why or why not?
2. What is 1 Corinthians 6:5 saying? Do you think having a wise person in the church to decide matters would be possible today? Would this work for believers and unbelievers both? Why or why not?
3. In 1 Corinthians 6:7, what do you think Paul meant by the phrase "already a moral failure for you"? What would be a suitable outcome? Could Matthew 18:15–17 be an answer? Why or why not?
4. How would you explain 1 Corinthians 6:12 to someone? What is the definition of "permissible"? Where else in the Bible is this mentioned? (Matthew 5:29; 1 Corinthians 10:23; 1 Timothy 4:8; 2 Timothy 3:16; Titus 3:8)
5. What does immorality mean? Why are we told to flee from it?
6. What did Paul mean when he wrote, "You have been bought with a price" (1 Corinthians 6:20a)? What price did Paul mean? Take a few minutes and consider this price and thank God for it.
7. What did the Holy Spirit highlight to you in 1 Corinthians 6 through the reading or the teaching?

WEEK 73

Lesson 23: 1 Corinthians 7

The Last Adam: Identifying Strongholds

Teaching Notes

Intro

First Corinthians 7 is a chapter I've heard multiple sermons and teachings on. It's a chapter you hear discussed at marriage retreats and pre-marriage counseling. Before we start digging in, I want to set up two things to help us understand the Scriptures—the context of the chapter and Paul's apostolic viewpoint. As we read through the chapter, we first need to understand some context. Then, once we have the context, I want to look through it with a different lens—an apostolic lens.

Context: Paul first visited Corinth in AD 51 (Acts 18). The Lord spoke to Paul to boldly do ministry in Corinth. He was there for a year and a half—Paul was invested. God gave Paul the city of Corinth to steward. The culture in Corinth was idolatrous and hedonistic. This chapter talks a lot about marriage. MacArthur helps depict this culture: There were four scenarios of "marriage" in the Roman culture of the time. From slaves being allowed to live together, to what we would call common law marriage, marriage by sale from the father, and then a nice, regular marriage.[1] There was most likely a lot of confusion about how believers in Corinth should navigate their new faith in their current culture. Thus, Paul had to navigate it too. Paul wrote this letter in AD 57—five years later. Paul was addressing questions they had.

Apostolic Viewpoint: Paul was an apostle writing to the new believers or saints (1 Corinthians 1:1–2). The word "apostle" comes from the Greek word *apostolos*, meaning "one who is sent out." This was originally a secular term used by Romans to describe someone who was sent out to acculturate newly acquired land. The roles of the apostles can be found in Ephesians 4:11–13. These verses line up with what the Lord spoke to Paul in Acts 18. Paul's role as an apostle was to equip the saints.

[1] John MacArthur, "To Marry or Not to Marry," Grace to You, November 30, 1975, https://www.gty.org/library/sermons-library/1828/to-marry-or-not-to-marry.

Chapter seven can be broken into three sections or audiences: the marrieds (vv. 1–11), the unequally yoked (vv. 12–24), and the singles (vv. 25–40).

Teaching

1 Corinthians 7:1: This first verse implies the Corinthians wrote a letter to Paul. Paul was writing this letter, in part, as a response to their letter. Celibacy was becoming a polarizing topic in the new church culture because people viewed celibacy as a higher form of spirituality. Remember the four types of marriages? These believers wanted to get it right, so they came up with rules. One of these rules was to hold celibacy in marriage, in high regard.

The Corinthians were asking: What is right? Am I supposed to get married? Should I just remain celibate? Paul's answer was basically, "Relax, it is OK to be celibate, and it's OK to get married and have a sexual relationship with your spouse."

1 Corinthians 7:2: Temptation can lead to sin. Paul was trying to take the culture of heaven and tie it to the culture of Corinth. Paul pointed out there were temptations all over Corinth, like prostitution and adultery. He encouraged the Corinthians to have a godly marriage—no more concubines, no more affairs, no more flirting. We are to find a spouse and stick with them, and them alone. Paul knew that in the kingdom of God you find a mate and stick with them or you stay single. Paul was trying to establish a foundation.

1 Corinthians 7:3: This verse is how Paul poured into marriages in this context. The conjugal rights represent the most intimate connection. There should be 100 percent openness in a marriage. That means what's mine is yours and what's yours is mine. There is nothing to hide and everything to share. Think of our covenant relationship with Jesus. He doesn't hold back His love. He wants to give us more. In a marriage, there should be exclusive sexual intimacy.

There are many reasons one would withhold conjugal rights: control, manipulation, fear, shame. Do any of those things sounds like they are from God? No. In our pre-marriage counseling, our pastor shared, "Before you get married, Satan will do anything he can to get you to have sex. After you get married, Satan will do anything he can to keep you from having sex." Don't give the enemy any foothold in your marriage. Paul identified the biggest stronghold the enemy could use to keep from advancing the greater move of God. The sexual strongholds in Corinth were huge.

1 Corinthians 7:4: This verse is not a license for control—physical or emotional. It is a mutual agreement to honor and respect one another.

1 Corinthians 7:5: This speaks to that stronghold again. When we no longer have that 100 percent openness in our marriages, the enemy has a little bit of a crack to wedge himself in. If you must deprive each other, fill that time with prayer and fasting, then come together again—as quick as possible, thus protecting yourself from unnecessary temptation. In the context of a safe and healthy marriage, if you get to the point where you are withholding or depriving your spouse of sexual intimacy, the sin has already taken place. Anger, disappointment, and frustration must be reconciled.

1 Corinthians 7:6–9: Paul acknowledged everyone's uniqueness, but wished everyone were single. It is OK to be single, like Paul. But if you don't think you are called to be single and you could fall into temptation, pursue marriage. Don't go on a spouse hunt, just prepare yourself to be married. Paul is not addressing things like sexual addiction. Get help if you need it.

1 Corinthians 7:12–14: What God joins together, let no man separate. We all know couples where one spouse is a believer and the other a nonbeliever (unequally yoked). Paul encouraged the believers in those marriages to stay married, sharing their faith and the love of God. Couples unequally yoked can have great or often hard marriages. Either way, encourage those couples you know. Pray for them and include their spouse in your activities.

1 Corinthians 7:25–40: Verse 26 refers to the call to be single. If you are called to be single, embrace it. Remain who you are and embrace who the Lord has created you to be. If you are single, devote your attention to the Lord. Marriage can hinder or distract from ministry. Don't allow yourself to be drawn into bitterness about being single.

Closing

Most people are called to be married. Just know when you are married your attention is going to be divided. Ministry can be tough for those married, but God will get you through that. It can be hard to balance. When you look though the apostolic lens of Paul at these verses, where Paul tries to bring the culture of heaven into the culture of earth, they are more than just good tips for marriage. They are tips for building on the foundation for the body. In the context of the Corinthian church, strong marriages build fortresses against the strongholds of idolatry and sexual immorality. As you study Scripture, try to understand the lens of the author. Paul was able to identify the strongholds and encourage new believers.

The Daily Word

Marriage is a covenant agreement between a man and woman who are joined together as one flesh in unity all the days of their lives. Joining together for all the days of your life is easier said than done, but God promises *nothing is impossible with Him!* Yes, even a strong, unified marriage is possible! Therefore, together in marriage, *keep your eyes on Christ and walk in the power of His Spirit.*

Marriage is one key to building up the kingdom of God. This is why the enemy seeks to destroy marriage. The enemy schemes to get through the crack in marriage to bring destruction. Therefore, don't withhold anything from your spouse. Don't withhold sharing information. Don't withhold serving one another. Don't withhold sexual intimacy. As you trust the Lord and walk in the Spirit, being open and vulnerable with your spouse creates strength in your marriage and eliminates opportunities for the enemy to creep through cracks. *Seek to have complete and pure devotion to Christ in every area of your marriage.* Christ will give you the strength and wisdom needed daily as you draw near to Him.

Do not deprive one another sexually—except when you agree for a time, to devote yourselves to prayer. Then come together again; otherwise, Satan may tempt you because of your lack of self-control. —1 Corinthians 7:5

Further Scripture: 2 Corinthians 11:3; Galatians 5:16; Ephesians 5:31–33

Questions

1. In Corinthians 7:4, what was Paul's intended meaning? How would you explain this to an unbeliever?
2. 1 Corinthians 7:20 (NASB 1995) says, "remain in that condition in which he was called." What does this verse mean?
3. According to 1 Corinthians, is it better to be married or single? What were the pros and cons for both?
4. What did the Holy Spirit highlight to you in 1 Corinthians 7 through the reading or the teaching?

WEEK 73

Lesson 24: 1 Corinthians 8

The Last Adam: My Brother's Keeper

Teaching Notes

Intro

As we've seen in the past few chapters, the church in Corinth had some real issues going on that Paul was trying to straighten out. Keep in mind the five problems of 1 Corinthians: (1) divisions; (2) sex; (3) food; (4) church etiquette; and (5) Christ's resurrection. Chapter 8 is all about the food that had been sacrificed to idols.

Teaching

1 Corinthians 8:1–3: In Corinth, there were several temples to Greco-Roman mythological figures in which sacrifices were made to the gods, idols, and even demonic powers. This was commonplace at the time. Throughout 1 Corinthians, little proverbs have been quoted that were common to life in Corinth. In verse one, Paul used another one: "We all have knowledge." There were different beliefs about eating food sacrificed to idols. All who held belief about it thought they "had the knowledge" about the issue. So Paul then added that knowledge inflates with pride while love builds up (v. 1b). Paul told the Corinthians that just because they "thought" they knew something, maybe they didn't know all of it (v. 2). My mentors always said, "We all walk in a measure of deception and a measure of revelation. You may think you're right, but you may be dead wrong." Paul said if we love God, we are KNOWN by Him (v. 3).

In this situation, I'd like to divide the church into two groups. (Remember all the divisions they were already having?) The first group was BIGGIEs; the second group was No-BIGGIEs. Both groups were right and both wrong. Those who thought it was a big deal to eat food sacrificed to God were in the BIGGIEs group; those who thought it was not a big deal were in the No-BIGGIEs group. Both groups were right.

1 Corinthians 8:4–6: In verse 4 are two more proverbial sayings: "An idol is nothing in the world" and "there is no God but one." Paul explained idols were nothing and there was only one God. Therefore, anything done for these who did not exist had no meaning because of the one true God and one Lord (vv. 5–6a). We are "from Him" and "for Him." All things are "through Him," and we exist only "through Him" (v. 6b).

1 Corinthians 8:7–13: Paul explained to the Corinthians that not everyone has this knowledge (v. 7). If they were coming right out of idol worship and sacrifice, then seeing someone participate in anything related to their old life would have been highly offensive and a struggle seeing another Christian brother or sister partaking in these things. Because their conscience was weak, they would be defiled. Paul reminded the Corinthians that what they ate didn't make them holy or defile them (v. 8). Food is a neutral thing, like money or alcohol or music or media. These things can all be used for evil or for good, but they themselves are neutral.

However, Paul cautioned his readers that what was good for them might not be OK for another brother or sister (v. 9). Believers have different opinions about tongues, displaying flags, and using big Christian words. We must be careful not to do something that would become a stumbling block to someone who is weaker. Just because we know something is OK or we know it is our right, we should not do it if it causes a brother/sister to stumble (v. 10). We read in verse 11, "the brother for whom Christ died"—this is not about comparison but about humbling ourselves and preferring one another (Romans 14:1–22). When we sin against others (causing them to stumble because they are weak), we sin against Christ (v. 12). Paul concluded by saying he would eat nothing that caused another brother in Christ to fall (v. 13).

Closing

In Genesis 4, the story of Cain and Abel is recorded. In verse 9, God asked Cain where his brother was, and Cain responded, "Am I my brother's guardian?" We have a duty, an obligation, a privilege, and an honor to guard our brothers and sisters in the Lord.

The Daily Word

Jesus taught His disciples the greatest commandment: *Love the Lord your God with all your heart, with all your soul, and with all your mind.* Then Jesus taught the second greatest commandment: *Love your neighbor as yourself.* The Apostle Paul gave similar guidelines to the church in Corinth. First, if anyone loves God, he is known by Him. Second, knowledge inflates with pride, but *love builds up.*

What do you learn from Jesus and Paul as you walk through this life with Christ and with others? Keep it simple. It's not about knowledge, and it's not about works or keeping the law. *As you love God, you will know God, and He will know you.* More than teaching, more than sacrifice, *God desires for you to love Him.* Then the Lord's love will overflow from your life into those around you. You don't need to force knowledge, justice, or judgment on them. As you love God, He will fill you with wisdom and grace for others. They will feel Jesus' transforming love through your life and will hunger for the love you offer them. Today, focus on loving God and loving others, and then trust the Lord to transform your heart and theirs.

About food offered to idols: We know that "we all have knowledge." Knowledge inflates with pride, but love builds up. If anyone thinks he knows anything, he does not yet know it as he ought to know it. But if anyone loves God, he is known by Him. —1 Corinthians 8:1–3

Further Scripture: 1 Samuel 15:22; Matthew 22:36–39; Romans 12:2

Questions

1. In 1 Corinthians 8:1 (NASB 1995), what do you think Paul meant when he said, "Knowledge makes arrogant"? Do you know anyone who has much head knowledge but lacks wisdom to use it properly? Could you be that person? What people group were known to be like this in Jesus' day? (Matthew 23:1–8; John 7:45–49)
2. What did Paul say about eating meat offered up to idols? To what "idols" do you offer yourself today?
3. Who were the "weak" Paul referred to in 1 Corinthians 8:9 (Romans 14:1; 1 Corinthians 10:27–28)? Are there any weak people in your life you may have caused to stumble?
4. In 1 Corinthians 8:12, why do you think Paul said, "And so, by sinning against the brethren and wounding their conscience when it is weak, you sin against Christ" (Psalm 51:4)? What does this say about the heart of God and how He wants us to live in relationship with fellow believers?
5. What did the Holy Spirit highlight to you in 1 Corinthians 8 through the reading or the teaching?

WEEK 73

Lesson 25: 1 Corinthians 9

The Last Adam: A Worker Worthy

Teaching Notes

Intro

Yesterday we studied chapter 8 and Paul's teachings on eating food that had been sacrificed to idols. Constable mentions that chapter 9 is a continuation of the discussion from chapter 8. He explains: "Evidently the Corinthian Christians had misunderstood Paul's policy of limiting the exercise of his freedom in order to help others (8:13). Some in the church had apparently concluded that because he did not exercise his rights, he therefore did not have them: for example, his right to material support (2 Corinthians 12:13)."[1] Therefore, some Corinthians did not want to submit to Paul's authority.

Teaching

1 Corinthians 9:1–14: Paul responded to their lack of trust in his authority by asking four Questions to point out his authority: *Am I not free? Am I not an apostle? Have I not seen Jesus our Lord? Are you not my work in the Lord* (v. 1)?2 All these Questions expect a positive response. Proof of his apostolic identity included:

- Only those who had seen the risen Lord in person received the title of apostle (Acts 1:21–22).
- Paul met the risen Christ on the road to Damascus (Acts 22:14–15).
- Paul also founded the church in Corinth (Romans 15:15–21).

According to Ephesians 4:11–12, God gave some the spiritual gift of apostleship. Are there apostles today? There are still countries that have people groups who have never heard the gospel. It's possible that in those situations, God would still give the gift of apostleship. I don't think we can say apostles and prophets are no longer needed.

---

[1] Thomas L. Constable, *Expository Notes of Dr. Thomas Constable: 1 Corinthians*, 156, https://planobiblechapel.org/tcon/notes/pdf/1corinthians.pdf.

[2] Constable, 157.

Paul then moved into the area of apostolic rights using another set of questions (v. 4). His first question was whether he had the right to eat and drink "at the expense of others. It means to accept financial support in his ministry."[3] His second question was about having the right to be accompanied by a Christian wife (v. 5). This is one of the few places in which Christian wives of the apostles are mentioned. According to this, Peter traveled with his wife. Constable explains that it was customary for the church leaders that Paul listed to travel with their wives in ministry, and the local churches would pay for the expenses of the ministers and their wives.[4] (Mark 1:29–31). Wives mattered in their ministries.

Paul's third question was whether he and Barnabas could not work to pay their own expenses (v. 6) (Acts 18:3). Paul reminded his readers he paid his own expenses, taking nothing from the church (v. 7). He even used three illustrations: soldiers, farmers, and shepherds, to explain he had the right to be paid by the congregation. In verses 9–10, Paul quoted Deuteronomy 25:4 to explain that according to the Mosaic Law, "God was teaching His concern for the maintenance of all who serve others, not just oxen."[5] (Philippians 4:15–16).

In verses 11–12, Paul was not asking for money but rather was pointing out he had earned support through his ministry (Romans 15:25–27). This is why churches financially support ministers and evangelists. People sow into Time to Revive and reviveSCHOOL, and we're grateful for that support. Constable explains Paul "chose rather to support himself, so his work of establishing the church might not suffer from the criticism that he was serving for the material benefits he derived from his converts."[6] Paul wrote that the Lord commanded those who preach the gospel would earn their living by the gospel (vv. 13–14).

In Luke 10:5–8, Jesus told those He sent out to go to a town and find a person of peace to stay with, eating and drinking what they were given, because "the worker is worthy of his wages." Time to Revive is dependent upon people of peace who come alongside us and support us in our ministry. We couldn't do what we do without them. When we come into a city, we just trust that the Lord will meet our needs.

1 Corinthians 9:15–27: In this section, Paul moved on to the subject of apostolic restraint and the fact that he had not used his apostolic rights for financial support (v. 15). Paul said that God called him to preach the gospel, and he would have been disobedient ("woe is me") if he had not followed that call (v. 16; Acts 9:3–6). Paul said he knew he would survive through God's provision, whether

---

[3] Constable, 157.

[4] Constable, 157.

[5] Constable, 157–58.

[6] Constable, 159.

through the support of others or through his own efforts (v. 17). His reward was to preach the gospel free of charge to all (v. 18).

Paul explained that he had apostolic freedom and was a free man, but he had made himself a slave to all in order to preach the gospel. He said he would do whatever it took to connect with both the Jews and the Gentiles (vv. 19–21). Paul said that to the weak he had become weak; he became all things to all people, in order to lead people to the Lord (vv. 22–23). Paul described runners in a race with only one winner and told his readers to run their "race" in such a way as to win the prize. He said he would run hard, discipline his body, and preach until he was done (vv. 24–27).

Closing

Paul says he's going to go until he drops; he's going to preach, teach, and deliver the good news until he's done. I love this picture. Let's do the same.

The Daily Word

Paul did not take advantage or leverage his position to receive benefits from people he shared the gospel with or did ministry alongside. He didn't make use of his rights; he did almost the opposite as he endured everything for the sake of the gospel. He didn't rely on position, power, or rank. Rather *he relied on the power and provision of the Lord.* He became all things to all people, so by every possible means, people would hear and receive the gospel.

Jesus said the pure of heart will see God, and the poor in spirit will inherit the kingdom of God. The Lord longs for your heart to praise Him and to trust Him in obedience. As your heart remains pure and as you live with humility, the Lord will allow you to hear from Him, to recognize His ways, and inherit the kingdom of God. You don't need to bend the rules, manipulate, lie, cheat, or take things under your own control. On the contrary, walk in obedience, no matter where the Lord has you go. The Lord will honor your obedience. He will meet every need. God promises He will be with you, and He will reward you. Whatever you do, do it in the name of the Lord Jesus, giving thanks to God the Father through Him.

If others have this right to receive benefits from you, don't we even more? However, we have not made use of this right; instead we endure everything so that we will not hinder the gospel of Christ. —1 Corinthians 9:12

Further Scripture: Matthew 5:3, 8; Ephesians 6:5–8; Colossians 3:17

Questions

1. In 1 Corinthians 9:4–5, Paul used himself as an illustration of giving up personal rights. What was his presentation regarding Christian rights? Do you think we have the right, as Christians, to choose not to share the gospel?
2. In 1 Corinthians 9:7–10, Paul went on to say Christian workers were deserving of a fair and adequate wage. Why then, according to 1 Corinthians 9:12–17, do you think he chose not to accept pay as a minister of the gospel?
3. What was Paul saying in 1 Corinthians 9:19–22? How can you become all things to all men?
4. Do you "run the race" to win? If not, why?
5. What did the Holy Spirit highlight to you in 1 Corinthians 9 through the reading or the teaching?

WEEK 73

Lesson 26: 1 Corinthians 10

The Last Adam: Warnings from Israel's Past

Teaching Notes

Intro

In this week's lessons, we'll cover some of the more controversial chapters in Paul's writings to the Corinthians. It's really easy to read through the Bible and then move on, but I challenge you to find out what God's Word says to you. In addition to listening to what I say, dig into the Word of God for yourself, planting the Word in good soil so that when tough times come, you will know what you believe.

Corinth was one of those cities that was kind of like Las Vegas. Paul wanted the believers in Corinth to learn from their forefathers, the Israelites. The Israelites enjoyed many blessings—protection from God, guidance from God, and miracles from God—yet "God was not pleased with most of them" (v. 5), because they turned their backs to God. In Paul's letters to Corinth, we'll see God wasn't pleased with the believers in Corinth either. He gave them an abundance of favor and grace through the Lord Jesus Christ, *The Last Adam* (1 Corinthians 15:45), who was for them "a life-giving Spirit." Yet the Corinthians gave in to society and the local culture just like the Israelites had done. Even though God's hand was on them, they chose to ignore Him and lived according to the culture and the flesh and the temptations of Satan.

Teaching

1 Corinthians 10:1–2: Paul used Israel as an example. All the Israelites were under the cloud and passed through the sea (v. 1). All were baptized into Moses in the cloud and in the sea (v. 2). Over and over and over, the Israelites experienced God's blessings. From a New Testament perspective, Tom Constable said, "Baptism is the outward expression of the believer's identification with the object of his or her faith."[1] The Israelites "were baptized into Moses," which indicated they

[1] Thomas L. Constable, *Expository Notes of Dr. Thomas Constable: 1 Corinthians*, 168, https://planobiblechapel.org/tcon/notes/pdf/1corinthians.pdf.

followed him. Their experiences "constituted a dry baptism."[2] Moses seemed to be a foreshadowing of Jesus. By following Moses, they submitted to his authority and expressed their identification with him. They experienced their faith in the Lord, but it came through Moses.

1 Corinthians 10:3–5: They ate the same spiritual food and drank the same spiritual drink (vv. 3–4a). This has to be connected back to verse 2. Every one of them experienced the presence of God. Everyone experienced this faith component in Moses because Moses had his faith in God. The spiritual food was the manna that fell from heaven (Deuteronomy 8:2–4). The spiritual drink was the water God brought forth from the rock (Exodus 17:1–7). This account showed the people riding on the faith of Moses, so Moses stepped up as the mediator by asking God what he should do with the people. Yes, the manna and water were literal, but in both instances, it was Moses talking to God on behalf of the people asking God to intervene. The Israelites drank from a spiritual rock—and that rock was Christ (v. 4b). Christ was present with them at all times. "But God was not pleased with most of them, for they were struck down in the wilderness" (v. 5). Only Joshua and Caleb made it through the wilderness.

1 Corinthians 10:6–13: Paul warned the Corinthians about falling into the same sins as the Israelites—worshipping idols (v. 7), sexual immorality (v. 8), testing the Lord and His patience (v. 9), and complaining (v. 10). Like the Israelites, the Corinthians seemed to say God was never enough. The church today often seems to say the same thing. Because the Israelites complained and went off-track of what God wanted for their lives, God killed them. Ten times in Exodus and Numbers, we're told about the Israelites complaining against God. God had a purpose—and He wants us to learn from their mistakes so we won't give in to them as well (v. 11). As *Nelson's Commentary* says, God is truly bringing about the end of all things.[3] Paul warned that those who think they stand strong must be careful lest they fall (v. 12). God will always bring about discipline when people think they are above Him. If we're not careful, we can fall into the same sin. We may think that because we have Jesus, then it's OK to go our own way. Instead of giving into the temptation, we should draw upon God who promises to help us escape from it (v. 13).

1 Corinthians 10:14–15: Although Paul understood the temptations they faced, he continued to warn the Corinthians against them (vv. 14–15). Rick Peterson

---

[2] Constable, 168.

[3] Earl D. Radmacher, Ronald B. Allen, and H. Wayne House, eds., *Nelson's New Illustrated Bible Commentary* (Nashville: Thomas Nelson, 1999), 1475.

gave four simple ways to deal with temptation.[4] First, avoid temptation whenever possible. Proverbs 4:14–15 says to avoid the path of the wicked. Second, flee from powerful temptations. Third, chronic temptation is something we need to confess and offer to Christ, and we need to ask for His cleansing work. Finally, resist temptation until it leaves.

1 Corinthians 10:16–22: From the manna and spiritual water, Israel participated in the presence of God and His provision, but they still gave in to idolatry (vv. 3–4). Likewise, the Corinthians partook of the cup and the bread of Christ (v. 16), and they participated in idol worship as well (vv. 18–20). Paul warned the Corinthians, "You cannot drink the cup of the Lord and the cup of demons. You cannot share in the Lord's table and the cup of demons" (v. 21).

1 Corinthians 10:23–24: Saying something is acceptable doesn't make it right (v. 23).

The whole point in Chapter 10 is we can't blend in with the world. We can't blend walking with the Lord in faith, having been baptized in one Spirit and having become one in the body of Christ, with walking with the world. Paul said if we're not careful, God's judgment will come and fall on us.

Closing

Avoid and flee temptation. Would you just confess what you're tempted with to a friend or your spouse? Confess those temptations and resist them, because Scripture says when you resist those things, the devil will flee.

The Daily Word

Paul encouraged the Corinthian believers to flee from idolatry. Even in the church today, idolatry remains a temptation. The enemy schemes and lures people to worship other idols. You may think, *What? Idolatry? Me? I don't struggle with bowing down and worshipping other gods!* Worshipping other gods refers to anything in your life that commands more time, loyalty, or devotion over the one true God—your Savior, Jesus Christ. Perhaps your idol is security, wealth, health, success, achieving a fit body, or following a sports team. Even your children's activities or family time may become an idol if you find yourself placing this time before quality time worshipping the Lord.

[4] Rick Peterson, "Pay Attention to Temptation!" Slide Share, December 6, 2008, https://www.slideshare.net/LindleyPreacher/nov-30dec-608-pay-attention-to-temptation-presentation.

The Lord says, "Glorify Me *with everything*." He didn't say to only worship the Lord with only half of you and worship other gods with your other half. If you are tempted in the area of idolatry, remember, the Lord is with you and will provide freedom. When you humble yourself and confess your sin of idolatry, the Lord will bless you with forgiveness and peace. He wants you to flee from all idolatry! So today, put on your running shoes and run after Jesus first and foremost and with everything you have!

Therefore, my dear friends, flee from idolatry. —1 Corinthians 10:14

Further Scripture: Exodus 34:14; 1 Corinthians 10:12–13, 31

Questions

1. Paul gave warnings to the Corinthians in 1 Corinthians 10:1–10. Where were those events in Scripture (Numbers 21:5–9; 25:1–9)? Why was Israel punished so harshly?
2. How would you explain 1 Corinthians 10:12–13? Do you agree with those verses? Have you ever felt tempted beyond what you thought you could handle? What did you do? Did God make a way of escape? Did you turn to Him for help? Why or why not?
3. Can you think of examples that explain what 1 Corinthians 10:21 means?
4. Meditate on 1 Corinthians 10:31 for a few minutes. Do you do everything to the glory of God? If not, why? What are some ways in which you can start giving God the glory?
5. What did the Holy Spirit highlight to you in 1 Corinthians 10 through the reading or the teaching?

WEEK 74

Lesson 27: 1 Corinthians 11

The Last Adam: Equal but Different Roles

Teaching Notes

Intro

In chapter 10, Paul told the Corinthian believers of how the Israelites turned their backs upon the Lord and earned God's displeasure. Sadly, the Corinthians were facing that displeasure as well. In chapter 11, Paul brought their attention to imitating Christ.

Teaching

1 Corinthians 11:1–12: Paul told the Corinthians they could imitate him because he imitated Jesus (v. 1). Isn't that what we want our children to do—model their behavior and beliefs after ours? I love this verse so much that I contemplated teaching only on this. Could I tell people to imitate my life because I imitate Jesus so completely? What are the things I need to avoid, or to flee, or resist for my life to be more like Jesus' life? In verse 1, Paul tied together everything he had been teaching up to this point with one summary statement: *Imitate me as I imitate Christ.*

In verse 2, Paul began what some people call a reprimand sandwich—start with something good, then reprimand, and finish with something good. He praised them for remembering him and keeping the traditions he taught them. "The traditions (as the other references show) were the central truths of the Christian faith, handed down at this stage (before the emergence of Christian literature) orally from evangelist and teacher to convert."[1] *Nelson's Commentary* explains, "The Corinthians had made many mistakes, but they were not totally corrupt. The Corinthians had followed the apostle's instructions in certain areas."[2]

In verse 3, Paul pointed out that Christ is the head of every man, man is the head of every woman, and God is the head of Christ. The word "head" can mean

[1] Charles Kingsley Barrett, *A Commentary on the First Epistle to the Corinthians*, Harper's New Testament Commentaries (New York: Harper & Row, 1968), 247.

[2] Earl D. Radmacher, Ronald B. Allen, and H. Wayne House, eds., *Nelson's New Illustrated Bible Commentary* (Nashville: Thomas Nelson, 1999), 1475.

either authority or origin.[3] The relationship between a man and a woman is not based on inferiority—Jesus is not inferior to God, and woman is not inferior to man. You cannot negate one of these statements without negating both, and that goes against everything the Bible teaches about God and Jesus.

Nelson's Commentary states, "Submission does not indicate inferiority, but subordination. Just as Christ and God are equally divine, men and women are equal beings. But just as Jesus and God the Father have different roles in God's plan of salvation, so men and women are given different roles."[4] I think we sometimes don't like the roles we have been given. But God clearly has a role and structure for each one.

In verse 4, "'Praying' involves expressing one's thoughts and feelings to God and specifically, asking things of God."[5]A man who prayed/prophesied with his head covered dishonored God. But a woman who prayed/prophesied with her head uncovered dishonored God (v. 5). Constable suggests three explanations for why a woman's head should be covered. First, she may have been missing a cloth or shawl to cover her head. Second, her hair may have been cut short and did not cover her head completely. Third, she may have left her hair down rather than putting it up as was customary for women to wear in public[6] (1 Corinthians 14:34; 1 Timothy 2:12; 1 Timothy 5:16; Titus 2:3–4). Based on these verses, Paul seemed to be saying women could pour teachings into women and children. This is where it gets controversial. According to MacArthur, "In the culture of Corinth, a woman's covered head, while ministering and worshiping, was a symbol to signify a subordinate relationship to her husband."[7] The head covering is a symbol of embracing her role. MacArthur continues, "The apostle is not laying down an absolute law for women to wear veils or coverings in all churches for all time but is declaring that the symbols of the divinely-established male and female roles are to be genuinely honored in every culture."[8] If there are no head coverings, then I still think God is saying men and women each have different roles in the church. What's happening in the church today is we're seeing these roles being blended into one.

---

[3] Radmacher et al., 1476.

[4] Radmacher et al., 1476.

[5] Thomas L. Constable, *Expository Notes of Dr. Thomas Constable: 1 Corinthians*, 188, https://planobiblechapel.org/tcon/notes/pdf/1corinthians.pdf.

[6] Gordon D. Fee, *The First Epistle to the Corinthians*, New International Commentary on the New Testament (Grand Rapids: Eerdmans, 1987), 495–97, 509–501.

[7] John MacArthur, *The MacArthur Bible Commentary* (Nashville: Thomas Nelson, 2005), 1588.

[8] MacArthur, 1588.

We need to go back to 1 Corinthians 11:3 and then look at verse 7, which states a man should not cover his head because he is God's glory and image, while a woman is man's glory. Verse 8 pulls it all together—the man did not come from woman, but the woman came from man. Paul said, man was not created for woman, but woman was created for man. When we don't focus only on head covering, we see man and woman were given different roles to fill, different but necessary, and important. This is not saying woman has a role that requires an apron at home, and she has no life, although that's the image many people have. According to this Scripture, woman was created for man so they could reflect the glory of God together.

Paul continued to explain, the woman should have a symbol of authority on her head because of the angels. This means that if angels were really watching, they would only see that there is a woman in submission to a man. The woman is not independent of the man, and the man is not independent of the woman (vv. 10–11). Constable shares four possibilities of what that symbol of "authority on her head" could be:

1. The symbol could be the man who has been given authority over her.
2. The symbol could be a veil over her head.
3. The head covering could show that women had new freedom in Christ.
4. The woman has authority over her head and can do whatever she pleases.[9]

Male and female are equal in the Lord, and they are different. What's happening in society is that men are leaving their families, and women are having to take on the man's role as well as their own. Woman came from man, man comes through woman, and everything comes from God (v. 12).

Closing

The bottom line is this: *Our job is to always reflect Christ.* Our personal agendas should be removed, because it's not about what we want—it's about what God wants. Our lives should be about having a personal relationship with Christ.

The Daily Word

Paul told the Corinthians, "Imitate me, as I also imitate Christ." Paul walked as Christ walked. He humbly knew the example he set for believers on how to live their lives. God is not calling you to live a perfect life so others will imitate your perfection. No, Paul was the first one to say, "God's grace is sufficient as God's

[9] Constable, 199–200.

power is made perfect in my weakness." *Paul may have appeared strong, but it was God's grace and power made perfect in Paul's weakness.* That's just how God works.

Therefore, imitating Christ includes walking in His power in order to love others, forgive others, and humbly give up your life for others. It's Christ's love working in you as you abide in Him. As people imitate you, they don't need to see perfection without any cracks or broken pieces. Allow others to see your cracks and broken pieces. It's in the brokenness the love and light of Jesus shines through you. And it's God's amazing grace and Christ's power you long for others to see.

Imitate me, as I also imitate Christ. —1 Corinthians 11:1

Further Scripture: 2 Corinthians 12:9; Philippians 2:5–8; 1 John 2:6

Questions

1. In your opinion, is 1 Corinthians 11:4–7 speaking literally about hair, or could it be pointing to something else? What other meaning could it have?
2. When reading 1 Corinthians 11:20–22, does this sound familiar to current church gatherings? Do you believe that this is a current problem? In what ways?
3. What did Paul mean by "sinning against the body" in 1 Corinthians 11:27? And what did he say needs to be done about it? What does that look like? Give some examples.
4. What did the Holy Spirit highlight to you in 1 Corinthians 11 through the reading or the teaching?

WEEK 74

Lesson 28: 1 Corinthians 12

The Last Adam: Unity in the Body of Christ

Teaching Notes

Intro

This week is a study, not of what Paul would have called "milk," but of "true meat" for the church. In chapter 10, we looked at how the Israelites experienced the presence of God and yet were still disobedient to Him. They took for granted what God had done for them. In chapter 11, Paul told the Corinthians to imitate him as he imitated Christ. He then worked through the structure of the church, of which God was the head, and the roles of men and women. Warren Wiersbe writes, "One of the marks of an individual's maturity is a growing understanding of, and appreciation for, his own body. There is a parallel in the spiritual life: as we mature in Christ, we gain a better understanding of the church, which is Christ's body."[1] In Scripture, besides referring to the church as the body of Christ, other terms are also used, such as: "a family, an army, a temple, and even the bride."[2] The concept of the church is not individualist, but corporate.

In three of his letters (1 Corinthians 12—13; Romans 12; Ephesians 4), Paul discussed three themes (unity, diversity, and maturity).[3] Today, we'll look at 1 Corinthians 12 around the first two of these three themes. The third theme (maturity) will be covered in chapter 13. The progression of these themes—from unity to diversity to maturity—is found in all three of Paul's letters mentioned above. This background is important to understand the spiritual gifts that are listed in the second part of chapter 12.

Teaching

1 Corinthians 12:1–7: Unity within the body. Paul wrote that the Holy Spirit had given believers something (v. 1). Wiersbe explains, "It was the Spirit who gave birth to the body at Pentecost and who ministers in and through the body. In the

[1] Warren W. Wiersbe, *The Bible Exposition Commentary: Matthew–Galatians* (Colorado Springs: David C. Cook, 1989), 607.

[2] Wiersbe, 607.

[3] Wiersbe, 607.

Corinthian church, unfortunately, the members were grieving the Holy Spirit by the carnal ways in which they were using spiritual gifts. They were like children with toys instead of adults with valuable tools, and they needed to mature."[4]

In verse 2, Paul referred to their Gentile heritage. *Nelson's Commentary* states, "Gentiles were looked upon as barbarian or learned which Paul uses to emphasize their state of ignorance. Because of their ignorance, they have been carried away or swept off their feet."[5] The phrase, "idols that could not speak," can also be interpreted as "dumb idols," an "expression that would be immediately recognized by the Corinthians familiar with the Old Testament idolatry."[6] Paul emphasized that only someone with the Holy Spirit within them could say, "Jesus is Lord," and no one with the Spirit of God could say, "Jesus is cursed" (v. 3).

Paul said there were different spiritual gifts that the Spirit distributes to believers (v. 4). There were different ministries but the same Lord (v. 5), and there were different activities that are activated by the same God (v. 6). *Nelson's Commentary* explains, "The Father provides the energy to the believer in exercising the gift."[7] Each believer is given a gift from the Spirit to use for the benefit of the church (v. 7). That means, "God works in believers to benefit the entire body, not simply the individual Christian."[8]

1 Corinthians 12:8–10: These gifts are the nine spiritual gifts in verses 8–10 that bring glory to God. I want to teach on these gifts because I'm convinced most of us don't know where to start in discovering and understanding our gifts. This is because the Holy Spirit scares us, and He shouldn't (Romans 8:14). These gifts must be expressed in love (1 Corinthians 13). These gifts are available to us today:

- Gift of Wisdom from the Spirit (v. 8): the ability to apply spiritual truth practically.
- Gift of Knowledge from the Spirit (v. 8): "This gift may have been revelatory in the first century, but it is today the ability to understand and speak God's truth, with insight into the mysteries of His Word, that cannot be known apart from God's revelation."[9]

---

[4] Wiersbe, 607.

[5] Earl D. Radmacher, Ronald B. Allen, and H. Wayne House, eds., *Nelson's New Illustrated Bible Commentary* (Nashville: Thomas Nelson, 1999), 1478.

[6] Radmacher et al., 1478.

[7] Radmacher et al., 1478.

[8] Radmacher et al., 1478.

[9] John MacArthur, *The MacArthur Bible Commentary* (Nashville: Thomas Nelson, 2005), 1592.

- Gift of Faith from the Spirit (v. 9): "The capacity to believe God for extraordinary deeds."[10]

Note there are no levels in any of these gifts. No gifts are greater than any other. All these are important to bring about the unity of Christ.

- Gift of Healing by the Spirit (v. 9): Most believers believe in healing, but they don't call it that. They pray for God to bring healing but don't expect God to heal through someone. Jesus used the gift of healing throughout His ministry. When people misuse or misrepresent the gift of healing, then people begin to question all of the gifts. Healing means the touch of God on someone.
- Gift of Miracles (v. 10): "The ability to do deeds similar to Moses, the prophets, or maybe some nature miracles one observes in the gospels."[11]
- Gift of Prophecy (v. 10): Revelation by the Holy Spirit for the purpose of encouragement.
- Gift of Discernment (v. 10): Distinguishing between spirits.
- Gift of Speaking in Tongues (v. 10): Speaking in different languages.
- Gift of Interpretation (v. 10): Interpretation of tongues.

In verse 11, Paul emphasized that the same Spirit was active in each of these gifts and gave the gifts to those He chose. All these gifts are still present, and the Holy Spirit distributes these as He chooses. These gifts are different parts of the body of Christ and are needed to complete the body.

1 Corinthians 12:14–20: Diversity in the body**.** There's much more in this passage as it considers what would happen if parts of the body tried to work independently from the rest. We are all necessary parts of the body.

Closing

Simply put—the gifts of the Spirit listed in the New Testament are still given today and used by God to bring unity to the church.

[10] Radmacher et al., 1478.

[11] Radmacher et al., 1478.

The Daily Word

As a demonstration of the Holy Spirit, each person has been gifted to benefit the body of Christ and build up the kingdom of God. God activates gifts in each person through the Holy Spirit to produce what is beneficial for the body. He gifts His people with wisdom, knowledge, faith, healing, miracles, prophecy, discernment, tongues, and interpretation of tongues. God is the same yesterday, today, and tomorrow. Therefore, His Spirit empowers the body of Christ today, just as He did years ago!

You may wonder: *What is my gift for the body?* Just as every part of your body works together for the greater good of the whole, the body of Christ *works together* to build up the kingdom of God. All the gifts *work together* and are necessary. Child of God, you have a part in the body of Christ. Earnestly ask the Holy Spirit to empower you with gifts to do His will. Then walk in humble obedience to the Holy Spirit prompting you. Trust Him and step out in faith. Pray for *healing.* Ask the Lord *for discernment* or *wisdom* in a situation. You never know how the Lord's power and giftings will move unless you are willing to step out in faith.

But one and the same Spirit is active in all these, distributing to each person as He wills. For as the body is one and has many parts, and all the parts of that body, though many, are one body—so also is Christ. —1 Corinthians 12:11–12

Further Scripture: Romans 12:4–5; 1 Corinthians 12:17–20; Ephesians 4:11–13

Questions

1. What will a person not do if they have the indwelling of the Holy Spirit? What will a person do or say if they have the Holy Spirit? (1 Corinthians 2:8–14; John 15:26; 1 John 5:6–8)
2. What are two ways Paul described the church? (1 Corinthians 12:4–6, 11, 27–31)
3. If the church is the body of Christ, how do you feel when people say they love Jesus but not the church? Is this possible?
4. What are three things Paul mentioned Christians should not be ignorant or unaware of? (Romans 11:25; 1 Corinthians 12:1; 1 Thessalonians 4:13)
5. What are some of the spiritual gifts mentioned in this chapter? Why is it important to the church that we are all given unique gifts? What are the issues that can arise from jealousy of each other's gifts?
6. What did the Holy Spirit highlight to you in 1 Corinthians 12 through the reading or the teaching?

Lesson 29: 1 Corinthians 13

The Last Adam: Love: The Superior Way

Teaching Notes

Intro

This lesson builds off yesterday's lesson on 1 Corinthians 12, which talked about the gifts the Holy Spirit has breathed into each believer. Nine of the gifts were listed in 1 Corinthians 12: wisdom, knowledge, faith, healing, performing miracles, prophecy, discernment (between good and evil), languages (tongues), and interpretation of languages (tongues). All of these gifts have to lead to one thing: love.

Teaching

1 Corinthians 13:1: When people speak in "human or angelic languages" (v. 1) or pray over you without doing so in love, then it's just confusing noises. When it's done without love, it's often done in pride as if the person speaking or praying is saying, "Hey, look at me. I can pray in tongues." This is just manufactured and sounds like Charlie Brown's teacher. In other words, you can't understand.

1 Corinthians 13:2: The person who exercises the gifts of prophecy (1 Corinthians 14:1 where Paul told them to desire this gift above all others) without love is nothing. Note that 1 Corinthians 14:1 also instructs believers to pursue love first. Love is most important; if you're just after the spiritual gifts then you're missing the whole message of the gospel.

Prophecy literally means "to speak before. The gift of prophecy is the divine enablement to reveal truth and proclaim it in a timely and relevant manner for understanding, correction, repentance, or edification. There may be immediate or future implications."[1] If you're speaking up to "expose sin or deception in others for the purpose of reconciliation,"[2] but love is not behind it, nobody wants to listen because it's just a loud noise. But if you have a heart and you want to

[1] Bruce L. Bugbee and Don Cousins, *Network: The Right People, in the Right Places, for the Right Reasons, at the Right Time* (Grand Rapids: Zondervan, 1994, 2005), 91.

[2] Bugbee and Cousins, 91.

"speak a timely word from God causing conviction, repentance or edification; see truth that others often fail to see and challenge them to respond,"[3] and you do this with love, then they will be drawn to Christ. If you come with the attitude that "I have this prophetic word," and you're just trying to stick it to somebody or to show how much the Holy Spirit has given to you, then you can abuse your spiritual gifts. But when you love people, it can be received. If you want people to "understand God's heart and mind through experiences He takes them through,"[4] all of that has to be filtered through the love of God. When you walk in prophecy that is based on love, you're discerning, compelling, uncompromising, outspoken, authoritative, convicting and confronting—all of it done because you love them. You can have the gift of prophecy, knowledge, faith, and giving to the point of sacrifice, but Scripture says it's worthless without love.

1 Corinthians 13:3: Giving everything to the poor, even sacrificing yourself, but not having love, you gain nothing. All of these gifts are worthless unless there is love. In these three verses, Tom Constable said Paul "was arguing for the necessity and supremacy of love."[5]

1 Corinthians 13:4–7: In these verses, we see "the character of love."[6] As we talk about these characteristics of love, it's important to keep the bigger picture in mind. Paul was talking to the Corinthian church, whose people at this point in time were not displaying any love but were abusing the gifts. There was division in the church. They were envying other gifts. Their behavior was disgracing the Lord. In this midst of those problems, Paul needed them to own up to this behavior and understand what true love was and how to express it. In these verses are 15 words that describe love. If we embrace 1 Corinthians 13:4–7, we just might see unity in the church. MacArthur explains them this way:

> - "Love suffers long." Bearing with a person's worst behavior, without retaliation, regardless of the circumstances.
> - "Love is kind." Diligently seeking ways to be actively useful in another person's life.
> - "Love does not envy." Delighting in the esteem and honor given to someone else.

---

[3] Bugbee and Cousins, 91.

[4] Bugbee and Cousins, 91.

[5] Thomas L. Constable, *Expository Notes of Dr. Thomas Constable: 1 Corinthians*, 247, https://planobiblechapel.org/tcon/notes/pdf/1corinthians.pdf.

[6] Constable, 247.

- "Love does not parade itself." Not drawing attention to oneself exclusive of others.
- "Love is not puffed up." Knowing one is not more important than others.
- "Love does not behave rudely." Not engaging any person in ungodly activity.
- "Love does not seek its own." Being others-oriented.
- "Love is not provoked." Not resorting to anger as a solution to difficulties between myself and others.
- "Love thinks no evil." Never keeping an account due on others.
- "Love does not rejoice in iniquity." Never delighting in another person's unrighteous behavior, nor will I join its expression.
- "Love rejoices in the truth." Finding great joy when truth prevails in another person's life.
- "Love bears all things." Being publicly silent about another person's faults.
- "Love believes all things." Expressing unshakeable confidence and trust in others.
- "Love hopes all things." Confidently expecting future victory in another person's life, regardless of the present imperfections.
- "Love endures all things." Outlasting every assault of Satan to break up relationships.[7]

1 Corinthians 13:8–13: These verses show "the permanence of love."[8] Love never ends. But prophecies, languages, and knowledge will come to an end. At some point, the gifts will come to an end: "When the perfect comes." *Nelson's Commentary* offered some options to interpreting verse 10:

1. The gifts ended at the end of the apostolic era.
2. The gifts ended with the completion of the canon of Scripture—all 66 books of the Bible.
3. The gifts will end at "the second coming of Christ, at which point the role and relationship of all believers and the church will be transformed, and the 'partial' will no longer be needed." [9]

---

[7] John MacArthur, *The MacArthur Bible Commentary* (Nashville: Thomas Nelson, 2005), 1598.

[8] Constable, 251.

[9] Earl D. Radmacher, Ronald B. Allen, and H. Wayne House, eds., *Nelson's New Illustrated Bible Commentary* (Nashville: Thomas Nelson, 1999), 1481.

Note that five times in verse 11, Scripture talks about the growth from childhood to adulthood. The revelation of God is ultimately incomplete until the end when we see Him face to face (v. 12). So we have these gifts and function in them until the perfect comes. Of all these gifts, faith, hope, and love remain—and the greatest gift is love (v. 13).

Closing

I want to encourage you to study the Word for yourself. Dig into 1 Corinthians 13. What do you see? What is the truth behind these words?

The Daily Word

You can have all the gifts of the Spirit and faithfully use them for the kingdom, but if you don't demonstrate love—then you gain nothing. Love is essential and greater than the gifts of the Spirit. If love is absent, then any gifts used are canceled out.

So how do you love? You love others out of the love you have been given from the heavenly Father. As you receive God's love, He will fill you up to love others as you walk in the Spirit. Love is number one in the kingdom of God. If you think, I don't know the gift God has given me, then start by loving others as Christ has loved you. Remember, God's greatest commandments are to love Him and love others. Today, take a deep breath and receive the love of your Father. Then go out and love others!

If I have the gift of prophecy and understand all mysteries and all knowledge, and if I have all faith so that I can move mountains but do not have love, I am nothing. And if I donate all my goods to feed the poor, and if I give my body in order to boast but do not have love, I gain nothing. —1 Corinthians 13:2–3

Further Scripture: Mark 12:29–31; 1 Corinthians 13:4–8a; Colossians 3:14

Questions

1. What's the problem with having spiritual gifts if they aren't accompanied with love?
2. In Corinthians 13:4–7, what are the qualities that characterize authentic, biblical love as mentioned? Which of these qualities do you need the Lord to help you with?
3. What did Paul say love was greater than? Why is love greater than these things? (1 John 4:8, 16)

4. What are the three great pursuits of the Christian life? What is your Christian life focused on? What are you truly seeking more of?
5. What did the Holy Spirit highlight to you in 1 Corinthians 13 through the reading or the teaching?

Lesson 30: 1 Corinthians 14

The Last Adam: The Priority of Prophecy

Teaching Notes

Intro

Paul genuinely cared for the church of Corinth. The believers were still pursuing idols from their former worship, trying to interweave the things of God and the things of the flesh. Throughout the letter, Paul reminded the Corinthians of the core essentials of what it meant to walk things out as the body of Christ. Today, I'm going to focus on the specific spiritual gift of prophecy.

Teaching

1 Corinthians 14:1–11: Paul told his readers to pursue love first and to desire spiritual gifts (v. 1a). It is a choice to love someone. This was so they could possibly prophesy (v. 1b). Paul showed prophecy as the higher gift. Those who speak in tongues speak to God not men and do not understand what they are saying (v. 2). But those who prophesy speak directly to people for edification (instruction or guidance of someone morally or intellectually), encouragement (giving support, hope, and encouragement), and consolation (giving comfort to someone after loss or disappointment). Paul said that one who prays in tongues builds himself up, while one who prophesies builds up the church (v. 4). Paul wished everyone could speak in tongues because it would build them up in the Lord, but more so that they could prophesy because that builds up the church and others in love (v. 5). (1 Corinthians 13:8—tongues and prophecy will stop only when the perfect comes, when Christ returns.)

That's why chapter 14 still makes sense. Paul then asked how he could be understood if he spoke in tongues; Paul would only be able to make a difference in believers through divine revelation, knowledge, teaching, or prophecy (v. 6). He offered the illustration that a musical instrument was only understood when it made notes that could be recognized (vv. 7–8). Paul emphasized that despite the fact there were many languages in the world, he only understood those whose meaning he knew (vv. 9–11).

1 Corinthians 14:12–19: Paul stressed that people use their spiritual gifts to build up the church (v. 12). Since God is a God of order, He wants order within the church. Therefore, tongues should not be used unless a person is present to interpret what is said (v. 13). Paul described that when he prayed in tongues, his spirit prayed, even singing in tongues (vv. 14–15). Around other believers, there needs to be interpreters to explain what has been said (v. 16), and to build up others (v. 17). Spiritual maturity means order is brought into using the gift of tongues with others (vv. 18–19).

1 Corinthians 14:20–40: Beginning in verse 20, Paul moved to how tongues should be used before nonbelievers. He cautioned the Corinthians not to be childish in thinking, but to be a babe in regard to evil (v. 20). Wiersbe explained verses 21–25 this way: "Paul made another point for the superiority of prophecy over tongues: a message in tongues (unless interpreted), could never bring conviction to the heart of a lost sinner. In fact, the unsaved person might leave the service before the interpretation was given, thinking that the whole assembly was crazy. Tongues were not used for evangelism, neither at Pentecost, nor in the meetings of the early church."[1] *Nelson's Commentary* adds, "When these non-Christians [who attended the services] heard the congregation prophesy, the message convicted them, so that they fell down on their faces and worshiped God."[2]

Don't close the door on speaking in tongues, because it is given to be a sign for nonbelievers. Just remember there has to be an interpreter to interpret for believers and unbelievers in order to edify them. Love is not selfish, arrogant, or boastful. Therefore, we only use tongues and prophecy to build up the church. In verse 26, Paul gave an outline of what the worship should include—everything included was to bring about edification, with only two (no more than three) speaking in tongues with interpreters (vv. 26–27). Without an interpreter, the person with tongues should stay silent (v. 28). While two to three prophets speak, others should evaluate so everyone is encouraged and can learn (vv. 29–31). Paul also said women should be silent in the churches—silent and submissive (v. 34). Her questions should be asked of her husband at home (v. 35). I know this can be a controversial issue and I'm not saying that I don't think women are gifted teachers. This is simply Paul putting order to gatherings. Keep digging and ask the Lord what this means to you. Next, it says anyone who thought he was a prophet or spiritual, should be able to recognize that what Paul wrote came from

---

[1] Warren W. Wiersbe, *The Bible Exposition Commentary: Matthew–Galatians* (Colorado Springs: David C. Cook, 1989), 614.

[2] Earl D. Radmacher, Ronald B. Allen, and H. Wayne House, eds., *Nelson's New Illustrated Bible Commentary* (Nashville: Thomas Nelson, 1999), 1483.

the Lord (v. 36–37). Everything, then, should be done in order as God intended (vv. 39–40).

Closing

John Piper defines *prophecy* as "a regulated message or report in human words usually made to the gathered believers based on a spontaneous, personal revelation from the Holy Spirit for the purpose of edification, encouragement, consolation, conviction or guidance but not necessarily free from a mixture of human error, and thus needing assessment on the basis of apostolic (Biblical) teaching and mature spiritual wisdom."[3] Piper provides seven practical suggestions about the gift of prophecy:

1. God gives gifts to those He chooses.
2. Not everyone will be prophets.
3. Desire to have the gift.
4. Be grateful to God for the gifts He has given to you and use them fully.
5. Make love your priority in all things.
6. Courageously speak out what God has told you.
7. Have humble expectations for the word of prophecy to be evaluated by spiritually mature believers.[4]

Embrace what God has given you and others as spiritual gifts.

The Daily Word

The Holy Spirit gives spiritual gifts for building up the body of Christ, such as speaking in tongues and prophesying. However, Paul warned the church, everything must be done decently and in order. Just like in today's church, Paul knew the gifts could easily cause division and confusion, which then voids and distracts from God's intended purpose. Paul instructed believers to walk in the Spirit and not despise prophecies, but he also instructed them to test them and hold on to what is good. The person who prophesies speaks to others for edification, encouragement, and comfort, just as the gifts of the Spirit are used to build up the body of Christ, not tear it down.

If you have what you believe is a prophetic vision or a word for another person, ask the Lord if it will edify, encourage, or comfort that person. Seek

[3] John Piper, "The New Testament Gift of Prophecy," Desiring God, March 26, 1990, https://www.desiringgod.org/articles/the-new-testament-gift-of-prophecy.

[4] Piper.

confirmation before you communicate. Trust the Holy Spirit, and as confirmation comes, communicate what you hear from the Lord. If you have a prophetic word that may bring fear, discouragement, or confusion, then perhaps you need to practice self-control and pray for the person, rather than release it immediately. Remember to pray at all times and give thanks, for this is the will of the Lord.

Therefore, my brothers, be eager to prophesy, and do not forbid speaking in other languages. But everything must be done decently and in order. —1 Corinthians 14:39–40

Further Scripture: 1 Corinthians 14:3; 1 Thessalonians 5:17–21; 2 Peter 1:20–21

Questions

1. According to 1 Corinthians 14:1, what spiritual gift did Paul encourage the Corinthian believers to especially desire (1 Corinthians 14:5)? What did he tell them to pursue? Is there a relationship between these two things?
2. There are three purposes for prophecy listed in 1 Corinthians 14:3. What are they? Have you ever witnessed a prophetic word that did not serve any of these purposes?
3. What does it mean to be an infant in regard to evil? (1 Corinthians 14:20)
4. Notice how many times "edifying" or "building up" (or "strengthened") is used in 1 Corinthians 14 (1 Corinthians 14:3, 4, 5, 12, 17, 26). Why do you think Paul stressed this?
5. Read 1 Corinthians 14:34–35, and then look at 1 Corinthians 11:5. Do you think the restrictions for women may be specifically for when prophecies are being evaluated, or how would you explain these verses? (1 Corinthians 14:29)
6. What did the Holy Spirit highlight to you in 1 Corinthians 14 through the reading or the teaching?

WEEK 74

Lesson 31: 1 Corinthians 15

The Last Adam: The Resurrection of the Dead

Teaching Notes

Intro

We've been looking at a series of issues causing disunity in the church. Paul told the Corinthians what it would look like to live out unity in the body of Christ. Paul emphasized that what should motivate the church was love. In chapter 14, Paul discussed the priority of the gift of prophecy. Next, we get into chapter 15. Constable explains, "From what [Paul] said in this chapter, he apparently knew that some of the church had adopted a belief concerning the resurrection that was contrary to apostolic teaching. They believed that there is no resurrection of the dead." These believers believed that while Christ was resurrected, believers would not be. "This chapter has been called 'the earliest Christian doctrinal essay,' and it is the only part of the letter which deals directly with doctrine."[1]

Teaching

1 Corinthians 15:1–9: Paul pointed out he had already delivered this information to the Corinthians and expected them to stand upon this foundation of Christ (v. 1). They were already saved by this message (v. 2). The most important thing, Paul stressed, was that Christ had died for our sins, was buried, and raised on the third day according to the Scriptures (vv. 3–4). Verses 3–4 give the good news—the entire gospel of Jesus—as simply as you'll ever read: Christ died for our sins; He was buried; He was raised on the third day. There is nothing that needs to be added to this or changed. This is *the message*. Paul then outlined all those who witnessed the resurrected Christ (vv. 5–8). MacArthur identifies all those Jesus appeared to, in order of appearance: Mary Magdalene; the other women; Peter; the ten disciples; the 11 disciples, including Thomas; the disciples on the road

[1] Archibald Robertson and Alfred Plummer, *A Critical and Exegetical Commentary on the First Epistle of St. Paul to the Corinthians*, International Critical Commentary, 2nd ed. (Edinburgh: T. & T. Clark, 1963), 329.

to Emmaus; in Galilee; 500 people; James and the apostles; Paul on the road to Damascus; and to all those at His ascension.[2]

1 Corinthians 15:10–19: Paul launched into his testimony, reminding the Corinthians how he had persecuted the church but was saved by God's grace (vv. 9–10a). Paul explained his effectiveness in ministry was because of God's grace (v. 10b–11).

Therefore, how could they deny the resurrection of the dead? If they denied that, they also denied Christ's resurrection and their faith was meaningless (vv. 12–19).

MacArthur gives six "What if?" statements of what would happen if Jesus' resurrection was not true:

- The preaching of Christ would be senseless and meaningless.
- Faith in Christ would be useless since He would still be dead.
- All the witnesses and preachers of the Resurrection would be liars.
- No one would be redeemed (saved) from sin.
- All former believers would have died as fools.
- Christians would be the most pitiable people in the world.[3]

1 Corinthians 15:20–28: Paul was banking his entire life that Christ was raised from the dead, and we are too! Christ is not on the cross, and He is not buried. He is at the right hand of the Father. Christ has been raised from the dead (v. 20a). Paul used three images to explain how we will be raised from the dead as well. First, Christ was "the *firstfruits* of those who have fallen asleep" (v. 20). "When Jesus was raised from the dead, it was God's assurance to us that we shall also be raised one day as part of that future harvest."[4] For believers, death is only "sleep," "the body sleeps, but the soul is at home with the Lord."[5] Second, "death came through a man"—*Adam*, and "resurrection of the dead also comes through a man"—Jesus (vv. 21–23). Third, Jesus came to earth to establish *the kingdom*, and when He comes again He will abolish "all rule and all authority and power" (v. 24). Jesus will reign until all enemies, including death, are put under His feet (vv. 25–26). When this happens, and everything on earth is subject to Christ, Christ will be subject to God, and God will be all in all (vv. 27–28).

---

[2] John MacArthur, *The MacArthur Bible Commentary* (Nashville: Thomas Nelson, 2005), 1605.

[3] MacArthur, 1607.

[4] Warren W. Wiersbe, *The Bible Exposition Commentary: Matthew–Galatians* (Colorado Springs: David C. Cook, 1989), 618.

[5] Wiersbe, 618.

1 Corinthians 15:29–34: So why are the dead raised (v. 29)? Paul answered why with three questions in this section. First, why do evangelism if there is no eternal hope? Second, why do we suffer and die for Christ daily if there is no hope (vv. 30–31)? Third, why would sin matter in our lives (vv. 32–34)? The fourth reason is found in verses 50–57.

1 Corinthians 15:35–49: Then, how are the dead raised? What kind of body will believers have? Paul gave three analogies to answer this question. First, Paul explained that when seeds are planted, what is grown is different from the actual seeds (vv. 36–38, 42–48). Therefore, there are heavenly bodies and earthly bodies (vv. 39–40). Second, Paul compared the differences in the flesh of humans, animals, birds, and fish (v. 39). Third, Paul compared the splendor of heavenly bodies versus earthly bodies (v. 40), and then used multiple couplets to enforce this comparison (vv. 40–41). When we question whether the resurrection of the dead exists, we are questioning our faith—our entire understanding of who Jesus is and what He came to do for us. *Nelson's Commentary* explains, "Jesus became spirit in the sense that His mortal existence and form were changed into that which is spiritual. As One now united with the Spirit in a glorified body, Jesus is no longer bound by His mortal body. He is alive in the Spirit, to give life to all who believe. This is why Paul speaks of the Spirit of life in Christ Jesus (Romans 8:2)."[6]

A lot of people have problems with the resurrection. MacArthur gives three options for how to view Jesus' resurrection: "(1) A great hoax (the resurrection is *false*); (2) mythology (the resurrection is *fiction*); (3) the supreme event of history (the resurrection is *fact*)."[7] MacArthur records the following theories:

- Jesus didn't really die.
- Only Jesus' spirit was resurrected, not His body.
- The disciples were seeing visions.
- Jesus' resurrection was only a story/parable that does not depend upon Jesus even being real.
- Jesus' dead body was stolen from the tomb. Those who had reason to take the body included the Jews, the Romans, the disciples, and Joseph of Arimathea.
- The disciples were confused and went to the wrong tomb that happened to be empty.

---

[6] Earl D. Radmacher, Ronald B. Allen, and H. Wayne House, eds., *Nelson's New Illustrated Bible Commentary* (Nashville: Thomas Nelson, 1999), 1487.

[7] MacArthur, 1609.

- The disciples intentionally made up the story of Jesus' resurrection for monetary gain.
- The disciples saw someone who looked like Jesus and thought it was Him.
- Jesus was raised from the dead through God's supernatural power.[8]

1 Corinthians 15:50–57: We will not all fall asleep, but we'll all be changed (v. 51). The sting of death is sin, but we were given victory through Jesus Christ our Lord.

Closing

For the gospel of Christ, always go back to 1 Corinthians 15:3–4. Do you believe that Christ was resurrected?

The Daily Word

Paul reminded the church of the simple gospel. Even today the gospel message can get overly complicated or even lost. Remember this truth that sets you free: Christ died for your sins. He was buried. He was raised on the third day. If you confess with your mouth and believe in your heart that God was raised from the dead, then you will be saved. That's the bottom line of the gospel. This simple truth will transform your life . . . and give you victory as you remain in Christ.

Yes! Because you believe Jesus was resurrected, then death has no sting. Jesus gives you victory over sin. Jesus gives you victory over death. Through your faith in Christ, you are victorious in all things! The world, the enemy, and the lies are all defeated because in Christ you have life, you have victory, and you have peace. Live today as an overcomer. Live today as a conqueror. Think about a stadium full of fans shouting after a sport team's victory over an opponent. Today, shout hallelujah, praise the Lord, and give thanks, honor, and glory to the Lord Jesus Christ because through Him, you have victory!

Death, where is your victory? Death, where is your sting? Now the sting of death is sin, and the power of sin is the law. But thanks be to God, who gives us the victory through our Lord Jesus Christ! —1 Corinthians 15:55–57

Further Scripture: Romans 10:9–10; 1 Corinthians 15:3–6; 1 John 5:4

[8] MacArthur, 1609.

Questions

1. The first part of 1 Corinthians 15 told of the many eyewitnesses to Christ's death and resurrection. Why do you think there were and still are so many people today who don't believe this? Do you think the same people who don't believe in the death and resurrection of Jesus also question the school history books they were taught from?
2. In 1 Corinthians 15:7, Paul went on to say Jesus appeared to James (His brother). Why did Jesus have to appear to His own brother (John 7:5)? Why do you think James did not believe? What book of the New Testament did James write later?
3. In 1 Corinthians 15:8, what does the phrase "abnormally born" mean (Acts 9:3–6)? Do you think this can still happen today, and, if so, has this ever happened to you or someone you know?
4. What does 1 Corinthians 15:21 mean? (Genesis 3; Romans 5:12–21)
5. Where else in Scripture can you find a similar account of what is said in 1 Corinthians 15:24–28 (Revelation 20:13–14)? How do you think Paul knew this, considering this letter was written before John wrote Revelation? (Psalm 8:6; Ephesians 1:22; Hebrews 2:8)
6. What is the significance of the trumpet sounding in 1 Corinthians 15:52? (Leviticus 23:24; Numbers 10:9–10; 29:1–6; Joel 2:1; Zephaniah 1:14–16)
7. Will everyone have to die a physical death (1 Corinthians 15:51–52)? Do you believe it's possible you could be one of those people who does not die a physical death? Why or why not?
8. What did the Holy Spirit highlight to you in 1 Corinthians 15 through the reading or the teaching?

WEEK 74

Lesson 32: 1 Corinthians 16

The Last Adam: Money and Opportunities

Teaching Notes

Intro

This week in our study of 1 Corinthians, we've dealt with some tough passages. To finish our study today with chapter 16, we're moving in a different direction. In chapter 16, Paul encouraged the Corinthians to bless the Jews in Jerusalem as they had been blessed by Christ. He asked them to give to the relief offering for the poor in Jerusalem.

Teaching

1 Corinthians 16:1–4: Paul explained he had been speaking to churches in his third missionary journey, to give money for him to collect when he arrived at each church (vv. 1–2). He explained that for accountability, he would send letters to all those who gave to let them know he had received the funds (v. 3). And, if they preferred, they could send someone to travel with Paul to keep track of the money until it reached Jerusalem (v. 4).

Why was Paul collecting money for Jerusalem? Wiersbe states Paul had two reasons for the offering. First, Paul wanted the Gentile believers to receive spiritual benefits by providing material gifts to the Jews (Romans 15:25–27). Second, at the Jerusalem Conference, Paul pledged to remember the poor (Galatians 2:10).[1]

Wiersbe also provides three reasons for the need in Jerusalem:

- The need in Jerusalem was great—many new believers (3,000 plus) had come into the Jerusalem church at Pentecost. That suggests the church had been overwhelmed caring for those who had no homes and no jobs in Jerusalem (Acts 2:41–47; 4:33–37; 11:27–30).
- The area had suffered a famine, further escalating the needs in Jerusalem.

[1] Warren W. Wiersbe, *The Bible Exposition Commentary: Matthew–Galatians* (Colorado Springs: David C. Cook, 1989), 621.

- "Paul's greatest motive for taking up the offering was to help unite Jewish and Gentile believers."[2] (Acts 17:21–25)

Wiersbe outlines five guidelines or principles of Christian stewardship from these first four verses:

1. "Giving is an act of worship." Paul told the Corinthian believers to put money aside on the first day of every week, not as a duty but as "spiritual sacrifices to the Lord" (Philippians 4:18).
2. "Giving should be systematic." Paul instructed the believers to bring the money to the church every week, systematically, so the offering would be complete when he arrived.
3. "Giving is personal and individual." Paul wanted every member to give, regardless of their financial circumstances.
4. "Giving is to be proportionate." Paul instructed believers to give as they were able, based on their specific circumstances (1 Corinthians 16:2; 2 Corinthians 8–9).
5. "Money is to be handled honestly."[3] Paul made sure his enemies had no reason to accuse him of mishandling the offerings received.

In 2 Corinthians 8—9 more information is given about the Jerusalem collection.

1 Corinthians 16:5–9: Paul explained his travel plans next, as well as the travel plans for some of the apostles (v. 5). He wanted to winter in Corinth, spending time there with the believers, rather than just passing through (vv. 6–7). However, first, Paul would stay in Ephesus until Pentecost because of the ministry opportunities that had opened to him (vv. 8–9). Paul's first travel plan was to go through Macedonia to Corinth, remain there for the winter, and then head to Judea. However, as time went on, he revised his first plan to go directly to Corinth, then visit Macedonia, pass back through Corinth, and then go on to Judea (2 Corinthians 1:15–16). That plan also had to be revised. Paul actually made "a quick and painful visit to Corinth, after which he returned to Ephesus. He then went on to Troas to wait for Titus (who had been sent to Corinth, 2 Corinthians 2:12–13; 7:5), visited Macedonia, and then went to Judea. He did not spend as much time at Corinth as he had hoped or as they had expected."[4] Even though Paul had already worked out his own travel plans, God changed his plans.

---

[2] Wiersbe, 621.

[3] Wiersbe, 622.

[4] Wiersbe, 623.

1 Corinthians 16:10–24: Paul closed the book of 1 Corinthians by writing about the people. Wiersbe points out, "Money and opportunities are valueless without people."[5] He wrote about their acceptance of Timothy when he visited, and that Apollos would come when he had an opportunity (vv. 10–12). He told them to "grow up," and to make sure their actions were done in love as they encountered these people (vv. 13–14).

In verses 15–18, Paul referenced Stephanas and his household, those whom Paul had baptized (1 Corinthians 1:16). Paul urged the believers to submit to people (these and others), who had devoted themselves "to serving the saints." Paul was encouraging them to be gracious to his own ministry team of workers.

Paul sent greetings from the churches of Asia, and Aquila and Priscilla. and the other believers there (vv. 19–20). Paul also sent his own greetings and reminded his readers the letter had come from his own hand (v. 21). He ended with a blessing: Our Lord comes. The grace of the Lord Jesus be with you (vv. 22–24).

Closing

Tomorrow, we move to Paul's second letter to the Corinthians.

The Daily Word

Paul exemplified a life surrendered to God's will. Even as he discussed his travel plans, he held them loosely, acknowledging only if the Lord wills. He also looked for open doors for ministry. He didn't fear man as he learned of people opposing him, calling it a closed door. Rather he called it a wide-open door for effective ministry. He embraced the persecution and walked with boldness and confident fear of the Lord.

Sometimes you make plans, and no matter what red flags or closed doors come your way, you don't consider they may be God trying to get your attention to redirect you for His good purposes. However, the Lord encourages His people to pray, "Thy will be done," trusting Him to make the path clear and walk in humility, even when it means changing plans or direction. The key is to open your mind to the plans you have and trust them to the Lord. Release control and allow Him to take the reins. Ask the Lord to open doors, and only go if He wills. As you live a life surrendered to the Lord's will, it doesn't mean there won't be opposition or sufferings. But with Christ leading the way, remember, you will be victorious.

[5] Wiersbe, 623.

I don't want to see you now just in passing, for I hope to spend some time with you, if the Lord allows. But I will stay in Ephesus until Pentecost, because a wide door for effective ministry has opened for me—yet many oppose me. —1 Corinthians 16:7–9

Further Scripture: Proverbs 3:5–6; Matthew 6:9–10; James 4:13–15

Questions

1. In 1 Corinthians 16:10–11, why did Paul tell the Corinthians to accept Timothy without being afraid, and to not despise him (Acts 16:1; 1 Timothy 1:2; 4:12)? Do you think we as a society look down on the youth of today? Are there reasons we should/shouldn't?
2. Do you think what Paul said in 1 Corinthians 16:13–14 still applies today? What do you believe he would want us to watch/stand guard/be on the alert for? How do we do all things in love?
3. What did the Holy Spirit highlight to you in 1 Corinthians 16 through the reading or the teaching?

WEEK 74

Lesson 33: 2 Corinthians 1

Treasure: The Writing of 2 Corinthians

Teaching Notes

Intro

Mindi's painting for 2 Corinthians includes a broken clay jar, the drapery cloth representing the Holy Spirit, and the veil that was lifted when Christ died and was resurrected. We'll get into the crown and the coins—there's a lot here. Just like 1 Corinthians, 2 Corinthians doesn't mince words. Like we've done before, in this first lesson on a new book of the Bible, we're going to spend a lot of time on the background, the author, and the date the letter was written. Today we'll talk about the "lost letter" to the Corinthians to set the tone for our study. Paul had a reason for continuing to communicate with the church at Corinth. Looking at a map, we see Corinth wasn't too far from Athens, located between the Aegean Sea and the Adriatic Sea. This city was a hotbed for whatever debauchery existed.

Paul was the writer of this second New Testament epistle. John MacArthur identified the most likely date of this letter. In Acts 18:12, Gallio was identified as the proconsul of Achaia. Paul's trial before him in Corinth probably took place shortly after Gallio assumed office. In probably AD 52, Paul left Corinth and sailed for Caesarea (Acts 18:18–22), thus concluding his second missionary journey. He returned to Ephesus on his third journey in AD 52, where he remained for about two and a half years (Acts 19:8–10). While in Ephesus, Paul wrote 1 Corinthians (1 Corinthians 16:8) around AD 55. Second Corinthians was written after Paul left Ephesus, most likely in late AD 55 or early AD 56, roughly five years after his visit to Corinth.[1]

In Paul's second missionary journey, he started the church at Corinth. He spent 18 months in that city. He left Corinth and then heard about immorality, idolatry, and a lack of patience among the believers in Corinth. In 1 Corinthians 5:9, Paul said he wrote them a letter telling them not to associate with immoral people. Many people call this the "lost letter" to Corinth. This letter did not become a part of Scripture. While Paul was in Ephesus, he heard more about the

[1] John MacArthur, *The MacArthur Bible Commentary* (Nashville: Thomas Nelson, 2005), 1614.

problems in the Corinthian church (1 Corinthians 1:11), which, in addition to the immorality, included division and rivalry. The Corinthians had responded to Paul's initial letter (1 Corinthians 7:1), asking him to clarify things. Paul then responded to the letter from the Corinthians with the letter we know as 1 Corinthians.[2] This background information sets the tone for 2 Corinthians. Paul intended to stay in Ephesus a little while longer, so he sent Timothy to check up on them.[3]

Paul heard some disturbing reports about false apostles inside the Corinthian community (2 Corinthians 11:13). These false apostles questioned Paul's character and taught people to turn away from Paul and from Christ. So 2 Corinthians was written in response to the reports the Corinthian church was getting further and further away from what they originally put their faith in. Paul left Ephesus determined to go back to Corinth. Second Corinthians 2:1 referred to this as a "painful visit." From Ephesus, Paul wrote what is called "the severe letter" (2 Corinthians 2:4), which he sent with Titus to Corinth (2 Corinthians 7). Paul left Ephesus after a riot (Acts 19) and went to Troas to meet Titus to hear about his visit to Corinth. In 2 Corinthians 7:7, Paul found out the Corinthians had repented of their rebellion against him. MacArthur said Paul wrote 2 Corinthians from Philippi.[4]

In the first seven chapters of 2 Corinthians, Paul defended his apostleship and explained his ministry. In chapters eight through nine, Paul urged them to resume their preparations for the Jerusalem collection. In chapters 10—13, Paul confronted the false apostles who were turning people away from Christ.

Teaching

2 Corinthians 1:1–11: Paul identified himself as an apostle of Christ "by God's will" (v. 1), and Timothy as his brother in the Lord. Paul followed his typical pattern of salutation in verse 2. In almost all of Paul's epistles, he included a salutation: a statement of the author and the recipients of the letter and a greeting. In verse 3, Paul urged them to "remember what God is to you."[5] This little verse emphasizes ways all of us could overcome tough times in our lives. First of all, praise God because He's God. Second, praise Him because He's the Father of our Lord Jesus Christ. Third, praise God because He's the Father of mercies. Fourth, praise Him because He's the God of all comfort. Mercy is what God

---

[2] MacArthur, 1614.

[3] MacArthur, 1614.

[4] MacArthur, 1615.

[5] Warren W. Wiersbe, *The Wiersbe Bible Commentary: New Testament* (Colorado Springs: David C. Cook, 2007), 504.

shows; comfort is what we receive. Paul praises God because God is with him in the midst of these attacks on his character, his ministry, his soul.

Here's what we should emphasize in everything contained in verses 4–11: our one word for 2 Corinthians is *Treasure*. Second Corinthians 4:7 says there is a treasure inside each one of us. As we go through these afflictions, pains, and sufferings, we get through them because we have the *Treasure,* Christ, inside us. That was the hope Paul could cling to; it was the extraordinary power that allowed him to go on.

Closing

As you read through 2 Corinthians, you will hear Paul be kind of harsh at times. But he's going to show mercy, grace, and comfort in this process because of the *Treasure*, Christ. This is the backdrop explaining why Paul continued to pour into the Corinthian church.

The Daily Word

When you think of comfort, what do you think of? Perhaps being wrapped in a cozy, soft blanket while sitting by a fire, drinking your favorite cup of tea or coffee, being hugged by a loved one at the end of a hard day, or snuggling with a puppy. These are all wonderful but temporary comforts. As Paul told the Corinthian church, God is the God of *all comfort*.

When you feel sad or disappointed, depressed or grieving a loss, God's presence will comfort you. God is there for you and will never leave you because He is constant. Therefore, turn to God. Read His Word. Listen to worship music. Rest in His presence through prayer. Spend time with other people seeking the Lord together. Oftentimes you hurt when those you care for hurt. Pray for God to comfort them and for them to trust His promises for their lives. Each and every one of God's promises is a yes. This means every one of God's promises is fulfilled. *Every promise is a yes.* With this truth in mind, find comfort in the Lord. You can stand in His faithfulness and say, "Amen!" God loves you even when life feels as though it's falling apart. Today, may the Lord comfort you and help you.

Praise the God and Father of our Lord Jesus Christ, the Father of mercies and the God of all comfort. —2 Corinthians 1:3

Further Scripture: Psalm 23:4; 86:17; 2 Corinthians 1:20

Questions

1. Why do you think God allows suffering and affliction? (Romans 8:16–18; Philippians 3:8; Hebrews 10:32–36)
2. According to 2 Corinthians 1:4, God comforts us in our affliction so we can comfort others with the comfort we received from Him. Have you ever gone through anything that was hard at the time but then was able to help someone else going through a similar situation because of what you had been through?
3. In addressing the Corinthians, why do you think Paul shared the excessive burdens he and Timothy endured in Asia?
4. According to 2 Corinthians 1, can God go back on His promises (Numbers 23:19; Jeremiah 4:28)? How do we know His promises? (Deuteronomy 6:9; Hebrews 10:16)
5. In 2 Corinthians 1:23, what did Paul mean when he said, "But I call on God as a witness, on my life, that it was to spare you that I did not come again to Corinth"?
6. What did the Holy Spirit highlight to you in 2 Corinthians 1 through the reading or the teaching?

Lesson 34: 2 Corinthians 2

Treasure: The Need for Accountability

Teaching Notes

Intro

Churches in the west, especially America, should pay special attention to 1 and 2 Corinthians because America could be a Corinth. We have influences from everywhere that we try to keep up and compete with. The American church has great influence, but we seem to struggle with accountability. When Paul wrote this letter, he wanted to put his best foot forward. He knew his heart and motive and the burden in his heart. The struggle was how to put that on paper.

Teaching

2 Corinthians 2:1–2: Paul said he would not come to Corinth again on a painful visit that would cause them grief or sorrow. He didn't want to bring hardship on them. Paul didn't want them to think the only reason he came to Corinth was to bring correction or to lord it over them. Instead, he wanted the Corinthians to know they were his joy and wanted to see the light (of Christ) coming out of them. But if allowed to continue down the paths they were on, Paul was afraid the light of the *Treasure* (2 Corinthians 4:7) would be covered up by the cracks in the pot instead of shining through the broken vessel.

2 Corinthians 2:3: What Paul really wanted to see was them flourishing in their faith, but if he didn't correct them, they wouldn't be the treasure they were supposed to be. Yes, many influences came into Corinth, but many influences also went out of Corinth. If the gospel was in its proper form, it would go out from Corinth. But, Paul was afraid the influences coming into Corinth were diminishing the gospel going out. If false teachers perverted the gospel, their treasure would be tainted.

2 Corinthians 2:4: This verse clarified Paul's motive for writing. He agonized over writing this letter to them. Paul wanted them to know he had written this harsh letter to them because of his abundant love for them.

2 Corinthians 2:5–7: If someone in the church caused grief, it would not affect Paul because he was not there; however, it would taint the message of the *Treasure* or the witness of the church. Most likely, Paul was referring to the incident in 1 Corinthians 5 of sexual immorality among the congregation. Paul had told them to deliver such a one "to Satan for the destruction of the flesh, so that his spirit may be saved" (1 Corinthians 5:5). Since they had done that, Paul now urged them to forgive and comfort the sinner so he would not "be overwhelmed by excessive grief" (v. 7).

Confronting a believer about sin in his/her life is never easy, but the *Treasure* must be protected and the message pure. Then, when you see genuine repentance, it's time to forgive and say, "Welcome home." As believers, maybe we should express to others our desire to walk in fellowship with God and invite them to hold us accountable when our words, attitudes, and actions need correcting. After all, any of us are susceptible to temptation. But if our heart's desire is to please God, if our purity of motive is to follow the ways of God, then we can hold each other accountable.

2 Corinthians 2:8–11: Redemption is sweet, so when one who has been confronted then repents, bring him/her back in and reaffirm your love for him/her. Paul's ulterior motive in writing was to find out if they would be obedient in all things (v. 9). Paul gave them permission to speak for him, saying that if they had forgiven someone, then Paul had also forgiven them (v. 10). Satan's greatest device, or scheme, is the lie that divides and conquers and it's deceitfulness of one fashion or another, which results in pride and ownership that will separate relationships. Satan's devices are very easy to detect in others yet very difficult to see in ourselves. Satan wanted to bring division in the church so the reputation of the gospel was soiled and the gospel could not be furthered throughout Corinth.

2 Corinthians 2:12–13: Paul had gone to Troas to preach the gospel, but when he could not find Titus there, he departed for Macedonia.

2 Corinthians 2:14–17: Going to Macedonia ended up being a good thing because God allowed Paul to preach the gospel there. Paul went on to say believers "are the fragrance of Christ" (v. 15). To those who refuse the gospel, believers are the "aroma of death leading to death," but to those who receive the gospel, believers are "an aroma of life leading to life" (v. 16). Believers bear the burden of both of these responses, which led Paul to ask, "Who is competent for this?" Paul put his reputation on the line and spoke the truth, the whole truth, and nothing but the truth. He spoke the sincere message of Christ (v. 17).

Closing

These are the burdens of the Word of God. This is the way of righteousness in the church today. I pray God will open the doors of accountability among us in the church and leaders of the church today.

The Daily Word

Have you ever thought about how you smell? Not physically *but spiritually?* Paul called the Corinthians the "fragrance of Christ." Just like a clerk puts a bottle of perfume on display at the department store, God puts you on display as His child, His ambassador, His vessel, *His aroma,* in order for you to represent Christ to the world around you. What does your aroma smell like today? As you abide in Christ, your aroma could smell like unity, life, forgiveness, love, peace, or comfort. So many victorious combinations exist as you walk with the Lord!

Remember, Satan comes to kill, steal, and destroy the intentions of Christ. Satan schemes for your aroma to be death, disunity, unforgiveness, strife, and anxiety. *Therefore, stand guard!* Don't fall into the traps and schemes of the enemy. The people around you will be drawn to your pure, humble, and sincere aroma as your love of Christ is displayed for all to "smell." Abide in Christ, and you will have the fragrance of Christ.

But thanks be to God, who always puts us on display in Christ and through us spreads the aroma of the knowledge of Him in every place. For to God we are the fragrance of Christ among those who are being saved and among those who are perishing. —2 Corinthians 2:14–15

Further Scripture: John 10:10; 2 Corinthians 2:10–11; Ephesians 5:1–2

Questions

1. In 2 Corinthians 2:4, Paul described the love he had for the church in Corinth. Do you share that kind of love for the people in your church family? If not, what are some practical ways you could?
2. In 2 Corinthians 2:5–11, Paul instructed the Corinthian church to forgive someone who caused them sorrow. Why did he do this? What could be the consequences for the church body if they don't forgive? Has one person/group in your church ever caused sorrow/quarreling/division among the rest of the people? If so, what was the outcome?

3. Why is it so hard, as Christians, to live a life of victory/triumph, as described in 2 Corinthians 2:14? (Romans 7:19)
4. What did the Holy Spirit highlight to you in 2 Corinthians 2 through the reading or the teaching?

WEEK 75

Lesson 35: 2 Corinthians 3

Treasure: Paul's Ministry

Teaching Notes

Intro

The first seven chapters of 2 Corinthians describe and affirm Paul's role as an apostle to pour into the church at Corinth. In spite of the problems in the church in Corinth, Paul still believed in them like a parent believes in a child.

Teaching

2 Corinthians 3:1–3: Paul asked if the Corinthians needed letters of recommendation from other churches or individuals to validate his ministry. The Corinthians themselves were Paul's letter of recommendation. They had turned to other apostles and taken on practices of the culture because they did not like the instruction Paul provided them. The proof of Paul's ministry wasn't in the things he knew. It was in the impact his ministry had on people like those in the church in Corinth.

Our word for 2 Corinthians is *Treasure*. Because of the treasure in them, the Corinthian church was meant to reflect Christ. They were Christ's letter to the world. They needed people to pour into them for accountability and their spiritual growth. The Corinthians were a letter written by the Spirit, not with ink. "So it is written: The first man Adam became a living being; the last Adam became a life-giving Spirit" (1 Corinthians 15:45). The Corinthians were given life through God's Spirit, not through any external code written on stone tablets.

2 Corinthians 3:4–6: Paul was not being arrogant in stating that the Corinthians were the proof of his ministry. Instead, his confidence was found in Christ. Paul recognized his competence in his ministry came from God. God made him a minister of the new covenant of the Spirit, which produced life.

Second Corinthians was likely written before AD 70.[1] If 2 Corinthians was written before AD 70, then the temple was still standing. It is possible the

[1] John MacArthur, *The MacArthur Bible Commentary* (Nashville: Thomas Nelson, 2005), 1614.

Corinthians might have been struggling with how to blend the worlds of faith in Jesus and the Mosaic Law.[2]

But Paul was a minister of the new covenant, which Paul argued produced life. In contrast, the letter (Law) killed. "Is the law therefore contrary to God's promises? Absolutely not! For if a law had been given that was able to give life, then righteousness would certainly be by the Law" (Galatians 3:21). The law simply could not produce life, but the Spirit could.

> "'The days are coming'—this is the Lord's declaration—'when I will sow the house of Israel and the house of Judah with the seed of man and the seed of beast. Just as I watched over them to uproot and to tear them down, to demolish and to destroy, and to cause disaster, so will I be attentive to build and to plant them' says the Lord. 'In those days, it will never again be said: The fathers have eaten sour grapes, and the children's teeth are set on edge. Rather, each will die for his own wrongdoing. Anyone who eats sour grapes—his own teeth will be set on edge. 'Look, the days are coming'—this is the Lord's declaration—'when I will make a new covenant with the house of Israel and with the house of Judah. This one will not be like the covenant I made with their ancestors when I took them by the hand to bring them out of the land of Egypt—a covenant they broke even though I had married them'—the Lord's declaration. 'Instead, this is the covenant I will make with the house of Israel after those days'—the Lord's declaration. 'I will put My teaching within them and write it on their hearts. I will be their God, and they will be My people'" (Jeremiah 31:27–34).

Paul commanded the Corinthians to stop blending the old with the new.

2 Corinthians 3:7–11: While the Law was characterized as "the ministry of death," Paul acknowledged that it still came with glory. Moses' face shone with the glory of God when he received the Law. However, Moses covered his face to hide the fact that God's glory faded off his face after some time. Wiersbe noted six deficiencies of the Law:

1. The Law could not justify the lost sinner—"know that no one is justified by the works of the law but by faith in Jesus Christ" (Galatians 2:16).
2. The Law could not give the sinner righteousness—"I do not set aside the grace of God, for if righteousness comes through the law, then Christ died for nothing" (Galatians 2:21).

[2] Warren W. Wiersbe, *The Wiersbe Bible Commentary: New Testament* (Colorado Springs: David C. Cook, 2007), 510.

3. The Law could not give the Holy Spirit—"I only want to learn this from you: Did you receive the Spirit by the works of the law or by hearing with faith" (Galatians 3:2)?
4. The Law could not give an inheritance—"For if the inheritance is from the law, it is no longer from the promise; but God granted it to Abraham through the promise" (Galatians 3:18).
5. The Law could not give life—"Is the law therefore contrary to God's promises? Absolutely not! For if a law had been given that was able to give life, then righteousness would certainly be by the law" (Galatians 3:21).
6. The Law could not give freedom—"But in the past, when you didn't know God, you were enslaved to things that by nature are not gods. But now, since you know God, or rather have become known by God, how can you turn back again to the weak and bankrupt elemental forces? Do you want to be enslaved to them all over again? You observe special days, months, seasons, and years" (Galatians 4:8–10).[3]

The new covenant's glory was much greater than that of the old.

2 Corinthians 3:12–18: Those under the law read the law as though a veil was over their faces. Their understanding has been darkened, and it could only be removed by professing faith in Christ. Paul made these comments as someone whose heart broke over his fellow countrymen, "I speak the truth in Christ—I am not lying; my conscience is testifying to me with the Holy Spirit—that I have intense sorrow and continual anguish in my heart. For I could almost wish to be cursed and cut off from the Messiah for the benefit of my brothers, my own flesh and blood" (Romans 9:1–3). Paul understood better than most the reality that the law brought death. He knew what was at stake, and he was willing to go to almost any lengths to see his Jewish brothers and sisters come to faith in Jesus.

Paul concluded the chapter by pointing out believers had access to God's very presence through the ministry of the Spirit. Moses had to climb a mountain to experience the presence of the Lord, but followers of Christ can experience God's presence anywhere, anytime. The "mirror" to which Paul referred was the Word of God. As believers look to God's Word we are transformed into the image of God in Christ, who lives inside believers.[4]

---

[3] Wiersbe, 510.

[4] Wiersbe, 511.

Closing

The result of the old covenant was death and bondage to sin. The result of the new covenant is life and freedom in Christ.

The Daily Word

Paul emphasized to the Corinthian church the ministry of the Spirit versus living under the Law. He described the Jewish people as having a veil covering their hearts to the truth and freedom found in Jesus Christ. However, with faith, God can remove the veil over anyone's heart. And when He does, freedom is found. Jesus came with a new covenant of grace and love. The Spirit of the Lord gives freedom.

Have you thought about the freedom you have in the Lord? Or do you find yourself still striving to keep up, do better, and find competence in yourself? The truth is you don't have to do more for God. Your competence comes from Him. He came to set you free. Imagine a five-year-old child running freely in a field with a fence around it. The fence around the open space protects the child from harm. But inside the fence, the child can run, play, and spin in circles with freedom and enjoyment. That same picture is for you today. Child of God, *twirl around in the freedom you have in Christ.* Cease striving and know God's got you just as you are. Be confident in His love for you and the freedom you have in the Spirit of the Lord.

Even to this day, whenever Moses is read, a veil lies over their hearts, but whenever a person turns to the Lord, the veil is removed. Now the Lord is the Spirit, and where the Spirit of the Lord is, there is freedom. —2 Corinthians 3:15–17

Further Scripture: John 8:36; Acts 13:38–39; 2 Corinthians 3:4–6a

Questions

1. What were the Judaizers boasting about? What did they accuse Paul of? What did Paul say was the proof of his ministry's authenticity? (Jeremiah 31:33; 32:38–39; Ezekiel 11:19; 36:26–27)
2. Since Paul was a smart and well-educated man, why did he not rely on his own adequacy (Acts 22:3)? Is there anything you are leaning on more than the adequacy that comes from God?
3. What are four characteristics of the Holy Spirit mentioned in 2 Corinthians 3? What did Paul describe when he mentioned the Spirit of the Lord?

4. What happens when a preacher keeps a congregation under rules and regulations of the law? What happens when there is unhealthy competition between Christians? What is the only way a life can be transformed and have freedom?
5. Compare 2 Corinthians 3:7–11 and Exodus 34:29–35. Why is the new covenant of grace far more superior to the old covenant? (Galatians 2:16, 21; 3:2, 18, 21; 4:8–10)
6. What did the Holy Spirit highlight to you in 2 Corinthians 3 through the reading or the teaching?

WEEK 75

Lesson 36: 2 Corinthians 4

Treasure: Treasure in Clay Jars

Teaching Notes

Intro

Paul dealt with a lot of conflict and a lot of other voices that breathed into the church at Corinth. As a result, Paul had plenty of reasons to be discouraged, but he refused to give up. At the beginning and the end of chapter four, he wrote, "We do not give up." Why? Because he knew who his *Treasure* was. Remember, *Treasure* is our word for who Jesus is in 2 Corinthians. That treasure was what Paul possessed in Jesus Christ.

Teaching

2 Corinthians 4:1: Verse 1 builds off chapter 3. Because Paul had this ministry and was shown mercy, he refused to give up. That is the theme of this chapter. What did "this ministry" look like, as Paul described it in chapter 3? This was a "ministry of death" (2 Corinthians 3:7), a "ministry of the Spirit" (2 Corinthians 3:8), and a "ministry of righteousness" (2 Corinthians 3:9). *This ministry kept Paul from being a quitter.*[5] Paul confessed early in this letter to the Corinthians that all the news he was receiving and all he was facing had brought him to despair (2 Corinthians 1:8).

2 Corinthians 4:2–4: *This ministry kept Paul from being a deceiver.*[6] Warren Wiersbe pointed out: "You can prove anything by the Bible, provided you twist the Scriptures out of context and reject the witness of your own conscience."[7] Remember, in the Gospels, even Satan used Scripture to tempt Jesus. He took just enough of the truth and twisted it. We do the same, sometimes with the best of intentions. How many times have you heard someone say, "God won't give you anything more than you can handle"? But the Bible doesn't say that. It's a twist

[5] Warren W. Wiersbe, *The Wiersbe Bible Commentary: New Testament* (Colorado Springs: David C. Cook, 2007), 512.

[6] Wiersbe, 513.

[7] Wiersbe, 513.

of one word in 1 Corinthians 10:13, which says, "No temptation has overtaken you." If God doesn't give you anything more than you can handle, then you don't need God. But we absolutely need God.

Instead, 1 Corinthians 10:13 promises God will provide a way out of every temptation we face. The Greek verb for deceit and distort (v. 2) is only found in this verse in the New Testament. It means "to dilute or adulterate." So why didn't more people listen to Paul's message? Because "the god of this age has blinded their minds of the unbelievers so they cannot see the light of the gospel of the glory of Christ" (v. 4). Paul also talked about this in Romans 11:25 and 2 Corinthians 3. Satan does not want people to see the glory of salvation, and he loves to use religious teachers to spread a false message. In this case, Satan used the Judaizers who twisted the Scripture to fit their interpretations.

2 Corinthians 4:5–6: *This ministry kept Paul from being a self-promoter.*[8] Paul practiced genuine humility by saying he was a slave because of Jesus. Paul was a strong personality and could have easily built up a fan club, but he didn't do that. It's easy to promote a pastor or person rather than Christ, but it's not about us—it's about Christ our Savior. God's light begins to shine through us when we promote Jesus through our testimony (v. 6).

2 Corinthians 4:7–12: In Mindi's wonderful painting for this book, the light shines out from behind the cracks in the clay pots, the broken vessel. Much of the time, we look at the pot—we look at what we can see. We make some really nice clay jars and then focus on what we can see. We make sure they are perfect, smooth, and wonderful, but it means nothing without what is inside the pots. Paul emphasized we should focus on what's inside the pots. The clay pots don't last because they aren't made of stone or concrete. They will age and break. The pot isn't of value—it holds what is of value. It's what's inside the clay pot that is valuable. What's on the outside doesn't compare in any way, shape, or form, to what's on the inside.

God didn't need to package Jesus. Paul said none of us have the best package. It's that whole element of "the Spirit gives life" (John 6:63) and "that life is the light of men" (John 1:4). That life is on the inside, and when we crack—for whatever reason—the light shines through (v. 7). The jars will be hard-pressed and squeezed but not crushed. We will be perplexed, but we will not despair (v. 8). The jars will be persecuted, but the treasure on the inside says you are not abandoned (v. 9a).

So much of the time, in our earthly flesh—in our clay jars—when we're persecuted, we think God isn't paying any attention to us. Paul wanted his readers

---

[8] Wiersbe, 513.

to understand that because of the treasure inside them, they weren't abandoned. Even when struck down, we won't be destroyed (v. 9b). We saw that when we studied Job, "Though my flesh be destroyed, I will see God" (Job 19:26). In the story of Gideon, it was the breaking of vessels that made the light shine forth and bring victory to God's people (Judges 7:20). Paul stressed that what's on the outside—this body—won't make it. But what's on the inside is glorious and wonderful—it's a treasure. Understand that if your jar doesn't have the light of Christ in it, then it's just empty.

2 Corinthians 4:13–18: In His resurrection, Jesus defeated death. Because Paul believed this, he could say: "We know that the One who raised the Lord Jesus will raise us also with Jesus and will present us with you" (v. 14). This *Treasure* inside made Paul sure that God would be glorified. Paul was also sure these trials were working for him and not against him.[9] Everything he went through was absolutely incredibly important. Therefore, he did not give up even though the outer person was being destroyed. Paul knew the inner person was being renewed every day (v. 16).

Yes, life is hard, but in the midst of it, keep your eyes, your heart, your soul, and your mind focused on what is unseen (v. 18). Wiersbe pointed out the contradiction here: light affliction versus the weight of glory; momentary versus eternal; destroyed versus renewed day by day.[10] In this life, we have light affliction—this life is hard—but it's nothing compared to the weight of glory, the joyous increase of glory, because this is momentary but that is eternal. Paul was sure of one more thing: he was sure the invisible world was real.[11] Instead of focusing on what is seen, Paul focused on the unseen (v. 18). What is seen—this body, this broken jar of clay—is temporary. What is unseen—the light inside—is eternal. It takes faith. Wiersbe said, "The things of this world seem so real because we can see them and feel them; but they are all temporal and destined to pass away. Only the eternal things of the spiritual life will last."[12]

Closing

In chapter 5, we'll see how all this gets applied. I'm joining with Paul in this: call me a crackpot. It's a compliment because of Christ inside of me.

[9] Wiersbe, 514.

[10] Wiersbe, 514.

[11] Wiersbe, 515.

[12] Wiersbe, 515.

The Daily Word

Paul encouraged the Corinthian church *to not give up*. He understood they were pressured in every way from the outside, and yet they weren't crushed. They were perplexed, persecuted, and struck down, but they were not in despair, abandoned, or destroyed. Yes, from the outside, their momentary troubles appeared devastating. But what the Lord saw on the inside was *the unseen work of the Holy Spirit*. The Lord was producing an absolutely incomparable eternal weight of glory.

Perhaps you feel like giving up today. Debt is mounting, your health problem seems incurable, you're facing devastation in your marriage, or you feel so much sadness and grief that you don't want to lift your head out of bed. *Don't give up, friend.* Press on. Keep going. Get up. God's power is at work *inside you*. You are His vessel. Yes, you have cracks, imperfections, and hardships, but you are beautifully and wonderfully made this way! These cracks enable the power of God, His strength and love, to shine through you to others. Hang on to the *hope* you have in Christ. God's power is at work within you! *Don't give up!* You will make it through!

Therefore we do not give up. Even though our outer person is being destroyed, our inner person is being renewed day by day. —2 Corinthians 4:16

Further Scripture: 2 Corinthians 4:7–9, 17–18; Galatians 6:9

Questions

1. In 2 Corinthians 4:1, what ministry did Paul say we have? (2 Corinthians 3:4–18)
2. How did Paul describe the life Christians should live according to the gospel? How can you keep yourself from distorting the Word of God?
3. Why are some people blinded to the light of the gospel? Who is the "god of this age"? (John 12:31; 14:30; 16:11)
4. Identify the paradoxes Paul described in the things he endured in his ministry (2 Corinthians 4:8–12). Do you have this confidence in the Lord when tough trials come your way?
5. Even though Paul went through some hard things, what did he say believers should not do? Where should they keep their focus? How do you focus on things that are unseen? (2 Corinthians 5:7; Hebrews 11:27)
6. What did the Holy Spirit highlight to you in 2 Corinthians 4 through the reading or the teaching?

WEEK 75

Lesson 37: 2 Corinthians 5

Treasure: Walk by Faith

Teaching Notes

Intro

Today, we're going to build on the message shared yesterday about the treasure in clay pots. In 2 Corinthians 4:1, Paul said he was called to this ministry and was determined not to give up. In 2 Corinthians 4:7, Paul described the treasure he had been given (we are the clay jar, Jesus is the *Treasure*). In 2 Corinthians 4:13, Paul said we have the same spirit of faith that leads us to speak. As we transition to 2 Corinthians 5, verse 1 tells us we have a building from God, an eternal dwelling not made by hands.

Teaching

2 Corinthians 5:1–5: Acts 18:1–3 tells us that while Paul ministered in Corinth, he supported himself as a tentmaker. Tents have one thing in common—you hope and pray they stay up, because one huge gust of wind can take them down. Tents are not durable; they are not a permanent structure. When saying "if our temporary, earthly dwelling is destroyed," Paul was talking about our bodies, which will be destroyed when we physically die. Praise God we have something else—"an eternal dwelling in heaven, not made with hands." Paul wasn't talking about a mansion in heaven—he was talking about a new, glorified body. We have this new, beautiful, eternal body that will never actually show weakness. That's the complete opposite of a weak, temporary body that has aches, pains, tingles, bad hips, or bad feet. The glorified body trumps 100 percent the temporary tent.

This new building comes because of the resurrection of Christ (1 Corinthians 15). Because of Christ's resurrection, we can say with confidence we will have a glorified body. Death can no longer sting us or have victory over us. Because we have this *Treasure* inside us, "we groan in this body, desiring to put on our dwelling from heaven" (v. 2). Warren Wiersbe put it another way: we're really just eager for Jesus to come back.[1] God prepared us for this purpose (the glorified

[1] Warren W. Wiersbe, *The Wiersbe Bible Commentary: New Testament* (Colorado Springs: David C. Cook, 2007), 515.

body) and gave us the Spirit as a down payment (v. 5). Paul urged us to endure this process because we have something better to look forward to. To help us get through this process, God gave us the Holy Spirit. Interestingly, the Greek word for "earnest" means "engagement ring. The church is engaged to Jesus Christ and is waiting for the Bridegroom to come to take her to the wedding."[2] We're waiting for His return.

2 Corinthians 5:6–7: We never have to worry about losing our salvation. We know that even while we're away from the Lord, we can be confident because of who Christ is inside us. We can truly "walk by faith, not by sight" (v. 7). This whole chapter is the key to understanding how to walk by faith. So how do we learn to do this? WikiHow offered some suggestions, which are listed in bold print:

1. **Focus on things that have eternal significance.** Get beyond focusing only on the things you can see.
2. **Obey the Bible and God's commands.**
3. **Prepare to look foolish.** It's okay to be an idiot for the Lord. The church is afraid to look foolish in the eyes of the world. People may be afraid to look foolish in front of a spouse or kids.
4. **Expect to face trials along the way.** Walking by faith is not easy, but God will always be with you.
5. **Stop waiting for an epiphany.** When we pray, "God give me a sign, and then I'll go," that is still walking by sight.
6. **Glorify God in all that you do.** Paul said this in 1 Corinthians 10:31.[3]

You don't have to have the [spiritual] gift of faith to walk by faith. John Piper offered this list:

- Admit you can do nothing without God (John 15:5).
- Pray for help (Psalm 50:15).
- Trust a specific promise (2 Chronicles 20:20).
- Act (Philippians 2:12–13).
- Thank God for His provision and goodness (Psalm 106:1).[4]

---

[2] Wiersbe, 515.

[3] "How to Walk by Faith: Part 2, Delve Deeper," WikiHow, updated June 16, 2022, https://www.wikihow.com/Walk-by-Faith.

[4] John Piper, "Practical Steps to Walk by Faith," Desiring God, July 7, 2016, https://www.desiringgod.org/labs/practical-steps-to-walk-by-faith.

In Romans 10:17, Paul wrote: "So faith comes from what is heard, and what is heard comes through the message about Christ." So when we hear these things, based on the Word of God, then we will walk out this faith. So what is the benefit of all this? In Ephesians 3:20, we read God will do "above and beyond all that we ask or think according to the power that works in us." In John 14:12, Jesus said, "The one who believes in Me will also do the works that I do. And he will do even greater works than these." You want to know how to walk by faith? Have the faith that you can do even greater works than Jesus. So admit you can't do this without Him; pray, asking Him to help you; trust in this specific promise; and then begin acting this out; then you can thank God for showing up.

Closing

While this chapter also talks about being ambassadors for Christ, I just felt God telling me to encourage you to walk by faith today.

The Daily Word

Paul challenged the Corinthians believers to *walk by faith, not by sight.* Faith is complete trust or confidence in someone or something. As a believer, you can have 100-percent complete confidence and trust in God. This requires you to let go of control and accept you are not all-knowing. Imagine yourself with a blindfold on, taking steps forward, and trusting the ground will be there as you take each step. However, perhaps there are holes in the ground. Faith is believing you will have the help you need even in the midst of the holes. *You will have help to keep on walking.*

It is time for you, child of God, to *walk by faith and not by sight.* God promises He will be there. He will never leave you. Jesus says rest in Him because you can do nothing apart from Him. God promises by faith you will do even greater things than Jesus, above and beyond what you can even imagine. So today, what is one action of faith you can take a step forward in? It may feel scary and unsettling, but most likely, that is the step of faith you need to take today. Trust that the Lord will help you navigate the unknowns ahead. Let go and let God.

For we walk by faith, not by sight. —2 Corinthians 5:7

Further Scripture: John 14:12; 15:5; Hebrews 11:1

Questions

1. How do you feel after reading 2 Corinthians 5:1? Spend a few minutes thinking about your "house" in heaven and your eternal body. Praise God for these gifts He has given you.
2. According to 2 Corinthians 5:7, "We walk by faith and not by sight." What does this mean to you? Give some examples of this in your own life.
3. Does 2 Corinthians 5:10 put a fear in your heart when you read it? What do you think you will receive on that day, either good or bad?
4. How would you practically explain 2 Corinthians 5:17 to an unbeliever? Do you believe this verse and walk in it? If so, how?
5. Do you fully believe 2 Corinthians 5:21? Do you share that with others? How can you practically share, "He, who has no sin, became sin for us"?
6. What did the Holy Spirit highlight to you in 2 Corinthians 5 through the reading or the teaching?

WEEK 75

Lesson 38: 2 Corinthians 6

Treasure: The Spirit Life

Teaching Notes

Intro

Before getting into chapter six, there are a few passages in chapter five to highlight that will qualify what we will study in this chapter:

"Indeed, while we groan while we are in this tent, burdened as we are, because we do not want to be unclothed but clothed, so that mortality may be swallowed up by life" (2 Corinthians 5:4). Our burden is this *Treasure* that is inside of us that wants to break out to the outside. This *Treasure* on the inside gives us the life we want; it consumes our life in the flesh with the life that is from God.

"From now on, then, we do not know anyone in a purely human way. Even if we have known Christ in a purely human way, yet now we no longer know Him in this way. Therefore, if anyone is in Christ, he is a new creation; old things have passed away, and look, new things have come. Everything is from God, who reconciled us to Himself through Christ and gave us the ministry of reconciliation" (2 Corinthians 5:16–18). In Christ, something new happened in our hearts. That's why we speak of being born again. Our old life passed away and we were given new life. What God has done in us and for us has given us a new identity and a new perspective.

"Therefore, we are ambassadors for Christ, certain that God is appealing through us. We plead on Christ's behalf, 'Be reconciled to God'" (2 Corinthians 5:20). God did not desire to simply alter the Corinthians' behavior. He wanted them to become brand-new people through Christ who were given work to do.

Teaching

2 Corinthians 6:1–2: Paul did not work with the Lord with his own agenda. Instead, Paul acknowledged he was "working together with Him" (v. 1). Paul allowed the Lord to set the agenda for his ministry and he obeyed. The grace the believers received from God wasn't something they could take off and put on. Identifying with Christ became who they were. Paul wanted the Corinthians to major in the new life experience in the Spirit.

2 Corinthians 6:3–10: Paul committed to walk so much in the life of the Spirit that no one could claim he was a hypocrite or inauthentic. Paul's overriding concern was the validation of his ministry. As long as he walked in the Spirit, the power and authority of his ministry could not be discredited. This standard was not just for Paul as a minister. The same standard applies to all believers. The particulars of what that looks like differs according to individuals, but all believers are to walk in the Spirit life to such an extent that the validity of their message cannot be discredited. Paul listed several qualifications of walking in the Spirit life that were born out of his own experience:

- Great endurance (v. 4)—we will walk through things that will take time and will be uncomfortable for us.
- Afflictions (v. 4)—unexpected difficult situations that come up against us.
- Hardship and difficulties (v. 4)—difficult things we must endure.
- Beatings and imprisonments (v. 5)—physical difficulties.
- Riots and labors (v. 5)—people physically coming against you; situations that require physical persistence and effort.
- Sleepless nights and times of hunger (v. 5)—burdens that cause us to not sleep; when pursuing God's mission leads you to a place where food is unavailable.
- Purity and knowledge (v. 6)—conviction; what has been made known by God.
- Patience and kindness (v. 6)—things that are worth having, but necessary to wait on; moral integrity, not just being nice.
- Holy Spirit and sincere love (v. 6)—authentic love that had to be shown because of the work of God on the heart.
- Message of truth, power of God, weapons of righteousness (v. 7)—the spiritual tools given to all believers.
- Glory and dishonor, slander and good report, as deceivers, yet true (v. 8)—opinion will be mixed; some would resist and seek to discredit the work of ministry.
- Unknown yet recognized, dying but living, disciplined yet not killed (v. 9)—unknown to people, but well known to God; the outward man perishes but the inward man is renewed daily.
- Grieving yet rejoicing, poor yet enriching many, having nothing yet possessing everything (v. 10)—Experiencing difficulty, but focusing on eternal realities; emptying oneself to see others blessed spiritually; laying down one's life to gain eternity.

Paul's qualifications will come up again in 2 Corinthians 11:23–27: "Are they servants of Christ? I'm talking like a madman—I'm a better one: with far more labors, many more imprisonments, far worse beatings, near death many times. Five times received 39 lashes from Jews. Three times I was beaten with rods by the Romans. Once I was stoned by my enemies. Three times I was shipwrecked. I have spent a day and night in the open sea. On frequent journeys, I faced dangers from rivers, dangers from robbers, dangers from my own people, dangers from the Gentiles, dangers in the city, dangers in the open country, dangers on the sea, and dangers among false brothers; labor and hardship, many sleepless nights, hunger and thirst, often without food, cold, and lacking clothing."

2 Corinthians 6:11–13: Paul loved the Corinthians and wanted them to know and enjoy the freedom of Christ of which he had been speaking. Paul endured everything he mentioned previously because of his love and concern for the church, but the Corinthians were "limited by [their] own affections" (v. 12). Paul encouraged the Corinthians to open their hearts to hear what he was saying to them.

2 Corinthians 6:14–18: Paul encouraged believers to "not be matched with unbelievers" (v. 14). Believers have *Treasure* on the inside that unbelievers simply can't understand. Paul then gave several examples of how different believers are from unbelievers (vv. 14–16). The point is that what was on the inside was more important than what was on the outside.

Closing

If we really believe we have *Treasure* on the inside of us, how important is it for us to guard it, treasure it, keep a high moral integrity, and compel us toward God because we love what He has done in our hearts.

The Daily Word

As a follower of Christ, you are a new creation, and your old ways have passed away. God's grace is upon you, and you have the Holy Spirit to empower you to walk in a new way of life. As you do, you serve as an ambassador for the Lord, representing Christ to others. As God's minister, *you have a responsibility to reflect Christ*, regardless of hardships and afflictions. Yes, the Lord says hardships will come, just as they did for Paul. But even through the hard, reflect Christ with patience, kindness, purity, knowledge, and wisdom as the power of the Holy Spirit works through you. Show sincere love and convey the message of truth.

This may seem like a list of things to do, but Christ doesn't intend for you to take on a checklist. Rather walk this out with thanksgiving and joy in the Lord.

Why? Because you are a new creation! Walk and rejoice in the power of the resurrected Savior. Walk in His saving grace. No matter how hard life may get, and all the Lord calls you to endure—*remember the Lord will give you His power through the Holy Spirit.* As an ambassador of God, walk by faith, trusting His grace will carry you through each step.

We give no opportunity for stumbling to anyone, so that the ministry will not be blamed. But as God's ministers, we commend ourselves in everything. —2 Corinthians 6:3–4

Further Scripture: 2 Corinthians 5:17, 20; 6:4b–7a; 1 John 2:4–5

Questions

1. What would receiving the grace of God in vain look like? (2 Corinthians 6:1)
2. Read 2 Corinthians 6:3. Since coming to Christ, have you "given cause for offense"? Have you seen offense discredit the ministry of reconciliation that we have been called to as believers? (2 Corinthians 5:18)
3. Paul mentioned afflictions and sufferings in 2 Corinthians 1:4–8 and then shared some of the details in 6:4–10. What else did he include besides afflictions and sufferings? With which details in this list can you personally identify?
4. Weapons of righteousness for the right hand and the left are mentioned in 2 Corinthians 6:7 (Nehemiah 4:16–18). What do you think these might be? (2 Corinthians 10:3–4; Ephesians 6:17–18; James 5:16)
5. What are ways we bind ourselves with unbelievers? (1 Corinthians 15:33)
6. What did the Holy Spirit highlight to you in 2 Corinthians 6 through the reading or the teaching?

WEEK 75

Lesson 39: 2 Corinthians 7

Treasure: The Superior Covenant

Teaching Notes

Intro

We are wrapping up this section of 2 Corinthians, which is a powerfully personal explanation of Paul's ministry. Wiersbe lays out for us this "week" that Paul wrote about to his readers.

- In spite of trials, Paul had a triumphant ministry (Chapters 1–2—Monday/ Tuesday).
- Paul had a glorious ministry (Chapter 3—Wednesday).
- Paul never thought of quitting, even under accusation (Chapter 4—Thursday)
- Paul's ministry was based on faith in God (Chapter 5—Friday)
- Paul challenged the hearts of the Corinthian believers (Chapter 6) and then gave his conclusion to this section (Chapter 7—Saturday).[1]

Teaching

2 Corinthians 7:1: This was Paul's natural conclusion to 2 Corinthians 6:14–18. Where Paul wrote about the need to separate from worldly influences so that we can live a close life with God. Basically, let's get it cleaned up and again have fellowship. Having spent most of his time dealing with problems in the church in Corinth, Paul began to express confidence and joy in the Corinthians to motivate them to faithful service. Wiersbe highlights a threefold encouragement in this chapter.[2]

---

[1] Warren W. Wiersbe, *The Wiersbe Bible Commentary: New Testament* (Colorado Springs: David C. Cook, 2007), 519.

[2] Wiersbe, 522.

2 Corinthians 7:2–3: Wiersbe wrote that Paul encouraged the church in verses 2–4.[3] This is probably where we will spend most of our time. The Corinthian Christians believed many bad things about Paul; that God wasn't using him and that he didn't have the kind of image, authority, or power an apostle should have. Why is it so difficult to assure people of our love?

Their problem was not an information problem, rather it was a problem with their hearts, which had been open to the world but not to Paul. In the "unequally yoked" passage, Paul told them to close their hearts to the world. Now it was time to open their hearts to him. Paul asked them to trust him—he had never done anything to wrong them. Paul was willing to die for them if necessary; they were in his heart.

2 Corinthians 7:4–7: Paul was boasting about them. This is really a great set of letters that are especially applicable to our times. In his book *Paul's Worst Church: Our Best Model?*, Pastor Church Warnock wrote, "I think it's time somebody came to the defense of the church in Corinth. Okay, so they're all dead now. But they live on in two of Paul's letters for all the world to see. I think Corinth, arguably Paul's worst church, may be our best model for the church today.

- *They were brand-new believers.* Phoebe came from Corinth (Romans 16:1–2).
- *They participated.*
- *They made mistakes, but out of enthusiasm.*
- *Their new faith was relevant to their world.* This was a community with false love everywhere. Once they understood what real love was, they were able to communicate and relate with others in their community.
- *They were a real church.* How many times do we put on a mask and hide all our garbage at home? We are called to be authentic and real. That's when we become a real church.[4]

2 Corinthians 7:5: Wiersbe wrote that Titus encouraged Paul in verses 5–10.[5] Note these are the churches in Macedonia: Philippi, Thessalonica, and Berea. It strikes me that the turmoil impacted the God-given rhythm of rest and work. It impacted Paul physically, emotionally, and spiritually.

---

[3] Wiersbe, 522.

[4] Chuck Warnock, "Corinth: Why Paul's Worst Church May Be Our Best Model," Chuck Warnock (blog), December 2, 2007, chuckwarnockblog.wordpress.com/2007/12/02/corinth-why-pauls-worst-church-may-be-our-best-model/.

[5] Wiersbe, 522.

2 Corinthians 7:6–7: What a huge encouragement! It was not easy for Paul to communicate or travel. We tend to take for granted how easy it is for us to communicate with others locally and around the world. Paul was encouraged by the reports Titus gave of his reception at Corinth. The Corinthians read Paul's "painful letter," repented of their sins, and disciplined the members who created the problem. Here is the accountability which we read earlier this year in Psalms and Proverbs—and the impact it can have.

2 Corinthians 7:8: The letter Paul referred to was probably written between 1 and 2 Corinthians. It helps to remember the sequence of events. Things were going badly among the Christians in Corinth, and in an attempt to get them on track, Paul made a quick, unplanned visit that only seemed to make things worse (2 Corinthians 2:1). After the failure of the visit, Paul decided not to visit Corinth again in person, but instead sent Titus to help them with a strong letter of rebuke. Paul was worried about how the Corinthians would receive the letter and whether it would turn them to Jesus or make them angry. Don't you think Paul was wrestling over Ephesians 4:14–16? In addition to speaking truth in love, Paul gave both correction and encouragement.

2 Corinthians 7:9–10: The letter was stern and had achieved its purpose. The Corinthians repented. This was not merely a passing regret. It was a true Godly sorrow in sin. Wiersbe illustrates the difference by comparing Judas to Peter: "Judas was full of regret and went and committed suicide. Peter wept and repented of his failure (Matthew 26:75—27:5)."[6] To repent simply means to change one's mind. Disobedient Christians need to repent, not in order to be saved, but in order to restore their close fellowship with God.

2 Corinthians 7:11–16: Paul recorded that the Corinthians encouraged Titus in verses 11–16. The experience of Titus in Corinth, and his report from there, was sure evidence the Corinthian Christians had a change of mind. I think it is good to slow down and savor this paragraph. Paul spelled out their handling of the matter of discipline. Paul praised the Corinthian Christians, and they seemed to be in a place of victory. But in the "sorrowful letter," mentioned in 2 Corinthians 2:1, there was no praise. What was the difference? The difference was their real repentance reported by Titus and commented on by Paul in this chapter.

[6] Wiersbe, 522.

Closing

This chapter shows how concerned Paul was about his relationship with the Corinthian Christians and that people were just as important to Paul as ministry. He didn't want to do ministry at the expense of his relationship with people.

One of the most difficult things to do is rebuild a shattered relationship. Unfortunately, there are many shattered relationships today—in homes, churches, and ministries—and they can be repaired and strengthened only when people face problems honestly, deal with them biblically and lovingly, and seek to get right with God. As we examine our own lives, we must determine to be a part of the answer and not the problem. Let us learn from Paul and the church in Corinth and allow God to use us to restore broken relationships.

The Daily Word

Paul wrote about the reality of the Corinthian lifestyle and how painful his visit with the Corinthians church had been. *Paul also expressed gratitude.* Even though watching the Corinthians had been painful at times, Paul's ministry had not been in vain. The Corinthians were similar to the church today—*sinners saved by grace who were learning how to live by the Spirit in faith and not by works.* The Corinthians were learning to live as broken vessels with God's powerful treasure inside. Therefore, Paul spent time affirming his gratefulness that grief leads to repentance.

There may be people in your life who need encouragement and guidance on how to walk with the Lord. These people could be peers, coworkers, neighbors, or even your children. Allow Paul's affirming and encouraging words to the church remind you to affirm others with your love for them. Perhaps today you need to encourage someone in your life, even in your own family. Even when frustrated, point out something positive, instead of dwelling on negatives or weaknesses. Build others up. Take a minute to love those in your life deeply, without any strings attached. The Lord is at work regardless of any fruit you may or may not see. The Lord is working all things out for His purposes.

I have great confidence in you; I have great pride in you. I am filled with encouragement; I am overcome with joy in all our afflictions.
—2 Corinthians 7:4

Further Scripture: Romans 1:8; 2 Corinthians 7:9–10; 3 John 1:4

Questions

1. Second Corinthians 7:1 is a call to cleanse ourselves from all defilement of flesh and spirit. How do we do this?
2. According to 2 Corinthians 7:5, Paul and his companions had been afflicted by fear from within. Does it surprise you that Paul experienced fear? What could have caused their fears? (2 Corinthians 1:8–10; 6:4–10)
3. Paul told the Corinthians that God comforts the depressed. How can we receive that comfort? (2 Corinthians 7:6)
4. There are two kinds of sorrow mentioned in 2 Corinthians 7:10. Describe each one. Do you think sometimes people "repent" out of worldly sorrow and not faith in Christ? If so, are they truly saved?
5. What did the Holy Spirit highlight to you in 2 Corinthians 7 through the reading or the teaching?

WEEK 75

Lesson 40: 2 Corinthians 8

Treasure: The Motivation of Giving

Teaching Notes

Intro

Second Corinthians 8—9 are an ongoing thought with themes Paul has carried throughout the entire letter. Our one word for 2 Corinthians has been *Treasure*: "Now we have this treasure in clay jars, so that this extraordinary power may be from God and not from us" (2 Corinthians 4:7). Jesus, the *Treasure* of believers, lives inside of us. In chapters 8—9, Paul talked about real treasure. Paul took up an offering of money from the churches to take back to poor believers in Jerusalem who were experiencing a famine. Paul collected this earthly treasure because of the *Treasure*, in Jesus, the churches possessed. "Yes, they were pleased and indeed are indebted to them. For if the Gentiles have shared in their spiritual benefits, then they are obligated to minister to Jews in material needs" (Romans 15:27). This continued a pattern in Paul's ministry: "In every way I've shown you that by laboring like this, it is necessary to help the weak and to keep in mind the words of the Lord Jesus, for He said, 'It is more blessed to give than to receive'" (Acts 20:35). Wiersbe highlighted four reasons Paul wanted to take up this collection for the Jerusalem church:[1]

1. To strengthen the unity of the church.
2. The Gentiles were debtors to the Jewish people.
3. Paul wanted to show he wasn't an enemy to the Jews.
4. Paul promised to remember the poor. "They asked only that we would remember the poor, which I made every effort to do" (Galatians 2:10).

Paul had to remind the Corinthians of this offering because the Corinthian church had not lived up to their end of the commitment: "Now I am giving an opinion on this because it is profitable for you, who a year ago began not only to do something but also to desire it. But now finish the task as well, that just as

[1] Warren W. Wiersbe, *The Wiersbe Bible Commentary: New Testament* (Colorado Springs : David C. Cook, 2007), 523.

there was eagerness to desire it, so there may also be a completion from what you have" (2 Corinthians 8:10–11).

Teaching

2 Corinthians 8:1–2: Wiersbe noted that when giving is motivated by grace, we give in spite of our circumstances.[2] Paul mentioned the churches in Macedonia gave in spite of less than ideal circumstances. Paul specifically mentioned these churches gave in abundance in spite of "their deep poverty," which Wiersbe defined as "rock-bottom destitution."[3] They even gave with an "abundance of joy" (v. 2), not begrudgingly. *Nelson's Commentary* pointed out the Macedonian churches' giving went "beyond their means."[4]

2 Corinthians 8:3–4: The Macedonian churches gave enthusiastically.[5] They "begged" (v. 4) for the opportunity to give to the Jewish believers because of the *Treasure* inside them.

2 Corinthians 8:5–9: Because of the treasure inside them, the Macedonian churches gave as Jesus gave.[6] Paul observed the abundance of spiritual gifts and graces the Corinthian church possessed: faith, speech, knowledge, diligence, and love (v. 7). Now, as a test to the genuineness of their love, Paul encouraged them to follow through on their commitment to help the Jerusalem believers. Their generosity ought to overflow from their love for Christ. Paul reminded the Corinthians of the example of Christ who, "Though He was rich, for your sake He became poor, so that by His poverty you might become rich" (v. 10).

The riches to which Paul referred were not earthly riches. Jesus didn't die so we could get a bonus or lake house. Instead, the riches we receive from our faith in Jesus are spiritual riches, namely salvation. *Nelson's Commentary* lists: "justification, regeneration, eternal life, glorification, Jesus purchases us from slavery to sin and makes us children of God"[7] as the riches that believers receive from Christ.

---

[2] Wiersbe, 523.

[3] Wiersbe, 523.

[4] Earl D. Radmacher, Ronald B. Allen, and H. Wayne House, eds., *Nelson's New Illustrated Bible Commentary* (Nashville: Thomas Nelson, 1999), 1505.

[5] Wiersbe, 524.

[6] Wiersbe, 524.

[7] Radmacher et al., 1505.

2 Corinthians 8:10–12: Wiersbe wrote we know giving is motivated by grace when we give willingly.[8] The Corinthians' giving was an investment. It would help them before the Lord in the same way the physical gifts would help the Jerusalem believers.

2 Corinthians 8:13–24: Grace-motivated giving is done by faith.[9] Paul encouraged the Corinthians to give out of their abundance into the poverty of others, with the idea in mind that others would sow out of their abundance, in the Corinthians' time of poverty. Verse 15 is a reference to the experience of the Israelites in the wilderness when they gathered manna:

"When they measured it by quarts, the person who gathered a lot had no surplus, and the person who gathered a little had no shortage. Each gathered as much as he needed to eat . . . But they didn't listen to Moses; some people left part of it until morning, and it bred worms and smelled. Therefore, Moses was angry with them" (Exodus 16:18, 20). The Israelites hoarded the manna in spite of God's commandment to only gather enough for one day. They kept the abundance thinking they would provide for themselves for the next day. We sometimes hoard giving to the kingdom out of concern for holding on for the next day. We don't always see giving as an investment into the kingdom of God. We don't always value the spiritual blessing we will receive from the Lord in our giving over the physical wealth that we choose to hold onto.

Titus went out with an unnamed brother to gather the funds for the collection. This brother had a desire to honor the Lord. This group of people was responsible for the collection as an act of accountability before the churches for the money they would receive. They were characterized by a "cooperative spirit" in their desire to see all the churches rally around this collection to benefit the Jerusalem church.[10]

Closing

The *Treasure,* Christ, inside the Corinthians was meant to motivate them to contribute to the needs of the church in Jerusalem. Paul reminded them of the blessings of giving and encouraged them to participate as Titus and the brother came to receive their gifts.

---

[8] Wiersbe, 524.

[9] Wiersbe, 525.

[10] Wiersbe, 526.

The Daily Word

Paul testified about the Corinthian church's generous spirit, even in the midst of their affliction and poverty. In a similar way, God sacrificially gave the world His Son Jesus. Jesus also demonstrated selfless, abundant giving as He gave up His life for the world so you could be saved from death and have eternal life.

As an imitator of Christ, you are called to give as Jesus gave—selflessly and generously. As a believer, the Lord calls you to offer your whole life to Him. Give of your finances, even when it makes you uncomfortable. Give of your time, even when your schedule is full. Always give of your life for the sake of the gospel. *Generous giving involves giving as the Spirit leads in faithful obedience*, even when it doesn't make sense or resemble what others around you are doing. The Lord calls you to follow Him and to not conform to the pattern of the world. How is the Lord calling you to give obediently today? Remember to trust in the Lord's faithfulness as you give from a place of obedience!

During a severe testing by affliction, their abundance of joy and their deep poverty overflowed into the wealth of their generosity. —2 Corinthians 8:2

Further Scripture: Ephesians 5:1–2; James 1:17; 1 John 3:16

Questions

1. Why did Paul inform the Corinthians about the Macedonian churches giving to those in need in Jerusalem? (2 Corinthians 8:1–8)
2. What does giving beyond your means or ability mean (2 Corinthians 8:3)? Have you ever given like this? If not, what holds you back?
3. What did Paul mean by saying the Lord Jesus Christ became poor for our sakes so that through His poverty, we might become rich? (2 Corinthians 8:9)
4. What outcome do you think Paul desired in 2 Corinthians 8:13–15? (Exodus 16:18)
5. What did the Holy Spirit highlight to you in 2 Corinthians 8 through the reading or the teaching?

WEEK 76

Lesson 41: 2 Corinthians 9

Treasure: Ministry of Giving

Teaching Notes

Intro

Our one word for this book of the Bible is *Treasure*, based on 2 Corinthians 4:7. This *Treasure* is Christ within us. Through the power of the Holy Spirit, God wants to speak through us, and to move through us. In 2 Corinthians 8—9, God says He has given us faith and speech and knowledge and discernment and the gift of giving. Paul wanted to make sure the Corinthians would be faithful to fulfill their promise to give to the Christians in Jerusalem. Giving to the Jewish believers was important because they launched this whole thing. Salvation came to the Jews first, and through them, to the Gentiles.

Warren Wiersbe referred to the giving described in 2 Corinthians 9 as "grace giving."[1] Wiersbe then walked through five encouragements that relate to giving. Paul wanted them to understand the benefits of giving, both for themselves and for those who received their gifts.

Teaching

2 Corinthians 9:1–5: According to Wiersbe, "*Your giving will provoke others.*"[2] When we give, others will also give. In a classic move, Paul said he wasn't going to talk about the offering anymore, then proceeded to do just that. Paul bragged about them to the Macedonians, which in turn, stirred the Macedonians to also give. Paul then said he was sending "the brothers" (v. 3), to pick up their gift, praying they would not be unprepared with their gift and therefore embarrassed (v. 4). Paul encouraged them to have their generous gift ready as they had promised (v. 5).

[1] Warren W. Wiersbe, *The Wiersbe Bible Commentary: New Testament* (Colorado Springs: David C. Cook, 2007), 527.

[2] Wiersbe, 527.

2 Corinthians 9:6–11: These verses, according to Wiersbe, show "*Your giving will bless you.*"[3] Paul used farming terms to make his point. When a farmer planted a lot of seeds, he would get a large crop. If he didn't plant a lot of seeds, he wouldn't get much of a crop. Wiersbe said there's a "principle of increase: we reap in measure as we sow."[4] In Luke 6:38, Jesus described the law of harvest: "Give, and it will be given to you . . . for with the measure you use, it will be measured back to you." Solomon made a similar statement in Proverbs 11:24–25. *Nelson's Commentary* said, "Giving is like sowing a seed. The amount of harvest is determined by the seed sown."[5] Proverbs 19:17 says God will reward those who show kindness to the poor. When you give, God will bless you.

Wiersbe also said there's a "principle of intent."[6] God loves a cheerful giver (v. 7)—one who gives enthusiastically and with joy when prompted by the Holy Spirit. Wiersbe then described a third principle: the "principle of immediacy."[7] When you hear from the Lord, then you need to give immediately. Don't take time to analyze it or disregard it. Just give as God directs. Paul quoted Psalm 112:9 in his statement in verse 9. Basically, the good person's acts of generosity endure forever and bring eternal blessings to those who receive them. Because God had provided "seed for the sower and bread for food," (v. 10), He also has the ability to give the provision and bring forth the increase.

The prosperity theology in America uses verses 10–11 to say that if you give, you will be enriched in everything. Since our society is confused about giving, the Gospel Coalition describes five errors about prosperity gospel.[8]

1. "The Abrahamic Covenant is a means to material entitlement." In Genesis 12:3, God promised to bless those who blessed Abraham. This means those who bless Israel will receive God's blessings while those who turn against Israel will be cursed. The prosperity gospel says if I pour all my money into Israel, then I'll get all kinds of money back. That's the wrong motive. But we should bless Israel simply because Scripture says that is what we're supposed to do.
2. "Jesus's atonement extends to the 'sin' of material poverty." Prosperity gospel claims Jesus' actions on the cross abolish the whole mentality of poverty

---

[3] Wiersbe, 527.

[4] Wiersbe, 527.

[5] Earl D. Radmacher, Ronald B. Allen, and H. Wayne House, eds., *Nelson's New Illustrated Bible Commentary* (Nashville: Thomas Nelson, 1999), 1505.

[6] Wiersbe, 527.

[7] Wiersbe, 527.

[8] David W. Jones, "5 Errors of the Prosperity Gospel," The Gospel Coalition, June 5, 2015, https://www.thegospelcoalition.org/article/5-errors-of-the-prosperity-gospel/.

(based on 2 Corinthians 8:9). They claim because of Jesus' death and burial, no longer are you poor.

3. "Christians give in order to gain material compensation from God." Based on Mark 10:30, the prosperity gospel claims giving brings 100 times more.
4. "Faith is a self-generated spiritual force that leads to prosperity." The prosperity gospel claims if you have the faith this can happen, then you will prosper. Instead, believers give by the grace of God that He's given us to give to someone else.
5. "Prayer is a tool to force God to grant prosperity." Prosperity gospel claims that if you pray for it, anything can happen.

Here's Kyle's heart in sharing this: He wants you to be aware of the wolves disguised in sheep's clothing in the church. It's not just the American church, it is churches all across the world. We twist the scriptures, and the focus is on materialism and not meeting needs.

2 Corinthians 9:12: Wiersbe pointed out, "*Your giving will meet needs.*"[9] According to Paul in this verse, when we give, we help people.

2 Corinthians 9:13: Wiersbe also said, "*Your giving will glorify God.*"[10] Your obedience to God's directive to give generously will bring glory to God.

2 Corinthians 9:14–15: Lastly, Wiersbe observed, "*Your giving will unite God's people.*"[11] When you receive money from someone, you begin to pray for them because your heart is for them (not because they gave you something). Because of that gift, other people begin to experience God as well.

Closing

Because of Christ, that *Treasure*—that gift, we have the chance to reflect Christ.

The Daily Word

When the Holy Spirit prompts you to give, obey His voice. The Lord promises the person who sows sparingly will reap sparingly, and the person who sows generously will reap generously. If the Lord prompts your heart to give a specific amount of money, then follow through and give. If the Lord prompts your heart to bring a

[9] Wiersbe, 529.

[10] Wiersbe, 529.

[11] Wiersbe, 529.

meal to a family, drive a carpool, spend time at the food pantry, or lead a discipleship group, but you don't think you have the energy, wisdom, time, or talent to make it happen, stop rationalizing and *instead walk it out in obedience*. Remember, the Lord is able to make every grace overflow to you so that in *every way*, you will always have *everything you need*, and you may excel in *every good work*.

The ministry of giving involves *a step of faith*. The ministry of giving *requires sacrifice*. The ministry of giving *takes obedience*. The ministry of giving *expects an extra measure of grace and power from the Holy Spirit*. The Lord promises that as you walk with Him in obedience, *He will make a way*. So, start walking in obedient giving. The more you let go of yourself and your things, the more room the Lord has to move in your life beyond what you can imagine! You can never out give God. His love, His grace, and His power will continue to *overflow* in your life.

Each person should do as he has decided in his heart—not reluctantly or out of necessity, for God loves a cheerful giver. And God is able to make every grace overflow to you, so that in every way, always having everything you need, you may excel in every good work. —2 Corinthians 9:7–8

Further Scripture: Romans 15:13; Philippians 4:13; 1 Timothy 1:14

Questions

1. How did Paul use the Corinthians and Macedonians to stir one another toward generous giving? (2 Corinthians 8:1–2; 9:2–4; Hebrews 10:24)
2. What seemed to be Paul's concern in 2 Corinthians 9:3–5? Have you ever boasted about a person or group and then they let you down?
3. What principle was Paul teaching in 2 Corinthians 9:8–10? Have you given generously and seen this principle proven true?
4. In 2 Corinthians 9:15, for which "gift" from God was Paul thankful? (2 Corinthians 9:8, 14)
5. What did the Holy Spirit highlight to you in 2 Corinthians 9 through the reading or the teaching?

Lesson 42: 2 Corinthians 10

Treasure: Battling Spiritual Warfare

Teaching Notes

Intro

We've been looking at 2 Corinthians 8—9, which have been all about giving. Our word for 2 Corinthians is *Treasure* (2 Corinthians 4:7). We have the *Treasure* inside of us. In 2 Corinthians 10, we'll see a big shift that seems not to fit with the verses and chapters before it. Chapter 10 is about the power of Christ in us against spiritual battle. Paul also used the opportunity to address the Judaizers who were making false claims against him.

Teaching

2 Corinthians 10:1–6: Wiersbe divides chapter 2 into three sections, the first dealing with, "How to Wage Spiritual Warfare."[1] This section is so important that if we don't get past these first six verses, I'll be okay with that. Paul began in "the gentleness and graciousness of Christ" (v. 1a). He then spoke against the Judaizers who said he was weak in person, but bold from a distance (v. 1b). *Nelson's Commentary* explains that "by saying 'I beg,'"[2] Paul was gently asking the Corinthians to deal with his critics before he came so he would not have to be stern with them." Paul described them as living in the flesh in verse 3, even as he himself lived in the flesh. But Paul would not behave "in an unspiritual way," because his warfare was not worldly but was through the power of God (v. 4). Wiersbe explains, "The powers of hell are still trying to destroy the work of God (Matthew 16:18)."[3] Paul continued that he would demolish arguments and high-minded theological thoughts that did not come from the knowledge of God (v. 5). Finally, Paul was ready to punish any who had been disobedient (v. 6).

[1] Warren W. Wiersbe, *The Bible Exposition Commentary: Matthew–Galatians* (Colorado Springs: David C. Cook, 1989), 664.

[2] Earl D. Radmacher, Ronald B. Allen, and H. Wayne House, eds., *Nelson's New Illustrated Bible Commentary* (Nashville: Thomas Nelson, 1999), 1507.

[3] Wiersbe, 665.

Verse 3 mentioned spiritual warfare. What is spiritual warfare? Spiritual warfare attacks us through many levels of revelation.

1. The first level is fleshly—the flesh versus the power of God, which the enemy (Satan) is trying to draw us into. We have to fight this with one of the weapons God has given us—by saying we will not engage in a fleshly battle with him.
2. The second level is speculations, arguments, and lies that become lodged within us. Satan cannot be in more than one place at a time, so we mostly face demonic assignments, such as fallen angels who have turned away. They attack us with lies about ourselves. In many cases, the enemy speaks into our lives when we are young through a traumatic event that makes us question our own worth. We feel devalued and insecure, and we interpret life through that lens.
3. The third level is lies about God that enter our hearts. These lies work with the lies in level 2 to create a web of deceit and misunderstanding within our hearts. This web of lies can cause us to question if the Holy Spirit is real, if Jesus will desert us, if God actually cares about us. This causes desperation and hopelessness about our lives and our faith. All these create strongholds in our lives that the enemy can use to try to defeat us. They happen before we are believers and we bring them into our relationship with Christ. When we open our hearts to Jesus, we have to open those areas as well.
4. The fourth level contains the fortresses and/or strongholds. If we feel devalued and get angry at perceived insults, we've created a stronghold where the anger resides. If we don't get to the root of the cause of the stronghold, we cannot experience freedom in Christ. Jesus has to cut out the root of the stronghold before we can be free.

We have the *Treasure* of God within us. How do we walk through these levels so we can defeat these levels?

1. We have to know the enemy's voice from God's voice. The enemy's voice sounds like us, but God's voice is a thought or a vision that we didn't put there. God's voice will sound like His character. The enemy is making himself sound really good, but his words have no substance.
2. Is God's voice setting us free, or is the enemy's voice putting us in bondage? If you hear a voice that is contrary to God's nature, then pray the opposite as Holy Spirit leads. Speak life and truth through Jesus, and the enemy's voice will go away.

Closing

Jesus, thank You for coming to set the captives free and to release the prisoners. You paid a high price for the captives to receive freedom. I pray those who hear or read this will experience You in a new and profound way. I pray these will press through the enemy's voice and lies to be able to know Your voice and hear You personally. Jesus, come set us free. Amen.

The Daily Word

As a follower of Christ, you must realize, just like the Corinthian church, you are in a spiritual battle. It's not a battle against flesh and blood *but a spiritual battle against rulers, authorities, world powers of this darkness, and spiritual forces.* What the Lord intended for good, the enemy wants to defeat.

To fight the battle, you must be aware of the war raging against you. Then the Lord says to renew your mind daily because you need the truth to stand firm, to resist the enemy, and to hear the voice of the Lord. The voice of the Lord speaks truth and life. The more you read His Word, the more you will recognize the Lord's voice in battle. The enemy speaks lies to you: "You aren't good enough. You aren't worthy. You are rejected. You can't succeed." Paul instructed the Corinthian believers to *take every thought captive.* This means that when these lies creep in, *stand and proclaim God's Word and the truth*: "You are perfectly and wonderfully made. You are clothed in righteousness. You are worthy. You can do all things through Christ who gives you strength." Believe the truth will set you free, and the enemy's voice will flee. Then you will find victory in the battle. Today, practice taking every thought captive and proclaim Jesus in the middle of your battle. He is with you, and He is freedom!

Since the weapons of our warfare are not worldly, but are powerful through God for the demolition of strongholds. We demolish arguments and every high-minded thing that is raised up against the knowledge of God, taking every thought captive to obey Christ. —2 Corinthians 10:4–5

Further Scripture: John 8:3; 10:10; Ephesians 6:12

Questions

1. In 2 Corinthians 10:1–2, Paul spoke about boldness in Christ. Do you think you walk with this type of boldness? Why or why not?

2. How would you explain 2 Corinthians 10:5 to someone? What does "bringing into captivity every thought to the obedience of Christ" mean? Is this easy to do or a struggle for you?
3. According to 2 Corinthians 10:15–16, for what reason did Paul want to increase the faith of the Corinthians? How would the Corinthians' faith allow Paul to travel farther?
4. What did the Holy Spirit highlight to you in 2 Corinthians 10 through the reading or the teaching?

WEEK 76

Lesson 43: 2 Corinthians 11

Treasure: Paul and the False Apostles

Teaching Notes

Intro

Yesterday's lesson on 2 Corinthians 10 encouraged us to experience freedom in the Lord because we have the *Treasure* in us—that is, Christ is inside us. Even in our weaknesses, we get to see the Lord work. Paul said the enemy would come and try to smash anything that had been established. In this case, it was the Corinthian church. Paul encouraged them to recognize the enemy in the camp and then talked about how to fight that enemy. Because Paul loved the Corinthian church, he wanted to be the shepherd that protected them from the enemy. Today, in 2 Corinthians 11, Paul said there were people inside the camp (the church) who were wolves disguised as sheep's clothing. Paul loved the church enough to call out the false apostles in their midst.

Teaching

2 Corinthians 11:1–6, 13–15: According to Warren Wiersbe, these verses show Paul's *jealousy over the church.*[1] Paul wanted them to "put up with" him (1) because he was "jealous over you with a godly jealousy" (v. 2). Paul painted a picture of a loving father who had promised his daughter to one husband. This was a picture of the local church being engaged to be married to Christ.[2] In Ephesians 5:22–27, Paul further described this picture. A similar image of becoming one with the Messiah is found in Romans 7:4. However, this marriage doesn't take place until Christ comes for His bride (Revelation 19:1–9). Until that happens, the church is supposed to remain pure without letting anything come into the picture to muddy the waters.

But the Corinthians were in *peril*—in danger of being unfaithful to Christ. And the *person behind the peril was Satan.*[3] Paul reminded them, "The serpent

---

[1] Warren W. Wiersbe, *The Wiersbe Bible Commentary: New Testament* (Colorado Springs: David C. Cook, 2007), 534.

[2] Wiersbe, 534.

[3] Wiersbe, 534.

had deceived Eve by his cunning" (v. 3), and they were also in danger of being deceived. If they couldn't make the distinction between the enemy's voice and God's voice, then how would they know what was wrong? In Genesis 3:1, the serpent was described as "the most cunning of all the wild animals." Satan then deceived Eve (Genesis 3:1–6) by questioning God's Word.

Satan continues to get us to question God's Word and to deny God's Word. Then Satan substitutes his own lie.[4] As believers, we get impatient. When we get impatient, we become unfaithful and lose our sincerity and devotion. We become defiled and then just let Satan creep in. Paul was so jealous over the Corinthians because they were giving in to their old way of life.

Paul pointed out that they were giving in to another Jesus, giving in to a different spirit, and giving in to a different gospel (v. 4). How many false religions are out there today that say Jesus was an incredible man but He wasn't God? Or yes, Jesus died on the cross, but He wasn't God? Or yes, Jesus is a Savior, but He isn't God? There's a different gospel out there today that combines works and faith—it's a counterfeit gospel. There's two ways to look at the "super-apostles" (v. 5). Maybe they aren't really super apostles, but the false apostles—the pseudo apostles—whose methods are deceitful. The other way to look at it is that the term refers to the genuine apostles of Christ who came before.[5] Though Paul had no professional training as a speaker (v. 6), he was very knowledgeable.

2 Corinthians 11:7–12: Next, Paul talked about "*his generosity to the church*."[6] Paul pointed out he had never charged them for anything (v. 7). *Nelson's Commentary* said, "At that time, professional philosophers and teachers in the Greek society charged people for teaching."[7] Paul labored as a tent maker and received support from other churches. But in Corinth's context, he preached the gospel free of charge. Paul even stated: "I robbed other churches by taking pay from them to minister to you" (v. 8). Other people supported me so I could minister to you, and this is how you're going to treat me? To maintain his integrity and to prevent people from holding it over him, Paul did not collect any financial support from them even though he could have (1 Corinthians 9:1–12). Instead Paul relied on the brothers from Macedonia to supply his needs so he would not be a burden on them (v. 9). Wiersbe said Paul had a father-figure mentality. Paul didn't want to be a burden on them.[8] This burdening image can also be translated "charge-

---

[4] Wiersbe, 534.

[5] Wiersbe, 535.

[6] Wiersbe, 535.

[7] Earl D. Radmacher, Ronald B. Allen, and H. Wayne House, eds., *Nelson's New Illustrated Bible Commentary* (Nashville: Thomas Nelson, 1999).

[8] Wiersbe, 535.

able." According to Wiersbe, "In the Greek, it literally means 'to grow numb.' The word comes from the image of the electric eel numbing its victim with its shock. A numbed part of the body would be a burden to the victim."[9] Because of the *Treasure* (Christ) in him, Paul was determined to continue his work. Paul refused to be the one who weighed them down (v. 20) because he loved them (v. 11). Paul's ministry was a labor of love. Paul did this so no one would have the opportunity to speak falsely against him (v. 12).

2 Corinthians 11:16–33: Paul described "*his anxiety for the church*."[10] Paul listed all the things he had gone through: the five times he had received 39 lashes (v. 24); the three times he was beaten with rods by the Romans; the stoning; the shipwrecks (v. 25). Paul listed the spiritual components and the physical hardships he had faced: dangers from rivers, robbers, the Gentiles, in the city, in the open country, the open sea, false brothers (v. 26). But then Paul mentioned "the daily pressure on me: my care for all the churches" (v. 28). Paul felt anxiety for the churches because he cared—he didn't want them to cave in or give in. He was willing to go through all this because he cared for them. Paul was willing to go through anything and everything so that they would just stay on the course.

Closing

Paul is really a father figure to the Corinthian church. He was warning them there was people creeping into the camp that were false apostles and that he needed every one to be aware of them. In Acts 20:24, Paul said, "But I count my life of no value to myself, so that I may finish my course and the ministry I received from the Lord Jesus, to testify to the gospel of God's grace."

The Daily Word

Paul cared for those he ministered to, and this deep love motivated him to press on through the most difficult of times. He told the church in Corinth: *I love you, like God loves you. I am weak. I am beaten up, and I have suffered much for you, all for the simple gospel and the truth that transforms lives. But it is worth it.* The pressure and alienation Paul experienced didn't stop him. He pressed on for the sake of the gospel so believers would follow the truth and not become wayward. Paul boasted only in the Lord, and the love he had for others kept him going.

[9] Wiersbe, 536.

[10] Wiersbe, 536.

Paul serves as an example to press on through hard times of ministry. You may minister in your home to your children, by teaching a Sunday school class, through leading a small group, serving the homeless, teaching from a large stage, or praying for others from your closet. As you follow Christ, the Lord will put people around you to love deeply. This great love will drive you, as it did Paul, to press on in your weakness, press on in the pressure, and press on in your weariness *for the sake of the gospel.* The Lord has you right where you need to be for a reason. Remember, you are not alone. Recall your great love for those around you and the desire within you for them to know Jesus. The Lord will give you the strength to press on in His great love.

As the truth of Christ is in me, this boasting of mine will not be stopped in the regions of Achaia. Why? Because I don't love you? God knows I do!
—2 Corinthians 11:10–11

Further Scripture: Acts 20:24; 2 Corinthians 11:27–30; Galatians 6:9

Questions

1. In 2 Corinthians 11:1–4, Paul spoke about false teachers and the Corinthians being swayed by those same teachers. When you look at the world today, could this be true for our time as well? In what ways?
2. Where else in Scripture is "bride" mentioned with concern to Christ, as in 2 Corinthians 11:2? (Ephesians 5:25–27; Revelation 19:7–9; 21:1–2)
3. In 2 Corinthians 11:23–27, Paul described the sufferings he endured spreading the Word of God. Have Christians, in this day and age, come close to suffering like this in the United States? In your opinion could we, as Christians, handle that kind of suffering?
4. What did the Holy Spirit highlight to you in 2 Corinthians 11 through the reading or the teaching?

WEEK 76

Lesson 44: 2 Corinthians 12

Treasure: Visions and Revelations

Teaching Notes

Intro

Paul was concerned that his church in Corinth was not being faithful to the Lord. Paul was pretty forward in his letter. There were people who crept into the camp and were discrediting Paul and his apostleship. Paul responded by boasting about who he is in the Lord, attempting to connect with the church in Corinth. Historically the Corinthians were fascinated with visions and revelations. So, Paul addressed this in chapter 12.

Teaching

2 Corinthians 12:1: Visions happen while a person is awake. You could be standing somewhere and all the sudden you feel as though you are in a different place—that is a vision. In this other place the Lord will show you something. A vision could take a long time or it could be very quick. This was the type of vision Paul was talking about. MacArthur notes six times visions are recorded in the book of Acts:

1. Visions lay out the foundation for you to walk it out with God (9:12).
2. Visions can be seen and heard (16:9–10).
3. The Lord can actually appear in visions (18:9).
4. Visions can be warnings (22:17–18).
5. Visions can give direction (23:11).
6. Visions can give encouragement and assurance (27:25–29).[1]

Paul boasted about these visions because he knew it was needed in order to connect with the Corinthian believers. Joel 2:28–32 explains visions and prophecies will be experienced until the coming of Christ. This means God continues

[1] John MacArthur, *The MacArthur Bible Commentary* (Nashville: Thomas Nelson, 2005), 1649.

to speak to people through dreams and visions today. Please don't discredit these things! Paul spoke about his revelations as well.

Revelations come from Christ (Galatians 1:12). Some of Paul's actions were dictated by revelations (Galatians 2:2). Mysteries were revealed to Paul through revelations (Ephesians 3:3). Clearly Paul had something to boast about.

2 Corinthians 12:2–4: Paul was talking about himself here but was still reluctant to boast. During his time, Jewish rabbis talked in third person. Paul could have been culturally speaking the Corinthians language. MacArthur wrote that, since Paul's experience in the third heaven "took place fourteen years before the writing of 2 Corinthians, the specific vision Paul relates cannot be identified with any incident recorded in Acts."[2]

Let's talk about the third heaven. Paul was not making a distinction between the third heaven and paradise; they are the same place. Revelation 2:7 states the tree of life is in Paradise, and Revelation 22:14 explains the tree of life is in heaven. According to MacArthur, "The first Heaven is the earth's atmosphere (Genesis 8:2; Deuteronomy 11:11; 1 Kings 8:35); the second is interplanetary and interstellar space (Genesis 15:5; Psalm 8:3; Isaiah 13:10); and the third is the abode of God (1 Kings 8:30; 2 Chronicles 30:27; Psalm 123:1)."[3]

At some point Paul received a call in his life, but he had yet to share everything. Whether he was caught up bodily into heaven (like Enoch in Genesis 5:24 or Elijah in 2 Kings 2:11) or his spirit temporarily separated from his body, it's not important. It is an interesting picture Paul paints in this Scripture.

2 Corinthians 12:5–6: MacArthur explains Paul "refrained from boasting out [his unique experience], however, because he wanted the Corinthians to judge him based on their observations of his ministry, not on his visions."[4] You don't just bank on the visions; you've got to walk it out. "Thorn in the flesh" is also translated as "stake for the flesh," which was a demonized person, not a physical illness. Nelson's Commentary explains three interpretations for what the thorn of the flesh could be:

1. A bodily ailment—some kind of physical ailment, such as ongoing headaches, ringing in your ears, a severe limp, or a heart defect.
2. The constant temptation of the flesh—such as pride, finances, anxiety, people pleasing, or fear.
3. Persecution or opposition.

[2] MacArthur, 1649.

[3] MacArthur, 1649.

[4] MacArthur, 1649.

Nelson's Commentary states, "Paul's thorn was a painful, humiliating experience given to prevent pride."[5]

Any number of things will humble you so you depend on the Lord and not yourself. Somewhere in Corinth was a person who was demonized. Possibly this person was Paul's thorn in the flesh who was trying to damage Paul's credibility.

2 Corinthians 12:9–10: Thorns of the flesh make us utterly dependent on God.

Closing

I encourage you to continue to dive into the rest of the verses in this chapter. We will continue the dialogue tomorrow.

The Daily Word

Paul discussed the thorn in his flesh, the thing the Lord allowed so Paul would remain weak and not exalt himself. He asked the Lord to take it away three times, and yet it remained. It may have been a physical ailment, a temptation, a constant need, or even persecution. It was through Paul's weakness that he discovered and understood that strength comes from the Lord, and God's grace is sufficient.

The world says, "You have to be strong and have it all together." But the Lord says, "*When you are weak, then I am strong.*" Stop trying to have it all together. Resist the temptation to be self-sufficient, strong, and independent. You don't need to hide your weaknesses. When you are weak, Christ is able to be strong within you. In your weakness, you allow His presence, power, and grace into your life. In your weakness, *His power is perfected because there is actually room to work.* Others will see Christ's power in your life, instead of your own strength. Therefore, you boast in the Lord and not in yourself. The gospel is all about Jesus and His grace working through you. Relax in your weaknesses. Just take a deep breath and inhale a little of God's grace for your life. Then expect the Lord's strength to shine through you.

But He said to me, "My grace is sufficient for you, for power is perfected in weakness." Therefore, I will most gladly boast all the more about my weaknesses, so that Christ's power may reside in me. So I take pleasure in weaknesses, insults, catastrophes, persecutions, and in pressures, because of Christ. For when I am weak, then I am strong. —2 Corinthians 12:9–10

Further Scripture: Romans 11:6; 2 Corinthians 4:7; 12:7–8

---

[5] Earl D. Radmacher, Ronald B. Allen, and H. Wayne House, eds., *Nelson's New Illustrated Bible Commentary* (Nashville: Thomas Nelson, 1999), 1511.

Questions

1. What kind of boasting was Paul talking about in 2 Corinthians 12:1 (2 Corinthians 11:30; Galatians 1:12)? Why did he say boasting was profitable?
2. Of whom could Paul have been speaking about that had the revelation in 2 Corinthians 12:2 (Acts 14:19–20)? What do you think he meant by the "third heaven" (Genesis 28:12; Revelation 4:2; 5:13)? Something to meditate on and ponder: since, according to Scripture, there is a third heaven, what are the first and second heavens (Genesis 1:1; Deuteronomy 10:14; Psalm 148:4)?
3. According to 2 Corinthians 12, why was Paul given a "thorn in the flesh"? Do you have anything in your life that you would consider a "thorn" in your flesh/life? If so, does it humble you or make you angry?
4. In 2 Corinthians 12:20–21, Paul listed some sins he feared he would find the Corinthians caught up in when he arrives there. Do any of these things sound accurate for the Christian church today? What can help us overcome these things? (Ephesians 4:2–3; Philippians 2:3; 1 Peter 5:5)
5. What did the Holy Spirit highlight to you in 2 Corinthians 12 through the reading or the teaching?

WEEK 76

Lesson 45: 2 Corinthians 13

Treasure: Final Warnings and Exhortations

Teaching Notes

Intro

Today, we're studying the final chapter in 2 Corinthians. Our word for this book is *Treasure*. The *Treasure*, Christ, is inside of us. Through our weaknesses and cracks, Christ is revealed. Let's walk through Paul's interactions with the Corinthians one last time. Acts 18 described the founding of the church at Corinth, which happened in roughly AD 50–52, during Paul's second missionary journey. Paul stayed there 18 months teaching the Word of God and ministering to them. In this process, Paul wrote the "lost letter" referred to in 1 Corinthians 5:9, in which he urged them not to associate with sexually immoral people and is a hotbed for idolatry. The letter we know as 1 Corinthians was written in roughly AD 55, probably two to five years after his time of ministry there.

As continuing communication with the Corinthians, Paul wrote this letter from Ephesus (1 Corinthians 16:8), while on his third missionary journey. Paul loved this church so much that, at one time, he made a "painful visit" to them (2 Corinthians 2:1). During this visit it did not go so well. There is a lack of respect and they did not value him. Because of this painful visit, he also wrote a severe letter (2 Corinthians 2:3). To summarize, there was a lost letter, then 1 Corinthians was written, followed by a painful visit, then the severe letter was written followed by 2 Corinthians, which was written from Macedonia, in roughly AD 55–56. In 2 Corinthians 12:14, Paul wrote that he longed for a third visit with them. Acts 20:1–4 explained why Paul never made this third visit.

Teaching

2 Corinthians 13:1–8: According to Warren Wiersbe, Paul warned the Corinthians.[1] According to Tom Constable, there are four views of interpreting the "two or three witnesses" of verse 1. "First . . . *the church* would *pass judgment* and, based on the testimony of the witnesses that Jesus Christ prescribed, should decide

[1] Warren W. Wiersbe, *The Wiersbe Bible Commentary: New Testament* (Colorado Springs: David C. Cook, 2007), 541.

who was right."[2] In other words, the witnesses would affirm whatever Paul said (Matthew 18:15–20). "Second, Paul may have viewed his three visits to Corinth as three 'witnesses' to his *innocence.* Third, he may have been referring to his *warnings* that he would not spare the Corinthians. Fourth, Paul may have meant the *witness of his fellow workers* when he returned to Corinth."[3]

Paul planned to deal with the Corinthians biblically when he dealt with their sin. Wiersbe said, "In dealing with sin in a local church, we must have facts and not rumors."[4] Deuteronomy 19:15 emphasized that wrongdoing could not be established by only one witness but required the testimony of two or three witnesses. Paul made a similar statement in 1 Timothy 5:19.

Paul's warning included the statement that he would not be lenient with those who continued to sin (v. 2). Verse 3 indicates the false teachers and apostles "were still seeking proof that Paul was a genuine apostle."[5] They accused Paul of being weak, but "Paul was going to use his apostolic authority and power to deal with any sin and rebellion."[6] MacArthur pointed out that by rebelling against Paul, the Corinthians and the Judaizers in that group were rebelling against Christ.[7] Paul would confront them by the power of God within him (v. 4). MacArthur said Paul would "come to Corinth armed with the irresistible power of the risen, glorified Christ."[8]

Paul then warned the Corinthians to quit worrying about him and to examine their own faith.[9] Paul was the spiritual father to the church at Corinth, so if his faith was counterfeit, then so was their faith. Paul hoped they would realize whether or not they were born again (vv. 5–6). So how can people examine themselves for evidence of faith? MacArthur listed several possibilities.[10] Are you walking out righteousness and holiness (Psalm 15)? Do you show justice, kindness, humility (Micah 6:8)? Matthew 5:3–12 lists the beatitudes. Are you poor in spirit? Do you mourn? Do you walk in gentleness? Do you hunger and thirst for righteousness? Are you merciful and pure in heart? Are you a peacemaker? Do you show the love described in 1 Corinthians 13:4–7? Is the fruit of the Spirit present in your life (Galatians 5:22–23)?

---

[2] Thomas L. Constable, *Expository Notes of Dr. Thomas Constable: 2 Corinthians*, 175, https://planobiblechapel.org/tcon/notes/pdf/2corinthians.pdf.

[3] Constable, 175.

[4] Wiersbe, 541.

[5] John MacArthur, *The MacArthur Bible Commentary* (Nashville: Thomas Nelson, 2005), 1652.

[6] MacArthur, 1652.

[7] MacArthur, 1652.

[8] MacArthur, 1652.

[9] Wiersbe, 542.

[10] MacArthur, 1652.

Does your thinking reflect Philippians 4:8? If you are in the faith, then you will grow in these areas. Does your life reflect the basics described in 1 Thessalonians 5:14–22? Are you walking with the Lord as described in 2 Peter 1:5–9? Do you walk in truth, obedience, and love (1 John)? Do you live by the pattern in Revelation 1:3? Nobody likes an examination. Because examinations hurt, and we're afraid of failure. But Paul challenged them to make this self-examination so they would not fail the test. Paul wanted them to pass the test (v. 7), and wanted them to do everything based on the truth (v. 8).

1 Corinthians 13:9–13: Paul then encouraged them.[11] Paul rejoiced when they were strong and wanted them to become fully mature (v. 9). Paul wanted them to succeed. He wanted them to be filled, equipped, and trained. The word Paul used for fully mature (v. 9) could also mean "to be fitted out, to be equipped . . . to set a broken bone, to adjust a twisted limb . . . to outfit a ship for a voyage . . . to equip an army for battle . . . mending nets." Paul wanted them to be strong.

Paul closed with five exhortations in verse 11: "Become mature, be encouraged, be of the same mind, be at peace, and the God of love and peace will be with you."

Closing

Thanks for slowing down and studying these two epistles. May you be greatly encouraged by Christ being the *Treasure* in the Corinthian church and in your life as well.

The Daily Word

Not many people look forward to their regular exam at the doctor, the dentist, or even taking their car in for a regular tune-up. They may think, *It's going to cost me money I don't want to spend. I think I'm fine, so why do I need to even go? What if I find out something is wrong? Then I have to deal with it!* However, after you go, you are usually thankful and relieved! Similarly, your faith in the Lord needs regular exams and check-ups as well.

As Paul ended his letter to the Corinthian church, he encouraged them to *examine themselves in the faith*. Examining your faith may look like meeting with a friend once a week to discuss Scripture, praying consistently with a prayer partner, or asking a close friend to hold you accountable concerning an area of temptation in your life. It may also look like regularly quieting yourself before the Lord and asking Him to search your heart for anything not aligned with Him. The Lord desires for you to rejoice, become mature in Him, remain encouraged, and feel peaceful. In order to grow spiritually, diligently set these regular "exams,"

[11] Wiersbe, 542.

whether you feel like it or not. Take time to make an "appointment" with a friend or ask the Lord to examine your heart today. Just do it!

Test yourselves to see if you are in the faith. Examine yourselves. Or do you yourselves not recognize that Jesus Christ is in you?—unless you fail the test. —2 Corinthians 13:5

Further Scripture: 1 Corinthians 11:28; 2 Corinthians 13:11; Galatians 6:4

Questions

1. Why is it important to have more than one witness before passing judgment on or punishing someone (Numbers 35:30; Deuteronomy 19:15)? Why did Paul state this to the church of Corinth in 2 Corinthians 13:1?
2. In 2 Corinthians 13:5, the Corinthians were called to examine and test themselves in the faith. What did Paul mean by this (John 14:19–21; Romans 8:10; 1 Corinthians 9:24–27)? Based on these verses, do you think all who call themselves Christians will go to heaven?
3. In 2 Corinthians 13:10, Paul said, "This is why I am writing these things while absent, that when I am there I will not use severity." Why do you think Paul chose to do this instead of waiting until he was with them to bring up these things?
4. How can we experience the grace, love, and fellowship of God the Father, God the Son, and God the Holy Spirit (Romans 5:5; Philippians 2:1)?
5. What did the Holy Spirit highlight to you in 2 Corinthians 13 through the reading or the teaching?

WEEK 76

Lesson 46: Galatians 1

Liberator: The Liberator

Teaching Notes

Intro

Galatians is famous for its description of the fruit of the Spirit. Secondarily, Galatians is known for its description of freedom in Christ. Because of this association, our word for Galatians is *Liberator.* Galatians 5:1 says, "Christ has liberated us to be free. Stand firm then and don't submit again to a yoke of slavery." Because of Jesus' work as our *Liberator,* we have freedom to live in the Spirit and display the fruit of the Spirit.

Galatians gets its name from a region in Asia Minor in what is most likely modern-day Turkey. It was a large region that included many churches. Paul is unquestionably the author, which is established in Galatians 1:1, "Paul, an apostle."[1]

Paul was originally from Tarsus, in the province of Silicia, which was near Galatia. As a result, Paul understood this region well. Paul studied under the famous rabbi Gamaliel as stated in Acts 22 and became a rising star within Judaism before his Damascus road experience with Jesus.[2] After this encounter, MacArthur noted Paul went from being "Christianity's chief persecutor to its greatest missionary."[3]

Galatians is one of 13 letters Paul wrote that are contained in the New Testament. This letter was written to a group of churches—"to the churches of Galatia" (Galatians 1:2). In Galatians 2, Paul describes a visit to the Jerusalem council. If this was the Jerusalem council of Acts 15, which most scholars date to AD 49, then Galatians was most likely written a few years later.[4]

Before Galatia became a province in the Roman Empire, the title referred to a smaller, ethnic region. The Romans created a large province and gave it the name Galatia. Because of the wide range of possible recipients, MacArthur notes

[1] John MacArthur, *The MacArthur Bible Commentary* (Nashville: Thomas Nelson, 2005), 1654.

[2] MacArthur, 1654.

[3] MacArthur, 1654.

[4] MacArthur, 1654.

that two schools of thought have emerged about how to understand Paul's references to the Galatians:[5]

1. Galatia was used in an ethnic sense—Galatia was a region in central Asia Minor inhabited by Galatians who were Celtic people. They had migrated to the region from Gaul in the third century BC. Then around 25 BC, Rome created the province of Galatia, which was inhabited by some people who were not ethnically Galatians.
2. Galatia was used in a political sense—Galatia described the entire province and was not limited to the original region inhabited by ethnic Galatians.

Paul founded churches in the southern Galatian cities of Antioch, Iconium, Lystra, and Derbe. MacArthur notes these cities were not located in the ethnic Galatian region. There is no record of Paul having founded churches in northern Galatia. However, it is difficult to say with certainty who the original recipients of this letter were. Paul traveled through the northern regions of Galatia, but there is no record of him conducting any evangelistic ministry in those areas (Acts 16:6; 18:23). At a minimum, it is reasonable to conclude that at least the four churches in southern Galatian whom Paul founded probably received it.[6]

MacArthur highlights two main reasons why Paul wrote Galatians:[7]

1. To emphasize justification by faith—Judaizers added observing the Law to faith, which Paul argued was contrary to the gospel.
2. Some were ignoring the decree of the Jerusalem Council—these false teachers argued that a person must first become a Jewish proselyte and observe the Mosaic Law before becoming a Christian.

Teaching

Galatians 1:1–5: Paul followed a pattern for beginning his letters. He identified himself (v. 1), addressed his recipients (v. 2), and offered a greeting (v. 3). Afterwards, Paul quickly moved into a short recitation of the gospel (vv. 4–5).

Galatians 1:6–9: Now, Paul addresses head-on his reason for writing. He was "amazed" the Galatians had turned away from the gospel he preached to them and embraced "a different gospel" (v. 6). Paul was so adamant the gospel of

[5] MacArthur, 1654.

[6] MacArthur, 1654.

[7] MacArthur, 1655.

justification by faith alone was the true gospel that he pronounced a curse on the deliverer of that gospel, even if it were an angel (vv. 8–9).

Galatians 1:10: Paul had no interest in listening to someone's message just to make them happy. Because he was in Christ, he gave no consideration to appeasing any person other than Jesus (v. 10).

Galatians 1:11–12: The gospel Paul preached was given by "a revelation from Jesus Christ" (v. 12). Paul's radical encounter with Jesus had completely changed him. "As he traveled and was nearing Damascus, a light from heaven suddenly flashed around him. Falling to the ground, he heard a voice saying to him, 'Saul, Saul, why are you persecuting Me?' 'Who are You, Lord?'
he said. 'I am Jesus, the One you are persecuting,' He replied. 'But get up and go into the city, and you will be told what you must do'" (Acts 9:3–6).

Galatians 1:13–17: *Nelson's Commentary* defined the "Judaism" Paul referenced in v. 13 as "the Jewish way of life, which was based partly on the OT and partly on additional traditions of the fathers."[8] While Paul "advanced in Judaism beyond many contemporaries" (v. 14), God had a different plan for his life. After his Damascus road experience, Paul went to Arabia for three years before consulting with anyone else.

Galatians 1:18–20: After his time in Arabia, Paul went to Jerusalem where he met with Peter for 15 days.

Galatians 1:21–24: Paul established how God did this work in his life through grace. As news about Paul's conversion spread, the churches glorified God because of what God had done in Paul's life.

Closing

Paul's life trajectory was changed by God. Jesus revealed Himself to Paul, and Paul received the *Liberator* and refused to go back to embrace the yoke of slavery again (Galatians 5:1).

[8] Earl D. Radmacher, Ronald B. Allen, and H. Wayne House, eds., *Nelson's New Illustrated Bible Commentary* (Nashville: Thomas Nelson, 1999), 1517.

The Daily Word

Isn't it interesting how people seem confident, filled with faith, and ready to be bold for Christ with the gospel as you pour into them? Yet sometimes you find that confident, bold person will quickly turn away from the message of the gospel and the truth. It's as though the seed of the gospel was snatched away from them! Even Paul found this to be the case as he ministered to others. He struggled with understanding how they could turn away so quickly.

Remember, the Lord asks you to plant the seeds of the gospel. The reality is that some seeds will grow strong; some seeds will struggle to grow; some seeds will get plucked away by the schemes of the enemy. The enemy, the deceiver, is on the prowl. Although your spirit may be willing, the flesh is weak. As a believer, continue to stay strong in the Lord. Continue to keep your eyes on the author of your faith. Remain steadfast in Him. Strength will arise as you keep your focus on the one true Son, Jesus Christ.

I am amazed that you are so quickly turning away from Him who called you by the grace of Christ and are turning to a different gospel—not that there is another gospel, but there are some who are troubling you and want to change the good news about the Messiah. —Galatians 1:6–7

Further Scripture: Matthew 13:19; John 10:10; 2 Peter 3:17–18

Questions

1. How did Paul become an apostle (1 Corinthians 9:1)? What was his calling as an apostle (Acts 9:15)? Did he fulfill what he was called to do? What has the Lord called you to do? Are you living out this calling?
2. What was the major issue with the Galatian churches? What was the gospel Paul said they had turned away from (1 Corinthians 15:1–11)?
3. How did Paul receive the gospel in the midst of persecuting the church (Acts 9:3–9)? How was this in contrast to how the Judaizers received religious instruction? How did you receive the gospel?
4. What did Paul's contact with other believers look like after he was converted? Where did Paul go if he did not immediately go to Jerusalem? How long did the Lord prepare him for ministry?
5. Did Peter and the other disciples receive Paul when he visited them (Acts 9:26–28)? Why were they suspicious of him? Whose approval did Paul ultimately care about?
6. What did the Holy Spirit highlight to you in Galatians 1 through the reading or the teaching?

WEEK 76

Lesson 47: Galatians 2

Liberator: The Meeting

Teaching Notes

Intro

Jewish believers seem to have had a hard time with the fact that Paul was willing to share the gospel with people who were down and out. Additionally, Paul didn't require these new converts, many of whom weren't Jewish, to observe the Law. The Gentiles embraced the gospel differently than many of the Jews did. This created some problems with Jewish believers who still operated under a faith and works understanding of salvation.

Teaching

Galatians 2:1–2: Wiersbe termed the meeting which Paul described as "The Private Consultation."[1] Paul, Barnabas, and Titus went to Jerusalem to inform the Jerusalem leaders about the gospel that he preached among the Gentiles. This was Paul showing honor to the leaders of the church and submitting to their leadership. He even went so far as to allow the Jerusalem leaders to determine if his gospel was correct (v. 2).

When it says Paul went up to Jerusalem (v. 1), we have to ask, which trip to Jerusalem was he referencing? Paul made at least five visits to Jerusalem.[2]

1. After his Damascus road encounter with Jesus—"When he arrived in Jerusalem, he tried to associate with the disciples, but they were all afraid of him, since they did not believe he was a disciple" (Acts 9:26–30; Galatians 1:18–20).
2. The famine visit—"Then one of them, named Agabus, stood up and predicted by the Spirit that there would be a severe famine throughout the Roman world. This took place during the time of Claudius. So each of the

[1] Warren W. Wiersbe, *The Bible Exposition Commentary: Matthew–Galatians* (Colorado Springs: David C. Cook, 1989), 690.

[2] Thomas L. Constable, *Expository Notes of Dr. Thomas Constable: Galatians*, 32, https://planobiblechapel.org/tcon/notes/pdf/galatians.pdf.

disciples, according to his ability, determined to send relief to the brothers who lived in Judea. They did this, sending it to the elders by means of Barnabas and Saul" (Acts 11:28–30; Galatians 2:1–10).

3. The Jerusalem Council—probably the visit that lines up the best with Galatians 2. Galatians 2 articulates what took place at the Jerusalem Council (Acts 15:1–29).
4. The end of Paul's second missionary journey (Acts 18:22).
5. His final visit that resulted in his imprisonment (Acts 21:15—23:35).

Barnabas and Titus accompanied Paul on this trip to Jerusalem. Barnabas' name means "Son of Encouragement." Barnabas was with Paul during the famine visit and on the first missionary journey, so he was in a unique position to vouch for Paul's preaching and ministry. Paul also brought Titus, a Gentile believer who most likely became a believer as a result of Paul's ministry: "To Titus, my true son in our common faith" (Titus 1:4).[3]

With whom did they meet? Galatians 2:9 specifically names "James, Cephas [Peter], and John." Peter and John were disciples of Jesus. Jesus had given Peter "the keys" to open the door of faith. John was one of the inner three of Jesus' disciples. James was Jesus' brother who did not initially believe in Jesus but who later became a leader in the Jerusalem church.[4]

Galatians 2:3–5: Wiersbe termed this "The Public Convocation."[5] Titus, a Gentile believer, had not been circumcised and did not feel "compelled to be circumcised." Circumcision was the mark that the Jewish people were in a covenant relationship with God. The fact that Titus had not been circumcised was a huge issue with some "false brothers" who managed to get into the meeting. Paul had been preaching a message of salvation by faith alone while some insisted on Jesus and works as the way to salvation. Paul understood Jesus to be the *Liberator*: "Christ has liberated us to be free. Stand firm then and don't submit again to a yoke of slavery" (Galatians 5:1). He refused to "give up and submit to these people . . . so that . . . the gospel would be preserved for you" (v. 5).

Galatians 2:6–10: Wiersbe called this section, "The Personal Confirmation."[6] While Peter, James, and John had prominent positions in the church, Paul knew

---

[3] John MacArthur, *The MacArthur Bible Commentary* (Nashville: Thomas Nelson, 2005), 1660–61.

[4] MacArthur, 1662.

[5] Wiersbe, 691.

[6] Wiersbe, 692.

that God does not show favoritism. Ultimately, Paul pursued God's affirmation and not the affirmation of these leaders. Peter, James, and John saw Paul had a different mission. While Peter had been sent to the circumcised, they recognized Paul had a unique call to the uncircumcised. *Nelson's Commentary* points out the leaders offered Paul "'the right hand of fellowship' [which] was a common sign of acceptance and friendship. It indicated full recognition of Paul by the representatives of the Jerusalem church."[7] Their only stipulation was that Paul "remember the poor" (v. 10), something Paul had already done and would continue to do.

At this point, everyone was on the same page. Paul and Peter had reached an understanding of their missions and understood one another's teaching and mission.

Galatians 2:11–14: Paul recounted an experience with Peter in which Peter acted hypocritically. Peter came to Antioch and ate with Gentiles until "certain men came from James" (v. 12). These men would have been Jewish believers who still taught circumcision. After they arrived, Peter removed himself from the Gentiles and other Jewish believers; even Barnabas followed his example (v. 13) "because he feared those from the circumcision party" (v. 12). Paul publicly confronted Peter because of their previous private conversation (v. 14).

Galatians 2:15–21: Paul reiterated that faith in Jesus alone justifies believers. He knew that observing the law would never lead to one's justification before God. If it were even possible for someone to earn righteousness before God through the law then Jesus would have died for nothing (v. 21).

Closing

The gospel of faith alone was meant for both Jews and Gentiles.

The Daily Word

Christ died and set you free from bondage, from laws, from performance, and from striving in your own strength to please God. Christ gave Himself *for you.* If Christ died but you still needed to keep the law for righteousness and abide by rules, then Christ would have died in vain. Rather, Christ died to set you free. *Your righteousness is found in Christ alone.* Your ego, your ways of keeping rules, and your attempts to appear perfect *died with Christ.* Your life is no longer about you. Doing things in order to earn God's approval are over and have been put to *death with Christ.* Now Christ lives in you, and you are righteous in Him.

[7] Earl D. Radmacher, Ronald B. Allen, and H. Wayne House, eds., *Nelson's New Illustrated Bible Commentary* (Nashville: Thomas Nelson, 1999), 1520.

Remember, Jesus died because He loves you and chose to give His life for you. Believe you are worthy for Him to love. When you feel as though you are failing and can't keep up, cease striving. Christ didn't come to earth and die so you would have to try to keep up. It's not about striving for perfection. Life in Christ involves *resting in Him alone.* It's about walking freely by faith in the grace Jesus gives abundantly. You are free from the law. Walk in that freedom. Praise the Lord!

For through the law I have died to the law, so that I might live for God. I have been crucified with Christ and I no longer live, but Christ lives in me. The life I now live in the body, I live by faith in the Son of God, who loved me and gave Himself for me. —Galatians 2:19–20

Further Scripture: Galatians 2:21; Ephesians 3:12; 1 Peter 2:16

Questions

1. Who was Titus? How did he become associated with Paul (2 Corinthians 2:13; 7:5–6; Titus 1:4–5)?
2. What did Paul need to discuss privately with the Jerusalem leaders (Acts 15:1–2)? Who told Paul to go to Jerusalem? What was the result of the meeting (Galatians 2:6)?
3. What was Paul's issue with Peter? How did Paul handle the conflict? How do you handle conflict when you see another believer in sin?
4. Why did Peter compromise his beliefs? What does the church compromise on today? What do you compromise on? Examine yourself and ask the Holy Spirit to reveal these things to you (2 Corinthians 13:5).
5. How did Paul's life reflect Galatians 2:20 (Romans 6:2–6; Ephesians 4:22)? How does your life reflect that verse?
6. What did the Holy Spirit highlight to you in Galatians 2 through the reading or the teaching?

Lesson 48: Galatians 3

Liberator: Faith in Christ

Teaching Notes

Intro

Galatians is the kind of book that has to be studied in its entirety to understand what it's talking about. And once you finish the book study, you need to go back to chapter 1 and read it again. Before we start the study, I want to provide a bit of background to prepare for the transition that chapter 3 makes into a discussion of "flesh" and "spirit." So far, we've talked about circumcision as the mark on the flesh and a new circumcision as the mark on the heart. We've all been foolish Galatians at times when there have been things about God and Christ we didn't understand.

Teaching

Galatians 3:1–5: The word "bewitched" (v. 1 KJV) can be understood as "turned your eyes to another." Chapter 2 was a strongly worded, divisive section of the letter that had cost Paul relationships. He continued the strong wording into chapter 3. Paul diminished the letter of the law in some of his other letters. His point is that faith is of the Spirit, not in obedience to the letter of the law.

Through my ministry and with the people I have walked with, I understand the Galatians. If the indoctrination of the truth was brought by people who thought they were of the truth, it's easy to set your conscience to their truth. Leonard Ravenhill said something like, "If you find a church that is comfortable for you, RUN!" The gospel is not meant to be comfortable. Focusing on comfort means the church is preaching the gospel of comfort, not its mission to the world, which is to help the words of Jesus permeate through the world and bring change.

We all can hear what we believe is truth and let it become our truth. But have we investigated that truth, so we know it is the truth of Jesus Christ as Savior and Lord? Paul talked about his experiences in the third heaven. He was given the ministry of revelation for the New Testament truth while in the third heaven. Therefore, Paul was unwilling to compromise ANYTHING that was given to him for ANY reason, including getting along with people. He met with people in the church, but they had not received the revelation of what the church could be. Paul was ready to minister to the Gentiles and bring the entire world into the kingdom of God. Paul could not allow the Galatians to not embrace that revelation and to keep focusing on the act of circumcision. As Kyle taught yesterday: "Hypocrisy keeps people from the truth of the gospel."

If the law (rules, denominational doctrine, bishop, or the way it's always been) is the boundary of your truth, then unless you have the revelation of the Spirit, you will back away even from Jesus in the reasoning of your mind and conscience. If you are going to walk into real revelation, you make the WORD your compass. Embrace FAITH, not reasoning.

Galatians 3:6–9: "Abraham believed God" because he had heard God speak to Him (using words) (v. 6). Faith comes by hearing the word of the Lord. That means all the nations have to hear it. That "word" from God is from the word *ramah,* which literally means "God speaks." Faith is receiving by the Spirit the Word of God and obeying the Word of God as it is instructed. Faith does not mean stepping into an unknown, but it is obedience to the word that comes from God. "All of the nations" will be blessed through that faith (v. 8) (Genesis 12:3). Father Abraham provided the spiritual seed that would bring spiritual sons to Abraham (v. 9).

Galatians 3:10–12: Paul quotes from Deuteronomy 27:26 to point out again that if someone chose to keep the law, he had to keep all of the law (all 613 individual laws)—something impossible for anyone to do (v. 10). But even if man could keep all the laws, he would not be justified by his actions (v. 11). Rather, man is justified by faith in Christ, and following the law is not based on faith (v. 12) (Romans 3:27–31; 4:13–14). Note that the law was given as a part of faith for the people in the time that they received it, because they had not yet been given the revelation of the Spirit. Into a world that was controlled by sin and death, Jesus brought the law of life through His death on the cross.

Galatians 3:13–22: Jesus was willing to be cursed in order that we, the Gentiles, could become children of God (v. 13) (Deuteronomy 21:23). Verse 14 is the entire gospel message in one sentence: "That the blessing of Abraham would come to the Gentiles by Christ Jesus, so that we could receive the promised Spirit through faith." Jesus brought a new law that was meant to capture and captivate our hearts. Because of His Spirit within us, we are able to overcome the hold that sin has on our lives.

Verse 16 sets out God's plan for the culture of the kingdom. God had a plan from the very beginning to bring all mankind to Himself. God brought us through the culture of sin (by Noah's ark), through the chosen people (through

Abraham), through their deliverance (by Moses) into a place where they could receive a new set of laws no one on earth had. God did all of this so that, when Jesus came in the New Testament, we could understand and accept the new principles He was to deliver. We would understand all of this because we have the history lessons through God's Word to explain it to us. Faith is all about obedience and requires something of us (vv. 16–17). We get to serve Christ in our liberation; we have been put into bondage to Jesus Christ through God's love.

Closing

The law was necessary to conclude that humankind cannot live justly on our own. This law then made the new covenant necessary—through the forgiveness of sin.

The greatest thing we can do in our own lives (and we're doing it in reviveSCHOOL) is to study the Bible chronologically through certain sections, and then go back and forth between the old covenant and the new covenant, in order to receive the revelation of Christ and of what God wants to do in our lives. If you want revelation in your life, don't attend another conference; get alone in the Word of God.

The Daily Word

Paul continued to emphasize to the Galatians that *believers are saved by faith alone and the righteous live by faith.* This faith comes by hearing the Word of God. The law of sin and death is no longer necessary. There is no longer a distinction between Jew and Greek, slave and free, male and female. The law of the Spirit is found in Christ. *You belong to Christ.* So *put on Jesus* like a piece of clothing every day and *walk in His Spirit.* It's the Spirit who works miracles in your life.

Spend time in the Scriptures because faith comes from hearing God's Word. God's power will become great within you. The Word of God leads you to Jesus. The Word of God leads you to the Spirit. Remember, through your faith in Christ, you are a son or daughter of the Most High King. You belong to Christ, you have freedom in Christ, and you are one in Christ.

For as many of you as have been baptized into Christ have put on Christ like a garment. There is no Jew or Greek, slave or free, male or female; for you are all one in Christ Jesus. And if you belong to Christ, then you are Abraham's seed, heirs according to the promise. —Galatians 3:27–29

Further Scripture: Romans 10:17; Galatians 3:11; 3:26

Questions

1. What did Paul call the Galatians? What did he mean by calling them that (Luke 24:25; 1 Timothy 6:9; Titus 3:3)?
2. Why is it impossible to be saved by the works of the law (Ephesians 2:8–9; Titus 3:5)?
3. What does Abraham's belief have to do with Gentile believers (Romans 4:11, 16)?
4. How did Jesus become a curse and a blessing for you (Deuteronomy 21:23; Isaiah 32:15; Ezekiel 36:26; John 7:37–39; 2 Corinthians 5:21; Hebrews 9:28; 1 Peter 2:24)?
5. Why was the law given if you are not saved by it (Romans 7:1–13)? Who was involved in the giving of the law (Acts 7:53; Hebrews 2:2)?
6. What did the Holy Spirit highlight to you in Galatians 3 through the reading or the teaching?

WEEK 77

Lesson 49: Galatians 4

Liberator: Sons and Heirs

Teaching Notes

Intro

Our theme for the book of Galatians is Christ, the *Liberator*, as described in Galatians 5:1: "Christ has liberated us to be free." Because Christ has set us free, there is no reason to go back to the law. In Galatians 4:1–7, Paul compares the old and the new; the flesh and the Spirit; and Hagar and Sarah. Paul had a heart for the Galatians and wanted to know why they were trying to go back to the old way of doing things or trying to integrate the false teaching of the Judaizers and imposters.

Teaching

Galatians 4:1–7: In the first seven verses, Wiersbe says Paul was trying to explain their adoption.[1] Paul made a comparison: they were once children in bondage, but God came in and released them from bondage. According to MacArthur, in verses 1–2 Paul referred to "a child too young to talk, a minor, spiritually and intellectually immature and not ready for the responsibilities and privileges of adulthood."[2] Because they were like underage children, they were under someone's guardianship and authority until they came of age (v. 2). In the beginning, they didn't understand the bigger picture. The "elemental forces" (v. 3) Paul mentions could refer to the demonic realm, the flesh, or the world. The Greek word for "elements" means "'row,' or 'rank,' . . . basic, foundational things like the letters of the alphabet."[3]

According to MacArthur, "In God's timetable, when the exact religious, cultural, and political conditions demanded by His perfect plan were in place,

[1] Warren W. Wiersbe, *The Wiersbe Bible Commentary: New Testament* (Colorado Springs: David C. Cook, 2007), 564.

[2] John MacArthur, *The MacArthur Study Bible: NKJV* (Nashville: Thomas Nelson, 1997), 1794, footnote for verse 1.

[3] MacArthur, 1794, footnote for verse 3.

Jesus came into the world."[4] MacArthur further points out: "As a father set the time for the ceremony of his son becoming of age and being released from the guardians, stewards, and tutors, so God sent His Son at the precise moment to bring all who believe out from under bondage to the law."[5] Paul describes the Son in a couple different ways: He was born of a woman (which emphasized Jesus' humanity) and born under the law (v. 4). Jesus had to be born under the law to fulfill the law. "Like all men, Jesus was obligated to obey God's law. Unlike anyone else, however, He perfectly obeyed that law. His sinlessness made Him the unblemished sacrifice for sins. . . . That perfect righteousness is what is imputed to those who believe in Him."[6]

MacArthur said adoption "is the act of bringing someone who is the offspring of another into one's own family. Since unregenerate people are by nature children of the devil, the only way they can become God's children is by spiritual adoption."[7] As believers, we have the Spirit of Jesus in us (v. 6). Because we are adopted as God's sons, then we are heirs of God (v. 7).

You don't have to work for it; you don't have to earn it. God already knows when He adopts you that you are a mess and that you're bringing baggage from the past. Throughout the book of Galatians, there's a theme of the Holy Spirit. Galatians 3:2 says we receive the Spirit by faith. Paul then said to stay with the Spirit and don't go to the flesh (Galatians 3:3). God supplies us with the Spirit, which even allows us to work miracles (Galatians 3:5). In Galatians 5, Paul tells us to walk by the Spirit, not by the flesh (Galatians 5:16). There's a constant fight between flesh and Spirit. But as God's children, we don't have to go back to the flesh.

Galatians 4:8–11: In these verses, Wiersbe says Paul lamented their regression.[8] Paul worried they were going back to their old ways. Sunday mornings are easy, but depending on faith and the Holy Spirit gets messy. Paul warned that walking in the bondage of religion leaves no room for the fruit of the Spirit. Paul freely observed the festivals they celebrated—the special days, months, season, and years (v. 10), and wondered if his efforts to share the gospel with them had been wasted (v. 11). This was just like the Israelites who wanted to go back to Egypt. They would rather be enslaved there, because they knew what they would be doing.

---

[4] MacArthur, 1795, footnote for verse 4.

[5] MacArthur, 1795, footnote for verse 4.

[6] MacArthur, 1795, footnote for verse 4.

[7] MacArthur, 1795, footnote for verse 5.

[8] Wiersbe, 566.

Galatians 4:12–18: In these verses, Wiersbe says Paul seeks their affection.[9] This was where Paul's shepherding side showed up. Paul begged them to become like him (v. 12). In 1 Corinthians 11:1, Paul told the Corinthians, "Imitate me, as I also imitate Christ." Paul had ministered to them during a time of physical illness (v. 13), which MacArthur said could have been malaria contracted from the coastal area of Pamphylia.[10] Paul wondered why they had received him so eagerly back then but didn't want to receive him now (vv. 14–15). Paul's illness had impacted his eyes to such a degree that he testifies in verse 15, "you would have torn out your eyes and given them to me," indicating the Galatians had truly cared for Paul. Paul warned them, "They (meaning the Judaizers) are enthusiastic about you, but not for any good" (v. 17). Today, there are people who will come into a congregation and their intent is not good. They are looking for something for themselves but have no intention of furthering or encouraging the body of Christ.

Galatians 4:19–20: Paul was implying he was at his wit's end and didn't know what to do with the Galatians.

Galatians 4:21–31: Paul then began to draw a comparison using an Old Testament story about Abraham. He compared the slave mentality versus the free. Hagar, from Mt. Sinai, bears children into slavery (v. 24); she represents bondage and flesh. Sarah on the other hand represents freedom: "But the Jerusalem above is free, and she is our mother" (v. 26). Quoting from Isaiah and from Genesis, Paul concluded his argument. "Therefore, brothers, we are not children of the slave but of the free woman" (v. 31). Paul walked through their adoption process and was saddened that they were turning away and going back to their old ways of doing things. Then he asked them which they wanted to be—the slave children or the free children, who can run because of the Spirit of God in them. Because Abraham didn't depend on the promise of God, we have Ishmael, which brings in the Islamic faith. Because of the Islamic faith, we have major issues between the descendants of Isaac and Ishmael. But what we really have is a picture of bondage and freedom. That freedom can only come through the *Liberator*—not through the Jews, the Muslims, or even Christianity. That freedom only comes through Christ. Christ is the one who says, "Because of Me, you are a child of God."

Closing

Pray through what you heard today and process it. Maybe go back and read through Galatians 4 again. Tomorrow will be a lot more lighthearted as we talk about the fruit of the Spirit.

---

[9] Wiersbe, 566.

[10] MacArthur, 1795, footnote for verse 13.

The Daily Word

You are an heir of God the Father. God is your father, your *Abba,* your heavenly daddy. You are no longer a slave to the law. You are no longer a slave to this world. You are no longer a slave to fear. You are no longer a slave to performing. Dear one, no matter what your life was like before Christ, as you believe in Him, *you are His child and receive an inheritance from Him, your heavenly Father.*

You may think: *I don't deserve this.* That is a lie from the enemy. You are worthy of all the glorious riches from your heavenly Father. He has a great love for you, the love of a father. You are a child of God, adopted into His family. *You are wanted.* You are chosen. You are worthy. You are an heir through Christ. So, when you feel as though you are not enough, when you feel you have no family and are alone, remember to stand on this truth—*You are an heir of God the Father.*

And because you are sons, God has sent the Spirit of His Son into our hearts, crying, "Abba, Father!" So you are no longer a slave but a son, and if a son, then an heir through God. —Galatians 4:6–7

Further Scripture: 2 Corinthians 6:18; Galatians 4:1; 1 John 3:1–2

Questions

1. In Galatians 4, what was Paul's fear for the Galatians? Why was Paul concerned about this (Galatians 4:8–9)? Have you ever turned back to weak and worthless things? Why do you think we do this as children of God?
2. In Galatians 4:14, why did Paul commend the Galatians? Do you find yourself avoiding people going through misery of some kind, or do you embrace them as the Galatians did for Paul when he first came to them? Give a reason for your answer.
3. In Galatians 4:16, Paul said: "Have I now become your enemy by telling you the truth?" Have you ever become someone's enemy by speaking the truth in love? What does Scripture say about this (Matthew 18:15–18; Ephesians 4:14–15; 2 Timothy 4:3–4)?
4. By telling the story of Sarah and Hagar in Galatians 4:21–31, what picture was Paul trying to paint (Romans 4:16; Galatians 3:8, 29)?
5. What did the Holy Spirit highlight to you in Galatians 4 through the reading or the teaching?

Lesson 50: Galatians 5

Liberator: Walk by the Spirit

Teaching Notes

Intro

Galatians 5:1 gives us our word for Galatians: Christ is the *Liberator*. Christ has liberated us to be free. Christ has bought us freedom, and for freedom Christ has set us free. The first half of the chapter calls us to walk in freedom, not bondage. The last half calls us to walk by the Spirit, not by the flesh.

Teaching

Galatians 5:1: The call to "stand firm" (v. 1) in the original language means to stand firm as a lifestyle and a habit, of standing firm and not submitting to the whole yoke of slavery. A tool called the Covenant Triangle, from Mike Breen, helps us understand how to not submit to the yoke of slavery.[1] Using the diagram of a triangle to illustrate his point, God is placed at the top point of the triangle. Our identity in Christ is on the lower right side. Obedience is on the lower left side of the triangle. Our identity is from the Father. We are adopted as His sons and daughters. When we flow in our obedience, from our identity, there is life. When our obedience flows from our identity in Christ, it becomes enlightening, liberating, and we enjoy our relationship with God. But when we go with the law, we use our obedience to gain our identity. We think if we work hard enough and do well enough, then we'll find our identity. But we can't earn our identity in our own strength. This leads to bondage. Paul urged the Galatians not to submit again to the yoke of bondage, to the ball and chain of the law.

Galatians 5:2–6: Paul warned that those who chose circumcision as the way to earn salvation would then be obligated to keep the entire law (vv. 2–3). If you are trying to be justified by the law, then you are alienated from Christ (v. 4). You can't add anything to Christ without subtracting Christ. You can't say it's Christ plus something. This element of "fallen from grace" (v. 4) doesn't mean the loss of eternal salvation but refers to an effective relationship with Christ. Through

[1] Mike Breen, *Covenant and Kingdom* (Pawleys Island, SC: 3DM, 2010), 111–13.

the Spirit and by faith, we are saved (v. 5). What matters is faith working through love (v. 6). This love is agape love. Hope (v. 5) is an assurance and a certainty that something is going to happen. Faith, activated by love and acting in love, leads to our assured hope in Christ.

Galatians 5:7–12: Running well (v. 7) is a continuous action, not running that was completed in the past (like running a 5K on Saturday). Obeying (v. 7) is also a lifestyle of continual obedience. Paul voiced his confidence that they would not accept any teaching that led them back to circumcision (the law) (v. 10). Paul said those teachers were taking them away from the truth. He warned them not to listen to those teachers so they wouldn't lose their freedom in Christ.

Galatians 5:13–15: Verses 1–12 say that it's easy to lose your freedom by slipping back into legalism and works based righteousness. But in verses 13–15, Paul instructed them not to abuse that freedom. Instead, they should serve one another, with "serve" denoting a lifestyle of serving others through love. In other words, love your neighbor as yourself. In no uncertain terms, Paul said, the gospel does not free you to sin. We have more reasons to love God than we ever did before, so that love causes us to want to love our neighbor. Obedience becomes the natural expression of our hearts. J. I. Packer wrote: "What work does Christ set his servants to do? The way that they serve him, he tells them, is by becoming slaves of their fellow-servants and being willing to do literally anything, however costly, irksome, or undignified, in order to help them. This is what love means, as he himself showed at the Last Supper when he played the slave's part and washed the disciples' feet."[2] Paul warned them that if they set aside love to "bite and devour one another" then they would be "consumed by one another" (v. 15).

Galatians 5:16–26: These verses describe the difference between the works of the flesh and the fruit of the Spirit. "Walk by the Spirit" (v. 16) denotes a lifestyle, not just a day or season of life. The Spirit is the daily, sustaining, inspiring, desiring power of the Christian's life. Why? Because the flesh and the Spirit are opposed to each other (v. 17). Again, this verse speaks to a lifestyle of wanting to do what God wants. The Spirit indwells every believer and asserts opposition to the flesh. Paul urges us to grow in this lifestyle by walking by the Spirit. Believers emerge triumphant when they allow the Spirit to work in them so they can walk with Him. Paul describes the "works of the flesh" in verses 19–21—sexual immorality, moral impurity—sex. We looked at this earlier in Song of Songs. When sex is done within the context of how God designed it, then it's beautiful and amazing.

[2] J. I. Packer, "Training for Christian Service," *The Evangelical Christian* (September 1961): 10–11.

But Satan likes to take that and twist it around and make it about our flesh and our pleasure. The Galatians lived in a world where sexual immorality was condoned as normal, but Paul said that was not how God designed it. Promiscuity, or debauchery (NIV), is more than just sexual; it's being ready for any kind of pleasure—a runaway pleasure. Idolatry is anything that takes the place of God. Sorcery or witchcraft comes from the Greek word from which we get pharmacy. It is drug use because so many who used witchcraft and magic in the ancient world used drugs. The relationship with sin destroys community: hatred, strife, jealousy, outbursts of anger (leads to bitterness), selfish ambitions (I want to be first), dissensions and factions (a party spirit that leads to rival ambitions in the church), envy (coveting), drunkenness, carousing, and anything similar. If you practice these, you will not inherit the kingdom of God (v. 21).

"But the fruit of the Spirit is love, joy, peace, patience, kindness, goodness, faith, gentleness, self-control" (v. 22). The fruit of the Spirit has been described as the under-armor. It comes out from within us when we fight this spiritual battle. This quote has been attributed to Francis Frangipane: "Too many religious folks are angry that the world is not more Christian, yet at ease with the fact that they themselves are not more Christlike." The fruit of the Spirit is fruit that all comes up together and is produced by the Holy Spirit: Love, joy, peace, patience, kindness, goodness, faith, gentleness, and self-control. This is the fruit of the Spirit, and it's got to be real. The only way it can be real in our lives is by the Holy Spirit. If we're going to walk by the Spirit, we have to incorporate the Spirit 24/7, 365 days of the year, for every year until the Lord returns. Be done with fake fruit, which is the result of trying to do it ourselves outside of a relationship with God. God has called us to walk by His Spirit so that the fruit comes from Him. The fruit all comes from one root, from one tree. We must live out the fruit of the Spirit in today's world.

> Love—sums up all true spiritual life. Love in ministry is described in 1 Corinthians 13. Joy—empowers us to be Christians. We can't create it.
> Peace—harmony and wellbeing.
> Patience—how patient was God with us? How can we live that out?
> Kindness—integrate inner character and outward expression of life.
> Goodness—goodness that is "good for something."
> Faith—faithfulness and fidelity.
> Gentleness—submission to the will of God. Not weakness but strength, like a horse in a bridle.
> Self-control—the mastery of self.

Closing

When you are in Christ and moved by the Spirit, and the unexpected comes, you will respond in ways you never thought possible, as His fruit is expressed in you. Are you growing in the fruit of the Spirit? Which one are you struggling with? Since we live by the Spirit, we must also follow the Spirit.

The Daily Word

Christ came to *set you free,* allowing you to *live in the Spirit, not the flesh.* The fleshly deeds include idolatry, strife, jealousy, outbursts of anger, dissensions, envy, and drunkenness. If your life shows any of these signs, then Paul says you are living in your flesh. You can't walk in both the Spirit and the flesh.

Imagine walking in the Spirit as a bumper car ride. Your bumper car connects by a metal bar to the power supply in the ceiling. As you drive your bumper car, the car is powered from above. The car won't move unless the power source and the bar are connected. In a similar way, your power to bear the fruit of the Spirit comes from the Holy Spirit. As you keep in step with Him, *His power flows through you* to produce fruit: love, joy, peace, patience, kindness, goodness, faithfulness, gentleness, and self-control. Ask yourself: *Am I connected to the power source and bearing fruit? Or am I striving on my own and continuing to produce the deeds of the flesh?* Today, stay connected to the power of the Holy Spirit and begin to watch the flesh fade away while His fruit remains in your life.

But the fruit of the Spirit is love, joy, peace, patience, kindness, goodness, faith, gentleness, self-control. Against such things there is no law. Now those who belong to Christ Jesus have crucified the flesh with its passions and desires. Since we live by the Spirit, we must also follow the Spirit.
—Galatians 5:22–25

Further Scripture: John 15:4–5; Galatians 5:1; Ephesians 5:18–20

Questions

1. Is there any other way in which we may be saved except through faith in Jesus (Matthew 7:13–14; Luke 13:23–24; John 14:6; Acts 4:12)? Do you think everyone who claims to be a Christian will go to heaven (Matthew 7:21–23)?
2. How should Christians use their freedom/liberty in Christ (Galatians 5:13)? How do you use your freedom?
3. How do we walk by the Spirit (Romans 6:12; 8:4–6)?

4. According to Galatians 5, what are the works/deeds of the flesh? Do you struggle with any of these? In contrast, what is the fruit of the Spirit? Do you see these in yourself? Do others see them in you?
5. What did the Holy Spirit highlight to you in Galatians 5 through the reading or the teaching?

WEEK 77

Lesson 51: Galatians 6

Liberator: Spiritual Work Ethic

Teaching Notes

Intro

I believe God so inspired Paul's letter to the Galatians that it can still be used by the "Galatian" churches today. Galatians 6 can be summarized as "the spiritual work ethic." We have a love/hate relationship in the church today with works. When it comes to salvation, it's not about our works but God's grace. However, as believers, we will develop a pattern of good works on the inside from the Holy Spirit living within us.

As Pastor Tom said when he taught Galatians 5, loving people should become natural. The fruit of the Spirit is supposed to be a matured fruit that comes out of our lives and becomes magnetic to those around us. Therefore, I believe there is a work ethic involved on behalf of the Spirit within us that doesn't come from the law. In teaching chapter 6, I am not bringing a works ethic into spiritual salvation. There is meant to be an intentional flip from what the law says about performing works and what the Spirit leads us to do. It's the tension between the flesh and the Spirit that is the entire subject of the book of Galatians.

Teaching

Galatians 6:1–5: In verse 1, Paul told the Galatians that if someone had fallen, guilty of sin, those who knew about it were to handle it as the Spirit led them, because they too could be tempted. They were to respond by restoring the guilty one with meekness, a component of the fruit of the Spirit. Contrast the passages that explain the punishment for not following the law to these verses in Galatians. Paul instructs them to bear each other's burdens as they fulfill the law of Christ (v. 2).

Note that the law accuses and shifts responsibility—if we sin, we know we sin. Sin is supposed to have consequences. The law made people into law enforcement officers, finding those committing sin and pushing them out. However, in the Spirit, we're not trying to get rid of people but trying to bring them in. Verse

1 reminds us that we know ourselves better than anyone. Sin would easily overtake us if we were not controlled by the Spirit.

According to verses 4–5, we are no longer looking to be someone important but are happy to have life in the Spirit. We become kingdom-minded people. Because we live under the Spirit, we can forgive those who have sinned and repented. Because we live under the Spirit, we should quickly repent because we know what we have done.

I recently preached on this passage in my own church and told my congregation that one of the areas in the church where we struggle with is accountability. I told the congregation I want to love God with everything I am. I want to follow His truth and obey His Word. That is the desire of my heart. I explained that since they now had the standard of what I want my life to be like, they have a standard to which they can hold me to. I want that to be the captivating work of my life, and I want it to be visible to those who are around me. I then asked those who wanted to live their lives for Christ to stand. I told them to look at all those standing there together and bear each other's burdens. That allows us to check on others, encourage them, and help them bear their burdens because we want them to make it in the kingdom of God. We should be able to commit ourselves to saying we love God, and we want people to hold us accountable to living that way. That opens up our understanding of these verses.

Galatians 6:6–10: Verse 6 is the law of reciprocation that those who teach/preach God's Word receive good things in return. The Spirit, not the law, desires this. The law makes this individual; the Spirit makes this corporal. In verse 7 is the universal law—what a man sows he will also reap. If a man sows fleshly things, he will reap fleshly things. But the man who sows to the Spirit reaps eternal life (v. 8). We should not be weary of doing good, for we reap when we are obedient (v. 9). Therefore, we should do good to all people as we are given the opportunity (v. 10).

Closing

All of us struggle with the flesh/spirit concept. It is easy to chase things that satisfy us for the moment. It is MUCH harder to wait for the reward when culturally the reward is immediate. When someone sees something they want in someone else, they get jealous. The Jews were supposed to be the people everyone else wanted to be like, but they didn't understand their Messiah. So, God pulled out another group of people who are to have exemplary lives that draw people to Him so they become jealous of what the people of God have.

The Daily Word

When you see a brother or sister in Christ sin, it can make you uncomfortable. Most people don't like others holding them accountable or confronting them in their sin pattern. However, as a follower of Christ, you are called to do this. So what do you do? When you feel led to confront a brother or sister in sin and help them seek restoration, ask yourself: *Am I fearing God or fearing man in this situation? Am I walking in the Spirit or walking in the law?*

As you walk in the Spirit, the Spirit will supernaturally lead *you to restore others with gentleness and love in just the right timing.* Walk with courage, and allow the Spirit to lead you, never quenching His influence in your life. Your role in the kingdom of God involves *holding others accountable and bearing their burdens with the love of Christ.* Can you imagine the difference gentle and loving accountability could make in the kingdom of God? Don't be afraid. If the Spirit is leading you, then most likely He is also preparing the other person's heart. That's the supernatural work of the Spirit and God's abundant grace producing unity.

Brothers, if someone is caught in any wrongdoing, you who are spiritual should restore such a person with a gentle spirit, watching out for yourselves so you also won't be tempted. Carry one another's burdens; in this way you will fulfill the law of Christ. —Galatians 6:1–2

Further Scripture: Psalm 56:4; Galatians 6:9–10; James 5:19–20

Questions

1. In Galatians 6:1, Paul told the Galatian believers to help restore a fellow believer who had strayed to get back to the right path. Have you ever found yourself in this type of a situation? What was the outcome?
2. How would you explain Galatians 6:7–9 to an unbeliever? Where else in Scripture is reaping and sowing mentioned (Proverbs 11:18; Hosea 10:12; 2 Corinthians 9:6)?
3. In your opinion, what was Paul saying in Galatians 6:15? What Scriptures back that up (Romans 6:14; 7:1–6; 2 Corinthians 5:17; Galatians 2:19; Ephesians 2:15; Hebrews 7:18–19)?
4. What did the Holy Spirit highlight to you in Galatians 6 through the reading or the teaching?

WEEK 77

Lesson 52: Ephesians 1

The Head: The Work of the Trinity

Teaching Notes

Intro

This lesson begins our study of Paul's letter to the Ephesians. Our phrase for Ephesians is *The Head* (Ephesians 1:22, 5:22–23). All 66 books in the Bible point to and reflect one thing—that Jesus Christ is the fulfillment of the entire Bible. *The Head* describes how Jesus is presented in Ephesians. The city of Ephesus was located in the Roman province of Asia (today it's located in modern Turkey). Paul identified himself as the author in Ephesians 1:1. Paul wrote the letter to the Ephesians while he was imprisoned in Rome (Acts 28:16, 30–31) between AD 60–62. While in prison, Paul wrote letters to the Ephesians, Philippians, Colossians, and Philemon, letters that are usually referred to as the Prison Epistles.[1]

Remember that Paul was originally called Saul from the tribe of Benjamin, a Jew who was one of the leaders of the anti-Christian movement. He was on the way to Damascus to arrest the Christians there when he met the resurrected Jesus on the road. Paul was transformed from going after the Christians to being one of the greatest preachers in early Christianity.

Paul first visited Ephesus on his second missionary journey. When he departed, he left Priscilla and Aquilla behind to continue the ministry there. Paul returned on his third missionary journey and helped strengthen the struggling church that Priscilla and Aquilla had begun, and left Timothy there to shepherd the ministry and counter the false teachers there.[2]

Paul's letter to the church in Ephesus was written nine to ten years after his visit there. Because the name of the city was not mentioned in the letter, many scholars believe the letter was meant to be circulated throughout the churches of Asia Minor, and was sent first to Ephesus.[3] According to Ephesians 6, Tychicus became Paul's courier to deliver the letter to the Ephesians.

---

[1] John MacArthur, *The MacArthur Bible Commentary* (Nashville: Thomas Nelson, 2005), 1680.

[2] Earl D. Radmacher, Ronald B. Allen, and H. Wayne House, eds., *Nelson's New Illustrated Bible Commentary* (Nashville: Thomas Nelson, 1999), 1530.

[3] Radmacher et al., 1530.

In my opinion, one of Paul's greatest messages was the letter he wrote to the Ephesians. Paul was in Rome under house arrest and waiting to be tried. Things didn't look good for Paul. Yet, Paul's focus was on those with whom he had shared Christ and his concern was that they were continuing to walk with the Lord faithfully.

Teaching

Ephesians 1:1–6: Paul began the letter with his usual greeting: "To the faithful saints in Christ Jesus at Ephesus. Grace to you and peace from God our Father and the Lord Jesus Christ" (vv. 1b–2). Paul named the blessings (grace and peace) that came from the Ones with authority (God the Father and Jesus Christ). Paul continued to remind his readers that they had been blessed through Christ with every conceivable spiritual blessing, and that they had been chosen by Him from before the beginning of the earth (vv. 3–4).

Nelson's Commentary explains being chosen as having "predestined us" (v. 5): "Predestination is not a cold-hearted determinism or set fate, but rather a loving choice on God's part."[4] Love is a choice more than an emotion. Regardless of what happens, we choose to love, just as God chose to love us. God chose us, predestined us, and adopted us (vv. 4–5). He favored us with His beloved Son (v. 6). The work of the Father comes through election.

Ephesians 1:7–12: The work of the Son is our redemption (vv. 7–8). Christ "made known to us the mystery of His will." *Nelson's Commentary* explains the term mystery this way: "The mystery is not a puzzle to solve, or knowledge only for the few and the initiated, as the mystery religions of Paul's day. In Paul's usage, the word *mystery* refers to an aspect of God's will that was once hidden or obscure, but now was being revealed by God (Romans 11:25)."[5] In the Old Testament, the people didn't understand the mystery, but it has been explained to us. As ambassadors of Christ, we can make known the mystery that came through Jesus Christ as Lord and Savior. We've also received an inheritance that was predestined according to God's will.

---

[4] Radmacher et al., 1531.

[5] Radmacher et al., 1532.

Closing

Ephesians 1 provides an explanation of the Trinity in our salvation: (1) God the Father's work through our election; (2) Jesus the Son's work through our redemption; and (3) the Holy Spirit's work to provide us protection.[6]

The Daily Word

God sent Jesus Christ into the world as a free gift for you to receive. Your heavenly Father is the giver of every good and perfect gift. When you believe in Jesus, you receive redemption through His blood, forgiveness of your trespasses, and the indwelling of the Holy Spirit. Because God—as Father, Son, and Holy Spirit—is rich in grace, He *lavishes grace after grace upon you.* Today, you need to believe the truth that you are worthy to receive His lavish grace. Lavish means *amazingly rich, elaborate, or luxurious.* Many parents desire to lavish their children with good gifts of all types and sizes. Your heavenly Father *is able* to do abundantly more than you can even imagine. He chooses to lavish you with what He knows you need most of all—grace with all wisdom and understanding.

Stand and receive this truth today. Your heavenly Father delights in showering you with gifts. He gushes over you with grace, wisdom, and understanding. Lift up your hands and receive His wonderful gifts!

We have redemption in Him through His blood, the forgiveness of our trespasses, according to the riches of His grace that He lavished on us with all wisdom and understanding. —Ephesians 1:7–8

Further Scripture: John 1:16–17; Ephesians 3:20; 2 Peter 1:2

Questions

1. What do you think some of the spiritual blessings are that are mentioned in Ephesians 1:3?
2. Who chose us for adoption, when were we chosen, and what was the process (Luke 19:10; John 15:16; Ephesians 1:4–6, 11; 2:18–19)?
3. According to Ephesians 1:4, as one of the chosen, how does God see us? Do you see yourself the way God views you, and if not, how do you see yourself? Which one is the correct view? How can you change your thinking (Romans 12:2; 1 Corinthians 2:12–16; 2 Corinthians 10:5; Philippians 4:8)?

[6] MacArthur, 1683.

4. In Ephesians 1:18–19, what were Paul's reasons for his prayer that the eyes of our hearts would be enlightened? How would you say that this prayer has been answered in your life?
5. Describe what Christ being *The Head* over the Church should look like (Ephesians 1:22; 3:10; 4:11–16; 5:23–32)? Ephesians 1:23 says, "And the church is his body; it is made full and complete by Christ, who fills all things everywhere with himself" (NLT). Is this how you see the American church as a whole? If not, how can that change?
6. What did the Holy Spirit highlight to you in Ephesians 1 through the reading or the teaching?

Lesson 53: Ephesians 2

The Head: A Brick in the Temple

Teaching Notes

Intro

Paul wrote Ephesians to be read aloud to all the churches. Would you read a letter you just received one paragraph at a time? Of course not. Therefore, these letters need to be read in completion in ONE sitting. I would encourage you to read it aloud as well, because the letter is best understood that way. It is incredibly important to get the whole concept of the letter before breaking it down into sections to study. Paul painted two pictures for us: (1) before Christ in verses 1–3, and (2) after Christ in verses 4–6. This picture is the transformation from death to life and is at the very heart of who we were and are.

Teaching

Ephesians 2:1–3: Paul used the word "dead" to describe how black the before picture was (v. 1). That death was the result of sin. Sin kills. It destroys. It annihilates. Some commentators note that Ephesians deals more with the spiritual realm and its forces than any other New Testament book. God wants you alive; Satan wants you dead. This struggle is the war we all must face (v. 2). Paul emphasized that we too lived under the same condition (v. 3). Culture defines freedom as the ability to do anything we want. The problem with that is our sinful state. The things we want are ultimately self-destructive. These cravings are so strong they'll cause us to rationalize everything from premarital sex and extramarital sex to running red lights or eating just one more Hershey's Kiss.

Paul described humankind as "by nature children under wrath." Wrath is God's holy anger against sin and judgment that results from sin. God hates sin, and He despises what sin does in our lives. But we tend to see the wrath of God in opposition to the love of God. Therefore, we feel forced to choose between them, and we opt to focus on God's love. In fact, the two are not opposites but are two sides of the same coin. God cannot be completely loving if He does not hate the things that rob us of life.

Ephesians 2:4–6: If God didn't love us, He wouldn't care about the consequences of sin in our lives. We WERE dead, and we gratified our sinful nature with our fleshly desires. Note that the word "dead" is not the focus of the sentence. We WERE dead, BUT death no longer holds on to us. We have hope found only in Jesus Christ. Paul began verse 4 with "BUT." Our merciful and loving God, because of the "love with which He loved us" (NASB), has made us alive (vv. 4–5). The penalty has been paid, and our bondage to sin has been broken forever. Not only have we been saved, God has also raised us from death in sin to life and has seated us with Christ in the heavens (v. 6).

Ephesians 2:7–10: Why would God do such a thing? God did it to show the world what He is like (v. 7). We are God's visual aid. When people look at us, they should see the reflection of the gift of love and salvation we have received. Verses 8–9 are the heart of the book of Ephesians, and they are the blue area on the TTR wristbands. Memorize these verses because they powerfully state the incredible message of salvation—salvation is by grace through faith. We are not saved BY works, but FOR works, not because we were told to, but in response to God's mercy (v. 10).

Put together the before and the after—we were purchased by Christ's life, death, and resurrection:

- We WERE dead, but NOW we are alive.
- We WERE unrighteous, but NOW we have been purified.
- We WERE objects of wrath, but NOW we stand before God forgiven.

In light of that, the church—as Christ's greatly loved bride—gets to do the hard and heart work of evangelism and missions. It's a costly, messy, much-resisted work that God has given us to do, but it's worth all the sacrifice, tears, and conflict. Is your spiritual life the before picture or the after picture? If before, I challenge you to read verses 8–10 every day this week. May God's Holy Spirit reveal what these verses mean in a real-life way. If after, anticipate the good works God has prepared for you this week. Look around to see what opportunities God has for you.

Ephesians 2:11–12: You have been chosen by God to be a metaphorical brick in His house. We should be the best building materials. But, before Christ, our lives were a barrier. The walls and dividers that separate us from God are real, both religious and sociological. The Jews were conscious of the privileges they had inherited, and the physical walls that separated them from all other peoples. Even in the temple, walls were built that separated the Jews from the Gentiles. Circumcision was the external sign of their special relationship with God. We were also separated from God by our sin (vv. 1–10).

Ephesians 2:13–18: "But now" reminds us the walls have been removed and the barriers between us and God are no more (vv. 13–14). Through Jesus' death, He reconciled (made peace) the Jews and the Gentiles to each other. The point is, Jesus came to tear down, destroy, and abolish the walls that separated us from one another in order to make us into one new, united people as His children. Our call is to stand for God's truth and to live and minister in God's grace.

Ephesians 2:19–22: Paul reminds his readers they are citizens of God's kingdom with all the rights and privileges that go with that citizenship. That means we are not two bodies—we are one. We are both the body of Christ and the temple of God as a dwelling place for the Holy Spirit. Mindi's painting shows the glory of God coming from the cornerstone, the stone Isaiah described as "a tested stone, a precious cornerstone, a sure foundation" and said that "the one who believes will be unshakable" (Isaiah 28:16). The cornerstone was the most important part of the structure and was carefully chosen as the strongest and the truest. The cornerstone set the direction of the building, supported its weight, and tied the rest of the structure together. That is exactly who Jesus is to us as the church—the One who ties us all together and holds us together (v. 21). As believers, we are a part of that building/temple, because that is where God abides.

Closing

If you are a brick, how do you see yourself? Are you someone who goes to church, or are you someone who is the church? There is a huge difference between those two Questions, and it is crucial to know your answer. There are people who just go to church, and then go home, and continue on with their daily lives unaffected.

But everything HAS changed. Christ died for us, His bride, in order for us to BE His church.

> Jesus died for us to fill the God-shaped vacuum in our lives. That's the good news.
>
> Jesus died for us so we can do the good works He prepared in advance for us to do, to fill the purpose-shaped vacuum in our lives.
>
> Jesus made us a brick and includes us as part of the holy temple.

We are God's workmanship who were created in Christ Jesus to do good works, works God has prepared for us to do in advance. Be a brick!

The Daily Word

God, who is rich in mercy and lavish in His grace, is also your peace. Christ came to be peace to those who believe by faith. When you rest in the Lord alone, when you cease striving, when you take a deep breath and humbly surrender your will with thanks, then *Christ will be your peace.* Open your hands and lift them up. Pray to the Lord: *"I believe in You. I receive Your mercy. I receive Your grace. I receive Your love."*

God has everything in His hands—the issues, the worries, the problems, and the heartaches. Christ came so you may have peace. He is the one and only true assurance for peace in your life, the only authentic peace found in this world. Only Jesus. Nothing else will bring you peace. Nothing. Therefore, stop searching and receive Him. Then slow down long enough to rest in His peace. Give Him thanks at all times for His peace.

For He is our peace, who made both groups one and tore down the dividing wall of hostility. —Ephesians 2:14

Further Scripture: Psalm 85:8; John 16:33; Ephesians 2:17

Questions

1. Read Ephesians 2:1 and Romans 6:23a. Describe the death Paul spoke about in theses verses.
2. In Ephesians 2:8–9, Paul taught that by grace we are saved through faith, not from works. How then are we to understand the good works mentioned in Ephesians 2:10 (Romans 9:32; 1 Timothy 6:18; Hebrews 10:24; James 2:26; 3:13)?
3. Is the peace mentioned in Ephesians 2:14 available to other hostile groups? What are some groups that are often hostile toward one another? Do you view Ephesians 2:16 as a message of hope to other groups besides Jews and Gentiles (Galatians 3:28)? What is the greatest enmity that has been reconciled (Romans 8:7–9; Ephesians 2:13; Colossians 2:13–14)?
4. Ephesians 2 informs us that Christ is our peace and He came and preached (proclaimed) peace. What is the first message of peace proclaimed in the New Testament (Luke 1:79; 2:10–14)? Where in the gospels can you find Jesus speaking of peace?
5. What did the Holy Spirit highlight to you in Ephesians 2 through the reading or the teaching?

Lesson 54: Ephesians 3

The Head: Paul's Ministry to the Gentiles

Teaching Notes

Intro

Dr. Tom Constable points out that in chapter 3, "Paul began to pray for his readers again (cf. vv. 1, 14), but he interrupted himself to tell them more about the church."[1]

Teaching

Ephesians 3:1–5: In the first five verses, Paul explains to the Ephesians what is important to him. John Eadie explains that in verse 1, "'For this reason' refers to what Paul had said in the first two chapters, about God's blessings that are now the possession of both Gentile and Jewish believers."[2] As we've already mentioned, Paul was under house arrest in Rome and was therefore "the prisoner of Christ Jesus" (v. 1b). Paul underscored that his ministry was for the Gentiles (v. 1c). In verse 2, the word "administration" can also mean stewardship, or managing someone's household.[3] Paul was explaining that he had been given the responsibility for stewarding God's grace to the Gentiles. *Nelson's Commentary* explains stewardship as "the work of a person who took care of all the financial affairs of a large household or business" and states, "Paul was entrusted with the stewardship of God's economy, to dispense the riches of Christ to God's household and to preach the Good News."[4]

In verse 3, Paul refers to the "mystery" that was revealed to him. *Nelson's Commentary* explains, "The dispensation (stewardship) that God gave Paul for the benefit of the Ephesians had previously been a mystery. Now God was

---

[1] Thomas L. Constable, *Expository Notes of Dr. Thomas Constable: Ephesians*, 64, https://planobiblechapel.org/tcon/notes/pdf/ephesians.pdf.

[2] John Eadie, *Commentary on the Epistle to the Ephesians*, 2d ed. (Edinburgh: T. & T. Clark, 1883; reprint ed. Minneapolis: James and Klock, 1977), 208–9.

[3] Constable, 65.

[4] Earl D. Radmacher, Ronald B. Allen, and H. Wayne House, eds., *Nelson's New Illustrated Bible Commentary* (Nashville: Thomas Nelson, 1999), 1535.

revealing this mystery more fully in Paul's ministry to the Gentiles. The mystery was that Jews and Gentiles were to have an equal status in the church, the body of Christ."[5]

The Bible Knowledge Commentary identifies the New Testament passages that reference the "mysteries"[6]:

- Matthew 13:11 and Luke 8:10 speak of the secrets of the kingdom of heaven and the kingdom of God, respectively.
- Romans 11:25 and 16:25–26 explains that Israel had a hardening of heart, and that the plan of salvation would come through Jesus.
- 1 Corinthians 4:1 and 15:51 speak of New Testament revelation and the rapture.
- Ephesians 1:9; 3:2–4 are about God's will, the administration of God's grace, and Christ. Ephesians 3:9 and 5:32 speak of Christ and the church.
- Colossians 1:26–27 speak of Christ in us.
- 2 Thessalonians 2:7 shares the secret power that comes with lawlessness.

Arnold Fruchtenbaum provides four characteristics of the church, which are described as a mystery:[7]

1. Jews and Gentiles are to be united in the church (Ephesians 3:1–12).
2. Christ dwells within each believer (Colossians 1:24–27).
3. The church functions as the bride of Christ (Ephesians 5:22–32).
4. The church will be raptured (1 Corinthians 15:50–58).

Fruchtenbaum explains, "These four mysteries describe qualities that distinguish the church from Israel."[8]

Paul explains that because the Ephesians were reading his words, they could now understand what Paul was saying about the mystery (v. 4). Paul explained that no one in earlier generations had been given this revelation and implied that this revelation was not just given to Paul (v. 5). *Nelson's Commentary* states, "People who lived in the other ages, before Pentecost, had a great deal of knowledge about God and His grace, as the OT demonstrates. However, that knowledge was

[5] Radmacher et al., 1535.

[6] Constable, 70.

[7] Arnold G. Fruchtenbaum, "Israel and the Church," *Issues in Dispensationalism*, ed. Wesley R. Willis and John Master (Chicago: Moody, 1994), 117–18.

[8] Fruchtenbaum, 117–18.

not as all-embracing as the revelation that we receive in Christ Jesus . . . equality with the Jews in one body was a secret never before revealed."[9]

Ephesians 3:6–13: Wiersbe explains that verse 6 shows the Gentiles "are fellow-heirs with the Jews and share in the spiritual riches God gave them because of His covenant with Abraham (Galatians 3:29)."[10] In verse 7, Paul explains he was "made a servant of this gospel by the gift of God's grace." Some translations use "minister" in the place of "servant." *Nelson's Commentary* states, "It took divine grace to transform Paul from a blasphemer into a saint, from a Pharisee into an apostle, and from a persecutor of Christians into a preacher of Christ. Then it took divine power and authority to enable Paul to function as a minister of God."[11] Paul repeats that the grace of this mystery had been given to him—one who was "the least of all the saints" (v. 8) (1 Timothy 1:15). Paul's assignment was to preach the gospel to the Gentiles (v. 8b) and explain the mystery of the church to everyone (v. 9). In verse 10, Paul said his work was "God's multi-faceted wisdom" and would be known to the rulers and authorities in the heavens. *Nelson's Commentary* explains, "God's manifold wisdom is to be displayed to the angelic beings by the members of the church . . . Angels are also learning about God's wisdom as they watch His grace working in us (1 Corinthians 11:10)."[12] This was all part of God's eternal plan (v. 11). Because of the work of Christ, we can have boldness and confidence in our access to God (v. 12). Paul told the Ephesians not to be discouraged that he was under arrest because it too was all part of God's plan (v. 13).

Ephesians 3:14–21: In verse 14, Paul begins to teach the Ephesians how to pray. Paul says he kneels before God who was/is the Father of everyone in heaven and on earth (v. 15). He prayed that the Ephesians would be strengthened by God's power through His Spirit (v. 16). Paul also prayed that the Ephesians would be firmly rooted in the love of Christ and to be able to understand the depth of God's love (vv. 17–19). Paul used this prayer to speak to the debate going on about whether the Jews and the Gentiles were meant to come together as the body of Christ. Paul's response was that God's love was beyond anything they could comprehend. In verse 20, Paul began his doxology—his benediction at the end of the prayer: "Now to Him who is able to do above and beyond all that we

---

[9] Radmacher et al., 1535.

[10] Warren W. Wiersbe, *The Bible Exposition Commentary: Ephesians–Revelation* (Colorado Springs: David C. Cook, 2003), 28.

[11] Radmacher et al., 1535.

[12] Radmacher et al., 1535.

ask or think according to the power that works in us—to Him be glory in the church and in Christ Jesus to all generations, forever and ever. Amen."

Closing

Because of God's grace and power, Paul believed God could bring the Jews and the Gentiles together to be the body of Christ. Jesus is *The Head* of the body.

The Daily Word

Paul knelt before God the Father and prayed for believers to be strengthened with power through the Holy Spirit. He wanted them to understand and comprehend God's vast love for them and be filled with the fullness of God. Paul cared for the spiritual health of the believers in Ephesus. He knew they could easily become discouraged, so he pressed in, got on his knees, and cried out honestly for believers.

Have you ever knelt while praying? If Paul modeled praying on his knees for those he cared about, then it may be wise to try it the next time you pray. Kneeling involves humility. It may make you physically uncomfortable or even self-conscience in a public setting. You are to give *everything* to Christ—*even do the uncomfortable things*. Kneel before the Lord and pray to Him, believing He is able to do above and beyond what you can ask or think according to His power at work within you. Bring Him all your worries for the day and ask Him to fill you with power through the Holy Spirit. Perhaps make kneeling prayer a new routine!

For this reason I kneel before the Father from whom every family in heaven and on earth is named. —Ephesians 3:14–15

Further Scripture: Psalm 95:6; Ephesians 3:20–21; Philippians 2:9–11

Questions

1. Paul, while in prison, laid out God's plan for His people in Ephesians 3:6. How did this plan differ from the old covenant (Hebrews 10:1–18)? Were there any similarities between the two?
2. In Ephesians 3:12, Paul said: "We can now come boldly and confidently into God's presence" (NLT). Where else in Scripture do we see coming before the throne (Hebrews 4:16)? Do you come boldly before God's presence? If not, why?

3. Have you ever prayed for something you thought to be unattainable? In Ephesians 3:20, Paul stated God can "accomplish infinitely more" than we might ask or think (NLT). Have you asked for the impossible (in your mind)? If so, what was it, and if not, why?
4. What did the Holy Spirit highlight to you in Ephesians 3 through the reading or the teaching?

WEEK 78

Lesson 55: Ephesians 4

The Head: Unity and Diversity in the Body

Teaching Notes

Intro

In chapter 3, Paul explained Christ was *The Head* of the church and both the Jews and the Gentiles were united in Him to be His body—the church. Ephesians 4 builds on this foundation.

Teaching

Ephesians 4:1–6: In verse 1, Paul calls the Ephesians to "walk worthy" of what God had called them to do. They were to walk with humility, gentleness, patience, accepting one another in love, and with the unity and peace that binds us all (vv. 2–3). Paul lists three virtues: humility, gentleness, and patience. Constable explains humility as "a proper assessment of oneself in God's program," gentleness or meekness as "the opposite of self-assertion . . . one whose emotions are under control," and patience or longsuffering as "endurance even under affliction."[1] The result of these virtues is "accepting one another in love, diligently keeping the unity of the Spirit with the peace that binds us" (vv. 2b–3) (Matthew 5:9). We are not called to be peacekeepers but to be bound by peace. This has to be intentional!

In verses 4–6, Paul lists seven ways that we have unity. We have one body in Christ (Ephesians 1:23); we have one spirit in the Holy Spirit (1 Corinthians 12:13; Ephesians 2:22); we have one hope of eternity through the resurrection (1 Peter 1:3; 3:15); we have one Lord (Ephesians 1:22–23; Colossians 1:18); one faith (Ephesians 2:8–9); one baptism through the death of Christ (Romans 6:3); and one God who is Father of all (Deuteronomy 6:4; 2 Kings 19:15). We are united through all of these.

Ephesians 4:7–11: Paul then moves from unity to diversity. All believers received God's grace according to Christ's gift (v. 7). Harold W. Hoehner explains,

[1] Thomas L. Constable, *Expository Notes of Dr. Thomas Constable: Ephesians*, 83–84, https://planobiblechapel.org/tcon/notes/pdf/ephesians.pdf.

"For Christ to have ascended to heaven, He first had to descend to 'the lower parts of the earth.' This is probably a reference to Jesus' tomb or grave."[2] Constable continues, "In His death, Jesus Christ gained the victory over sin, and He redeemed those whom He would give as gifts to the church."[3] Jesus descended to us to save us and then ascended back to heaven where He personally gave each of us gifts (vv. 8–11). Note that verse 11 is one of TTR's key verses.

Ephesians 4:12–14: These gifts (apostles, prophets, evangelists, pastors, and teachers) were given for (1) the training of the saints in ministry and (2) the building up of the body of Christ (v. 12). These gifts are given for a specific time—"until we all reach unity in the faith and in the knowledge of God's Son" while we grow in the stature of Christ's fullness (v. 13). All of these things will continue until these conditions come to fruition.

According to Cindy Jacobs' ministry website:

- Every month, 1,800 pastors leave the ministry.
- In ten years, 40 percent of pastors will no longer be in ministry.
- 50 percent of all pastors feel they are not able to do the job.
- 80 percent of pastors believe their ministries affect their families negatively.
- 40 percent of pastors have experienced depression or burnout that required a leave of absence from their ministries.
- 33 percent experienced burnout within their first five years of ministry.[4]

Please understand that we've said to the pastor, "We want you to do it all." But Paul tells the Ephesians that if they want the work of the church to continue, he needs multiple voices, not just the voice of one man (the pastor). So let's talk about some of these other voices using he fivefold ministry.

Apostle: Visualize a drawing of your hand. The position of the apostle is represented by the thumb. The thumb does not work in opposition of the rest of the fingers but rather works with the fingers to do the work assigned to the entire hand. Apostles function in administration and (together with prophets) lay the foundation with proper doctrinal and spiritual structure (Ephesians 2:20). An apostle is a foundation layer, pioneer, or entrepreneur within the body of Christ

[2] Harold W. Hoehner, "Ephesians," in *The Bible Knowledge Commentary: New Testament*, ed. John F. Walvoord and Roy B. Zuck (Wheaton, IL: Scripture Press, Victor Books, 1983), 613–45.

[3] Constable, 90–91.

[4] "Do You Know Why Fivefold Ministry Is Essential?," Generals International, https://www.generals.org/blog/do-you-know-why-fivefold-ministry-is-essential.

(1 Corinthians 3:10). The term apostle or Apostolos in the Greek means "one who is sent out" and was originally used by the Romans to describe someone who was sent out to acculturate newly acquired land. They ask: "Are we leading the people of God to the new place God is calling them?"

Prophet: The prophet is the first or pointer finger, functions in revelation, and points the way for believers. The office of the prophet is different from the gift of prophecy—it carries a governmental authority and role of higher responsibility. The gift of prophecy is for edification, exhortation, and comfort, whereas the prophet flows in areas of guidance, instruction, rebuke, judgment, and revelation. Prophets know God's will and are particularly attuned to God and His truth for today. They question the status quo and ask, "Are the people of God hearing His voice and responding appropriately?" The title means "one who hears and listens to God."

Shepherd: The ring finger or wedding ring finger symbolizes the shepherd's commitment to and care of his flock. The pastor is bound to the local saints in a shepherding relationship to nurture and protect. They are caregivers of the community, focusing on the protection and spiritual maturity of God's flock, cultivating a loving and spiritually mature network of relationships, and making and developing disciples. Their title means, "one who shepherds God's people," and they ask, "Are the people of God being protected and prepared for a Christian lifestyle?"

Evangelist: The middle finger signifies the Evangelist and represents the outreach ministry extended to evangelize the world. They are soul winners, but there are also many in the body of Christ who have a burden to win souls who do not hold this office. Evangelists are not primarily soul winners but are called to stir up the church and move the people into action. Evangelists recruit others to the cause. Their title means "one who brings good news." They ask: "Are new people entering into God's kingdom?"

Teacher: Teachers are the littlest finger, which is essential and provides balance. The teacher grounds the church in truth through instruction in the principles of the Word of God. The teacher's heart is for truth, and their desire is to dissect the Word of God to make sure the church thoroughly understands the truth of Scripture. They are often expositors, theologians, or have a specific burden or emphasis in some special area of truth to teach the body of Christ. Teachers understand and explain. They help others remain biblically grounded to better discern God's will, guiding others toward wisdom, helping the community remain faithful to Christ's Word, and constructing a transferable doctrine. Their title means, "one who seeks and shares the truth," and they ask: "Are the people of God immersing themselves in Scripture and biblical principles? Are they living them out?"

Closing

Some of you question if the roles of apostles and prophets are still present today. Based on what I read in the Bible and what I've experienced, I think they are.

The Daily Word

As a believer, God desires you to live a life worthy of the calling you have received. You may think to yourself, *I don't even know my calling!* In general, Jesus instructed believers to seek first the kingdom of God as you love God and love others. God may have other specific callings and tasks of obedience for you along the way, but begin with first seeking the kingdom of God daily. Jesus says the world will know of His great love as Savior when believers live in unity. Unity is a key in the kingdom of God.

A supernatural power and beauty ignite in the kingdom when believers walk out their specific gifts with humility and love. So how do you foster and uphold unity of the Spirit? *Walk in humility, gentleness, and patience, accept each other with love, and be diligent to keep peace.* It's as though Paul gave believers a recipe for unity. With humility, recognize you can't walk this out in your own strength. Ask the Lord to fill you up with the power of the Holy Spirit, and see what happens. There is no way to have unity of the Spirit without walking in humility.

Therefore I, the prisoner for the Lord, urge you to walk worthy of the calling you have received, with all humility and gentleness, with patience, accepting one another in love, diligently keeping the unity of the Spirit with the peace that binds us. —Ephesians 4:1–3

Further Scripture: 2 Chronicles 7:14; 1 Corinthians 1:10; 1 Peter 5:5–6

Questions

1. Do you feel you have been called by God? Paul told the people to "lead a life worthy of your calling, for you have been called by God" (v. 1 NLT). What does this "calling" look like for you in your life?
2. Paul said Christ gave the church gifts—apostles, prophets, evangelists, pastors, and teachers—to equip God's people for the works of service (ministry). Does everyone fall into one of these categories? Do you feel you fall into one of them? If so, which one? Is your church operating with these five gifts? If not, does it feel like something is missing?

3. Ephesians 4:22 says "to throw off your old sinful nature" (NLT). Where else in Scripture does it say something similar (2 Corinthians 5:17; Colossians 3:5–10)? Does your Spirit need renewing and rejuvenating? Take a few minutes and ask God to renew your mind and heart.
4. What did the Holy Spirit highlight to you in Ephesians 4 through the reading or the teaching?

Lesson 56: Ephesians 5

The Head: Walk in Love and Light

Teaching Notes

Intro

MacArthur summarizes the message of chapter 5 as "God's standards for faithfulness in the church."[1]

Teaching

Ephesians 5:1–7: In verses 1–2, Paul tells his readers to be imitators of God. *Nelson's Commentary* explains, "Believers are to follow the example of God's actions. He loved us when we were still His enemies. As imitators, believers should demonstrate that type of self-sacrifice love."[2] MacArthur describes being imitators of God as "the very purpose of sanctification, growing in likeness to the Lord while serving Him on earth." MacArthur continues, "The Christian life is designed to reproduce godliness as modeled by the Savior and Lord, Jesus Christ, in whose image believers have been recreated through the New Birth."[3] According to 1 Peter 1:15–16, there is no greater calling or purpose than imitating the Lord—to look more like Him every day. That allows us to walk in love.

Verse 2 describes Jesus' life as a "sacrificial and fragrant offering to God." MacArthur explains Christ's offering on the cross "for fallen mankind pleased and glorified His heavenly Father, because it demonstrated, in the most complete and perfect way, God's sovereign, perfect, unconditional, and divine kind of love."[4] In Leviticus, five offerings were commanded by God.

MacArthur outlines the first three as: "(1) the burnt offering (Leviticus 1:1–17), depicting Christ's perfection; (2) the grain offering (Leviticus 2:1–6), depicting Christ's total devotion to God in giving His life to please the Father; and (3) the peace offering (Leviticus 3:1–17), depicting His peacemaking between God

[1] John MacArthur, *The MacArthur Bible Commentary* (Nashville: Thomas Nelson, 2005), 1697.

[2] Earl D. Radmacher, Ronald B. Allen, and H. Wayne House, eds., *Nelson's New Illustrated Bible Commentary* (Nashville: Thomas Nelson, 1999), 1538.

[3] MacArthur, 1697–98.

[4] MacArthur, 1698.

and man."[5] These three were a soothing aroma to the Lord. MacArthur explains of the last two, "The sin offering (Leviticus 4:1—5:13) and the trespass offering (Leviticus 5:14—6:7), were repulsive to God because, though they depicted Christ, they depicted Him as bearing sin (Matthew 27:46). In the end, when redemption was accomplished, the whole work pleased God completely."[6]

We should imitate Christ in all our actions. We cannot allow sexual immorality or greed to be in our lives (v. 3) or allow coarse and foolish talking or joking to come from our mouths (v. 4). *Nelson's Commentary* explains, "The Christian's life must not be degraded by filthiness, foolish talking, coarse jesting" because they "do not honor God nor give Him thanks for redeeming us."[7] Paul said those who were immoral, greedy, or an idolater had no inheritance in God's kingdom and would face God's wrath (vv. 5–6). God does not tolerate sin. Paul stressed that the Ephesians should guard themselves against false teachers who "deceive you with empty arguments" (v. 6) and warned them, "do not become their partner" (v. 7), so that nothing would get in their way of being pure, holy, and clean.

Ephesians 5:8–14: Paul moves on to contrast living in light with darkness. MacArthur explains, "Darkness describes the character of the life of the unconverted as void of truth and virtue in intellectual and moral matters."[8] Paul explained the believers had been in darkness before Christ but now lived in the light (v. 8). The believers should be walking in LOVE and in LIGHT. Living in the light allows us to have the fruit of that light—goodness, righteousness, and truth—so we can discern what pleases God (vv. 9–10). Believers should avoid the fruitless works of darkness and expose the shamefulness of what is done in darkness instead (vv. 11–12). On the other hand, what is shown by the light is seen clearly (vv. 13–14).

Closing

We are to pay attention to how we walk as the wise in Christ, so we bring glory to Him.

The Daily Word

Have you ever seen a little child wear a pair of their daddy's shoes and attempt to walk around, pretending to be his or her daddy? It can look kind of clumsy and funny, but the *heart of the child longs to walk like his or her daddy.* In a similar way,

[5] MacArthur, 1698.

[6] MacArthur, 1698.

[7] Radmacher et al., 1538.

[8] MacArthur, 1698.

as a follower of Christ, you are to *imitate your heavenly Father*. You are to walk in love and light just as Christ the Messiah loved you and sacrificed His life as a fragrant offering to God. What does it look like for you to walk selflessly in love and light? Be wise, not unwise. Think about others first, not just what's best for you. Don't be foolish but understand what God's will is. Be filled with the Spirit. Give thanks and praise to the Lord. Fear the Lord, not man. Walk in the light of Christ, not in darkness.

Today, imagine putting on the shoes of your heavenly Father, and, as you walk in His shoes, *imitate His love*. It may feel clumsy at first, but with time as you grow, it will feel more natural, and the love of your heavenly Father will overflow from your life. *Walk in His love* so you can *walk out His love*.

Therefore, be imitators of God, as dearly loved children. And walk in love, as the Messiah also loved us and gave Himself for us, a sacrificial and fragrant offering to God. —Ephesians 5:1–2

Further Scripture: Ephesians 5:15–21; 1 Peter 1:14–16; 1 John 1:6–7

Questions

1. According to Ephesians 5, what are some of the things that will bring God's wrath? What can we do to avoid His wrath?
2. What did Paul advise the church in Ephesus to do to avoid being deceived?
3. In Ephesians 5:16, what did Paul say to do? What does it mean to you to make the most of your time? Do you think this is in line with what God wants you to do with your life?
4. Ephesians 5:22–30 speaks of how husbands and wives should act toward one another. Why is this important, and what relationship did Paul compare this to in this chapter?
5. What did the Holy Spirit highlight to you in Ephesians 5 through the reading or the teaching?

WEEK 78

Lesson 57: Ephesians 6

The Head: Children and Parents

Teaching Notes

Intro

This is the last chapter in Ephesians, and it's kind of a biggie—talking about spiritual war and the armor of God. In Ephesians 6:10–20, Paul encourages the Ephesians to prepare themselves daily for spiritual warfare. The Ephesians were fighting an enemy they could not see. We are fighting an enemy we cannot see. As we fight this spiritual war, we are to take up the armor of God and constantly be in prayer. I thought this is where I would spend our entire teaching time today, but as I studied the Word, I never made it past verse four. As I read through these verses on children, I realized they are not just for children but for parents too. We are going to start with the children's side and look at the four reasons children should obey their parents. Then we will look at the parents' side. In these first four verses, God convicted me about the type of parent I need to be.

Teaching

Ephesians 6:1: According to Paul, he was writing to "children" who were Christian. They knew the Lord. He had a starting point with these kids. By no means am I a perfect parent or my kids perfect children. When I talk through this, I am attempting to walk through Scripture and show you how Paul's writings have helped me.

Children should obey their parents in everything because it pleases the Lord (Colossians 3:20). Obeying parents is an action that reflects who that child is in the Lord. MacArthur wrote, "The child in the home is to be willing to be under the authority of parents with obedient submission to them as agents of the Lord over him, obeying parents as if obeying the Lord Himself."[1] Parents are in charge of children because that is the way God designed it. They are to submit to one another. When you have wives who submit to husbands,

[1] John MacArthur, *The MacArthur Bible Commentary* (Nashville: Thomas Nelson, 2005), 1705.

husbands who love their wives, and children who submit to parents, you see harmony in the house.[2]

Another reason children should obey their parents is because obedience is right.[3] Wiersbe wrote, "There is an order of nature, ordained of God, that argues for the rightness of an action. Since the parents brought the child into the world, and since they have more knowledge and wisdom than the child, it is right that a child obey his parents."[4] In today's culture we are told parents should obey their children in order to make them happy. That is contrary to the way God wants it to be.

Ephesians 6:2: Obedience is a commandment. Wiersbe wrote, "The righteousness of the law is still a revelation of the holiness of God, and the Holy Spirit enables us to practice that righteousness in our daily lives (Romans 8:1–4)."[5] We are able to walk out the act of honoring our parents because of the Holy Spirit. Wiersbe wrote, "All of the 10 commandments are repeated in the New Testament epistles for Christians to observe except 'Remember the Sabbath day, to keep it holy.'"[6] What comes to your mind when you hear the word "honor"? Honor means more than simply to obey. It is to show respect and love, to care for, and to seek to bring honor.[7] There is this tension, as a parent walking in the Spirit, of wanting your kids to listen but they don't always do that, because they are living in the world.

Ephesians 6:3: Obedience brings blessing.[8] Read this verse again. If your child dies early, does it mean they were disobedient? No. I want you to understand this is not always the case. If your children do honor you and are obedient, they will escape a good deal of sin and danger and avoid things that could shorten their lives.[9] The further away a parent is from the way of the Lord, the more disobedient their kids will be.

Ephesians 6:4: "Fathers" was from a Greek word that referred to mothers and fathers. This is for both parents. MacArthur wrote that, "In the pagan world of

---

[2] Warren W. Wiersbe, *The Bible Exposition Commentary: Ephesians–Revelation* (Colorado Springs: David C. Cook, 2003), 53.

[3] Wiersbe, 53.

[4] Wiersbe, 53.

[5] Wiersbe, 53.

[6] Wiersbe, 53.

[7] Wiersbe, 53.

[8] Wiersbe, 53.

[9] Wiersbe, 53.

Paul's day, and even in Jewish households, most fathers ruled their families with ridged and domineering authority. The desires and welfare of wives and kids were seldom considered."[10]

Parents must not provoke their kids.[11] Wiersbe wrote, "Paul told the parents, 'Don't use your authority to abuse the child.'"[12] The opposite of provoke is encourage. It is important to praise your kids. Wiersbe wrote, "By being inconsistent and unfair in discipling, and by showing favoritism in the home, by making promises and not keeping them, and making light of problems that, to the children, are very important [you are provoking your kids]."[13]

Parents must nurture their kids.[14] The word "nurture" used here is the same word used in Ephesians 5:29, which also means to nourish. A parent needs to meet more than just a child's physical needs (food, shelter, clothing). They must also provide both emotionally and spiritually, with love and encouragement. This is not to say that there is not a time for discipline, but we can't be so legalistic with our kids that we fail to be nurturing. I don't want my kids to fail, so sometimes I forget the nurturing part of parenting and focus on the task at hand. That is provoking my kids. I have to challenge myself to teach by example, to teach a more balanced way of life. A good example of this teaching is found in Luke 2:52—Jesus' parents taught and nurtured Him.

Parents must discipline their kids.[15] Wiersbe wrote, "The word 'nurture' carries with it the idea of learning through discipling . . . consistent, loving discipline gives assurance to a child."[16] Don't be afraid to discipline your children.

Parents must instruct and encourage their kids.[17] All of that has to be based on the Word of God.

Closing

When I read these verses, I see Paul saying, "Children need to please the Lord by honoring and obeying their parents, this is what is right. Parents need to look at themselves to make sure they are imitating God." Obviously, the Ephesians were struggling with this. The enemy was and is attacking the family life, breaking up families. Any area that your conscience isn't settled, let the Holy Spirit begin to move. Even in Scripture we see parents neglecting their children: David

[10] MacArthur. 1703.

[11] Wiersbe, 53.

[12] Wiersbe, 53.

[13] Wiersbe, 54.

[14] Wiersbe, 54.

[15] Wiersbe, 54.

[16] Wiersbe, 54.

[17] Wiersbe, 54.

pampered Absalom, Eli failed to discipline his sons, and they brought disgrace to the nations, and Isaac pampered Esau while his wife favored Jacob, which led to a divided house. We have lost focus on our families. We need parents to step up in their relationships with Christ and their children. Kids need their parents. We need to reflect Christ in our parenting.

The Daily Word

Remember you are in a spiritual battle as a follower of Christ. This battle is not against flesh and blood but against the spiritual forces of evil in the heavens. The devil schemes against you to steal, kill, and destroy everything in your life as you seek to bring glory to the Lord. He wants your time, your joy, your unity, your strength, and your thoughts.

In the midst of the battle, the Lord calls upon you to *stand strong* against the schemes of the devil. The Lord gives you spiritual armor to protect against the tactics of the devil. When the enemy goes after your marriage or your parenting, your children, or your ministry, walk with the sandals of readiness and the gospel of peace. When fiery darts of doubt enter your mind, hold up your shield of faith. The Lord your God is mighty within you. Walk in the power of the Spirit. You have victory! Don't get discouraged and give in! *Instead, be strengthened by the Lord and keep your armor on.* When you forget to put on your armor, or when you don't invite the Lord into your battle, you will grow weary. Therefore, *set your mind on Christ.* The enemy's schemes are defeated in Jesus' mighty name.

Finally, be strengthened by the Lord and by His vast strength. Put on the full armor of God so that you can stand against the tactics of the Devil. For our battle is not against flesh and blood, but against the rulers, against the authorities, against the world powers of this darkness, against the spiritual forces of evil in the heavens. —Ephesians 6:10–12

Further Scripture: 2 Corinthians 10:3–5; Ephesians 6:4; 6:13–17

Questions

1. Where else in Scripture do we see that children are supposed to honor their father and mother (Exodus 20:12; Deuteronomy 5:16; Matthew 15:4; 19:19; Mark 7:10; Luke 18:20)? In comparison to the other commandments, what is unique about this one? In your opinion, how would the world be different today if children were to always obey this commandment?

2. In Ephesians 6:4 (NLT), what do you think the statement, "Fathers, do not provoke your children to anger," means (Colossians 3:21)? Can you think of any examples of this in the Bible (2 Samuel 14)? In your own life?
3. Name the six things we are to "put on" to guard ourselves from the evil one (Ephesians 6:14–17). How often do you wear your armor of God? Why is this important?
4. What does it look like to "pray at all times in the Spirit" (Ephesians 6:18)?
5. What did the Holy Spirit highlight to you in Ephesians 6 through the reading or the teaching?

WEEK 78

Lesson 58: Philippians 1

Exalted One: Paul's Ministry to the Gentiles

Teaching Notes

Intro

The book of Philippians is the thirty-third book in our study and is another of Paul's prison epistles (letters). The letter to the believers in Philippi, like so many of Paul's letters we've studied so far, continues to unfold Paul's journey in Acts. Philippi was the first church in Macedonia that Paul began. Paul wrote the letter from Rome during his first imprisonment there around AD 60–62. Evidence of that is found within the letter (Philippians 1:13; 4:22), in the book of Acts (28:16, 30–31), in Ephesians (6:18–20), and in Colossians (4:2–4). Some scholars, however, believe the book was written from Caesarea, located on the sea, near the end of Paul's two-year imprisonment there.[1] According to Philippians 1:20, Paul anticipated his imprisonment was coming to an end.

The city of Philippi was named originally Krenides, or The Little Fountains, which referred to the little springs nearby. The city was renamed in honor of Philip II of Macedon, who was the father of Alexander the Great. Nearby gold mines attracted many people to the area. Philip conquered the city and the surrounding area in the fourth century BC, and the city became part of the Roman province of Macedon in the second century BC. Its fame really came years later when, in 42 BC, after the assassination of Julius Caesar in the Roman senate, the armies of Antony and Octavian, both of whom had supported Caesar, defeated the armies of Brutus and Cassius, both of whom had opposed Caesar. The city/region then became a Roman colony of the new Roman Empire.[2]

Paul founded the church at Philippi during his second missionary journey. When Paul arrived in Philippi, only a small Jewish population existed there. The Jewish population was so small that less than ten men were there for a synagogue to exist, so Jewish women in the city went outside the city along the Gangites River. Paul met the women there (Acts 16:13), and preached the gospel to them. The first believer in Philippi was a woman named Lydia. She was

[1] John MacArthur, *The MacArthur Bible Commentary* (Nashville: Thomas Nelson, 2005), 1708.

[2] MacArthur, 1708–9.

also a successful businesswoman, with wealth and a large home for the church to meet in. She invited Paul and Silas to stay with her there. Opposition came immediately through another woman, a demon-possessed girl who was a fortune teller and a slave. In response to her shouts and curses, Paul cast out the demon, making her master angry because she could no longer make money for him. Paul and Silas were grabbed by the crowd and taken before the magistrate, who had them beaten and imprisoned them in the jail in shackles (Acts 16). Their chains were broken and the gates were opened through an earthquake, but Paul and Silas stayed where they were. When the jailer found them, he accepted Christ as well as those in his household. The next day, the magistrates found out they had treated Paul and Silas illegally, since they were both Roman citizens, and they asked Paul and Silas to leave. Paul visited Philippi two more times—once at the beginning of his third missionary journey as he moved on toward Athens and Corinth and a second time on his return. Paul loved the church in Philippi (Philippians 4:15–16). The church in Philippi had generously given to the Jerusalem offering. They also sent a delegation to Rome to check on Paul, which included Epaphroditus, who came to minister to Paul. Epaphroditus became seriously ill, either while he was on his journey to Rome or while he was with Paul. Paul sent Epaphroditus back to Philippi for his health, and sent his letter to the church there with him.[3]

MacArthur identifies five purposes for Paul's letter to the church in Philippi. First, Paul wrote to say thanks for their generous gifts. Second, Paul wanted to explain why he sent Epaphroditus back to Philippi. Third, Paul wanted to give them an update of his circumstances in Rome. Fourth, Paul encouraged them toward unity. Fifth, Paul warned the believers there against the dangers of false teachers.[4] Paul also wrote about the *Exalted One* (2:5–11) who humbled Himself, even unto death on the cross (Mark 10:45). The second theme of the book is that of joy. The theme is so prevalent Paul used five different Greek words throughout the book for joy, and mentioned joy 15 different times.[5]

Teaching

Philippians 1:1: The first 11 verses contain Paul's greeting. Paul used the word "slave" or "bondservant" to describe his position in Christ (v. 1). MacArthur explains the word "denotes a willing slave who was happily and loyally linked to his master" (James 1:1; 2 Peter 1:1; Jude 1).[6] He addressed "all the saints . . . who are in Philippi, including the overseers and deacons." Paul did not know

[3] MacArthur, 1709–10.

[4] MacArthur, 1710.

[5] MacArthur, 1711.

[6] MacArthur, 1711.

all the believers there because the church had continued to grow since he had been there.

Philippians 1:2–8: He continues with his customary greeting of grace and peace from God the Father and the Lord Jesus Christ (v. 2). His statement in verses 3–6 was not customary but seems to express a very personal relationship between him and the Philippian congregation. He prayed for them without condemnation but with joy because they had never stopped doing the work of Christ from the beginning. Paul had no concern that the church there would go astray from what they had been taught about the work of Christ. They had been real partners with him, and there was deep affection between them (vv. 7–8). The phrase "in the day of Christ Jesus" in verse 6 does not refer to the day of the Lord, but "looks to the final salvation, reward, and glorification of believers."[7]

Philippians 1:9–11: Paul acknowledged he missed them deeply with the "affection of Christ Jesus." This phrase is based on the strongest Greek word "to express compassionate love—a love that involves one's entire being," and "refers to the internal organs, which are the part of the body that reacts to intense emotion."[8] Paul told them he was praying for them, that their love would continue to grow in knowledge and discernment (v. 9). He wanted them to be able to discern what is superior and pure and blameless (v. 10). The result Paul desired was that the Philippians would be filled with God's righteousness and bring glory and praise to Him (v. 11).

Philippians 1:12–26: In verses 12–26, Paul shares his circumstances with the Philippians. First, he explains his being in prison had "resulted in the advance of the gospel" and had shown the imperial guard and the people of Rome that he was in prison for the sake of Christ (vv. 12–13). Second, he shared that other believers had become more fearless in speaking the gospel message after seeing his imprisonment (v. 14). Third, however, Paul's enemies were beginning to speak out against him because they "were jealous of his apostolic power and authority, his success and immense giftedness"[9] (vv. 15–17). Fourth, Paul stated it didn't matter why people preached or what their motives were as long as Christ is still proclaimed! In the remainder of the chapter, Paul gave account of all the hardships he had endured and his desire that no matter what happened in his life, he would bring glory to his Lord, Jesus Christ.

---

[7] MacArthur, 1711–12.

[8] MacArthur, 1712.

[9] MacArthur, 1713.

Closing

Paul stressed that, for him, living meant giving his entire life to Christ's calling, and dying meant being in the presence of his Lord.

The Daily Word

The church of Philippi encouraged and supported Paul during his ministry. As Paul wrote to them, he remembered them with joy and gave thanks to the Lord for them because of their partnership in the gospel.

Today, think back over your walk with the Lord. Remember those people in your life who encouraged and supported your growth in the Lord. You don't have to be a full-time missionary to have people partner with you in the gospel. Perhaps a youth pastor, a teacher at school, a friend from work, or an older sibling encouraged your walk with the Lord. *Take time today to thank the Lord for their partnership in your life.* Next pray for them. Pray for their love to continue to grow in knowledge and discernment so that they can continue to approve the things that are superior, pure, and blameless. Pray they are filled with the fruit of righteousness that comes through Jesus Christ. Then, take time to write them a note or send a quick text letting them know you give thanks to God every time you remember them and the impact they had on your life.

I give thanks to my God for every remembrance of you, always praying with joy for all of you in my every prayer, because of your partnership in the gospel from the first day until now. —Philippians 1:3–5

Further Scripture: Philippians 1:9–11; 2 Timothy 2:1–2; Titus 2:3–4

Questions

1. Paul was confident God would complete the work He began in the saints. Describe the work that God is doing in us and the work we are doing through His equipping (Ephesians 2:10; Philippians 1:6; 2:13; 2 Timothy 2:15; Hebrews 13:20–21).
2. Read Paul's prayer for the church in Philippians 1:9–11. What specific things did he ask for them? Ask the Lord who He would have you pray a similar prayer for, and then start praying this for them regularly.
3. How did Paul's circumstance of imprisonment actually advance the gospel (Philippians 1:12–14)? How have you experienced or witnessed when a difficult situation helped the gospel to be shared?

4. What might it look like for Christ to be preached out of selfish ambition (Philippians 1:17)? What was Paul's response to the gospel being preached this way?
5. Explain Paul's instruction to the Philippians to conduct themselves worthy of the gospel of Christ in Philippians 1:27 (Ephesians 4:1–3; Colossians 1:10).
6. What did the Holy Spirit highlight to you in Philippians 1 through the reading or the teaching?

Lesson 59: Philippians 2

Exalted One: Jesus' Incarnation

Teaching Notes

Intro

Our phrase for Philippians to represent how we see the Lord within the book is *Exalted One* from Philippians 2:9. Chapter 2 is the essential passage for Christians, and it also goes after all the false religions.

Teaching

Philippians 2:1–4: MacArthur summarizes the first four verses as Paul's call "to be united by humility."[1] Verse 1 provides descriptors of what this looks like: "encouragement in Christ," "consolation of love," "fellowship with the Spirit," and "affection and mercy." "Consolation of love" can be understood as "to come alongside and help, counsel, exhort," and refers to "the Lord coming close and whispering words of gentle cheer or tender counsel in a believer's ear."[2] "Fellowship" describes "the partnership of common eternal life provided by the indwelling Holy Spirit."[3] While these statements each begin with "if," it can be understood best as "since." Since the believers already had these things in their lives, Paul gave what their lives would be like when they lived it out in Christ—they would live in complete unity and humility with each other (v. 2). They would think the same (being like-minded), have the same love that Christ has for them, share that same love with others, and share the common goal (intent on one purpose). Achieving these in unity would make Paul's joy complete. Since they were in unity, Paul encouraged them to do nothing that put themselves first to break that unity (v. 3a). They were to see others as more important than themselves (v. 3b–4). MacArthur defines "selfish ambition" as "strife," which leads to "factionalism, rivalry, and partisanship," and defines "conceit" as "empty conceit" that refers to "the pursuit of personal glory, which is the motivation for selfish

[1] John MacArthur, *The MacArthur Bible Commentary* (Nashville: Thomas Nelson, 2005), 1715.

[2] MacArthur, 1715.

[3] MacArthur, 1715.

ambition."[4] "Consider others as more important than yourselves" is "the basic definition of true humility."[5] Paul's instruction does not mean we cannot look after our own interests, but the balance of looking after others with the same passion that we look after our own interests.

Philippians 2:5–11: In verse 5, Paul encouraged the Philippians to live out their lives in selfless humility just as Christ did (Matthew 11:29; John 13:12–17). The early church possibly sang verses 6–11 as a hymn. Christ exists in the form of God (v. 6). Paul used an unusual word for "being" (v. 6 NIV) instead using a Greek word that "emphasizes the essence of a person's nature—his continuous state of condition," and he chose the word for form that "denotes the essential, un-changing character of something—what it is in and of itself."[6] Jesus was, is, and will always be God. But Jesus laid that aside to take on the "form of a slave" and was like men. He emptied Himself of His godly attributes (intentionally), took on the form and frailties of man (without sin), and died on the cross (not for anything He had done, but for what we had done) (vv. 7–8) (Matthew 27:46; 2 Corinthians 8:9; Colossians 1:22; Hebrews 2:14,17; 4:15). John 1:1 expresses this constancy of Godship, and in verse 14 the statement "The Word became flesh" shows Him emptying Himself to take on the form of a man. MacArthur explains what it means theologically for Christ to empty Himself of His Incarnation as God (represented by the term kenosis):

> "This was a self-renunciation, not an emptying Himself of deity nor an exchange of deity for humanity. Jesus did, however, renounce or set aside His privileges in several areas: (1) heavenly glory—while on earth He gave up the glory of a face-to-face relationship with God and the continuous outward display and personal enjoyment of that glory; (2) independent authority—during His Incarnation Christ completely submitted Himself to the will of His Father; (3) divine prerogatives—He set aside the voluntary display of His divine attributes and submitted Himself to the Spirit's direction; (4) eternal riches—while on earth Christ was poor and owned very little; and (5) a favorable relationship with God—He felt the Father's wrath for human sin while on the cross."[7]

Wiersbe describes those in Scripture who did not have the attitude of Christ, and who were actually the opposite of Christ:

---

[4] MacArthur, 1715.

[5] MacArthur, 1715.

[6] MacArthur, 1715.

[7] MacArthur, 1716.

1. Lucifer (Isaiah 14:12–15): "He was once the highest of the angelic beings close to the throne of God, but he desired to be on the throne of God. Lucifer said, 'I will!' But Jesus said, 'Thy will.'"[8]
2. Adam (Genesis 3:1–7): "Lucifer was not satisfied to be a rebel himself; he invaded Eden and tempted man to be a rebel. Adam had all that he needed; he was actually the 'king' of God's creation, but Satan said, 'You will be like God!'"[9]

John Henry Jowett said, "Ministry that costs nothing, accomplishes nothing."[10] Both Lucifer and Adam wanted to jump to the top. Lucifer tried to tempt Jesus to do the same. Yet Jesus gave up His life for us. It cost Him everything.

In verse 9, God made Jesus the *Exalted One* for what He had done and put Him above every name, those in heaven, and on earth, and under the earth. All people, regardless of whether they have accepted Christ as Savior and Lord, will bow before Him and confess that He is Lord (vv. 10–11). All people include "the angels in heaven (Revelation 4:2–9), the spirits of the redeemed (Revelation 4:10–11), obedient believers on earth (Romans 10:9), the disobedient rebels on earth (2 Thessalonians 1:7–9), demons and lost humanity in hell (1 Peter 3:18–22)."[11] They will ALL bow to Christ.

Closing

Wiersbe emphasizes, "Others is the key word in the vocabulary of the Christian."[12] The bottom line is our relationship with Christ determines how we are to live with one another:

- We are to prefer one another (Romans 12:10).
- We are to edify one another (1 Thessalonians 5:11).
- We are to bear one another's burdens (Galatians 6:2).
- We are not to judge one another (Romans 14:13).

When you have the attitude to love others and put them first, that is when you'll have the attitude of Jesus Christ. I pray that as we reflect the emptying that

---

[8] Warren W. Wiersbe, The Bible Exposition Commentary: Ephesians–Revelation (Colorado Springs: David C. Cook, 2003), 74.

[9] Wiersbe, 74.

[10] Wiersbe, 74.

[11] MacArthur, 1717.

[12] Wiersbe, 74.

Christ did as He loved us, we will empty ourselves as well. May the only thing others see is Christ in our lives.

The Daily Word

"Consider others as more important than yourselves." These words from Paul are pretty countercultural. Everything in today's culture says: me first, bigger, more, better, improve yourself, help yourself, and strengthen yourself. And yet the Lord says, *make your attitude like Jesus*. Jesus humbled Himself. He submitted to walk in obedience to the point of death, something He certainly didn't earn or deserve. He put the needs of the entire world above His own life and gave everything up. That's the attitude of Jesus—completely surrendered in humility.

As you go through your day, ask yourself: *Am I considering others more important than myself? Am I walking in humility? Am I looking out for others' interests and not just my own?* It can be convicting. However, this perspective puts people and tasks in proper alignment. Hold the door open for someone or be the last person to get in line. Pause before you speak and listen to hear the heart of a person. Act in obedience, even if it means giving up your schedule. Do something without being recognized. The Lord says to humble yourself, and in due time, the Lord will lift you up. Rest in this promise.

Do nothing out of rivalry or conceit, but in humility consider others as more important than yourselves. Everyone should look out not only for his own interests, but also for the interests of others. —Philippians 2:3–5

Further Scripture: Philippians 2:5–8; James 4:6; 1 Peter 5:6–7

Questions

1. Put in your own words the attitude Christ Jesus had and we too are to have (John 6:38; 17:5; Philippians 2:3, 5–8). Who exalted Christ above all others (Ephesians 1:20–22; Philippians 2:9–11)? How will this be displayed to the glory of God the Father?
2. Paul encouraged the Philippians to continue to work out their salvation with fear and trembling (Philippians 2:12–13). How does Ephesians 6:5–6 help you understand what that should be like?
3. How does Philippians 2:14 convict or challenge you? What is the outcome when we do this? (Philippians 2:15–16)
4. What does it mean in Philippians 2:15, "you shine like stars in the world"? (Matthew 5:14–16; John 8:12; Ephesians 5:8; Colossians 1:13)

5. The words "joy" and "rejoice" are mentioned by Paul multiple times throughout Philippians (joy—Philippians 1:4, 25; 2:2, 29; 4:1) (rejoice—Philippians 1:18; 2:17, 18, 28; 3:1; 4:4, 10). Why do you think Paul put this emphasis on joy and rejoicing? Do you experience joy and practice rejoicing regularly, and if not, how can you change that?
6. What did the Holy Spirit highlight to you in Philippians 2 through the reading or the teaching?

WEEK 78

Lesson 60: Philippians 3

Exalted One: Reaching for the Goal

Teaching Notes

Intro

Our one word or phrase for the book of Philippians is *Exalted One.* In chapter 3, Paul continues to speak into the Philippians about doing the will of God. Wiersbe divides chapter 3 into three sections: Paul's past (vv. 1–11); Paul's present (vv. 12–16); and Paul's future (vv. 17–21).[1]

Teaching

Philippians 3:1–11: Wiersbe describes Paul, looking at his past, as "the accountant," with the outcome being new values.[2] Paul explains he was writing to look out for them—to protect them (v. 1). His concern was about the Judaizers who blended faith and works together into one view of Christianity (v. 2). Paul used three terms for them. First, Paul called them "dogs," the same term the Jews used for Gentiles. By using the term "dogs," Paul was "comparing these false teachers to the dirty scavengers so contemptible to decent people."[3] Wiersbe explains these false teachers "snapped at Paul's heels and followed him from place to place 'barking' their false doctrines."[4] Second, Paul called them "evil workers" who "taught that the sinner was saved by faith *plus* good works, especially the work of the law."[5] Paul explained that their good works were really evil works because it put the emphasis on what the workers did instead of what Christ did for them. Finally, Paul called them "those who mutilate the flesh." The Judaizers taught that circumcision was required for salvation, while Jesus' death on the cross replaced the requirement for physical circumcision with spiritual circumcision. Wiersbe sums up the problems with the Judaizers' teaching: "The Bible has nothing good

[1] Warren W. Wiersbe, *The Bible Exposition Commentary: Ephesians–Revelation* (Colorado Springs: David C. Cook, 2003), 83.

[2] Wiersbe, 83.

[3] Wiersbe, 84.

[4] Wiersbe, 84.

[5] Wiersbe, 84.

to say about 'flesh,' and yet most people today depend entirely on what they themselves can do to please God. Flesh only corrupts God's way on earth. It profits nothing as far as spiritual life is concerned. It has nothing good in it. No wonder we should put no confidence in the flesh!"[6]

Paul explains that "we" (the believers) "are the circumcision" and therefore do not put any confidence in physical circumcision (v. 3). Paul went on to explain that he had once depended upon his own circumcision and his position as a Jew to be right with God (vv. 4–6). At one time, Paul could have boasted about his achievements under the law. Wiersbe states, "People who depend on religion are usually boasting about what they have done. The true Christian has nothing of which to boast. His boast in only in Christ!"[7] Paul had been a true Jew; now he was a complete Christian, and he lived by a new standard. Wiersbe describes this change in Paul: "When he looked at himself or looked at others, Saul of Tarsus considered himself to be righteous. But one day he saw himself as compared with Jesus Christ! It was then that he changed his evaluations and values, and abandoned 'works righteousness' for the righteousness of Jesus Christ."[8]

Paul then shared all he had gained through spiritual circumcision. First, Paul had received the surpassing value of knowing Jesus Christ our Lord—he had gained a personal relationship with Christ (v. 8a). Second, Paul had received the righteousness from God that is based on faith in Christ Jesus (v. 9). Third, Paul was now in fellowship with Christ (v. 10). There was nothing Paul could do to receive these things; it came only as a gift of grace from Jesus Christ. Paul's goal was "to know Him and the power of His resurrection!" Paul was willing to suffer for Jesus because he knew Him personally. Like an accountant, Paul counted all the blessings he had received from Christ in the past.

Philippians 3:12–16: In these verses, Wiersbe describes Paul's present as "the athlete" with "new vigor."[9] Paul explains he has not yet attained the goal of being fully mature spiritually but that he works toward that goal with every effort in Christ (v. 12). He describes himself as a runner pressing toward the finish line (v. 13). Note Paul had only ONE goal and he spent his time focusing on that one goal—"the prize promised by God's heavenly call in Christ Jesus" (v. 14). Paul encouraged the Philippians to live the same way (v. 15).

---

[6] Wiersbe, 85.

[7] Wiersbe, 85.

[8] Wiersbe, 86.

[9] Wiersbe, 83.

Philippians 3:17–21: In these verses, Wiersbe describes Paul's future as "the alien" with a "new vision."[10] Paul encourages his readers to follow and imitate him, not the Judaizers (v. 18). Paul describes the enemy teachers in verse 19: "Their end is destruction; their god is their stomach; their glory is in their shame. They are focused on earthly things." But we as believers are citizens in heaven. We do not run to win that citizenship because it is already ours. Therefore, we are aliens here on earth, but our home is in heaven (v. 20).

Closing

Paul emphasized he was who he was BECAUSE of Christ:

- Paul knew he had been *accepted in Christ* (John 1:12; 15:15; Romans 5:1). He could renounce the lie that he was rejected, unloved, dirty, or shameful because in Christ, the truth is, that he is completely accepted by Christ.
- Paul knew he had been *made secure in Christ* (Romans 8:1–2, 28, 33–34). He could renounce the lie that he was guilty, unprotected, alone, or abandoned, because in Christ, he was totally secure.
- Paul knew he was *significant in Christ* (Matthew 5:13–14; John 15:5, 16; Acts 1:8). He could renounce the lie that he was worthless, inadequate, helpless, or hopeless, because in Christ, he was significant.

You too have been accepted by Christ. You too have been made secure in Christ. And you too are significant in Christ.

The Daily Word

Are you a person with goals? After Jesus transformed Paul, his life was no longer about his accomplishments and achievements. He considered those a loss compared to knowing Jesus Christ his Lord. Paul clearly stated his life goals: *knowing Jesus personally, experiencing the power of the resurrection, partnering with Jesus' suffering, and being conformed even to His death.*

As you go through life, the world may entice you to set goals for your career, to achieve a certain lifestyle, to travel with your family, or even for retirement. However, Paul emphasized, none of "the stuff" really mattered to him for his own life. He had one thing on his mind and that was *to know Jesus Christ fully*—even if knowing Christ fully meant suffering, dying to himself daily, or physically dying. Paul desired to live out the resurrected power of Jesus every day of his

[10] Wiersbe, 83.

life. He didn't look back but focused on the future instead. Today, ask the Lord to reveal to you a goal for your life. As you fix your eyes on Jesus, *what's your one thing?* Write it down, post it where you will see it, and then ask the Lord to help you go after it.

My goal is to know Him and the power of His resurrection and the fellowship of His sufferings, being conformed to His death, assuming that I will somehow reach the resurrection from among the dead. —Philippians 3:10–11

Further Scripture: Psalm 27:4; Matthew 6:33; Philippians 3:13–14

Questions

1. Who did Paul refer to as "dogs" in Philippians 3:2 (Acts 15:1)? What were the evil workers teaching (Galatians 6:12–13)?
2. What were Paul's credentials that allowed him to boast about his flesh more than anyone else? How did Paul's attitude about those things change when he met Jesus?
3. Where are Christians not to place their confidence? Where should your confidence be placed? What or who do you put your confidence in more than Christ?
4. What benefits did Paul experience when he started following Christ?
5. What one thing did Paul want to do? Is this your way of thinking too?
6. Where is your true citizenship located? What will happen when you get there?
7. What did the Holy Spirit highlight to you in Philippians 3 through the reading or the teaching?

WEEK 78

Lesson 61: Philippians 4

Exalted One: Everyday Reminders

Teaching Notes

Intro

This is the last chapter of the book of Philippians. This letter was not written to a church in crisis but was a letter of appreciation and encouragement. As Paul wrapped up the letter, he built momentum in the encouragement to keep spreading the good news. In chapter 4, Paul gave some last minute, basic everyday reminders that were necessary for the church to mature.

Think about some of the everyday reminders in our world today:

- Employees must wash hands before returning to work.
- Please do not feed the animals.
- Caution—Hot Coffee
- Zero Entry Pool—No Diving
- Please turn off the lights when leaving

We know these things—they're obvious! But people still think we need to be reminded. Paul left his readers a list of reminders that were important to remember.

Teaching

Philippians 4:1–2: Paul's words were for "my beloved" (v. 1 NASB). Paul ministered with the Philippians and helped them build the church there. He had a long-term relationship with them, which allowed him to speak into them and made them willing to listen. Paul referred to them as "my joy and my crown," a reminder of all they had accomplished together. Paul used the word "entreat" (ESV) meaning to address, to speak to, to instruct or teach, before addressing an estrangement between two women, Euodia and Syntyche (v. 2). We don't know what their disagreement was about, and it's the only time Paul gave names. He then gave instruction equally without taking sides. The language he used was a gentle reminder. In verse 2, Paul asked them to agree with each other in the Lord.

His first everyday reminder then was: Pursue unity within the body. He wanted the women to model to the leaders how to maintain unity before their disagreement got out of hand.

Philippians 4:3: Paul used the phrase "true companion" (ESV) to show the relationship he had with his church leaders, that enabled him to speak into and encourage them. He was saying, "Hey, Skipper, remember the good old days when we labored together? Can you go help these women out?" His second everyday reminder is: Good relationships are relational currency.

Philippians 4:4: Paul instructed them to show great joy in the Lord. The everyday reminder is: Don't be a party pooper. In other words, do not bring discouragement to a joyous occasion!

Philippians 4:5–6: Be reasonable, and don't let anxiousness rule you. Doesn't anxiousness produce unreasonableness at times? If you've ever been anxious or been around someone who is anxious, you'll know that anxiety can make some decisions seem irrational. I believe reasonableness in the context of anxiousness is an antidote. The everyday reminder is: Keep calm. Be steady. Stay ready (with prayer).

Philippians 4:7: This everyday reminder is: Allow God to overwhelm you with His peace.

Philippians 4:8: Paul told the Philippians to dwell on what is true, honorable, just, pure, lovely, commendable, excellent, and worthy of praise. The everyday reminder is: Do the right thing. Stay true to what you believe and know about the Lord.

Philippians 4:9: Paul told them to practice the things they had learned because he had given them this list of reminders of what to do. Reminder: Do the right thing. Everything Paul reminded them of had purpose and had a greater meaning connected to the reminder.

Philippians 4:10–20: Paul thanked the Philippians for sending him money when he apparently didn't specifically request it. Imagine the emotions and the affirmation of his leadership he must have felt as he wrote this. The people he poured into over several trips were living out the example he set and were now pouring back into his life. It seems they were looking for an opportunity to bless Paul and thank him for his ministry to them. Paul wanted the people around him to be blessed for the fruit they harvested.

Closing

God knows the needs of doing ministry. Sometimes, He will put in our mind who to bless and how much, only to find out later that was the exact need of the recipient. Paul wrote this letter to the Philippians as a way to encourage them and thank them for walking along side of him in ministry.

The Daily Word

Peace comes from Jesus. You can search the entire world, but only Jesus' peace will satisfy. To paraphrase Paul's words, "Don't worry. Pray. Give thanks. Make your requests known to God." Then begin to praise and thank the Lord. It's from this place of humility, surrender, and gratefulness that the God of peace will come upon you. Is it a formula? No. Is it law? No. It's a promise. Paul says, "*Do what you have learned, received, heard and seen in me, and the God of peace will be with you.*"

Each day may bring new things to worry about—the "what ifs" and "I don't knows" of life. But remember, nothing good comes from worrying. Really. So just stop. Make your requests known to God. From that moment on, just give thanks. Focus your thoughts on whatever is true, honorable, just, pure, lovely, commendable, and morally excellent. Don't waste your time thinking about the junk you worry about! As you focus on what is lovely and true, Jesus' peace will come. Try it today, and witness the Lord transform your mind and your heart.

Don't worry about anything, but in everything, through prayer and petition with thanksgiving, let your requests be made known to God. And the peace of God, which surpasses every thought, will guard your hearts and minds in Christ Jesus. —Philippians 4:6–7

Further Scripture: Matthew 6:34; Ephesians 5:20; Philippians 4:8–9

Questions

1. Where did Paul, here on earth, derive his joy from (1 Thessalonians 2:19–20; 3:9)?
2. What are Christians to do in the midst of all situations and circumstances (John 16:33; James 1:2–4)?
3. What is a great antidote to anxiety (Psalm 1:2; Matthew 6:26–33)? What is the result of trusting God with all our anxieties and worries? (Isaiah 26:3)
4. What are things that, as Paul mentioned, Christians should be thinking about? What does it mean to think on whatever is true? (John 16:13; 17:17; Ephesians 4:20–21; 2 Timothy 2:25)

5. What is the context behind Philippians 4:13? How was Paul able to do all things (2 Corinthians 12:10; Galatians 2:20; Ephesians 3:16–20)? Does that work for us too? Why?
6. Why did Paul say God would provide all the needs of the Philippians (Proverbs 3:9; Philippians 4:18)? Have you or your church ever experienced God supplying your needs in times when you knew without a doubt that it was God?
7. What did the Holy Spirit highlight to you in Philippians 4 through the reading or the teaching?

WEEK 79

Lesson 62: Colossians 1

Firstborn: The Firstborn

Teaching Notes

Intro

We are continuing to look at Paul's letters, with his letter to the Colossians, who were so named as inhabitants of the city of Colosse. There is a good chance Paul never visited Colosse. This letter was to be read to the church in Colosse and by the neighboring church in Laodicea (Colossians 4:16). Paul wrote Colossians and Philemon in AD 60–62 when he was a prisoner in Rome (Colossians 4:3, 10, 18; Philemon 1, 9, 10, 23).[1] Colossians and Philemon mention the same people: Timothy, Aristarchus, Archippus, Mark, Epaphras, Luke, Onesimus, and Demas,[2] the people Paul both ministered and surrounded himself with.

The city of Colosse was located in what is now modern-day Turkey. MacArthur wrote, "Colosse was . . . about 100 miles east of Ephesus in the region of the seven churches of Revelation 1–3."[3] The city lay alongside the Lycus River surrounded by valleys and mountains. Colosse was a thriving city in the fifth century as a manufacturer of black wool and dyes and a main junction on the trade routes. During Paul's day Gentiles primarily populated the main route through Laodicea and the surrounding settlement area. This is important to note because with a mixed population of Jews and Gentiles there was a greater opportunity for heresy to arise. There would have been a temptation to intermix Jewish legalism and pagan mysticism with new teachings of Christianity.[4]

The church at Colosse was started during Paul's three-year missionary journey in Ephesus. The church was not founded by Paul but rather Epaphras (Colossians 1:5–7), who had accepted Christ when Paul was teaching in Ephesus. Several years after the church was founded, a heresy arose that threatened the church. The main heresy spreading through the church was Gnosticism, the belief "God is good, but matter is evil, that Jesus Christ was merely one of a series

[1] John MacArthur, *The MacArthur Bible Commentary* (Nashville: Thomas Nelson, 2005), 1729.

[2] MacArthur, 1729.

[3] MacArthur, 1729.

[4] MacArthur, 1729.

of emanations descending from God and being less than God (a belief that led them to deny His true humanity), and that a secret, higher knowledge above scripture was necessary for enlightenment and salvation."[5]

The church in Colosse also incorporated Jewish legalism into their fundamental beliefs. MacArthur wrote that the Colossians had embraced "the necessity of circumcision for salvation, observance of the ceremonial rituals of the OT law (dietary laws, festivals, Sabbaths), and rigid asceticism."[6] The Colossians also worshipped angels and mystical events. Epaphras found the direction of the Colossian church so upsetting that he journeyed to Rome to seek instruction and counsel from Paul. This is a cool picture of submission and discipleship.

Colossians, along with Ephesians, Philippians, and Philemon, are referred to as prison epistles because Paul wrote them during his imprisonment in Rome. Colossians was written as a warning against the heresy they faced. Epaphras did not return the letter; rather, Tychicus and Onesimus returned it. Onesimus was a runaway slave who was being returned to his master Philemon, who was a member of the Colossian church.[7]

We always have one word that we use for each book. The word we are using for Colossians is *Firstborn.*

Teaching

Colossians 1:1–14: I am not going to teach on the first 14 verses. Paul's greeting is in the first few verses. Then in verses 3–8 Paul expressed thankfulness and was very complimentary to the church. In verses 9–14 Paul had a prayer. These verses were to serve as an edifying word and encouragement. Then there comes a transition into addressing heresy in the rest of the chapter.

Colossians 1:15–23: These verses are about the deity of Christ. The Colossians questioned whether or not Jesus was really God. Remember, Gnosticism denies the deity of Christ. But Jesus is God. The meaning of the word "image" (v. 15) used here in the Greek also means copy or likeness. MacArthur wrote, "Jesus Christ is the perfect image—the exact likeness—of God and is in the very form of God (John 1:14; 14:9; Philippians 2:6), and had been so from all eternity. . . . Paul emphasizes that [Jesus] is both the representation and manifestation of God. . . . He is fully God in every way"[8]

---

[5] MacArthur, 1729.

[6] MacArthur, 1729.

[7] MacArthur, 1730.

[8] MacArthur, 1733.

I really want us to focus on the word *Firstborn* used in verse 15. MacArthur wrote, "The Greek word for firstborn can refer to one who was born first chronologically but most often refers to preeminence in position or rank."[9] In the Greek and Jewish culture Paul was writing to, the "firstborn" was the son who was left an inheritance, regardless of birth order. For example, the nation of Israel would be considered the "first nation." Although they are not the first nation to exist, they were the chosen people of God (Exodus 4:22; Jeremiah 3:19).[10]

MacArthur wrote,

> Firstborn in this context clearly means highest rank, not first created (cf. Psalm 89:27; Revelation 1:5) for several reasons: (1) Christ cannot be both "first begotten" and "only begotten" (cf. John 1:14, 18; 3:16, 18; 1 John 4:9); (2) when the "firstborn" is one of a class, the class is in the plural form (cf. v. 18; Romans 8:29), but "creation," the class here, is in a singular form; (3) if Paul was teaching that Christ was a created being, he was agreeing with the heresy he was writing to refute; and (4) it is impossible for Christ to be both created and the Creator of everything (v. 16). Thus, Jesus is the firstborn in the sense that He has the preeminence (v. 18) and possesses the right of inheritance "over all creation" (cf. Hebrews 1:2; Revelation 5:1–7, 13).[11]

Closing

God made the universe through Christ. God came in human flesh to give up His body so we can be forgiven. We barely scratched the surface of this chapter. Hopefully this will paint a picture of where you can begin studying more about Christ and His deity.

The Daily Word

Sometimes in this crazy world where truth becomes blurred, *you need to refocus.* What is actual truth? Go back to God's Word to strengthen and establish what you believe. Paul went back to the basics with the church in Colossae. He emphasized Christ is supreme over creation because *He created everything.* Yes, God created everything in heaven and on earth, the invisible and the visible—thrones, dominions, rulers, and authorities. Truth to remember: *God created everything.*

---

[9] MacArthur, 1733.

[10] MacArthur, 1733.

[11] MacArthur, 1733–34.

When things in your life seem overwhelming, remember, as the firstborn over all creation, *Christ is before all things, and by Him all things hold together.* Truth to remember: *Jesus holds all things together.* He is there in the mess. He is there in the joy. Jesus is holding all things together at all times. He holds things together because He loves you, He cares for you, and *He created it all.* Try to picture God holding all things together in your life. Trust God to be the superglue and rubber band for your life. He's with you, holding all things together in your life because His love for you will never fail.

For everything was created by Him, in heaven and on earth, the visible and the invisible, whether thrones or dominions or rulers or authorities—all things have been created through Him and for Him. He is before all things, and by Him all things hold together. —Colossians 1:16–17

Further Scripture: John 1:2–3; Romans 8:28; Hebrews 1:1–3

Questions

1. In Colossians 1:7–9, what was Paul's response to the news he received from Epaphras about the church in Colossae? What did he specifically pray for them (Colossians 1:9–12)?
2. How has God qualified (enabled) us to share in the inheritance of the saints (Romans 5:8; Ephesians 2:8–9; Colossians 1:12)? Do you ever forget that Christ is the One who already met the requirements for salvation? (Colossians 2:10)
3. How would you explain to someone that Christ is the image of the invisible God (John 14:9; Colossians 1:15; 2:9; Hebrews 1:3)? How are we made into the image of Christ? (Romans 8:29; 2 Corinthians 3:18; Galatians 3:27; Ephesians 4:22–24)
4. In Colossians 1:21–22, how are those reconciled to God through Christ's death presented to Him? In Colossians 1:23, why do you think Paul continued his teaching with the words, "If you continue in the faith" (ESV)?
5. What did the Holy Spirit highlight to you in Colossians 1 through the reading or the teaching?

WEEK 79

Lesson 63: Colossians 2

Firstborn: The True Nature of Christ

Teaching Notes

Intro

I want us to go back to the end of Colossians 1 today before we move on to Colossians 2. Paul was describing his ministry—that God made him a steward of sharing the news that Jesus is the *Firstborn* (Colossians 1:15, 25). Paul's job was to share the "mystery" that had been revealed, that the Jews and the Gentiles were to be one in Christ (Colossians 1:26–27). He desired that everyone would mature in Christ and become the image of Him (Colossians 1:28). Paul acknowledged that all he did was through the power of Christ in him (Colossians 1:29). His thought carried on into chapter 2.

Teaching

Colossians 2:1–4: Paul agonized for those he could not get to personally (v. 1). He wanted them to be encouraged and joined in love so they would be assured of their understanding and have the knowledge of God's mystery in Christ (v. 2). Paul prayed that they would have all the treasures of wisdom and knowledge that are found in Christ (v. 3). Paul was in prison and had never met any of those in Colosse and Laodicea, but he prayed with passion for them as though they were his best friends. He explained why he prayed so diligently for them in verse 4—so no one would come in and deceive them with false teachings ("persuasive arguments").

Colossians 2:5: Wiersbe describes verses 5–7 as presenting the "nature of progress" in Christ.[1] Paul told his readers he was with them in spirit and rejoiced over how well they were doing. He then gave three pictures to explain spiritual progress. First, he used the image of an army with the words "ordered" and "strength" in verse 5. Wiersbe explains "ordered" as "the arrangement of the army in ranks, with each soldier in his proper place," while "strength" or "steadfastness" "pictures

[1] Warren W. Wiersbe, *The Bible Exposition Commentary: Ephesians–Revelation* (Colorado Springs: David C. Cook, 2003), 124.

the soldiers in battle formation, presenting a solid front to the enemy."[2] The soldiers were arranged in order and were placed at the front line to fight the enemy—Paul's picture of what believers were to do.

Colossians 2:6: Paul uses the image of the pilgrim who walked along the journey. A pilgrimage was a long journey, and the pilgrim was the one who undertook the journey. Paul exhorted his readers to "walk in Him" on the journey of spiritual growth to maturity (Ephesians 2:2, 10; 4:1; 5:2, 8, 15).

Colossians 2:7: Here, Paul uses multiple images. "Rooted" refers to a tree that has deep and permanent connection to the ground. "Established" or "built up" speaks to a building that has been built on the foundation of faith. "As you were taught" refers to all they had been taught in faith. "Overflowing" creates a picture of a river whose banks have overflowed (Ezekiel 47; John 7:37–39).

Wiersbe summarizes the importance of these images:

> If [a Christian's] spiritual roots are deep in Christ, he will not want any other soil. If Christ is his sure foundation, he has no need to move. If he is studying and growing in the Word, he will not be easily enticed by false doctrine. And if his heart is overflowing with thanksgiving, he will not even consider turning from the fullness he has in Christ. A grounded, growing, grateful believer will not be led astray.[3]

Colossians 2:8–10: Paul warned his readers not to fall prey to those who used philosophy and deceit to persuade them but instead to stay based in Christ (v. 8). Keep your eyes on Christ or those who deceive will take you "captive" by coming in and kidnapping you from the faith.

Closing

Even in the seminary world, there is the danger of getting caught up in acquiring wisdom and losing focus on the relationship with Christ. That is the heart of our desire in reviveSCHOOL—that we pour into the lives of others with Scripture, making disciples in Christ through His truth. Our world today mirrors that of the Colossians, and we have to stay focused on Christ, drawing on the fullness of God's nature that is present in Him (vv. 9–10). Anything else is false teaching, deceitful, and dangerous to His gospel.

---

[2] Wiersbe, 124.

[3] Wiersbe, 125.

The Daily Word

After you receive Christ, you begin to walk with Him and grow in the mystery of the gospel. Like a student studying to become a teacher, a doctor, or a hairstylist, the time comes when you need to walk out what you have learned. Though you will never stop learning, it's time to start using your skills. As a believer who has accepted Christ as Lord and Savior, *start walking in faith as the Lord leads, trusting the Holy Spirit to fill you with all wisdom and knowledge.*

The more you walk in Christ's strength and not your own, *the deeper your roots grow in Him.* The storms may come, but they won't blow you over! You will not be shaken because you are established in your faith. Abide in Christ's presence in order to nourish your roots in Him. Walk with an attitude of praise and thanksgiving, worshipping the Lord your Savior. As you worship the Lord, the peace of Christ will be with you, providing what you need for what lies ahead.

Therefore, as you have received Christ Jesus the Lord, walk in Him, rooted and built up in Him and established in the faith, just as you were taught, overflowing with gratitude. —Colossians 2:6–7

Further Scripture: Jeremiah 17:7–8; Romans 10:9–10; Colossians 2:2

Questions

1. In Colossians 2 (NKJV), Paul used words like "steadfastness" (v. 5), "rooted and built up" (v. 7), "established in the faith" (v. 7), and "complete in Him" (v. 10). What do you think his purpose was?
2. In Colossians 2:3, what did Paul refer to as treasures? How are these things treasures, and where can they be found?
3. How do these treasures protect us from being deceived with well-crafted (persuasive) arguments? (Colossians 2:8)
4. What advantage is there to following religious commandments and teachings of men so that you appear wise or spiritual (Colossians 2:20–23)? Have you ever made decisions based on whether you would appear spiritual, having nothing to do with walking in the Spirit?
5. In regard to the body of Christ, what nourishes and promotes growth? (Ephesians 2:19–22; 4:11–16; Colossians 2:19)
6. What did the Holy Spirit highlight to you in Colossians 2 through the reading or the teaching?

WEEK 79

Lesson 64: Colossians 3

Firstborn: The Danger of Heresy

Teaching Notes

Intro

Paul began to talk in Colossians 3 about the practical applications of the doctrine he presented in chapter 2. For us, that is a big part of why we are doing this school—so we can apply things we're learning from Scripture. I am taken back to King Josiah in 2 Kings 22—23. Josiah found the laws of the Lord and told the Israelites they needed to get back to those teachings. We are calling our people back to walk faithfully in what the Word says. I hope and pray we can apply these things to our lives.

Wiersbe wrote, "We must keep in mind that the pagan religions of Paul's day said little or nothing about personal morality. A worshipper could bow before an idol, put his offering on the altar, and go back to live the same old life of sin. What a person believed had no direct relationship with how he behaved, and no one would condemn a person for their behavior."[1] As Christians, our faith defines how we conduct ourselves.

The previous chapters were written to correct the heresy of Gnosticism, a Greek philosophy that said everything created was inherently evil. Only "spiritual" realities were good. So, they did not believe God created the world or Christ came in a physical body. Paul corrected this by stating clearly that Christ is the creator and sustainer of all, the supreme head over the church and over all authorities.

Gnosticism affected a person's morality in one of two ways:

> Gnostics indulge. Since the body is evil and the spirit is good, nothing done in the body could harm the spirit. They gave into every sensual desire and denied themselves nothing. Because they had God's grace, they could do whatever they wanted with their bodies. We see that today!

[1] Warren W. Wiersbe, *The Bible Exposition Commentary: Ephesians–Revelation* (Colorado Springs: David C. Cook, 2003), 133.

Asceticism reasoned that because the body is bad it should be denied every pleasure. They hoped denial of the body would elevate the spirit. Paul's opponents at Colosse were ascetics. The strict Jewish laws meshed with their harsh, self-denial rituals. Paul warned that such rituals were useless and had no spiritual value (Colossians 2:20–23).

Their rejection of the deity of Christ led them to seek salvation through their intellect or through the abuse of their bodies. This is the backdrop of what Paul was dealing with in Colosse. Paul stressed that it's not about philosophy, legalism, or carnality. It is about Christ.

Teaching

Colossians 3:1–2: "So if" in verse one means "Since then." Because the Colossians knew Christ and had "been raised with the Messiah." they were to "seek what is above" (v. 1). Paul encouraged the church to focus their minds on the eternal realities of heaven because of their relationship with Christ. The word used for "set your affection" emphasized this was an ongoing decision.[2]

Colossians 3:3–4: Paul emphasized that the Colossians old life was dead. The work of the cross was not just to forgive the Colossians from their sin so they could go to heaven. The work of the cross made them a new creation and compelled them to live differently from the way they lived before. Because of their faith in Christ, the Colossians "life is hidden with the Messiah in God" (v. 3). The grammar of the word "hidden" meant it was something God accomplished in the past that had a present reality. Now Jesus "is your life" (v. 4). Paul emphasized this point in Galatians 2:19b–20: "I have been crucified with Christ and I no longer live, but Christ lives in me. The life I now live in the body, I live by faith in the Son of God, who loved me and gave Himself for me." When the Colossians understood that Christ lived in them, it would be a game-changer for how they lived their everyday lives. Jesus said He was the light of the world (John 8:12), but He also told His disciples they were the light of the world (Matthew 5:14). How could both be true? Because Christ indwells believers, His light can shine through us as we live out the reality of Christ in us. We don't have to strive to be light; rather we can simply let His light shine through us.

Paul stated Christ would one day be "revealed." One day Jesus will be seen in His full glory. In the same way, we "will be revealed with Him in glory" (v. 4). Paul seems to be asking, "Why would you want to live for anything else? Jesus has provided us with so much more than we could ever want to live for!"

---

[2] Earl D. Radmacher, Ronald B. Allen, and H. Wayne House, eds., *Nelson's New Illustrated Bible Commentary* (Nashville: Thomas Nelson, 1999), 1566.

Colossians 3:5–9: Because of the gnostic heresy the Colossian church encountered, Paul outlined practices that belonged "to your worldly nature" (v. 5). None of the practices outlined in verse 5 were to characterize the life of the believer. In the event they did, Paul called the Colossians to repent and return to living biblically faithful lives because Jesus had better things for them to walk in. Ephesians 5:3 admonished believers that "sexual immorality and any impurity or greed should not even be heard of among you, as is proper for saints."

Colossians 3:10–11: Paul told his readers to release past habits. The "new self" Christ gave believers bore "the image of your Creator" while the old self was only flesh. This change happened through "knowledge according to the image of your Creator" (v. 10). Ephesians 1:17 says, "I pray that the God of our Lord Jesus Christ, the glorious Father, would give you a spirit of wisdom and revelation in the knowledge of Him."

Colossians 3:12–17: Paul said old habits were to be replaced with new ones. As "God's chosen ones," believers are holy and loved. In light of the salvation they received, the Colossians were to live out their relationship with Jesus. Their lives would be marked by characteristics that marked Jesus' life: compassion, kindness, humility, gentleness, patience, forgiveness, and love (vv. 12–14). Love was to be the highest expression of Christlikeness. All of these characteristics worked themselves out as believers devoted themselves to "teaching and admonishing one another in all wisdom . . . singing psalms, hymns, and spiritual songs, with gratitude in your hearts to God" (v. 16).

Nelson's Commentary says God's peace "rules in our hearts when we are completely surrendered to God's will, and thus our whole being is unified in obedience to Him."[3]

Closing

You have been given everything you need as a follower of Jesus to walk in victory and to live a life worthy of the calling Jesus placed on your life. You don't have to fall back into the old nature. You can walk in your new nature in victory. When Christ is revealed, it will all be worth it!

[3] Radmacher et al., 1567.

The Daily Word

Child of God, you are chosen. You are holy. You are loved. Let that soak in just a minute. Receive these promises over your life today. You don't have a reason to doubt or question. The enemy will put lies in your mind but take those thoughts captive. Believe this today: *You are chosen. You are holy. You are loved.*

Now because you walk with these promises over your life, you have a responsibility to represent Christ's love—to be His hands and feet to others. Therefore put on *compassion, kindness, humility, gentleness, patience,* and *forgiveness.* Put them on like clothing each day! And above all this, *put on love, which binds everything in unity. Above all, love.* Love others just as you have been loved. Remember, you received Christ's love as a gift. Jesus received you just as you are with an unconditional love. He modeled how you are to love others. No matter what you face today, *put on love,* remembering you walk as a chosen, holy, and loved child of God.

Therefore, God's chosen ones, holy and loved, put on heartfelt compassion, kindness, humility, gentleness, and patience, accepting one another and forgiving one another if anyone has a complaint against another. Just as the Lord has forgiven you, so you must also forgive. Above all, put on love—the perfect bond of unity. —Colossians 3:12–14

Further Scripture: 1 Corinthians 13:13; Ephesians 2:8–9; 1 John 5:2–3

Questions

1. Meditate on Colossians 3:5–9. In your own life, is there anything on that list you need to repent of and lay down? If so, take a few minutes now and pray about that.
2. Colossians 3:13 says we must forgive as God has forgiven us. Pray and ask the Lord if there is someone you need to forgive. If someone comes to mind, pray and tell the Lord you choose to forgive them. Do this for anyone who comes to mind.
3. Specific statements were made for the husbands and wives in Colossians 3:18–19. Where else in Scripture is this relationship spoken of (Ephesians 5:22–25)?
4. What did the Holy Spirit highlight to you in Colossians 3 through the reading or the teaching?

WEEK 79

Lesson 65: Colossians 4

Firstborn: The Master/Servant Relationship

Teaching Notes

Intro

Chapter 4 begins in an awkward spot—in the middle of a paragraph. In chapter 3, Paul wrote about rules for Christian households—wives were to submit to their husbands, children were to submit to their parents, and bond servants were to submit to their masters. In Colossians 4:1, Paul ended these household instructions and told the masters of the slaves to be honorable (right and fair) to their servants.

In that context, we will be talking about masters/servants, bosses/workers, and leaders/teams today. Paul was communicating that it is not wise to do ministry alone and is always wise to do ministry as a team. Look at the partnerships and teams represented in Scripture:

- Peter and John
- Peter, John, and the Apostles
- Peter, John, the Apostles, and the men of Cypress and Cyrene
- Aquila and Priscilla
- Timothy and Silas
- Barnabas and Mark
- Barnabas and Paul

I believe Paul was in the business of building teams of people whom he knew could carry the torch of spreading the gospel throughout the world. Not only did Paul practice what he preached in terms of building a team, he also practiced what he preached when it came to maintaining a team—his ongoing leadership of people. Note that Paul was already in a master/bond servant-type relationship. There are three ways we can look at the master/bond servant relationship. A bondservant is (1) someone who was unwillingly serving a master; (2) a servant who was willingly serving a master without compensation; or (3) someone who was willingly serving a master with compensation. For the purpose of this discussion, we'll be looking at the last two options—someone who was willingly serving.

Teaching

Colossians 4:1–4: Paul instructed the masters to treat their servants justly and fairly (v. 1). Justly can be understood as "rightly," and fairly can be understood as "favorably." Ephesians 6:5–9 gives an extended explanation of how masters were to be treated and how masters were to treat their servants—both masters and servants were to treat each other as they would obey Christ, "do God's will from your heart" (v. 6). In Colossians 4:2, Paul instructed them to pray continuously for each other and to be watchful to see how God was using the team. In verses 3–4, Paul asked for prayers for his team ("us") that God would continue to open the door for them to share God's Word, and to give Paul the words to make God's Word clear. Paul then encouraged them to walk in wisdom and speak with graciousness before others (vv. 5–6).

Colossians 4:7–14: In verse 7, Paul began to name his team:

- **Tychicus** (vv. 7–8) was mentioned four times in Paul's letters (Ephesians 6:21–22; Colossians 4:7; 2 Timothy 4:12; Titus 3:12). Paul sent Tychicus to Colosse to bring word of Paul's imprisonment and to encourage the people there. Tychicus must have been dependable and had a shepherd's heart, and Paul wanted to make sure he was treated *fairly*.
- **Onesimus** (v. 9) was previously a slave who ran away from his master, met Paul, and was saved. Paul sent Onesimus with a mentor, Tychicus, and Paul wanted him to be treated *justly* (Philemon 10–12, 17–19).
- **Aristarchus** (v. 10a) accompanied Paul through some of his most difficult circumstances—a riot, imprisonment, a shipwreck—and he stayed with Paul in spite of these. Paul wanted Aristarchus to be treated *rightly* because he had endured a lot and earned their respect.
- **Mark** (v. 10b) wrote the Gospel of Mark and had accompanied Paul on his first journey together with Barnabas as an assistant. John Mark ultimately abandoned them and went home—he quit. Paul refused to take John Mark on the second journey with Barnabas, but was reconciled with him later (2 Timothy 4:11). Since Mark had been restored, he wanted Mark to be treated *justly*.
- **Justus** (v. 11) was a fellow worker and a comfort to Paul. Paul wanted him to be treated *fairly*.

- **Epaphras** (vv. 12–13) was the founder of the church in Colosse (Colossians 1:7–8), and was a servant of Christ (Colossians 4:12). Epaphras was a hard worker and one of Paul's prayer warriors. He was even Paul's roommate. Paul wanted him treated *fairly*.
- **Luke** (v. 14a) wrote the Gospel of Luke and the book of Acts. He accompanied Paul to Jerusalem and to Rome and was a great support partner and encourager. Luke had credibility with the Greeks because he was a physician. Paul wanted him treated *fairly*.
- **Demas** (v. 14b) was labeled as a fellow worker (along with Mark, Luke, and Aristarchus) in Philemon 24, but he fell in love with the world and deserted Paul (2 Timothy 4:10). Note that no adjectives were given to describe him, making it seem he has lost favor with Paul. Paul wanted him to be treated *justly*.

Colossians 4:15–18: In chapter 2, Paul explained he had never met the believers in Laodicea, but he continued to pour into them (v. 15). Paul also instructed that the letter to the Colossians be shared with the Laodiceans and that the Colossians were to read the letter he sent to Laodicea (v. 16). This suggests there may have been another letter from Paul that did not make it into Scripture. Paul then encouraged Archippus, even from a distance, because he had a desire to see God's kingdom grow, and he knew it takes an army of believing laborers to do so (v. 17). This is a great example of leadership and discipleship. This is why we don't do ministry alone! Paul concluded his letter with words of grace.

Closing

Paul had a love for the church, for the laborers who worked within it, and for the cause of Christ. Paul demonstrated this through the way he poured into the churches and laborers and the way he demonstrated concern for them consistently throughout his ministry.

The Daily Word

Paul wrote this letter to the Colossian believers while imprisoned for declaring the gospel message. As he concluded the letter, Paul mentioned several of his coworkers in ministry. Paul was not alone; he had other people alongside him, walking out their faith and using their gifts as ambassadors for the gospel. For example, Tychicus and Onesimus were sent with news about Paul as encouragement. And Paul's teammate, Epaphras, continued to pray for the believers. Paul cared deeply for the believers and gathered like-minded people to help him in his calling.

No matter how you serve the Lord with the gifts He has given you, *surround yourself with others to help walk out your calling*. If you don't have anyone, ask the Lord to provide someone to help you, someone to pray for you, and someone to sharpen you. Just as iron sharpens iron, the Lord created you to work with others to sharpen your own faith. Devote yourself to prayer and continue to give thanks for open doors for the message of Jesus Christ.

I have sent him to you for this very purpose, so that you may know how we are and so that he may encourage your hearts. He is with Onesimus, a faithful and dearly loved brother, who is one of you. They will tell you about everything here. —Colossians 4:8–9

Further Scripture: Colossians 4:12–13; 1 Peter 4:10; 3 John 1:8

Questions

1. In Colossians 4:5, what are some examples of living wisely?
2. How can you make your conversations "gracious, seasoned with salt" (Colossians 4:6)? What do you think this phrase, "seasoned with salt," means? How do we balance these conversations with those who are not "seasoned with salt"?
3. What did the Holy Spirit highlight to you in Colossians 4 through the reading or the teaching?

WEEK 79

Lesson 66: 1 Thessalonians 1

Coming Lord: Greetings and Thanksgiving

Teaching Notes

Intro

This is Paul's first letter to the church at Thessalonica. Paul spent about three weeks, or three Sabbaths, in Thessalonica, which prompted him later to write two letters to this church. We can learn so much from Paul about the steps of beginning a work in a new city: model, assist, watch, and leave. Our phrase for this book is *Coming Lord.* First Thessalonians 4 is a chapter of hope and comfort, because it encourages us to keep our perspective on Jesus as the *Coming Lord*: "We who are still alive at the Lord's coming will certainly have no advantage over those who have fallen asleep" (1 Thessalonians 4:15b). "Fallen asleep" refers to those who have died. Verses 16–17 describe Jesus' return from heaven and the reunion of those both dead and alive with Him. Paul concluded this letter by encouraging the people in Thessalonica to "be kept sound and blameless for the coming of our Lord Jesus Christ" (1 Thessalonians 5:23b).

Paul identifies himself as the writer in two places: 1 Thessalonians 1:1 and 2:18. Silas and Timothy traveled with Paul on his second missionary journey. Acts 17 says that these men visited Thessalonica and started the church in that city. Paul's two letters were written while he was ministering in Corinth around AD 51. According to John MacArthur, "The date has been archaeologically verified by an inscription in the temple of Apollos at Delphi near Corinth."[1] In Acts 18, Paul referred to Gallio, who was proconsul in AD 51. Since Galatians was probably written around AD 50, this letter would have been Paul's second canonical correspondence.

Thessalonica is modern-day Salonica, a modern city with an old look located by the water. It lies near the ancient site of Therma on the Thermaic Gulf, which reaches into the Aegean Sea. It became the capital of Macedonia in 168 BC. They enjoyed the status of a "free city," meaning they were ruled by their own citizenry.[2] This is supported by Acts 17:5–9, which states that some of the Jews "dragged

[1] John MacArthur, *The MacArthur Bible Commentary* (Nashville: Thomas Nelson, 2005), 1747.

[2] MacArthur, 1747.

Jason and some of the brothers before the city officials." Thessalonica was part of the Roman Empire and was referred to as "the mother of all Macedonia."[3] Two hundred thousand people lived in the area. Paul travelled from Philippi to Thessalonica, a distance of roughly 100 miles.

As was his custom, when Paul entered the city, he looked for a synagogue where he could teach the gospel to the local Jews. Acts 17:1–4 paints the best picture of Paul's entry into the city. For three Sabbaths, Paul proclaimed Jesus as the Messiah in the synagogue. Some of the Jews, as well as the Greeks and God-fearing women, joined Paul in believing the gospel. The Jewish leadership then became jealous, formed a mob, and started riots in the city until they brought Jason and some of the other brothers before the city officials. The brothers sent Paul and Silas away to Berea. Paul then traveled on to Athens while Silas and Timothy stayed in Berea. Silas and Timothy eventually joined Paul in Athens. Later Timothy was sent back to Thessalonica and Silas back to Philippi. In Acts 18, Paul went on to Corinth (v. 1), where Timothy and Silas joined him (v. 5). Paul wrote the first letter to the Thessalonians after Timothy brought a report to him about the status of the church in Thessalonica.

Teaching

1 Thessalonians 1:1–4: Paul began the letter with his usual greeting, "Grace to you and peace" (v. 1). Paul said he constantly remembered them in his prayers (v. 2). He never stopped praying for the churches he established. Paul recognized their "work of faith, labor of love, and endurance of hope in our Lord Jesus Christ" (v. 3). As Paul traveled, he heard how well these new believers were doing. Their "work produced by faith" indicated they were hearing something from the Holy Spirit and walking it out. Their "labor motivated by love" meant they were actually doing something to express their love. And all the while, they were holding onto their hope. They were anchored in the Lord.

1 Thessalonians 1:5–8: Even though Paul spent only three weeks in Thessalonica, the believers there became an example "to all the believers in Macedonia and Achaia" (v. 7) because God did something special there. We have four words that describe the steps Paul took: model, assist, watch, and leave.

Model: In verse 5a, Paul modeled the gospel for them in word, in power, and in the Holy Spirit with assurance, conviction, and passion. People need to hear the gospel (Romans 10:17), and Paul modeled sharing the Word. If we truly believe Christ went through death, burial, and resurrection, then we need to speak about it (2 Corinthians 4:13). Paul also came to them in power. This word comes from

[3] MacArthur, 1747.

the Greek word *dunamis* meaning the force, might, ability, and strength that inherently resides in something by its very nature. In other words, the Spirit of God gave them power and enabled them to share the gospel. We need the power of God (Acts 1:8) to be His witnesses. Not only does the Spirit enable us to share the gospel, but the gospel is the power of God. They are interchangeable. Romans 8:14 says, "All those led by God's Spirit are God's sons." As we share the gospel, we must do so with much assurance, confidence, conviction, and passion because we actually believe the gospel. The Spirit of God brings forth the fire when we believe that everything about the gospel is true.

Assist: We can't lead people from afar. We have to get in the mix, into the streets and neighborhoods, to share the gospel. Paul assisted them in the process of sharing the gospel (v. 5b).

Watch: The Thessalonians became imitators of Paul and of the Lord, welcoming the message with joy from the Holy Spirit. Paul was able to watch them as they began to imitate the faith Paul modeled.

Leave: From Thessalonica, the message went all over Macedonia and Achaia and "in every place that your faith in God has gone out" (v. 8). Who knows how far their witness extended? Even though Paul and Silas left Thessalonica, the message continued to spread. That was an effective move of God.

1 Thessalonians 1:9–10: They turned to God from idols (v. 9) and were waiting in confident hope for Jesus' return (v. 10). This is a message we can replicate wherever we go: model, assist, watch, and leave. But it starts and ends with Jesus.

Closing

This is why I get excited about 1 Thessalonians, because even though Paul only spent 3 weeks with the people that lived there, it was enough for them to be an effective witness for Jesus. I pray you're encouraged as well.

The Daily Word

When you share the gospel with others, you don't share with just words and methods. You testify with the Holy Spirit's power and passion. Christ's power transforms lives. As the Lord leads you to share the gospel, remember it's not about you or how well you articulate the message. It's the passion, it's the testimony, and it's the Holy Spirit's presence and power *working through you and working in the lives of those listening* to the good news. *The Holy Spirit touches hearts*, not the fancy words.

It's in the moments when the Holy Spirit's power moves that lives will change. Therefore, live out your testimony to others. When you walk in obedience—when you walk in the power of the Holy Spirit, the message of your faith in God will travel. If you want to see change in your community, in your family, or in your marriage, then walk in the power of the Holy Spirit with deep conviction, in humility, in faith, in love, and in hope. As you endure all things, the Holy Spirit's power will touch and transform lives!

For our gospel did not come to you in word only, but also in power, in the Holy Spirit, and with much assurance. You know what kind of men we were among you for your benefit. . . . For the Lord's message rang out from you, not only in Macedonia and Achaia, but in every place that your faith in God has gone out. —1 Thessalonians 1:5, 8

Further Scripture: 1 Corinthians 2:4; 1 Thessalonians 1:3; 2 Timothy 1:7–8

Questions

1. How was the church in Thessalonica started (Acts 17:1–9)?
2. Since Paul's initial converts were Jewish, what did he make sure they understood perfectly (Acts 17:2–3; 1 John 2:13)?
3. What characteristics of the church in Thessalonica made it such a joy to Paul?
4. How did the gospel come to those in Thessalonica (1 Thessalonians 1:5)? Why can you feel confident sharing the gospel with others (Isaiah 55:11; Matthew 28:19–20; Romans 1:16; 1 Corinthians 2:4–5)? Serving others in the name of Jesus is wonderful and beneficial, but why is it also important to eventually speak the gospel (Romans 10:13–17)?
5. What were the dangers that Paul noticed among the Thessalonians? Compare 1 Thessalonians 1:3 to 1 Thessalonians 1:9–10.
6. What did the Holy Spirit highlight to you in 1 Thessalonians 1 through the reading or the teaching?

WEEK 79

Lesson 67: 1 Thessalonians 2

Coming Lord: Paul Modeled Discipleship

Teaching Notes

Intro

The church at Thessalonica was a baby church, and Paul wanted to come alongside them and help them grow. In this chapter, Paul talks to them about perseverance through tribulation. In chapter 1, Paul came to the church as an evangelist. In this chapter, Paul reveals himself as a shepherd who is getting them ready for the *Coming Lord*.

Teaching

1 Thessalonians 2:1–6: Warren Wiersbe said Paul revealed himself as the faithful steward in these verses.[1] Evidently, Paul's motives for coming to Thessalonica were questioned and challenged, probably by the Jews and pagan Gentiles, after Paul left the city. Paul responded by saying his visit had not been in vain (v. 1). Even though Paul suffered outrageous treatment in Philippi, he preached the gospel with boldness in Thessalonica (v. 2). This spiteful treatment was described in Acts 16:22–24. Paul's exhortation (admonition and encouragement) was a comforting and strengthening presence for this young church (v. 3). Paul didn't speak from error (which basically means leading someone astray) or uncleanliness (referring to impurity in a moral or lustful sense or with wrong motives) or in deceit (this word describes a lure, like a fishing lure used to bait or trick the fish).

Paul said that first of all they had been "approved by God to be entrusted with the gospel" (v. 4). "Approved" is the Greek word *dokimázō*, which means to test, to examine, or to scrutinize to see whether or not a thing is genuine. Because of what Paul experienced, he felt that he was approved, that he had passed the test, and that he had been entrusted with the gospel. As followers of Christ, we have also been entrusted with the gospel and approved to carry this message forth. In 2 Corinthians 5:17–21, Paul said believers are new creations in Christ

[1] Warren W. Wiersbe, *The Wiersbe Bible Commentary: New Testament* (Colorado Springs: David C. Cook, 2007), 708.

who have become Christ's ambassadors to carry the message of reconciliation to the world. Paul did not preach the gospel using flattering speech to please men in order to gain a following for himself (v. 5). He knew God tested the heart. The only thing that mattered to Paul was pleasing the Lord. He wanted the words from his mouth to be truth, and he didn't worry about how people would react. King David also hated the sin of flattery as revealed in Psalm 12:2: "They speak vanity every one with his neighbour: with flattering lips and with a double heart do they speak" (KJV). In 2 Timothy 4:3–4, Paul warned Timothy that a day would come when they would not "tolerate sound doctrine but . . . they will turn away from hearing the truth and will turn aside to myths." Peter warned believers to beware of false teachers who would deny Jesus and exploit them with deceptive words (2 Peter 2:1–3 NKJV). Paul, just like Jesus, went forth in truth and let the people decide whether or not they wanted to follow that truth. The word "covetousness" means a greedy desire to have more.

1 Thessalonians 2:7–8: In these verses Paul presents himself as having the characteristics of a loving mother.[2] Basically, Paul modeled discipleship. He brought the gospel to them and invested in their lives. *Nelson's Commentary* says, "While a professional nurse would know how to provide for the physical needs of an infant, a mother cherishes her own children with maternal love. Paul emphasizes the extent of his love: he would have sacrificed his own life for them if necessary."[3] This is a huge challenge for us: Do we care about young believers that much? Would we be willing to pour our lives into them, whatever it takes? Wiersbe said, "Babes in Christ sensed his tender loving care as he nurtured them."[4] It takes time and energy to nurture young children, and Paul showed great patience with them.

1 Thessalonians 2:9–12: Paul also showed himself as the concerned father.[5] Paul was a spiritual father to this church, just as he was to the church in Corinth (1 Corinthians 4:15–16). Paul modeled for this early church what the heart of a father looks like. Paul labored and toiled night and day so he wouldn't be a burden on them as he shared the gospel with them (v. 9). Paul's work was a model to them as a father.[6] In Hebrews 12:14, we're told to make every effort to live in peace with everyone. In 2 Peter 1:5, Peter said to make every effort to add

---

[2] Wiersbe, 709.

[3] Earl D. Radmacher, Ronald B. Allen, and H. Wayne House, eds., *Nelson's New Illustrated Bible Commentary* (Nashville: Thomas Nelson, 1999), 1574.

[4] Wiersbe, 709.

[5] Wiersbe, 709.

[6] Wiersbe, 709.

goodness to your faith. Ephesians 4:3 says, "diligently keeping the unity of the Spirit."

The second thing Paul modeled as a spiritual father was his walk.[7] Paul not only shared the message; he also lived it (v. 10). The Thessalonians watched Paul when the tensions rose in times of high stress to see how he would respond. Third, Paul modeled how to be a spiritual father through his words.[8] Paul spoke words into their lives that edified and encouraged them. Paul exhorted, comforted, and charged them as a father with his own children to walk worthy of God's calling (v. 11–12). In the Great Commission, Jesus told the disciples to go into the world and make disciples, teaching them to obey everything He commanded (Matthew 28:19–20).

1 Thessalonians 2:13–20: Paul was thankful that they received the Word of God and welcomed it effectively (v. 13). The word "effectively" denotes with work, with energy, and with power. In verses 14–16, this church went through a time of persecution. Paul comforted and encouraged them to keep going. Maybe you have faced the same thing. You feel like you are growing in the Lord, but all of a sudden you are starting to face oppression. Maybe your own family is pushing you aside because you are starting to walk in faith and you are growing in the Lord. Paul's message to you is: keep going and keep growing. One of the great values of the local church is that we stand together in times of difficulty and encourage one another. As Wiersbe said, "A lonely saint is very vulnerable to the attacks of Satan. We need each other in the battles of life."[9] In 2 Corinthians 4:16–18, Paul encouraged believers not to lose heart but to focus on the eternal.

In verses 19–20, Paul told the Thessalonians that they were his glory and joy. Paul's joy would come from seeing them in the presence of Christ and that kept him going. He encouraged them to keep going because Jesus is coming back, and it will all be worth it.

Closing

Paul modeled discipleship as a faithful steward, a loving mother, and a concerned father. Paul modeled discipleship through his work, his walk, and his words. Wiersbe said that Paul encouraged them to "lay hold of the spiritual resources you have in Jesus Christ. You have the Word of God within you, the people of God around you, and the glory of God before you. There is no need to give up."[10] Peter also encouraged believers not to be surprised when they suffer for

[7] Wiersbe, 710.

[8] Wiersbe, 710.

[9] Wiersbe, 713.

[10] Wiersbe, 713.

the sake of the gospel but instead to rejoice at the revelation of His glory (1 Peter 4:12–14). The Lord is encouraging us today. Sometimes it's not easy, but there's a prize coming: Jesus Christ!

The Daily Word

Just as the Lord led Paul to share the gospel, the Lord will lead you to share the gospel with others. As you go, remember to walk in obedience to the Lord. Don't focus on pleasing others. Don't worry about what others will even think of you. Rather, follow the voice of the Lord. If He is nudging you to share truth, to love someone with His love, to be His hands and feet in a specific way, *then follow that voice*. Fear the Lord, not others.

Oftentimes you feel a nudge to say or do something, but all kinds of "what ifs" and "I don't knows" pop into your mind discouraging you. Press on and *listen to the voice* of the Lord, which will always align with the Word of God. Walk obediently with pure motives, and you will see the Lord. God wants to move in your life and in others' lives in ways you can't imagine! Have a heart that cares enough for others to walk obediently to the Lord's voice!

For our exhortation didn't come from error or impurity or an intent to deceive. Instead, just as we have been approved by God to be entrusted with the gospel, so we speak, not to please men, but rather God, who examines our hearts. —1 Thessalonians 2:3–4

Further Scripture: Proverbs 29:25; Isaiah 30:21; 1 Thessalonians 2:8, 11–12

Questions

1. Explain why Paul's visit to the Thessalonians was not in vain (1 Thessalonians 1:5–8).
2. Why did Paul bring the gospel to the Thessalonians? What did Paul argue was not his purpose? Why must you be a good steward of sharing the gospel (Luke 16:1–2; 1 Corinthians 4:1–2)?
3. Paul made it a point to say he did not use flattery to persuade the Thessalonians with the gospel. Why would flattery be a bad approach (Psalms 12:2; 36:2; 78:36; Mark 7:6)?
4. Who was Paul ultimately seeking to please with his teaching? Do you have the tendency to want to please men more than God? How can you learn from Paul in this area?

5. In 1 Thessalonians 2:10–11, what illustration did Paul use to describe his ministry? Compare that verse to 1 Thessalonians 2:7.
6. What did the Holy Spirit highlight to you in 1 Thessalonians 2 through the reading or the teaching?

WEEK 79

Lesson 68: 1 Thessalonians 3

Coming Lord: Encouraging and Praying for the Church

Teaching Notes

Intro

One of Paul's practices was to pour into the cities to make sure the people were shepherded and grounded in the Word of God. To make sure the people in Thessalonica were taken care of, Paul sent Timothy to help them. In the first two chapters of this book, Paul explained how the church was born and how they were nurtured. In this chapter, Paul talks about their level of maturity. Our word for this book is *Coming Lord*, which comes from 1 Thessalonians 4:16–17. Paul wanted to make sure this group of believers would be ready for Christ's return.

Teaching

1 Thessalonians 3:1–2: Paul sent Timothy to strengthen and encourage the believers in Thessalonica (vv. 1–2). There is nothing better than discipleship done in person, face to face, where you can see each other. Though Paul couldn't return, he sent Timothy, a fellow worker, believer, minister, and deacon, who was not afraid to work. If we're going to get ready for the *Coming Lord*, we have to strengthen and encourage the people we have poured into. Paul sent Timothy to help them grow in their faith—which he mentions five times in the first ten verses of this chapter. What is so important about growing in faith?

1 Thessalonians 3:3–5: Paul wanted them to grow in their faith so they wouldn't be "shaken by these persecutions" (v. 3). By stating, "we are appointed to this," Paul implies God knows His followers will suffer. When we go through times of persecution and tribulation, it is to refine and strengthen us. According to MacArthur, "Paul reminded the Thessalonians of this divine appointment so that they would not think that: (1) God's plan was not working out as evidenced by Paul's troubles, or (2) Paul's afflictions demonstrated God's displeasure with him."[1] If Jesus went through it and Paul went through it, why would

[1] John MacArthur, *The MacArthur Bible Commentary* (Nashville: Thomas Nelson, 2005), 1754.

the Thessalonians be any different? In Matthew 5:10–12, Jesus said, "Those who are persecuted for righteousness are blessed. . . . You are blessed when they insult and persecute you . . . because of Me. Be glad and rejoice, because . . . that is how they persecuted the prophets who were before you." Paul sent Timothy to put his arm around them as they suffered through hard times so they would be strengthened through this process. While he was there, Paul warned them persecution was coming (v. 4). Now he sent Timothy to check on them because he feared "the tempter had tempted you and that our labor might be for nothing" (v. 5).

1 Thessalonians 3:6–8: Paul sent a helper because he was afraid and concerned about persecution, and he was afraid they might be turning away.[2] Timothy returned to Paul with good news: their faith and love was strong, they had good memories of Paul, and they wanted to see him again (v. 6). Paul was encouraged that they were standing firm in the Lord (vv. 7–8). MacArthur said, "Pictured here is an army that refuses to retreat even though it is being assaulted by the enemy."[3] Paul sent them this letter to let them know he was excited for them. Wiersbe said this letter shows, "God's Word is food to nourish us (Matthew 4:4), a light to guide us (Psalm 119:105), and a weapon to defend us (Ephesians 6:17).[4]

1 Thessalonians 3:9–13: Not only did Paul send them a helper and write them a letter, but Paul also prayed for them.[5] Paul was excited by the change he saw in them (v. 9), and he prayed night and day to see them again to teach them more (v. 10). Paul wasn't criticizing them; he wanted them to experience the fullness of God in their lives. Paul loved them so much he went before almighty God and prayed their love would spill over, not only to Paul but also to everyone in order to radically impact Thessalonica and spread to other cities in the area (vv. 11–12). Paul also prayed God would make their hearts "blameless in holiness before our God and Father at the coming of our Lord Jesus with all His saints" (v. 13). In his prayer, Paul basically said, "Hey, Jesus is coming, and I need your hearts to be ready. I need you to walk in holiness so you reflect Him. And sometimes I believe the only way that can happen is if I pray for that in your lives."

---

[2] Warren W. Wiersbe, *The Wiersbe Bible Commentary: New Testament* (Colorado Springs: David C. Cook, 2007), 714–15.

[3] MacArthur, 1754.

[4] Wiersbe, 715.

[5] Wiersbe, 715

Closing

Jesus is coming back, and Paul wanted them to be ready!

The Daily Word

Paul and Silas intentionally sent Timothy to the Thessalonian church to help strengthen and encourage the believers there out of care and concern for them and their faith. Timothy returned with great reports of their strong faith, even amidst expected persecution. Paul continued to pray for them and encouraged them to stand firm in the Lord.

As believers, speaking words of encouragement is critical. How often do you take time to encourage a missionary or a pastor, a spouse, child, friend, or coworker? Encouragement brings life to a person's soul. As a believer, stand firm and speak life, hope, and encouragement to others. Today, take a few minutes to encourage and pray for someone the Lord puts on your heart. Call them or write them a note. As a guide, follow Paul's prayer for the Thessalonian church: *"May the Lord cause* [insert person's name here] *to increase and overflow with love for one another and for everyone, just as you also do for* [insert person's name here]. *May He make* [insert person's name here]*'s heart blameless in holiness before our God and Father at the coming of our Lord Jesus with all His saints. Amen."*

But now Timothy has come to us from you and brought us good news about your faith and love and reported that you always have good memories of us, wanting to see us, as we also want to see you. Therefore, brothers, in all our distress and persecution, we were encouraged about you through your faith. —1 Thessalonians 3:6–7

Further Scripture: 1 Thessalonians 3:12–13; Hebrews 3:13; 10:24–25

Questions

1. In 1 Thessalonians 3, Paul talked about the afflictions he and his fellow travelers had suffered for their beliefs. Do you think you would be willing to suffer like Paul did for the sake of the gospel? Meditate on how much Paul went through (Acts 14:19; 2 Corinthians 11:24–27).
2. How would you compare your love for the church to Paul's love for the Thessalonian church? Is it a genuine, selfless, sacrificing love? If not, how could you change that?

3. First Thessalonians 3:13 says, "May He make your hearts blameless in holiness before our God and Father at the coming of our Lord Jesus with all His saints." How do you establish your heart without blame?
4. What did the Holy Spirit highlight to you in 1 Thessalonians 3 through the reading or the teaching?

WEEK 80

Lesson 69: 1 Thessalonians 4

Coming Lord: Call to Sanctification and Comfort of Christ's Coming

Teaching Notes

Intro

When you're grieving because you've lost someone, you want to know where they are. First Thessalonians 4 is considered the funeral chapter because you can find hope in the process of grieving, if you're walking with the Lord. Remember, in 1 Thessalonians 3, Paul sent Timothy to comfort the believers at Thessalonica because they were being persecuted. In this chapter, Paul continues to urge them to get ready for the *Coming Lord*. Today we'll talk about what it will look like when He comes.

Teaching

1 Thessalonians 4:1–8: Paul wanted the Thessalonians to walk in holiness.[1] By following the commands given to them by Paul through the Lord Jesus, they would please God (vv. 1–2). According to Wiersbe, the word "command" (v. 2) was a military term referring "to orders handed down from superior officers."[2] In order to walk in holiness, we have to actually obey what God has asked us to do. The Great Commission doesn't mean talk about it, put pictures up about it, write a vision statement, or change your mission statement. We have to actually do it.

Then Paul gave specific instructions. Thessalonica was a city where many people from many cultures traveled through, and it was a city of sexual immorality. Paul said they had to "abstain from sexual immorality" (v. 3) so they could experience the purity that pleases God. Paul called them to control their own bodies instead of participating in the lustful desires of the Gentiles, who did not know God (vv. 4–5). When you walk in holiness, you do it to please God, to obey God,

[1] Warren W. Wiersbe, *The Wiersbe Bible Commentary: New Testament* (Colorado Springs: David C. Cook, 2007), 717.

[2] Wiersbe, 717.

and to bring glory to God. Paul reminded them God will deal with His children when they sin (v. 6). Because God calls believers to sanctification, those who reject this instruction reject God (vv. 7–8). Sanctification is the process of being sanctified or made holy. The only way that can take place is through the work Christ did on the cross—that work allows us to be cleansed, forgiven, and set free—to be removed from the sin of the past so we can come to the table clean. Holiness means set apart. Sanctification, holiness, and righteousness all have the same underlying principles. God has not called us to walk in the old way of doing things. He's called us to be set apart and new in who we are in Christ. Peter wrote: "But as the One who called you is holy, you also are to be holy in all your conduct" (1 Peter 1:15). We need to be set apart from the world and walk in light.

1 Thessalonians 4:9–10: Paul wanted the Thessalonians to walk in harmony.[3] Paul heard some really good things about their loving care for others in Thessalonica and throughout the region in Macedonia (vv. 9–10). He encouraged them to do so even more. There are four words for love: *eros*, the physical, erotic type of love; *storge*, which is family love such as parents for their children; *philia*, which is "the love of deep affection, such as in friendship or even marriage" and can be described as brotherly love; and *agape*, "the love God shows toward us. It is not simply a love based on feeling; it is expressed in our wills. Agape love treats others as God would treat them."[4]

1 Thessalonians 4:11–12: Paul wanted the Thessalonians to walk in honesty.[5] Constable said by living a quiet life, you won't disturb others; by tending to your own affairs you won't mess with somebody else's business; and by providing for your own family you won't be a burden to others.[6]

1 Thessalonians 4:13–18: If we're anticipating the coming of the Lord, we should be ready. Our house should be in order. When we talk about the rapture, we have to remember no one knows when Jesus is coming. People have predicted His return. People have prophesied His return. But nobody knows when He will return; therefore, the best thing we can do is to walk out our faith and always be ready.

---

[3] Wiersbe, 718.

[4] Wiersbe, 718.

[5] Wiersbe, 719.

[6] Thomas L. Constable, *Expository Notes of Dr. Thomas Constable: 1 Thessalonians*, 46–47, https://planobiblechapel.org/tcon/notes/pdf/1thessalonians.pdf.

According to Wiersbe, in verses 13 and 15 we have a revelation: we have God's truth.[7] Because we have God's truth, we have hope. The phrase "those who are asleep" refers to those who have died. In response, Paul said what he revealed to the Thessalonians came straight from the Lord (v. 15a). Paul emphasized that Christ is coming back again. Practically speaking, Jesus is at the right hand of God in heaven. When Paul said Jesus would bring with Him those who have died, Paul implied that those who believed in Jesus and are now dead are with Jesus (v. 14). Therefore, we can have hope that we will again see believers who have died. Those who are alive when Christ returns have no advantage over those who have already died (v. 15b). The timing doesn't matter since we are all going to be with the Lord. The revelation is that Christ is coming back. When He comes back, He's bringing with Him those who have died before us. He will resurrect those who are dead. This passage is used at funerals because it gives us hope we will again see those who have died, if they have put their trust in the death, burial, and resurrection of Christ. We just don't know when.

The Lord will descend from heaven with three sounds (v. 16). He will descend with a shout. We don't know what that means, but we can surmise everyone will hear it. He will descend with the archangel's voice, and we will hear that. There will be a trumpet sound, which is usually the sound for war. The battle is coming, and we had better get ready.

We will then see the rapture.[8] Living believers will be caught up together with the dead in the clouds to meet the Lord in the air (v. 17). This word rapture has excited so many people. We've had books written about the rapture. The word means to be caught up, to seize, or to carry off. Dr. Kenneth Wuest explains different meanings for this word. It could mean "to catch away speedily," like when the Spirit moved Philip after he led the Ethiopian to Christ. It could mean "to seize by force," possibly implying Satan may try to keep us from leaving earth. It could mean "to claim for one's own self," as when Christ comes to claim His bride. Other meanings could be "to move to a new place" or "to rescue from danger." Those who take this final view use this verse to claim believers will be taken before the tribulation.[9]

Christian believers will be forever with the Lord.[10] The coming of the Lord will allow all believers, whether dead or alive at the time of His coming, to be together.

---

[7] Wiersbe, 720.

[8] Wiersbe, 721.

[9] Wiersbe, 721.

[10] Wiersbe, 722.

Closing

Christ could come at any given moment, so please get ready. When does this rapture happen? Does it happen before the seven years of tribulation; does it happen in the middle, after three and a half years; does it happen after the seven years of tribulation? It doesn't matter when it happens. We should not be caught off guard regardless of what our viewpoint is. Our view must be, if Christ is coming back, we have to get ready. Let's walk in holiness, harmony, and honesty, because then He can recognize His children because they look like Him.

The Daily Word

Paul cared deeply about the church and encouraged them to walk and please God and to live a life of sanctification, not of impurity. He encouraged them because Jesus will return one day, and *Paul longed for the church to live ready for Jesus' return.*

The same is true today! Are you living ready for Jesus' return? As a believer, God called you to *grow in Him*, which is the process of sanctification. As a believer, you are set apart, you are righteous, you are holy, you are forgiven, and your sins have been removed. But even as a follower of Christ, temptations come your way. Sexual impurity and immorality remain rampant in today's culture, just as it was in Paul's. Even still, you are called to resist and flee from impurities, stand firm, and run toward growing in Christ. Don't mess with things in the flesh. Don't mess with momentary satisfaction. Abstain from sexual immorality. *Seek sanctification. This is God's will for your life.* In doing so, you will be ready for Jesus' return. Make today matter for the kingdom by not giving into impure temptations. His return is coming. *Be ready.*

For this is God's will, your sanctification: that you abstain from sexual immorality, so that each of you knows how to control his own body in sanctification and honor, not with lustful desires, like the Gentiles who don't know God. —1 Thessalonians 4:3–5

Further Scripture: Luke 12:40; 1 Thessalonians 4:7, 15–17

Questions

1. In 1 Thessalonians 4:3, why do you think Paul told the Thessalonian church to abstain from sexual immorality? Based on Scripture, do you think sexual sin is worse than other sins (1 Corinthians 6:13, 18–19; Galatians 5:17)? Why or why not?

2. Based on what Paul said in 1 Thessalonians 4:9–10, did the Thessalonian church love each other well? Do you see this in the church today?
3. Read 1 Thessalonians 4:16–17. How do you think Paul knew this?
4. What did the Holy Spirit highlight to you in 1 Thessalonians 4 through the reading or the teaching?

Lesson 70: 1 Thessalonians 5

Coming Lord: The Day of the Lord

Teaching Notes

Intro

Yesterday, we only scratched the surface in talking about the rapture. Today, we'll dig a little deeper. I'm not an expert to say that the rapture has to be pre-tribulation, mid-tribulation, or post-tribulation. The rapture is described in 1 Thessalonians 4:16–17. There will be an unbelievable heavenly party in the clouds when we are raised up to meet Jesus in the air—seems like it would be in the first heaven because we're still in the earth's atmosphere. This is the rapture. When will that happen? The Lord could come back at any given moment. This should not frighten us, but it should give us hope and drive us to tell others about Christ. Remember, our theme for 1 Thessalonians is *Coming Lord.* Please get ready; He is coming back.

Teaching

1 Thessalonians 5:1: Why did Paul create this theological stir by saying they did not need anything written to them about the times and seasons? Paul talked about the rapture because they needed to get ready for it, but since they didn't know when Jesus was coming back, they needed to walk out their sanctification. In Acts 1:7, Jesus told His followers, "It is not for you to know times or periods that the Father has set by His own authority." Though they could not know when Jesus would come back, in the meantime, He gave them (and us) the power of the Holy Spirit (Acts 1:8). Scripture says that until all the Gentiles have a chance to hear the gospel, Jesus is not coming back. So we are holding Him back because we have not done what He commissioned us to do.

1 Thessalonians 5:2: When you think about the day of the Lord, what do you think of? In Genesis, there was some discussion that sometimes a day means twenty-four hours; sometimes a day actually means a whole week. It might not mean, instantly, everything takes place and unfolds in twenty-four hours. We have to recognize that God's timetable is completely not on our clock—we can't even grasp what that implies. But let's talk about this day of the Lord mentality. *Nelson's Commentary* says that there are two things implied: (1) we'll see God's judgment against sinful people, and (2) we'll see God's eternal reign over His people.[1] The day of the Lord "is that time when God will judge the world and punish the nations. At the same time, God will prepare Israel for the return of Christ to earth to establish His kingdom."[2] The day of the Lord could imply Jesus' second coming. When some people refer to the day of the Lord, they go to Jeremiah 30:7 and call this day the time of Jacob's trouble. Some people say the day of the Lord could be called the tribulation because as soon as Jesus comes, the tribulation starts. When the day of the Lord occurs, you can expect the birth of the kingdom to take place.[3] The image of "the Day of the Lord will come just like a thief in the night" (v. 2b) is used by Jesus in Matthew 24:42–44, "you also must be ready, because the Son of Man is coming at an hour you do not expect."

1 Thessalonians 5:3–7: The words "When they say" in this verse refer to the unsaved, the unbelievers. Judgment is coming to those who don't trust Christ (v. 3). But believers won't be surprised because they are aware of His coming (v. 4). Believers are "sons of light and sons of the day" (v. 5) who "must stay awake and be serious" (v. 6). If you are functioning in drunkenness, then you won't be prepared for His return (v. 7). For twenty centuries, we have been given the promise that the Lord could come back at any time.[4] Peter wrote: "Dear friends, don't let this one thing escape you: With the Lord one day is like a thousand years, and a thousand years like one day" (2 Peter 3:8). God is on a completely different calendar, so we have to live like Jesus could return any day. Several passages in Isaiah talk about the birthing pains. In Matthew 24:8, we're told that birthing pains are the beginning of birth pains.

1 Thessalonians 5:8–11: We have to be constantly functioning in faith, hope, and love (v. 8). We put on the armor of faith by believing that God will show up and Jesus is the Messiah. We put love on our chests by exemplifying Christ and giving up our lives for others. We put on the helmet of the hope of salvation by knowing that He is coming back for us in this process. Wiersbe said, "It is time to wake up, clean up, and dress up."[5] Regardless of when the rapture happens,

---

[1] Earl D. Radmacher, Ronald B. Allen, and H. Wayne House, eds., *Nelson's New Illustrated Bible Commentary* (Nashville: Thomas Nelson, 1999), 1580.

[2] Warren W. Wiersbe, *The Wiersbe Bible Commentary: New Testament* (Colorado Springs: David C. Cook, 2007), 723.

[3] Wiersbe, 723.

[4] Wiersbe, 723.

[5] Wiersbe, 724.

when we meet Him in the clouds, "we will live together with Him" (v. 10). It doesn't matter if it happens before the tribulation, during the tribulation, or after the tribulation—we will be with Christ. If there's a chance we're going to have to go through tribulation, we need to be prepared for that.

1 Thessalonians 5:12–28: These verses talk about how to lead your family, how to integrate and partner with your family, and how to do this with the body of Christ.

Let's review some information about the tribulation. Most people describe the tribulation as a seven-year period when the Antichrist comes into play and initiates peace. For the first three and a half years, it's calm and good and the temple is rebuilt. In the middle of the seven years, the Antichrist says he is God. For the next three and a half years, it's all-out tribulation and wrath.

People who believe that the rapture is coming before the seven years of tribulation cite 1 Thessalonians 1:10, which says Jesus rescues us from the coming wrath, and 1 Thessalonians 5:9, which says God did not appoint us to wrath. This pre-tribulation view says that if God did not appoint us to wrath, then we won't have to go through the seven years of tribulation. Wiersbe takes this view because (1) it's the nature of the church that we will not taste God's wrath (John 5:24); and (2) the promise of Christ's imminent return, instead of being an unknown time, would have a time line established by the signing of the peace treaty.[6] One valid argument against this is that Christ suffered, and He allowed believers who suffered to trust in Him and glorify God.

Second Thessalonians 2:3 says, "[That day of the Lord] will not come unless the apostasy comes first and the man of lawlessness is revealed." This verse says we have to see the Antichrist come into play. So, this verse would validate the mid-tribulation or post-tribulation or pre-wrath viewpoints of the rapture. The abomination of desolation (Matthew 24:15) takes place when the Antichrist reveals himself and claims to be God.

Revelation 6:16–17 implies that there are believers going through the tribulation because they want to be hidden from the face of God and the wrath of the Lamb. These verses support the mid-tribulation and post-tribulation viewpoints. Revelation talks about seven seals that Jesus breaks open, and that God's wrath is not poured out until the seventh seal.

Revelation 7:9 and 14 describe a great multitude standing before the throne and before the Lamb (v. 7). They were identified as "the ones coming out of the great tribulation" (v. 14). This comes after Revelation 6, and the sixth seal being opened, stating the day of wrath had come. Revelation 7 describes 144,000 who were sealed to go through the wrath and the rapture. The term "great tribulation"

[6] Wiersbe, 725.

was language that Jesus used in Matthew 24:15 for the part of the tribulation that comes after the abomination of desolation. This supports the argument that the rapture takes place mid-tribulation or post-tribulation.

Matthew 24:29–31 says, "Immediately after the tribulation of those days . . . they will see the Son of Man coming . . . and they will gather His elect from the four winds." Possibly verses 30–31 describe the rapture as coming after the tribulation. This is a great argument for a post-tribulation or pre-wrath view.

Closing

We don't know if we'll meet Christ pre-tribulation, mid-tribulation, or post-tribulation, but it should cause every one of us to get ready.

The Daily Word

Jesus is returning. That is a fact. You just don't know exactly when. Paul thought it would be in his lifetime. You may think it will be in your lifetime. The question to ask is . . . *are you living as though Jesus could return today?* You are called to *live ready* for His return. Are you walking in the light or the darkness? Are you awake or sleeping as a follower of Christ? Are you filled with the Spirit or drunk and unaware? Are you equipped for the battle that wages war around you? Paul made it pretty clear: *Live in the light. Stay awake and be serious for Jesus. Put on the armor of faith. You are in a battle.* It's real, and it's happening. If you had a houseguest arriving tonight, wouldn't you get ready? The same is true for Christ's return. *Live ready!*

How do you live ready? God longs for you to pursue what is good for one another. God's will is for you to rejoice always, pray constantly, and give thanks in everything. As you prepare yourself for Jesus' return, focus on these things: rejoicing, praying, and giving thanks. By doing so every day, you will be ready for His return and others will see the light of Christ in you. Live ready!

For you are all sons of light and sons of the day. We do not belong to the night or the darkness. So then, we must not sleep, like the rest, but we must stay awake and be serious. For those who sleep, sleep at night, and those who get drunk are drunk at night. But since we belong to the day, we must be serious and put the armor of faith and love on our chests, and put on a helmet of the hope of salvation. —1 Thessalonians 5:5–8

Further Scripture: Matthew 24:27; Romans 13:12; 1 Thessalonians 5:16–18

Questions

1. How will the day of the Lord come? In what two ways was the day of the Lord characterized in the Old Testament (Isaiah 2:1–3; 11:1–9; 30:23–26; Joel 2:1–2; Amos 5:18–20; Zephaniah 1:14–17; Zechariah 14:1, 7–11)?
2. How does Christ both unite and divide (John 7:43; 9:16; 10:19; 1 Corinthians 1:10; Galatians 3:28; 1 Thessalonians 4:17)?
3. In 1 Thessalonians 5:6, what did Paul mean by the word "sleep"? What should the believer in Christ be doing instead (Romans 14:10–11; 1 Corinthians 3:11–15; 9:24–27; 2 Corinthians 5:10)?
4. What has God not appointed for believers (Revelation 6:12–17)? What has He appointed for them instead (1 Thessalonians 1:10)? In light of these truths, does this spur you on to share your faith with others?
5. What three things did Paul say are God's will for you in Christ Jesus? What five admonitions did Paul give relating to the Spirit and prophecies?
6. What did the Holy Spirit highlight to you in 1 Thessalonians 5 through the reading or the teaching?

WEEK 80

Lesson 71: 2 Thessalonians 1

Faithful Lord: Eternity in the Presence of God

Teaching Notes

Intro

So far we've done 556 lessons out of 730, and it's never too late to jump in and get started with this study. The Word of God is alive and active today and it brings instruction as well as encouragement into our lives. Second Thessalonians looks back at some of the issues in 1 Thessalonians but with a different perspective. Paul claimed authorship of the book twice (2 Thessalonians 1:1; 3:17). Timothy and Silas (or Silvanus) were with Paul when he wrote the letter. Second Thessalonians was written around late AD 51 or early AD 52, a few months after 1 Thessalonians was written; both were written from the city of Corinth.[1] Our phrase for 1 Thessalonians was *Coming Lord*, and for 2 Thessalonians, it is *Faithful Lord* (2 Thessalonians 3:3). The Lord is faithful to what He said, and He will return.

Paul was on his second missionary journey and spent three Sabbaths in Thessalonica. Paul's time there is recorded in Acts 17: his arrival (vv. 1–2); his teachings about Jesus (vv. 2–3); the response of new believers (v. 4); the response of the Jews (vv. 5–9); and him being sent out of the city to Berea by the Christian brothers (v. 10). From Berea, Paul went on to Athens alone while Timothy and Silas stayed behind. They later rejoined Paul in Athens (v. 15). From Athens Paul sent Timothy back to Thessalonica and Silas on to Philippi. In Acts 18:1, Paul left Athens to go to Corinth, and Timothy and Silas rejoined him there.

When Timothy arrived in Corinth, he made his report to Paul about what was happening in Thessalonica and Paul wrote his first letter in response to Timothy's report. Paul spent eighteen months in Corinth and wrote several letters from there. MacArthur suggests, "Perhaps the bearer of the first letter brought Paul back an update on the condition of the church, which had matured and expanded (1:3); but pressure and persecution had also increased. The seeds of false doctrine concerning the Lord had been sown, and the people's behavior

[1] John MacArthur, *The MacArthur Bible Commentary* (Nashville: Thomas Nelson, 2005), 1762.

was disorderly."[2] Paul's second letter to the Thessalonians was in response to "the seeds of false doctrine concerning the Lord [that] had been sown," and wrote to the believers who were "(1) discouraged by persecution and needed incentive to persevere; (2) deceived by false teachers who confused them about the Lord's return; and (3) disobedient to divine commands, particularly by refusing to work."[3] Paul's desire was to offer comfort to those who had faced persecution, correction for those who had received false teachings, and confrontation for those who had been disobedient.[4] Paul not only addressed these issues, but he presented solutions as well.

Teaching

2 Thessalonians 1:1–4: Verses 1–2 hold Paul's greeting, and verse 3 expresses Paul's thanks for the Thessalonians whose faith was flourishing and their love for each other was increasing. In fact, Paul boasted about the Thessalonians to other churches, telling them of the Thessalonians endurance in their faith against the afflictions they were enduring (v. 4).

2 Thessalonians 1:5–8: Paul pointed out they would be counted worthy of God's grace and His kingdom for their suffering (v. 5), and God would repay those who had persecuted them (vv. 6–8). Some scholars quote verse 7 as support for the coming rapture of the saints before the tribulation begins. Those who have suffered from persecution and affliction will receive rest when Jesus is revealed with His angels. They will no longer fear "flaming fire on those who don't know God and on those who don't obey the gospel of our Lord Jesus" (v. 8). The tribulation will last for seven years, and these scholars say Thessalonians 1:7 shows Jesus will pull His believers out before the tribulation takes place.

Other scholars believe that 1 Thessalonians 4:13–18 emphasizes that believers will be spared from the tribulation while 2 Thessalonians 1:7–8 speaks to the vengeance that will come against those who do not know God. Those that hold this interpretation believe the rapture will come at the end of the tribulation.

2 Thessalonians 1:9–12: Verses 9–10 clearly point out those who do not know Christ will face eternal destruction. Because of this eternal destruction, Paul prayed for the Thessalonians that God would find them worthy (vv. 11–12). Paul prayed they would continue the work of faith as a witness for Christ so that Christ's name would be glorified in them.

---

[2] MacArthur, 1763.

[3] MacArthur, 1763.

[4] MacArthur, 1763.

Closing

Paul stressed the importance of believing in Christ. Those who do will receive eternity in the presence of God; those who do not will receive eternal destruction.

The Daily Word

Paul validated the faith of the Thessalonian church and the persecution and afflictions they endured. He boasted and testified about their faith to others. Paul also continued to pray and encourage the church to press on and do the work of the Lord because eternity was at stake.

You may be facing persecution right now from family members who don't understand why you are walking by faith and following Christ. You may face insults from friends who want you to join the crowd or do perverse or impure actions. Yet you choose to remain pure in your body and in your thoughts. You need to hear . . . *well done!* Even in the midst of this culture, *stay strong, friend.* Remember you are worthy of your calling. The Lord will strengthen you with power so you can press on in faith, sharing the good news with those around you. Christ is glorified in and through you. *Do not give up.* God's judgment is coming; therefore, press on, go, and share His love with others in the strength of Jesus Christ!

We must always thank God for you, brothers. This is right, since your faith is flourishing and the love each one of you has for one another is increasing. Therefore, we ourselves boast about you among God's churches—about your endurance and faith in all the persecutions and afflictions you endure. —2 Thessalonians 1:3–4

Further Scripture: Matthew 5:11–12; Acts 1:8; 2 Thessalonians 1:11–12

Questions

1. In 2 Thessalonians 1, it appears the church in Thessalonica was growing by leaps and bounds. Paul says their faith grew and their love abounded in 2 Thessalonians 1:3. In this modern age, is this seen in the church anymore? Why or why not?
2. Second Thessalonians 1:6 states not to seek revenge with someone who wronged us but to let the Lord do it. Where else in Scripture are we told the Lord fights for us (Exodus 14:14; Deuteronomy 3:22; 20:4; Joshua 23:10; Romans 12:19)?

3. What is your definition of faith? The church in Thessalonica believed what Paul spoke of without seeing. Are they any different from you? Is their faith different from yours? Do you place all your faith in Jesus and the message of the cross? If not, what is stopping you?
4. What did the Holy Spirit highlight to you in 2 Thessalonians 1 through the reading or the teaching?

WEEK 80

Lesson 72: 2 Thessalonians 2

Faithful Lord: Stand Firm

Teaching Notes

Intro

Our phrase for 1 Thessalonians is *Coming Lord* and for 2 Thessalonians is *Faithful Lord.* The reality is Christ is coming whether we are prepared or not, and we don't know when that will be (Matthew 24:36). In chapter 2, Paul continued his discussion about the end times, focusing on the Antichrist.

Teaching

2 Thessalonians 2:1–7: In these verses Paul talks about the rapture of the church. False teachers claimed the Thessalonians were in the last days, so they had quit their jobs and were waiting on His return. Yet Matthew 24:36 says no one will know the time of His return, not even Jesus Himself, only the Father knows. We should keep watch and be ready (Matthew 24:42). Verse 1 introduces the subject of the coming of Christ. Verse 6 states that the Antichrist is currently restrained so he will be revealed at the proper time. Who is restraining the Antichrist? Possibly the Holy Spirit. Notice the first reference to the restrainer is "what," which is gender neutral.

Verse 2 states the Thessalonians should not be easily upset by a spirit, a message, or a letter from Paul, that states the day of the Lord has come. Apparently, a false letter was being passed through the Thessalonians that claimed Jesus had returned. Paul says don't get caught up in the false teachings that you missed the day of the Lord. When Christ returns, we will all know. Today, when someone claims to be Christ, that is a false spirit, an Antichrist spirit.

Verse 3 seems to support a mid-tribulation or post-tribulation time for the rapture. It states the day of the Lord will not happen until the Antichrist is revealed, suggesting believers will remain at least three and a half years into the time of tribulation before being raptured. "The man of lawlessness" and "the son of destruction" both refer to the Antichrist. Verse 4 states the Antichrist will exalt himself as an object of worship and even sit in God's temple, proclaiming himself to be God.

Here's the progression of prophetic events of the end times:

1. The rapture of the church will take place at some point. We must be ready at any time.
2. The leader of ten European nations will make a seven-year peace agreement with Israel. That leader will be the Antichrist (Daniel 9:26–27). When that happens we should all get ready.
3. After three and a half years, the Antichrist is going to break the agreement (Daniel 9:27).
4. The Antichrist will move to Jerusalem and set up his image in the temple and declare that he is God (2 Thessalonians 2:3–4). That means the third temple will have to be built for that to happen.
5. The Antichrist will begin to control the world and force it to worship him. At that time, God will send a great tribulation (Matthew 24:21–22).
6. The nations will gather at Armageddon and will fight the Antichrist (Revelation 16:16). At some point, we will see the sign of Christ coming to fight the Antichrist in Israel.
7. King Jesus will return to earth, defeat His enemy, be received by the Jews, and establish His kingdom (Revelation 19:11).
8. Jesus will reign for 1,000 years (Revelation 20:4–6).

For me, all this points to one question: How can the Lord use us as His witnesses during all this?

In verse 5, Paul reminded the Thessalonians that he had already told them what was to happen, so they shouldn't fall prey to false teachers and false teachings. Wiersbe points out Satan has been at war with God since he tried to take God's throne for himself, giving examples of Satan in the Garden with Adam and Eve (Genesis 3), and God declaring war against Satan and his family (Genesis 3:15). Wiersbe emphasizes, "Satan has always wanted to be worshipped and served as God. He will one day produce his masterpiece, the Antichrist, who will cause the world to worship Satan and believe Satan's lies."[1]

2 Thessalonians 2:8–12: Jesus will bring the Antichrist to nothing with one breath and the brightness of His coming (v. 8). The coming of the Antichrist will be accompanied by false Christians (Matthew 13:38), false ministries (2 Corinthians 11:13), and a false gospel (Galatians 1:6–9; 2 Thessalonians 2:9). Basically the Antichrist will be Satan's puppet. These will all perish because they did not accept the truth of Jesus' redemption of them (v. 10). Therefore, God will give the

[1] Warren W. Wiersbe, *The Bible Exposition Commentary: Ephesians–Revelation* (Colorado Springs: David C. Cook, 2003), 196–97.

unrighteous "a strong delusion so that they will believe what is false, so that all will be condemned" (vv. 11–12a). Wiersbe explains that many will die:

> It is important to note that these people did have opportunity to believe and be saved. God has no delight in judging the lost (Ezekiel 33:11). God is "not willing that any should perish, but that all should come to repentance" (2 Peter 3:9). These people will be judged and will suffer forever because they would not receive and believe the truth. In fact, their hearts will be so evil that they will not even have any *love* for the truth.[2]

Closing

How can we describe the Antichrist who is yet to come? Wiersbe identifies these descriptors of what the Antichrist will look like when he comes:

1. He will be a peacemaker (Revelation 6:1–2). He'll be a political leader that pulls ten nations together into one block; and they ultimately give him their authority (Revelation 17:12–13).
2. He will be a protector (Daniel 9:24–27). This applies to Israel, Jerusalem, and the temple but not to the church.
3. He will be a peace-breaker (Daniel 9:27). After three and a half years, he will break the peace by proclaiming himself to be God from the temple.
4. He will be a persecutor (Revelation 13:15–17). After the agreement of the ten nations is broken, he will bring about intense persecution and tribulation (Matthew 24:21). Citizens will be required to bear the mark of the beast to be able to buy or sell anything (Revelation 13:16–17).
5. He will be a prisoner (Revelation 19:11–21). When Christ returns the Antichrist will become God's prisoner.[3]

When you look for Jesus' return, don't let any false teachings confuse you. Jesus will not return until after the Antichrist appears and proclaims himself publicly from the temple in Jerusalem to be God.

The Daily Word

Paul continued to warn believers about the end times. He specifically cautioned about the coming of the Antichrist—the lawless one, based on Satan's working, who would come with all kinds of false miracles, signs, and wonders. When you

[2] Wiersbe, 199.

[3] Wiersbe, 199.

hear of the Antichrist, the lawless one, or false miracles, signs and wonders, *do not fear*. Don't worry. Don't question the power or the working of Jesus, the Resurrected Savior. Fear is the reaction Satan wants you to have, the place he wants to deceive you to stay in.

As a believer, stay informed and alert about the end times and the types of deception, lawlessness, and evil on the horizon. *But do not fear.* Rather, continue to thank God for His love for you. *Stand firm and hold on to the truth you have been taught.* God chose you for salvation through sanctification by the Spirit and through believing in the truth. Walk out your calling. The Lord's presence and power will never leave you as you walk with Him. He will give you everything you need for the day the lawless one comes. You will find victory in God alone! Therefore, walk in that victory!

For the mystery of lawlessness is already at work, but the one now restraining will do so until he is out of the way, and then the lawless one will be revealed. The Lord Jesus will destroy him with the breath of His mouth and will bring him to nothing with the brightness of His coming. The coming of the lawless one is based on Satan's working, with all kinds of false miracles, signs, and wonders. —2 Thessalonians 2:7–9

Further Scripture: Luke 12:25; Romans 8:38–39; 2 Thessalonians 2:13–15

Questions

1. Even in Paul's time, people believed the return of the Lord was upon them. Two thousand years later, are we seeing the things Paul spoke about in 2 Thessalonians 2:2–12 come to pass? Do you feel the Lord's return is soon? Why or why not?
2. In 2 Thessalonians 2:11, Paul says that God will send them "a strong delusion so that they will believe what is false." Do you know people who are deceived or have believed the lies of the enemy? Have you spoken truth to them? Have you prayed for them? If not, take a few minutes to lift them up in prayer that their eyes and ears will be opened.
3. Do you realize God "chose" you for salvation just as He did the believers in Thessalonica? In 2 Thessalonians 2:13, Paul told the Thessalonians God chose them, just as He did us, for salvation. Take a few minutes to lift praises up to God for His saving grace, unfailing love, and for choosing you as His own.
4. What did the Holy Spirit highlight to you in 2 Thessalonians 2 through the reading or the teaching?

WEEK 80

Lesson 73: 2 Thessalonians 3

Faithful Lord: Church Discipline

Teaching Notes

Intro

Matthew 5:17 has been the theme verse for all of reviveSCHOOL: "Don't assume that I came to destroy the Law or the Prophets. I did not come to destroy but to fulfill." Jesus is in every part of the Law and the Prophets. We can see Him throughout the Bible. As both letters to the Thessalonians have dealt with the Lord's return, they have fulfilled the prophecies of Daniel 9 by pointing to Jesus. Our phrase for 2 Thessalonians is *Faithful Lord.*

Teaching

2 Thessalonians 3:1–2: At the conclusion of his second letter to the Thessalonians, Paul asked for the church's prayers for his ministry. Paul specifically asked the church to pray that the Lord's message would spread to new places in the same way that it did among the Thessalonians. Paul asked for prayer along similar lines in 1 Timothy 2:1–2: "First of all, then, I urge that petitions, prayers, intercessions, and thanksgivings be made for everyone, for kings and all those who are in authority, so that we may lead a tranquil and quiet life in all godliness and dignity." Paul did not want to become content with the work he had already done. Instead, he wanted to see the gospel continue to spread to new places.

Paul also asked for the church to pray "that we may be delivered from wicked and evil men" (v. 2). Constable proposed that these were likely the unbelieving Jews that Paul encountered in Corinth.[1]

2 Thessalonians 3:3–5: Regardless of your views on the rapture, the Lord will be faithful to strengthen and guard you while you await His return. Paul encouraged the Thessalonians to focus on Jesus, specifically that they would be drawn towards "God's love and Christ's endurance" (v. 5).

---

[1] Thomas L. Constable, *Expository Notes of Dr. Thomas Constable: 2 Thessalonians*, 39, https://planobiblechapel.org/tcon/notes/pdf/2thessalonians.pdf.

2 Thessalonians 3:6–13: Paul prayed that the church would walk in holiness. To demonstrate how serious this admonition was, Paul invoked the name of Jesus to warn the church to stay away from anyone who would get in the way of their pursuit of Jesus. Paul encouraged the church to imitate him and his companions, specifically in how they worked to support themselves. Constable linked this admonition to an unidentified false teaching that infiltrated the church, which possibly led some of the Thessalonians to quit their jobs and live off the charity of the church.[2] Paul also encouraged the Philippian church to imitate him: "Join in imitating me, brothers, and observe those who live according to the example you have in us" (Philippians 3:17). This was not arrogance on Paul's behalf, but confidence in his pursuit of Christ. Truly being prepared for Christ's return did not mean sitting back idly and just waiting. Instead, it meant actively pursuing Christ, working, and advancing the gospel every day. Ultimately, Paul could charge others to imitate him because of 1 Corinthians 11:1: "Imitate me, as I also imitate Christ."

Paul and his companions worked while he was in Thessalonica, even though he had a right to be supported by the church. They gave up their right to the church's support to set an example of work for the believers to follow. In fact, part of their message while in Thessalonica was that those who did not work should not eat. Paul exhorted these people to resume their work and to "not grow weary in doing good" (v. 13) as they awaited Christ's return.

2 Thessalonians 3:14–15: If any of the offending brothers refused to listen to Paul's exhortations in his letter, Paul encouraged the church to shun him in order to bring shame and hopefully repentance. Constable noted that, in this instance, social pressure is put to good use when it leads to a brother's repentance.[3] It is important to note that the person Paul taught the church to shun would have been in sin because of a false teaching. This was not simply because another believer did something the others didn't like. Paul did not want this process to be mean-spirited. He encouraged the church to not "treat him as an enemy, but warn him as a brother" (v. 15).

2 Thessalonians 3:16–18: Paul concluded his letter with a prayer for God to give the church peace and a wish for the church to continue to experience the grace of Christ.

---

[2] Constable, 42.

[3] Constable, 45.

Closing

Nelson's Commentary outlines a four-step process for practicing church discipline, or "denying fellowship with a believer who is in known and open sin":[4]

1. Meet with them one-on-one. Confront the fellow believer about his/her sin privately.
2. Take another church member. If they are unrepentant, take others with you.
3. Announce it to the church. If they are still unrepentant, inform the church of the person's unrepentant attitude.
4. Ask the person to leave the church. If the person still remains unrepentant, it is at this point permissible to ask them to leave the church.

The goal of this process is to see the person come to repentance: "Brothers, if someone is caught in any wrongdoing, you who are spiritual should restore such a person with a gentle spirit, watching out for yourselves so you also won't be tempted" (Galatians 6:1). Church discipline should be exercised in order to prepare the body for the return of Christ.

The Daily Word

"But the Lord is faithful." No matter what evil men do, no matter what life brings, no matter when the Lord returns, Paul reaffirmed this message to the Thessalonian church: The Lord is faithful. God is faithful to strengthen you and guard your heart from the evil one. You may need to be reminded today of this simple yet powerful truth: But the Lord is faithful. You may be facing an outstanding medical bill you just don't know how you will pay—*but the Lord is faithful.*

You may have a child whose heart seems to be swept away by culture and lies from the enemy—*but the Lord is faithful.* You may be dealing with a marriage, a relationship, a business, or a dream that seems to be failing—*but the Lord is faithful.* As you press on and seek the Lord in all your ways, the Lord will be faithful. He has promised that He will be faithful for a thousand generations! Whatever the weight on your shoulders may be, remember God's promise—*He is faithful.* God will walk with you. God will give you strength. God will guard

[4] Earl D. Radmacher, Ronald B. Allen, and H. Wayne House, eds., *Nelson's New Illustrated Bible Commentary* (Nashville: Thomas Nelson, 1999), 1590.

you as you go. God will direct your heart to love and grant you endurance to press on. Hold on to His faithfulness through it all. *He is faithful.*

But the Lord is faithful. —2 Thessalonians 3:3

Further Scripture: Deuteronomy 7:9; 1 Corinthians 1:9; 2 Thessalonians 3:3b–5

Questions

1. In 2 Thessalonians 3:4, Paul stated his confidence in the Lord that the brethren in Thessalonica would continue to do what was commanded. Who gave the commands they were to follow, and what were they (1 Thessalonians 4:1–12)?
2. Read 2 Thessalonians 3:6 and explain why Paul was commanding the brethren to keep away (withdraw) from every brother who led an idle (undisciplined, disorderly, unruly) life (2 Thessalonians 3:7–12).
3. Have you ever grown weary in doing good (2 Thessalonians 3:13)? If so, how did you combat it?
4. What did Paul firmly direct the Thessalonians to do if anyone did not obey the instructions given in the letter (2 Thessalonians 3:14–15)? Why would Paul want the disobedient to feel ashamed (Psalm 51:17; 2 Corinthians 7:9–10)?
5. What did the Holy Spirit highlight to you in 2 Thessalonians 3 through the reading or the teaching?

WEEK 80

Lesson 74: 1 Timothy 1

Our Mediator: Advice to Timothy

Teaching Notes

Intro

Today, we begin our study of the first of Paul's letters to his "beloved son Timothy."[1] MacArthur documents that the meaning of Timothy's name is "one who honors God." Timothy was brought up in the faith by his grandmother Lois and his mother Eunice, both of whom were devout Jews who became followers of Christ (2 Timothy 1:5). His father was a Greek and was probably not a believer. Timothy was from the city of Lystra (Acts 16:1), which was a Roman city in Galatia, now Turkey. Paul traveled through Lystra on his first missionary journey, met Timothy there, and probably led Timothy to Christ, becoming his "beloved son" (Acts 14:6–23). On his second journey, Paul visited Lystra again, and chose to take Timothy with him on the rest of his journey (Acts 16:1–3). Timothy was a young man, possibly in his late teens or early twenties (1 Timothy 4:12). Acts 16:2 states Timothy also had a reputation of godliness. MacArthur outlines the relationship of Paul and Timothy, stating, "Timothy was to be Paul's disciple, friend, and co-laborer for the rest of the apostle's life, ministering with him in Berea, Athens, Corinth, and accompanying him on his trip to Jerusalem."[2] During Paul's first imprisonment in Rome, Timothy was with him and stayed with him until Paul was released. Timothy then went to Philippi. Timothy also served as Paul's representative, visiting many of the churches Paul had started. At the time of Paul's first letter, Timothy was serving as pastor to the Ephesian church (1 Timothy 1:3).[3]

Paul's relationship with Timothy was as a mentor in discipleship. Every believer needs a mentor to help prepare them for taking on the role that God calls them to. Paul not only poured into Timothy, he trusted Timothy to carry on the work of ministry, even sending Timothy out in his own place. What an awesome

---

[1] John MacArthur, *The MacArthur Bible Commentary* (Nashville: Thomas Nelson, 2005), 1772.

[2] MacArthur, 1772.

[3] MacArthur, 1772.

example of how discipleship should work, and it mirrors what Jesus did in His own ministry. Our phrase of how Jesus is presented in 1 Timothy is *Our Mediator* (1 Timothy 2:5–6). He is the constant reminder of discipleship. Hebrews 13:23 states that, at some point, Timothy was put in jail and later released.[4]

Paul claimed authorship in verse 1, and the early church agreed. Some modern scholars, however, question if Paul actually wrote 1 and 2 Timothy and Titus. These scholars offer five arguments:

1. The historical information given in the Pastoral Epistles do not agree with Acts' presentation on Paul's life. However, there's nothing in Acts that mentions the Prison Epistles. For some scholars, this is missing historical support. Acts ends before Paul's last days in prison or his execution; none of his last letters would have been mentioned.
2. The false teachers Paul referred to was the form of Gnosticism present in the second century.
3. The way the church was organized in the Prison Epistles reflects the church of the second century. However, the church structure was the same as what Paul established in Acts 14 and Philippians.
4. The major themes of Paul's other letters are not mentioned in the Prison Epistles. Paul still talked about the importance of God's Word, of salvation, of election, and of what the church is meant to be. Paul's voice can be clearly heard in 1 and 2 Timothy and Titus.
5. The Greek words used in the Prison Epistles are not found in any other writings of Paul's or anywhere else in the New Testament.[5]

I share this because it is important to know that there are always critical viewpoints and different interpretations of any passage in the Bible. Part of studying scripture is to know that people read it differently, and it can be healthy to be aware of different viewpoints. Just so you know, I agree with MacArthur that Paul wrote all three of these books between AD 62–64—1 Timothy and Titus shortly after he was released from prison the first time, and 2 Timothy while imprisoned the second time, not long before he was executed.[6] After Paul was released from prison the first time, he revisited many of the churches he had started, including the church in Ephesus. Paul had left Timothy in Ephesus earlier to deal with four problems: "false doctrine, disorder in worship, the need for qualified leaders, and

[4] MacArthur, 1772.

[5] MacArthur, 1772–73.

[6] MacArthur, 1773.

materialism."[7] He followed up with Timothy from Macedonia with this letter about how to handle each of these issues.

Teaching

1 Timothy 1:1–11: Wiersbe explains Paul first emphasized that Timothy should *teach sound doctrine.*[8] Paul told Timothy not to listen to anything that included empty speculations about God (vv. 1–4, 6–7), but to teach sincere faith with a pure heart (v. 5). Paul went on to say that the law was not meant for the righteous, but for the unrighteous, which he then lists 14 examples: lawless, rebellious, ungodly, sinful, unholy, irreverent, those that kill their parents, murderers, sexually immoral, homosexuals, kidnappers, liars, perjurers, and "whatever else is contrary to the sound teaching" (vv. 8–10). Paul emphasized that all this was based on the gospel which had come from God (v. 11).

1 Timothy 1:12–17: Paul then instructed Timothy to *preach the gospel.*[9] Paul shared his personal testimony in verses 12–17, which was impossible for him to do without sharing the gospel of Christ and what that had meant to his life. Paul described who he had been before he met Jesus (v. 13) and what he had experienced in Christ (v. 14). Paul described himself as the worst sinner of all time (v. 15). Yet, Paul acknowledged the mercy and grace he had received through Christ Jesus, and to whom he gave all glory (vv. 16–17).

1 Timothy 1:18–20: Paul instructed Timothy to *defend the faith.*[10] Paul reminded Timothy of the prophetic words that had been spoken over him, so Timothy could hold on to that knowledge and find strength in it to engage in battle, in faith, and in conscience (vv. 18–19a). Wiersbe points out Paul went from an army image in verse 18 to a naval image in verse 19, describing professed Christians who "make shipwreck" of their faith by rejecting their good consciences in order to defend ungodly lives.[11] Paul went on to mention two of these who were shipwrecked—Hymenaeus and Alexander—and said he had turned them over to Satan (v. 20).

---

[7] MacArthur, 1773.

[8] Warren W. Wiersbe, *The Bible Exposition Commentary: Ephesians–Revelation* (Colorado Springs: David C. Cook, 2003), 210.

[9] Wiersbe, 212.

[10] Wiersbe, 213.

[11] Wiersbe, 213.

Closing

Here's the takeaway from these verses for the church today, a spiritual inventory to examine what we are doing:

- Are we teaching sound doctrine in the church?
- Are we proclaiming the gospel?
- Are we defending the faith?

Paul knew that if Timothy practiced these things, there would be a true movement of faith in the church in Ephesus. As Christ is *Our Mediator*, the same is true for the church today.

The Daily Word

In this letter of advice to Timothy, Paul remembered his life before Christ. He remembered his days as a blasphemer, a persecutor, and an arrogant man. He shared his testimony so others would know about the grace and mercy he received from Jesus Christ, his Lord. *Because Paul testified to others*, his testimony of God's mercy *impacted and transformed* others' lives for eternity, bringing honor and glory to God.

If you have received Jesus as your Savior, then like Paul, you have a testimony. You have a story about who you were before Christ and who you are now after Christ. Not everyone has the same story. You may think, *My story isn't as dramatic as Paul's.* Don't compare! Guess who wrote your story? Jesus. He's the author and perfecter of your faith. If you question your testimony, you are questioning God's story in your life. Fill in the blanks to help you begin: "I give thanks to Christ Jesus my Lord who has strengthened me, because He considered me faithful—I was formerly a [fill in the blank] and [fill in the blank] person. But I received mercy. I am a new person in Christ." Now, *go and share your story* with at least one other person! Share from your heart the story the Lord has written and the mercy He has had on your life.

I give thanks to Christ Jesus our Lord who has strengthened me, because He considered me faithful, appointing me to the ministry—one who was formerly a blasphemer, a persecutor, and an arrogant man. But I received mercy because I acted out of ignorance in unbelief. —1 Timothy 1:12–13

Further Scripture: Psalm 66:16; Mark 5:19; 1 Timothy 1:16

Questions

1. In 1 Timothy 1:2, how did Paul refer to Timothy? Have you been a spiritual father or mother to someone? How about a son or daughter? If so, how has this relationship helped you to grow and mature in the faith?
2. Paul shared with Timothy the goal of his instruction to the men who were teaching strange doctrines. What was his goal (1 Timothy 1:5)? What does not holding to this goal lead to (1 Timothy 1:6–7)? Have you known anyone who seemed to be a believer, but was teaching strange doctrine?
3. Paul shared some of his personal testimony. What did he hope would be evident through sharing his story (1 Timothy 1:12–16)?
4. Timothy was told to "fight the good fight" (1 Timothy 1:18b NASB). What does this mean? How are you being encouraged to fight the good fight by others? How do you encourage others?
5. What did the Holy Spirit highlight to you in 1 Timothy 1 through the reading or the teaching?

WEEK 80

Lesson 75: 1 Timothy 2

Our Mediator: Instructions for Praying for Men and Women

Teaching Notes

Intro

In chapter 2, Paul addresses the issue of having balance within the church (1 Corinthians 14:40). Remember, Paul was pouring into his young apprentice Timothy, who was pastor of the church in Ephesus, instructing him how to do that.

Teaching

1 Timothy 2:1–4: In verse 1, Paul established the priority of prayer: "First of all, then, I urge," then he outlined four types of prayer—petitions (or supplications), prayers, intercessions, and thanksgivings for everyone, not just themselves. Wiersbe differentiates among these four:

- Supplications as "offering a request for a felt need."
- Prayers are "an act of worship, not just an expression of our wants and needs . . . reverence in our hearts as we pray to God."
- Intercessions are when we draw near to God on behalf of others. "It suggests that we enjoy fellowship with God so that we have confidence in Him as we pray."
- Thanksgivings "not only give thanks for answers to prayer, but for who God is and what He does for us in His grace."[1]

Paul explains "everyone" (v. 1b) that was to be included in prayer—he mentions kings and those in authority (v. 2a). That means that we are to pray for President Trump and all those who represent us in government. Our prayers should not be about taking sides or praying only for those with whom we agree, but should be for everyone. Think about what the authority did to Paul—imprisonment,

[1] Warren W. Wiersbe, *The Bible Exposition Commentary: Ephesians–Revelation* (Colorado Springs: David C. Cook, 2003), 215.

execution—and yet he prayed for them! Why do we pray? Because it allows us to live tranquil, godly lives. I challenge you to stop posting negative things about people, and pray for them instead. I challenge you to pray for the deacons and ministers on your church staff, even if you disagree with them. Paul describes this kind of prayer as good and pleasing to God (v. 3). We pray for God's will to be done, which is for everyone to be saved (John 3:16) and understand the truth of Christ's death on the cross (1 John 2:2; 4:14).

1 Timothy 2:5–7: Paul explains why we can talk to the Father—because Christ is *Our Mediator*. He goes between us and God on our behalf (v. 5). *Our Mediator* gave Himself as our ransom, which was a testimony at God's proper time. In the Old Testament, Job wrote there was no one who could intervene for him with God (Job 9:33). To some extent, Moses took that role for the Israelites (Galatians 3:19). In verse 6, Jesus can do that for us because He paid that price for us with His life—"a ransom for all" (Matthew 20:28). Paul stated that for these purposes he was appointed a preacher, an apostle, and a teacher for the Gentiles (v. 7).

1 Timothy 2:8–15: In 1 Corinthians 11:4–5, Paul stated both men and women should pray. Both men and women prayed in the early church. Verse 10 does not contradict the 1 Corinthians 11 passage. Rather, Paul was establishing order for prayer in the church. In every prayer they prayed, men were to lift up "holy hands" without anger or argument (v. 8). Throughout Scripture, people are seen in various positions—standing with outstretched hands (1 Kings 8:22), standing (Luke 18:11), kneeling (Daniel 6:10), sitting (2 Samuel 7:18), bowing the head (Genesis 24:26), falling on the ground (Genesis 17:3), and lifting the eyes (John 17:1). Those postures express what the person is feeling. What is most important is not the posture of the body but the posture of the heart.[2]

Paul outlines three requirements for prayer: "holy hands," which means living a holy life; "without anger," which means to be "on good terms with one another"; and without argument, which means without "disputing" or having "open disagreements with others."[3]

In verses 9–10, Paul explains the requirements for women—to dress modestly and decently, without elaborate hairstyles, jewelry, or expensive clothes. Instead, they are to be clothed in good works that show "the true values of godly character and Christian service."[4] Further, women are to learn in silence with full submission (v. 11). Wiersbe explains that the word "silence" is a poor

---

[2] Wiersbe, 216.

[3] Wiersbe, 216–17.

[4] Wiersbe, 218.

translation of the Greek word. The same Greek word is translated as "peaceable" in 1 Timothy 2:2. Paul's instructions were because "some of the women abused their newfound freedom in Christ and created disturbances in the services by interrupting."[5] Further, "submission" can be best understood as "recognizing God's order in the home and the church, and joyfully obeying it."[6] Submission is about a rank under authority and order, not value or worth. There are seasons when children submit to the parents, when employees submit to their bosses, when citizens submit to their government. Jesus submitted to the Father. This model God has put in place doesn't mean we're less than another person, but it allows order within the body of Christ.

Before we look at verse 12, I want to remind you we have had very few controversial passages in reviveSCHOOL. If you do not agree, don't quit reviveSCHOOL. I am just trying to communicate from my experience what the Bible says. If you do not agree, that is fine!

In verse 12, Paul said he did not allow women to teach men or have authority over them. Paul outlines how older women should teach younger women (Titus 2:3–4) and how Timothy had been taught by women in his home (2 Timothy 1:5; 3:15). Women had an unbelievable ministry in the Bible. Think of the women who were at the cross and those at the empty tomb. Think of Lydia, Priscilla, and Dorcas. In Romans 16, Paul greeted at least six women by name, and Phoebe actually delivered a divine letter. Women clearly have a role in communicating in the church.

In verses 13–14, Paul gave his reasons why he gave these instructions to women. First, Adam was created before Eve, and Adam was not deceived, but Eve was and transgressed (sinned). There was deception because there was a violation of God's given orders. But women will be saved through childbearing and in faith, love, and holiness with good judgment (v. 15). The Savior was "born of a woman" (Matthew 1:18; Luke 1:34–35; Galatians 4:4).

Closing

Slow down and process what is Paul saying here to Timothy. If you are okay with prayer, with petition, intercessions, and giving thanks, what is the rest of the text portraying. I am by no means dimensioning the role a woman can have. There are qualities of my wife that make her an unbelievingly strong leader in the Lord. God is using her in an incredible way, just as he can use any women here. Just please do it according to scripture and in order. It is a hard line to walk, but my prayer is that you ask Holy Spirit to show you what this text is saying.

---

[5] Wiersbe, 218.

[6] Wiersbe, 217.

The Daily Word

Paul instructed Timothy on how to fight the spiritual battle the church faced as it followed Christ. He told Timothy to pray—petitions, prayer, intercession, and thanksgiving. Paul said to pray every kind of prayer. Paul urged the church to pray for everyone: authorities, outsiders, family, friends, enemies, and those who persecute others. You have the responsibility to pray for everyone. Why? Because it is good, and it pleases God.

Today, *take time to pray for others*. Try setting a timer for ten minutes and commit to pray during that time. Ask the Lord to bring specific people to your mind and make a list of names. Then pray all kinds of prayers.

Petitions: Ask in bold confidence from God's Word.
Prayer: Communicate to the Lord, your heavenly Father.
Intercession: Lift up the needs of others before the Lord.
Thanksgiving: Thank the Lord for everyone, even recalling His mighty attributes and answered prayers.

Pray for others as you press on in the spiritual battle. Prayer pleases God as He longs for all to be saved and know the truth.

First of all, then, I urge that petitions, prayers, intercessions, and thanksgivings be made for everyone. —1 Timothy 2:1

Further Scripture: Matthew 5:44; Ephesians 6:18; 1 Timothy 2:3–4

Questions

1. According to 1 Timothy 2, who are the subjects of prayer? Does this mean we only pray for those in authority we agree with? Take time today and pray for those in authority as well as others the Holy Spirit brings to your mind.
2. The word "good" is a keyword in Paul's pastoral letters. What are some things Paul said are good, starting with 1 Timothy 2:3 (1 Timothy 1:8, 19; 3:7, 13; 4:4; 2 Timothy 1:14; Titus 2:7)?
3. What is the good news we as believers have today that Job complained to God about not having (Job 9:33)? What does the mediator do on our behalf (Matthew 20:28)?
4. Why does it seem God makes distinctions between male and female roles in the church (1 Corinthians 14:40)?

5. What did Paul not permit women to do? What are the two reasons he used to back up his claim?
6. What did the Holy Spirit highlight to you in 1 Timothy 2 through the reading or the teaching?

WEEK 81

Lesson 76: 1 Timothy 3

Our Mediator: Requirements for the Overseer

Teaching Notes

Intro

We're continuing to work through Paul's first letter to Timothy with instructions for how Timothy is to pastor the church in Ephesus. Shepherding is hard work. Our phrase for the book of 1 Timothy is *Our Mediator*. Christ, *Our Mediator*, through His death and resurrection, allows us to come to the Father in prayer (1 Timothy 2:5–6). In chapter 3, Paul provides Timothy with instructions for who can serve as lay leadership within the church. The lay leadership of deacons and elders is necessary if Timothy is to succeed as pastor of the church and the church is to fulfill its call in Ephesus. As we work through this passage, I want you to pull back and look at those in your congregation. Ask yourself if your church is following the requirements Paul set out for Timothy. Paul wanted the elders and deacons to be installed so his work would not be corrupted (1 Timothy 3). Paul was establishing a team, another layer of people, to help protect the congregation from false teachers.

Teaching

1 Timothy 3:1–7: In verse 1, Paul names the position of overseer, a term synonymous with pastor or bishop (or elder as stated in Titus 1). *Nelson's Commentary* explains the overseer is "the person who oversees a congregation."[1] Then deacons are described (vv. 8–13) and are given the responsibility of overseeing "the internal affairs of the church."[2] It is a type of Acts 6:4 model. Paul emphasized an overseer was one who "desires a noble work" (v. 1b) and provided 15 requirements for an overseer/pastor (vv. 2–7). These can seem to be a bit ritualistic, and they are definitely hard to live up to.[3] All these have been adapted from Constable.

---

[1] Earl D. Radmacher, Ronald B. Allen, and H. Wayne House, eds., *Nelson's New Illustrated Bible Commentary* (Nashville: Thomas Nelson, 1999), 1600.

[2] Radmacher et al., 1600.

[3] David A. Mappes, "Moral Virtues Associated with Eldership," *Bibliotheca Sacra* 160:638 (April–June 2003): 202–18.

1. *Above reproach*: Constable explains the overseer "should possess no observable flaw in his character or conduct. That is, there should be no cause for justifiable criticism, now or in his past, that anyone could use to discredit him and bring reproach on the name of Christ and the church."
2. *Husband of one wife*: This requirement has been interpreted four ways: he is required to marry; he can only be married once; he must be monogamous, so only married to one person at a time; and he must be "a moral husband." Paul seems to have been writing about someone's current condition, not his past.
3. *Temperate*: "Sober, vigilant, clear-headed, and well-balanced."
4. *Prudent*: "Self-controlled . . . sensible . . . such a man, such a bishop, will not speak rashly, will be a person of sound judgment, will be master of himself, and of his situation."[4]
5. *Respectable*: "Orderly, of good behavior, dignified and decent in his conduct."
6. *Hospitable*: "One who opens his home to the early church. This was an especially essential quality in the early church, since there were few public accommodations for traveling ministers and much need[ed] to take in needy Christians temporarily." It is from the Greek word meaning "loving the stranger."
7. *Able to teach*: "Apt, qualified, and competent to explain and defend the truth of God," requiring "ministry skill or gift."
8. *Not addicted to wine*: "Not a brawler, playboy, slave of drink, or drunkard."
9. *Not pugnacious or violent*: He is not to be "a person who resorts to physical or verbal violence to vent his anger or to settle disputes."
10. *Gentle*: "Patient and forbearing."
11. *Uncontentious*: "A person who is not quarrelsome . . . not a fighter or a brawler."
12. *Free from the love of money:* The disqualifier is the love for not possession of money. "This means the candidate's attitude toward material wealth ought to be one of healthy detachment."[5]
13. *Manages his own household well*: "Has control of his family" (Proverbs 24:3–4; 27:23; Ephesians 6:4; Titus 1:6).
14. *Not a new convert*: "Evidence that he can function as an elder . . . without becoming 'conceited' . . . 'blinded' or 'beclouded.'" Does the new convert reflect the other fourteen characteristics?

---

[4] Guy H. King, *A Leader Led* (London: Marshall, Morgan & Scott, 1962), 59.

[5] Philip H. Towner, *1–2 Timothy & Titus*, The IVP New Testament Commentary (Downers Grove, IL, and Leicester, England: InterVarsity Press, 1994), 87.

15. *A good reputation outside the church*: To be above reproach with and before nonbelievers.

1 Timothy 3:8–13: There's another list in these verses of 12 requirements for deacons. The deacons are the doers—they get the work done in the church to allow pastors to oversee the spiritual matters of the church.

Closing

We did not have time to look at the rest of this chapter, but I encourage you to prayerfully read through it and ask God to show you the importance of each in the work of the church.

The Daily Word

God is a God of order and peace. Therefore, Paul instructed the church regarding the order and expectations for church leadership—the elders and deacons. At first glance it may appear like a checklist of how to behave and conduct yourself so you can become a church leader. Paul spoke frankly when he said those who can't manage their own households can't be expected to lead and manage a church body. Even so, Paul's heart reflected God's heart—*to maintain peace in God's household, the church of the living God, the pillar and foundation of truth.*

When your life possesses the qualities Paul listed for church leadership, it's an outward sign of your inward relationship with the Lord. Your life reflects your love and devotion to following Christ. This is important for church leadership because the God of peace and order understands a leader in the church must be strong in the Lord in leading his own household. As you follow God with everything in you, He gives you all you need to lead a godly life. Your household will actually reflect God's peace and order. Today, ask yourself: *Does my life, my character, and my household reflect my love for the Lord?*

I write these things to you, hoping to come to you soon. But if I should be delayed, I have written so that you will know how people ought to act in God's household, which is the church of the living God, the pillar and foundation of the truth. —1 Timothy 3:14–15

Further Scripture: 1 Corinthians 14:33; 1 Timothy 3:5; 2 Peter 1:3

Questions

1. What are the 15 qualifications for a man to meet if he desires to serve as a bishop/pastor? Do you agree every Christian should exhibit these characteristics?
2. What are the 12 qualifications for someone to serve as a deacon? What are the differences and similarities between the qualifications of a deacon and a bishop/pastor?
3. Why is it important for a man be able to manage his own household in order to be a leader in the church?
4. What is the encouragement given to those deacons who serve well in the church?
5. What are the basic facts of the mystery of godliness? Back up these claims with other Scripture (Matthew 3:16; 28:2; Luke 24:51; John 1:14; Acts 10:34; Romans 10:18; 16:26; 1 Peter 1:20; 1 John 1:2; 3:5).
6. What did the Holy Spirit highlight to you in 1 Timothy 3 through the reading or the teaching?

WEEK 81

Lesson 77: 1 Timothy 4

Our Mediator: The Characteristics of Godly Ministers

Teaching Notes

Intro

As Paul continued to write this letter, he began to talk to Timothy from his role as an older pastor to a younger one. Warren Wiersbe outlines Paul's expectations of Timothy in chapter 4—Paul called Timothy to be a *good minister* by preaching the Word (vv. 1–6), a *godly minister* by practicing the Word (vv. 7–12), and a *growing minister* by progressing in the Word (vv. 13–16).[1]

Teaching

1 Timothy 4:1–6: In verses 1–2, Paul told Timothy the Holy Spirit said some would leave the faith in later times, following deceitful spirits and the teaching of demons. *Nelson's Commentary* suggests, "Paul may be referring to various prophecies inspired by the Holy Spirit concerning defection from God's truth, or he might be speaking of a revelation the Spirit had given to him."[2] Paul's statement does not necessarily mean these people would walk away from the faith. It could mean they would stop walking out their faith in obedience to God.[3] Demons are fallen angels who are Satan's minions. They are deceitful spirits and will work to pull us away from God, using things like the spirit of pride or the spirit of fear. Even as believers we still have to deal with demons (Matthew 16:21–23). Even Jesus' closest disciples (Peter, James, and John) had to fight the demons, like in Matthew 16, when Jesus told Peter, "Get behind me, Satan!" Another example of the results of demons is found in the lives of Ananias and Sapphira in Acts 5:1–10. They lied to the Holy Spirit about what they had received from selling

---

[1] Warren W. Wiersbe, *The Bible Exposition Commentary: Ephesians–Revelation* (Colorado Springs: David C. Cook, 2003), 224–26.

[2] Earl D. Radmacher, Ronald B. Allen, and H. Wayne House, eds., *Nelson's New Illustrated Bible Commentary* (Nashville: Thomas Nelson, 1999), 1602.

[3] Radmacher et al., 1602.

some land, testing the Spirit of the Lord. The church today has to acknowledge and talk about the enemy.

Some of the false teachings are listed in verse 3—forbidding marriage, which God designed, and requiring abstinence from certain foods that God had created and blessed. Paul emphasized everything God created is good and sanctified (set apart) by the Word of God and prayer (v. 5) and should not be rejected when received with thanksgiving (v. 4). In verse 6, Paul points out that as a good servant of Christ, Timothy needed to continue to nourish himself through God's Word. One way to be a good servant of Christ is to point out the false teachings so they do not influence believers.

1 Timothy 4:7–12: Paul encourages Timothy to practice the Word of God as well as preaching it. Paul told him to have nothing to do with irreverent and silly myths but rather to train (exercise) himself in holiness (v. 7). *Nelson's Commentary* explains that the word "train" or "exercise" was the term used "for the physical training of Greek athletes. True spirituality requires one to train at godliness in one's walk with the Lord."[4] Paul explained training of the body has only temporary results while training in godliness is eternal (v. 8). *Nelson's Commentary* explains verse 9 as Paul's admonition that "no one can deny" what he had written.[5] Paul stated believers were to labor and strive because their hope was in God, the Savior of everyone (v. 10). The statement, "'especially of those who believe,' draws a contrast between God's common grace to all and His special saving grace to those who trust Him as their Savior."[6] Therefore, Paul encouraged Timothy to teach the things he had just listed in verse 10 (v. 11). Timothy was to be a godly example, regardless of how young he was (v. 12). *Nelson's Commentary* explains the word "young" used here usually included men up to the age of 40 and Timothy was probably between 35 and 40 years old at the time. *Nelson's Commentary* continues, "The antidote for his *youth* was his life."[7] Timothy was told to be an example through the words he said (Ephesians 4:15), through his behavior (Galatians 5:16; Titus 1:16; 1 John 2:6), in the love of God (1 John 4:18–21), in the attitude of the Holy Spirit, in the faith (through trust in God) (1 Timothy 1:14; 2:15; 6:11), and in purity (in sexual matters and thoughts) (Philippians 4:8; Colossians 3:25).[8]

---

[4] Radmacher et al., 1602.

[5] Radmacher et al., 1602.

[6] Radmacher et al., 1602.

[7] Radmacher et al., 1602.

[8] Radmacher et al., 1602.

1 Timothy 4:13–16: Finally, Paul instructs Timothy to keep growing in the Lord. Paul stated he wanted to come to Ephesus, but until he could, he instructed Timothy to publicly read Scripture (Acts 13:15), encourage believers to obey the Word, and to teach God's Word (v. 13). Paul then instructed Timothy not to neglect the spiritual gift he had received through prophecy and the laying on of hands by the council of elders (v. 14). This past experience for Timothy was a part of his being commissioned for the work he was called to do and probably happened while he was still in Lystra (Acts 16:1). Paul further instructs Timothy to practice using his given gift. Paul wanted Timothy to be committed to using those gifts (v. 15). Paul closed this section by instructing Timothy to pay attention to his own life and in his teaching to make sure he was doing what God had called him to do. In all this, Timothy was to persevere and continue on with the ministry he had been given (v. 16).

Closing

Paul understood how important it was for Timothy to continue to grow in the Lord, even as he led the believers in Ephesus. Paul's instructions are relevant to us today. We are called to His work and gifted specifically to do His work. We are successful only when we focus on growing spiritually through the Holy Spirit within us.

The Daily Word

Paul was honest with Timothy, advising that as Timothy dealt with church life, some people would depart from their faith. They would be deceived and lured by hypocrisy. Timothy, even though he was a young man, needed to continue to live as an example to believers in speech, in conduct, in love, in faith, and in purity, thus reflecting his own devotion and strength in the Lord.

Like Timothy, no matter how young or old you may be, the Lord calls you to live as an example to others through your speech, conduct, love, faith, and purity. Do you have to be perfect? No! God does not ask for perfection. Instead, as you *daily seek* the Lord's presence and His Word, *God's grace will transform your speech, conduct, love, faith, and purity.* Your transformed life will serve as a godly example to others by the way you talk with patience and self-control, the way you show undeserved kindness, or the way you choose purity over immodesty. You represent God's love as you live your life. Today, *spend time with Jesus.* Time in His presence transforms your life and will serve as an example for others, spurring them on in their own faith in the Lord.

Command and teach these things. Let no one despise your youth; instead, you should be an example to the believers in speech, in conduct, in love, in faith, in purity. —1 Timothy 4:11–12

Further Scripture: John 13:35; Romans 12:2; 1 Timothy 4:1–2

Questions

1. According to 1 Timothy 4:1, what will cause some to fall away from the faith? What are some of the "doctrines of demons" (NKJV) (Ephesians 6:12; James 3:14–15; 2 John 7–11)?
2. What benefits come from godliness? (1 Timothy 4:8; 6:6)
3. In 1 Timothy 4:10b, what do you think Paul meant when he said the living God is the Savior of all people, especially of believers?
4. In what specific ways was Timothy told to set an example for believers (1 Timothy 4:12)? How is your example to others in these five areas?
5. Read 1 Timothy 4:16. Why did Paul instruct Timothy to keep a close watch on how he lived and what he taught?
6. What did the Holy Spirit highlight to you in 1 Timothy 4 through the reading or the teaching?

Lesson 78: 1 Timothy 5

Our Mediator: The Widows and Elderly

Teaching Notes

Intro

This is the 78th lesson in our study of Paul's letters. His words drip with wisdom and practical advice for us. In 1 Timothy, Paul as the older minister poured into his young protégé, Timothy. In chapter 5, Paul presents practical church issues that need to be taken care of correctly.

Teaching

1 Timothy 5:1–2: Paul began by instructing Timothy not "to ignore older members [but] to love and serve all of the people, regardless of their ages."[1] He lists four groups of individuals in verses 1–2, reminding Timothy of their value regardless of their age. Rebuke means to speak sharply to someone (v. 1a). Younger men had no business speaking to older men without respect. This is part of God's order that we are to speak to those who are older with respect. Paul includes older women in his instructions for showing respect to and also said to treat younger women with pure motives as he would his sisters (v. 2).

1 Timothy 5:3–16: Paul also instructed that all widows should be honored, and those who are "genuinely widows," meaning they had no family to support them, should be both honored and supported, even with financial support if needed (v. 3). However, if the widow had family, her family was to honor and support her by learning to practice godliness (v. 4). *Nelson's Commentary* states, "Honoring our parents includes caring for them physically and financially as they grow older."[2] This pleases the Lord. Without family support, it is the church's responsibility to care for them while they devote themselves to petitions and prayers

[1] Warren W. Wiersbe, *The Bible Exposition Commentary: Ephesians–Revelation* (Colorado Springs: David C. Cook, 2003), 228.

[2] Earl D. Radmacher, Ronald B. Allen, and H. Wayne House, eds., *Nelson's New Illustrated Bible Commentary* (Nashville: Thomas Nelson, 1999), 1604.

(v. 5). Those who are self-indulgent or ungodly are no longer the responsibility of the church (v. 6).[3]

By doing what was right, the believers in the congregation maintained a good reputation in the community, and the church was held blameless (v. 7). Paul's condemnation was strong though for those who did not take care of the widows in their families. He described them as being worse than unbelievers, having actually denied their faith (v. 8).

Paul gave requirements for the widows who would receive the support of the church. They were those who were at least 60 years old, the wife of one husband, were known for good works—having brought up her children, shown hospitality, washed the feet of the saints, helped the sick, and done other good works (vv. 9–10). *Nelson's Commentary* explains why the age limit was so set: "The reason for this refusal [of women under 60] is that younger widows may grow wanton, which means to experience sexual desire, and thus desire to marry, presumably an unbeliever, since the marriage is said to be outside their first faith" (vv. 11–13).[4]

Paul wanted the younger women to marry and have children so Satan would not be able to use them (vv. 14–15). In verse 16, Paul repeated his admonition for the family, including female believers, to help support the widows in their families so the church could help the genuine widows (v. 16).

1 Timothy 5:17–25: In verse 17 Paul moved on to support for the elders. He stated it was okay to pay those who worked hard at preaching and teaching and were good leaders because "the worker is worthy of his wages" (v. 18). In verse 19, Paul explained an accusation should not be brought against an elder without two or three other witnesses. This is still about showing respect.

However, when someone was found guilty, Paul instructed Timothy to publicly rebuke the sinner so others would be afraid of the consequences of their sin (v. 20). Paul knew "discipline must be exercised in the church. But it should be done without prejudice (personal bias) or partiality (preferential treatment) (vv. 21–22)."[5] Paul cautioned Timothy to take his time in appointing an elder and to make sure he was not pulled into the sins of others (v. 22).

Paul interrupted his chain of thought in writing with a personal message for Timothy in verse 23. Paul told Timothy to add a little wine to his water to help with his stomach issues and his frequent illnesses.

Finally, he reminded Timothy that some sins are obvious from the beginning, but others will not surface until later (v. 24). He also pointed out that some

[3] Radmacher et al., 1604.

[4] Radmacher et al., 1604.

[5] Radmacher et al., 1604.

good works are obvious from the time they are done, while others won't become known until much later (v. 25).

Closing

Paul's advice for Timothy was for how to bring order within the body of Christ, how to enlist leaders, and how to treat the church's widows. In all situations, Paul reminded Timothy to treat the people in the church with respect, even when they needed discipline. In all he wrote, Paul's underlying concern was for the members of the congregation and for Timothy as their pastor.

The Daily Word

Paul advised his co-laborer Timothy as an older man pours into a younger man in the ministry, giving instructions on the characteristics for the church and the church's responsibility to care for widows and elders.

The heart of our heavenly Father is to look after His children. Specifically here, Paul discussed widows. God the Father has a caring and nurturing heart. As God's ambassador, you are called to care for widows. Take a minute to think about your community, your neighborhood, your family, or even your workplace. Ask the Lord how you can care for widows as a follower of Christ. Check in on them from time to time. Ask them to dinner. Mow their grass. Take them to doctors' appointments. Yes, it means going out of your way to care for someone else. Yes, it means setting aside your own agenda for someone else. But that is the heart of your heavenly Father! He loved you so you could unselfishly love and care for others. He will give you strength, wisdom, and joy as you trust Him to obediently care for widows. Open your eyes to see the widows in your life. It's what you are called to do.

Support widows who are genuinely widows. —1 Timothy 5:3

Further Scripture: Psalm 68:5; Ephesians 6:20; James 1:27

Questions

1. According to 1 Timothy 5, how important is it for children and grandchildren to take care of the widows in their families? How good of a job do you think we do at this today as a society? Whose job is it to take care of widows who have no family?
2. What did Paul say was best for younger widows and why?

3. In 1 Timothy 5:17, Paul said, "The elders who are good leaders should be considered worthy of an ample honorarium, especially those who work hard at preaching and teaching." Who was Paul talking about here? As the church, do we do a good job taking care of our leaders? Throughout Paul's letters to the different churches, he mentioned taking care of their leaders several other times (Galatians 6:6; 1 Thessalonians 5:12). Why do you believe he did this?
4. What are the stipulations for receiving an accusation against an elder of the church? Why is this important (Matthew 18:16)? In your opinion, do we hold our leaders accountable enough for their wrong actions in the church today? Do we give them too much grace or not enough grace?
5. What did the Holy Spirit highlight to you in 1 Timothy 5 through the reading or the teaching?

WEEK 81

Lesson 79: 1 Timothy 6

Our Mediator: Paul's Proverbs of Ministry

Teaching Notes

Intro

Paul's first letter to Timothy concludes with chapter 6, a chapter that has a military theme (1 Timothy 6:12). Paul urged Timothy to fight for the things that were important for the church in Ephesus, and he called Timothy to rise up against the false teachers and their teachings that were harming the Ephesian church. The message is still good for the church today. We need to fight for what we know to be true without backing down.

First Timothy 6 reads like a selection of Proverbs. Paul had multiple thoughts he wanted to make sure he shared with Timothy before he closed his letter.

Teaching

1 Timothy 6:1–2: Paul gives instructions for how slaves are to treat their masters because of their relationship with God. I don't know how to even address these verses because of the context of slavery. So, we'll just read what the Bible says and move through this. Wiersbe interprets this for today as believers showing respect for their bosses, regardless of whether those bosses deserve that respect.[1] Therefore, those who were slaves were required to show respect to those in authority, whether they were believers or not and to work harder for their brothers in Christ than for nonbelievers.

Constable explains, "Paul urged the adoption of proper attitudes toward others that would normally make it easier to produce proper actions. Christian slaves were to 'regard' their masters as worthy of all 'honor,' if, for no other reason, than that God had placed their masters in a position of authority over them."[2]

[1] Warren W. Wiersbe, *The Bible Exposition Commentary: Ephesians–Revelation* (Colorado Springs: David C. Cook, 2003), 224.

[2] Thomas L. Constable, *Expository Notes of Dr. Thomas Constable: 1 Timothy*, 117, https://planobiblechapel.org/tcon/notes/pdf/1timothy.pdf.

1 Timothy 6:3–10: Anyone who teaches false doctrines, who does not agree with the teachings of Christ, was conceited and had "a sick interest" in disagreements and verbal battles (vv. 3–4). *Nelson's Commentary* explains: "These false teachers were more interested in theory and debate than putting the truth into practice. They had a morbid desire to argue over words."[3] Paul explained the false teachers were driven by financial gain through their teachings (v. 5). Paul described them "deprived of the truth," meaning their arguments were useless.

In verses 6–7, Paul stresses finding contentment in Christ, not in material gain. Verse 7 refers to Job 1:21, reminding Timothy mankind is born with nothing and takes nothing with them when they die—except for the gift of eternal life through Christ. Nothing else lasts permanently. All that is necessary on earth to be content is to have essential needs met—food and clothing (v. 8) (Matthew 6:25–28, 34; Luke 12:25; John 14:27; Philippians 4:11–12). However, those who focus on gaining riches are open to temptations, traps, and foolish desires (v. 9a). This focus will plunge them into ruin and destruction (v. 9b). Is that temporary or eternal? *Nelson's Commentary* explains ruin and destruction as "ruin and irretrievable loss."[4] It continues: "This loss may be experienced in this life, as through a wrong purpose for living, or it may be experienced in the afterlife if material desires lead a person away from Christ."[5]

Paul explained the problem with these often-recited words: "For the love of money is a root of all kinds of evil" (v. 10a). Note Paul said the love of money is a root, not the root of evil. Money is not bad, but the love, the desire, the craving of money is the problem.

1 Timothy 6:11–16: Craving money can lead people away from Christ because their attention is taken from Him to the pursuit of riches. Paul instructed Timothy, as a "man of God," to run from the temptations and traps of money and wealth and to pursue the righteousness of God (v. 11). Paul instructed Timothy to "fight the good fight for the faith" and hold onto the things of God (v. 12). Paul told Timothy to flee from temptations (1 John 2:15–17), follow God's righteousness (Romans 7:18–25), and fight the good fight until Christ returns (v. 14) (2 Peter 3:10–16; 1 John 2:28). Paul reminded Timothy God would make things happen in His timing because He is God (v. 15). He is sovereign, immortal, and eternal (v. 16).

---

[3] Earl D. Radmacher, Ronald B. Allen, and H. Wayne House, eds., *Nelson's New Illustrated Bible Commentary* (Nashville: Thomas Nelson, 1999), 1605.

[4] Radmacher et al., 1606.

[5] Radmacher et al., 1606.

1 Timothy 6:17–19: Paul told Timothy to tell those who were rich not to be arrogant about their wealth or make it most important but to focus on God instead (v. 17). Timothy was to tell them to do what is good, to be generous, and to share what God had given them (v. 18), storing up the things of God that matter rather than the things of life that do not (v. 19).

1 Timothy 6:20–21: Paul returned to Timothy personally in the last verses of the chapter. Paul encouraged him to guard what had been entrusted to him, and to guard against using irrelevant and empty speech and contradictions that came from false teachings (v. 20). Paul emphasized the false teachings were so dangerous they had already pulled people away from God. He closed with a blessing that included everyone in the church in Ephesus: "Grace be with all of you" (v. 21).

Closing

Paul used four words that begin with F to give Timothy steps to follow:

1. *Flee* from temptations
2. *Follow* God's righteousness
3. *Fight* the good fight
4. Remain *Faithful* to God and His teachings.

We are to do all of this until Jesus comes back.

The Daily Word

So many worldly things fight for your attention, your love, and your focus: beauty, sports, fame, money, success, knowledge, trends, social media influence . . . you name it. They continue to add up but still leave you feeling as though you don't have enough. And then the lie creeps in that *you* are not enough.

God says to flee from these harmful desires, cravings, and love for things of this world. They can skew your mindset and draw you away from the Lord. Paul instructed Timothy to run from these things and follow God by pursuing righteousness, godliness, faith, love, endurance, and gentleness. Keep it simple—*run from the worldly things and pursue God.* As you intentionally abide in God's love day after day, you will hunger to know Him, you will desire to look like Him, and you will enjoy the things of the Lord more than the things the world offers you. You will find satisfaction in Him, and strength will arise for the spiritual battle you fight daily. The enemy is fighting to be your first love. But press on and stand firm in your faith in the Lord. Run away from worldly things and pursue God.

Victory comes with Jesus by your side as you fight the good fight for the faith. Walk in that promise today.

But you, man of God, run from these things, and pursue righteousness, godliness, faith, love, endurance, and gentleness. Fight the good fight for the faith; take hold of eternal life that you were called to and have made a good confession about in the presence of many witnesses. —1 Timothy 6:11–12

Further Scripture: Jeremiah 29:13; 1 Timothy 6:6; James 4:7

Questions

1. In 1 Timothy 6:1–2, Paul spoke of relationships between slaves and their masters. What relationship could this be compared to today? Why is important for us to respect those in authority over us (Exodus 22:28; Acts 23:5; Romans 13:1; Titus 2:9)?
2. What was Paul warning believers against in 1 Timothy 6:3–5 (Romans 16:17–18; 2 Timothy 3:8)?
3. First Timothy 6:6 says, "Now godliness with contentment is a great gain." How content are you with what God has given you? Do you seek after more things or more of God?
4. According to Paul, is it a bad thing to have money? Think about this in the context of 1 Timothy 6:7–10. Was Paul saying money in itself is a bad thing? What instructions did Paul give to the rich people (1 Timothy 6:17–19)?
5. In 1 Timothy 6:12, what did Paul mean in, "Fight the good fight for the faith" (2 Timothy 2:2–4; 4:7–8; Hebrews 12:1–2)?
6. What did the Holy Spirit highlight to you in 1 Timothy 6 through the reading or the teaching?

Lesson 80: 2 Timothy 1

Righteous Judge: Be Not Ashamed of the Gospel

Teaching Notes

Intro

Today begins our study of Paul's second letter to Timothy. In 1 Timothy, we saw how Jesus is *Our Mediator*. In 2 Timothy, Jesus is presented as the *Righteous Judge* (2 Timothy 4:8). Because of Jesus' death and resurrection, we are victorious. Through Him, we can receive the crown of righteousness. In our study on 1 Timothy, we learned Timothy's name means, "one who honors God."[1] He was brought up in the Word of God by his mother Eunice and his grandmother Lois. His father was Greek and was probably not a believer (Acts 16:1). Timothy was from the city of Lystra, which was a Roman city in Galatia (which is now Turkey). Paul traveled through Lystra on his first missionary journey (Acts 14:6–23), met Timothy there, and probably led Timothy to Christ, and he became Paul's "dearly loved son." On his second journey, Paul visited Lystra again and chose to take Timothy with him on the rest of his journey (Acts 16:1–3).

MacArthur outlines the relationship of Paul and Timothy, stating, "Timothy was to be Paul's disciple, friend, and co-laborer for the rest of the apostle's life, ministering with him in Berea, Athens, Corinth, and accompanying him on his trip to Jerusalem."[2] During Paul's first imprisonment in Rome, Timothy was with him and stayed with him until Paul was released. Timothy then went to Philippi. Timothy also served as Paul's representative, visiting many of the churches Paul started. At the time of 1 Timothy, Timothy was serving as pastor to the Ephesian church (1 Timothy 1:3).[3] Hebrews 13:23 states that, at some point, Timothy was put in jail and later released.[4]

Paul wrote 1 Timothy and Titus shortly after he was released from his first imprisonment in Rome (AD 62–64).[5] Paul wrote 2 Timothy during his second

[1] John MacArthur, *The MacArthur Bible Commentary* (Nashville: Thomas Nelson, 2005), 1772.

[2] MacArthur, 1772.

[3] MacArthur, 1772.

[4] MacArthur, 1772.

[5] MacArthur, 1801

imprisonment (AD 66–67) and shortly before his execution. During his second imprisonment, Paul had little hope he would be released (2 Timothy 2:9; 4:6–8, 13), and he wrote Timothy to give him his final words of advice and encouragement.[6] MacArthur compares these two periods of imprisonment for Paul:

> Unlike Paul's confident hope of release during his first imprisonment (Philippians 1:19, 25, 26; 2:24; Philemon 22), this time he had no such hopes. In his first imprisonment in Rome, before Nero had begun the persecution of Christians (AD 64), he was only under house arrest and had opportunity for much interaction with people and ministry (Acts 28:16–31). At this time, five or six years later (c. AD 66–67), however, he was in a cold cell (2 Timothy 4:13), in chains (2 Timothy 2:9) and with no hope of deliverance (2 Timothy 4:6).[7]

Within the letter, Paul gave Timothy six exhortations: (1) remain faithful in his work (2 Timothy 1:6); (2) teach and live by strong doctrine (2 Timothy 1:13–14); (3) avoid mistakes (2 Timothy 2:15–18); (4) accept he would face persecution for his faith (2 Timothy 2:3–4; 3:10–12); (5) remain confident in God's Word; and (6) preach God's Word without ceasing (2 Timothy 3:15—4:5).[8] Paul wanted Timothy to remain strong in his faith and in his calling.

Teaching

2 Timothy 1:1–12: Wiersbe summarizes these voices as courageous enthusiasm.[9] Paul expressed his call to the ministry (v. 1), his love for Timothy (v. 2), his prayer support for Timothy (v. 3), his joy in his relationship with Timothy (vv. 4a, 5), and his desire to see Timothy (v. 4b). Paul seemed to be acknowledging he was not experiencing that joy while imprisoned the second time and longed to be with his beloved son in Christ.

Having joy is important in the Bible. Robert Driskell gives seven things that are important to know about joy: "Worldly joy is fickle and temporary" (Job 20:5, 18); "in the Old Testament, joy was associated with the true worship of God" (1 Chronicles 15:16; Ezra 3:12; 6:16); "joy is a gift from God" (Galatians 5:22); "doing God's will increases our joy" (2 Corinthians 1:24; 2:3; Philippians 1:4; 2:2); "circumstances cannot take away our joy" (2 Corinthians 6:10; 1 Peter 4:13); "the only thing that can steal our joy is sin"; and "Christians should always

---

[6] MacArthur, 1801.

[7] MacArthur, 1801.

[8] MacArthur, 1801.

[9] Warren W. Wiersbe, *The Bible Exposition Commentary: Ephesians–Revelation* (Colorado Springs: David C. Cook, 2003), 240.

rejoice" (1 Thessalonians 5:16–18).[10] C. S. Lewis stated, "Joy is the serious business of heaven."[11] Paul longed to experience that joy with Timothy.

In verse 6, Paul encouraged Timothy to continue to use ("keep ablaze") the gifts he had received from God. The picture Paul made was that he was sitting in his cell, reviewing his ministry, and remembering a holy time when he and others laid hands on Timothy to commission him for ministry (v. 6). General Booth of the Salvation Army said, "The tendency of fire is to go out; watch the fire on the altar of your heart. Anyone who has tended a fireplace fire knows that it needs to be stirred up occasionally."[12] The laying on of hands is seen throughout Scripture for blessing, healing, and consecration (Numbers 27:18; Mark 10:16; Luke 4:40; Acts 8:17; 1 Timothy 5:22; Revelation 1:17).

Paul then reminds Timothy that fearfulness does not come from God, but power, love, and sound judgment do (v. 7). Paul explains his own situation and tells Timothy not to be ashamed of him in prison or who Timothy is in Christ (v. 8); for Christ has rescued us (saved us) from death and punishment (the process of justification) and called us into a holy calling to be set apart for Him (vv. 9–10). Paul again reviewed his own calling as a herald, apostle, and teacher, and reminds Timothy he suffered because of these callings (vv. 11–12).

2 Timothy 1:13–18: Paul reminds Timothy he had been given spiritual authority and was to hold on to the strong doctrinal teaching he had received (v. 13). Paul reminds Timothy they had shared the gospel for two years, with many converts. Yet all of those in Asia had turned away, including Phygelus and Hermogenes (vv. 13–15). However, Onesiphorus had not fallen away; he had visited Paul often in prison and was not ashamed of his chains (vv. 16–17). Paul prayed Onesiphorus and his family would receive God's mercy (v. 18).

Closing

This is 2 Timothy 1. We'll continue the story tomorrow.

---

[10] Robert Driskell, "Bible Study on Joy: 7 Things You Need to Know," What Christians Want to Know, https://www.whatchristianswanttoknow.com/bible-study-on-joy-7-things-you-need-to-know/.

[11] C. S. Lewis, *Letters to Malcolm: Chiefly on Prayer* (San Diego: Harvest, 1964), 92–93.

[12] Ralph Earle "2 Timothy," in *Ephesians-Philemon*, vol. 11 of The Expositor's Bible Commentary, ed. Frank E. Gaebelein and J. D. Douglas (Grand Rapids: Zondervan, 1978), 395.

The Daily Word

In Paul's final letter to Timothy, he encouraged Timothy to continue sharing the gospel of Jesus Christ with a spirit of power, love, and a sound mind, not being ashamed of his testimony from the Lord. Paul instructed Timothy to *rely on the power of God.*

As you seek to share the gospel, to live your life for Christ, to be bold in your faith, you may feel fearful, even embarrassed, ashamed, or awkward. Ask yourself: *Am I relying on my own strength and knowledge or fully relying on the power of God?* Imagine a water skier trying to stand up on the water. If the skier tries to force himself out of the water in his own strength and muscle, he'll never get up. But when the skier focuses on positioning his body, aligning his eyes to focus on the boat, and allowing the power of the boat for the strength, that's when he is successful to get up on the water.

In a similar way, as you share your testimony, keep your eyes and heart focused on the power from the Lord. Let go of your agenda and control. As you align yourself with the Lord, relying on the power of God, sharing the gospel will flow out from you supernaturally. Fear will fade away, and power will arise!

So don't be ashamed of the testimony about our Lord, or of me His prisoner. Instead, share in suffering for the gospel, relying on the power of God. —2 Timothy 1:8

Further Scripture: John 14:26; Philippians 4:13; 2 Timothy 1:7

Questions

1. In 2 Timothy 1:6, Paul told Timothy to "fan into flame" (ESV) his God-given gift. Do you have a similar experience? Whose responsibility is it to fan the flame? Are you walking out your gifting? If not, why?
2. We know the spirit of fear (2 Timothy 1:7) is from the enemy and that God gives us power, love, and a sound mind to combat it. Have you ever had a spirit of fear come over you? How did you handle it? Did you seek God for power, love, and a sound mind?
3. In 2 Timothy 1:14, Paul told Timothy to guard "that good thing entrusted to you." Guard from who or what?
4. What did the Holy Spirit highlight to you in 2 Timothy 1 through the reading or the teaching?

WEEK 81

Lesson 81: 2 Timothy 2

Righteous Judge: The Process of Discipleship

Teaching Notes

Intro

Every time I think of 2 Timothy 2, I think of a billboard I used to drive by in Charlotte, NC. The sign repeated, "Disciples making disciples making disciples . . ." and each time the word "disciples" was presented, it got a little smaller. That's what the Christian life is all about . . . disciples making disciples making disciples.

Remember that Paul was writing his last letter before his execution and it went to Timothy, his son in the faith. The letter contains his last teachings and encouragements to Timothy on how to continue his ministry. Wiersbe identifies seven different pictures of what a minister could look like in chapter 2: "the steward, the soldier, the athlete, the farmer, the workman, the vessel, and the servant."[1]

Teaching

2 Timothy 2:1–2: Paul told Timothy to be strong in the grace that Christ had shown him (v. 1). Paul then instructed Timothy to teach what he had been taught to those who would pass those teachings on to others (v. 2). This is a picture of stewardship through discipleship (1 Corinthians 4:17; 11:1). MacArthur explains, "Timothy was to take the divine revelation he had learned from Paul and teach it to other faithful men—men with proven spiritual character and giftedness, who would in turn pass on those truths to another generation."[2] We need faithful individuals to continue to communicate God's divine revelation to others. Timothy understood this instruction and followed it with urgency. He knew it was necessary and timely. Without doing this, false messages can infiltrate what is taught within the church.

Sadly, for many believers and even staff members, they have no idea where to start in this process, or they hesitate to start because they don't know what the

[1] Warren W. Wiersbe, *The Bible Exposition Commentary: Ephesians–Revelation* (Colorado Springs: David C. Cook, 2003), 244–48.

[2] John MacArthur, *The MacArthur Bible Commentary* (Nashville: Thomas Nelson, 2005), 1806.

outcome will be. Discipling someone takes major time. When we examine the lives of Paul, James, and John, ten keys become evident to us at Time to Revive:

1. *Pray.* Ask the Lord for a disciple (Mark 1:35–38).
2. *Look* for a disciple that the Lord has prepared, and discern if they are open (Mark 1:19).
3. *Call.* Reach out to the disciple; make initial connection (Mark 1:20a).
4. *Respond.* Positive or negative, the disciple will respond to the "call" in some form (Mark 1:20b).
5. *Relate.* "Do life" with the disciple; build intentional relationship (Mark 1:29–31).
6. *Establish.* Assist them in seeking God's purpose for their life (Mark 6:6b–13).
7. *Share.* Teach and work through hard Biblical truths together (Mark 10:35–45).
8. *Endure.* Model and assist the disciple in enduring hardships (Mark 14:32–36; Acts 12:2).
9. *Remain.* A disciple that remains in the Lord bears fruit (Acts 3:1–11).
10. *Replicate.* While the two continue in relationship, the disciple is able to carry out the great commission by finding someone to disciple, and the disciple-maker prays for a new disciple (Acts 4:3–4).

There is someone out there that God has already prepared for you to disciple. You've just got to find that person.

2 Timothy 2:3–10: I want to give you the rest of the pictures of the roles of the pastor that Wiersbe identified in the rest of chapter 2:[3]

- The Soldier (vv. 3–4, 8–13)
- The Athlete (v. 5)
- The Farmer (vv. 6–7)
- The Workman (vv. 14–18)
- The Vessel (vv. 19–22)
- The Servant (vv. 23–26)

In ministry and in discipleship, all of the roles come into play. At times, we'll take on all of them.

[3] Wiersbe, 244–48.

Closing

In order to make disciples, we must steward what we have been given. As we carry out the message of discipleship, the kingdom of God advances. The challenge for every one of us is to ask the Lord to show us who we are making disciples with. Ask Him, "who am I pouring into that is making disciples?" My hope is you have a chart and this chart is growing. If you don't have anybody, it's never too late to start. Begin by praying, start looking around, and be prepared to call someone to ask them if you can pour into their life. I thank Paul for this model, and my prayer is we can live this out as Paul challenged Timothy to do.

The Daily Word

When you hear the word "discipleship," what comes to your mind? Do you think, *I don't know how,* or *I don't have time for that,* or *that's only for people who work in the church*? Paul instructed Timothy to commit himself to discipling faithful men the things that Timothy heard from Paul. Paul desired for Timothy to continue to pass on the truth of the gospel to others.

Like Timothy, the Lord calls you to make disciples. Pray and ask the Lord *who* to pour into with the love of Christ. The Lord calls you to commit to faithful men and women who are willing to grow in their walk with the Lord. It may look like meeting for coffee once a week and intentionally discussing what you are learning in the Word, doing life together, and praying for one another. Discipleship is committing to a relationship with the purpose of spurring one another on to grow in your walk with Jesus Christ. Let go of all the "what ifs" and "I don't knows." Remember, the Holy Spirit gives you the power, strength, and wisdom. He will fill you up and equip you. Today, ask the Lord to lead you to someone to disciple.

And what you have heard from me in the presence of many witnesses, commit to faithful men who will be able to teach others also. —2 Timothy 2:2

Further Scripture: Matthew 28:19–20; John 1:45; Titus 2:3

Questions

1. Do you consider yourself to be a soldier? What about a soldier of Jesus Christ? In 2 Timothy 2:3, Paul told Timothy to suffer with him as a soldier of Jesus. Do you see yourself in this role? Why or why not?
2. How would you explain 2 Timothy 2:11–13 to an unbeliever? Do these verses make sense to you?

3. In your opinion, how can 2 Timothy 2:22 be done? How can a person pursue righteous living, love, faithfulness, and peace? Do you enjoy time spent with like-minded believers? Do you think you do that enough?
4. What did the Holy Spirit highlight to you in 2 Timothy 2 through the reading or the teaching?

Lesson 82: 2 Timothy 3

Righteous Judge: Continue in God's Truth

Teaching Notes

Intro

As we continue with our study in 2 Timothy, we will specifically look at a verse in the Word of God toward the end of the chapter. I wonder what we are passing on to the next generation. Dalton Thomas said:

> The last words we have from Paul before he lost his head for the Gospel are an admonition to his own beloved, adopted son in Christ to live into his own promises and purposes determined by the Author [Creator]of his days . . . the book of 2 Timothy is what spilled out of Paul's pen when he knew he had reached his numbered days' end. The stakes were not low for Paul and they wouldn't be for Timothy. Paul had discipled this young leader; he did not simply 'share the Gospel' with him, or even stop at sharing his life with Timothy. He entrusted the Gospel with him. And he knew the Lord was about to remove him from Timothy's life for the rest of this age. We are all responsible for our own lives in God, but Timothy was about to feel the absence of his "father." As the aged apostle weighed how to word his final letter, Paul challenged his young "evangelist" from Ephesus with perhaps unexpected words: "Son, soldier up."[1]

Teaching

2 Timothy 3:1–5: In verse 1, Paul used the phrase "But know this" to get Timothy's attention for the long term. "Difficult times" can also be translated "perilous," meaning a hugely stressful situation. That word is used only one other time in the New Testament in Matthew 8:28 when Jesus met the two demon-possessed men in Gadarenes. "In the last days" is a broad New Testament term and refers to the now, because Jesus initiated the last days. Peter announced it as fulfillment of prophecy that began at Pentecost (Acts 2:17). It has been used about the final judgment (John 6:39–40, 44, 54; 11:24; 12:48). It is especially appropriate for

[1] Dalton Thomas, *Pilgrim Field Journal*, vol. II (Frontier Alliance International's Annual, 2019).

the season immediately before Jesus' return. For Christians in the United States today, we do not think much about the coming of Christ. We get tired of waiting and concerned with other things, so this chapter is a challenge for us.

The reason Christians will be persecuted in troubled and perilous times grows out of the distorted values of the people around and among them. In verses 2–5, Paul identifies 20 characteristics of people who often unintentionally (due to their blindness) and sometimes intentionally, create a climate of trouble for those who take Jesus seriously. In this list, Paul used compound words for "love"—*philos* love, not agape. These people love people or things—a misdirected love. These people are also lovers of self. The biblical roots of this self-love are found in the encounter with Satan in the Garden when he told Adam and Eve to go ahead and eat so they would be like God. Love of self is the basic sin from which all others flow. The moment a man makes his own will the center of life, divine and human relationships are destroyed, and obedience to God and charity to men become impossible.

The love of money is not new, but it is easier today to pursue our love for money (v. 2). The characteristics of boasting, pride, and blasphemy each show that the individual considers himself or herself more important than anyone else. As you read through the list, each shows a characteristic about love of self. Pastor David Guzik said, "We don't have to choose between pleasure and God. Serving God is the ultimate pleasure"[2] (Psalm 16:11). We do not have to choose between the love of pleasure and the love of God. Living for God will give you many pleasures, but only as you love God first and refuse to love the pleasures themselves. In verse 5, Paul points out those who are "holding to the form of godliness but denying its power." In our self-obsessed world, people feel free to have a salad-bar religion; they pick and choose what they want. They want to feel spiritual but don't care about being biblical. Paul said to avoid these people! Paul explains why in verses 6–8.

2 Timothy 3:6–9: In verses 6–7, Paul describes these dangers. Paul knew these dangers were in the world in his day and would be increasingly present in the last days before Christ's return. He seemed especially concerned that they would creep into households—it is one thing to have such evil present in the world and another to allow it into our homes. Note that the idolatry of misdirected love is tragic; when it becomes evangelistic, the trouble multiplies. There's caution there for us as well: in our homes, on our TVs and computers (Deuteronomy 6:4–9). Verse 7 describes people who hear, even repeatedly hear, good sermons, but they don't meditate on those words or apply what they hear. Guzik wrote:

---

[2] David Guzik, *1–2 Timothy, Titus, Philemon* (Santa Barbara, CA: Enduring Word Media, 2013), n.p.

One should know if they are indeed one of these captives that Paul mentioned, bound by the influence of this end times rejection of God and celebration of self. There is one effective way to know: walk away from any king of worldly influence and see if there are chains that make your escape difficult. Take a week off from letting anything marked by the spirit of the last days into your household—and see if chains bind you back to those things.[3]

Verses 8–9 explain that Jannes and Jambres resisted Moses and therefore also resisted the truth. These names were never given in the Exodus account, but Jewish tradition holds that they were Egyptian magicians who opposed Moses before Pharaoh, even matching Moses' miracle for miracle for part of the time (Exodus 7:8–13, 19–23; 8:5–7, 16–19). Even as Jannes' and Jambres' power had limits, so does Satan's power. Even in the last days, God is still in control.

2 Timothy 3:10–12: In verse 10, Paul began to talk about struggles in the Christian life. He began, "But you," showing that Timothy was not like those he had been discussing. Timothy "followed" what he had been taught, meaning he modeled it and lived out Paul's example. Paul then reminded Timothy of the specific persecutions he endured at Antioch (Acts 13:50), at Iconium (Acts 14:5), and at Lystra (Acts 14:19) (v. 11). Paul emphasized that all who live in Christ will be persecuted (v. 12). Read that again. Oswald Chambers wrote, "An average view of the Christian life is that it means deliverance from trouble. It is deliverance *in* trouble, which is very different."[4] Rich Mullins said, "Never forget what Jesus did for you. Never take lightly what it cost Him. And never assume that if it cost Him His very life, that it won't cost you yours."[5] Persecution must not stop Christians today.

2 Timothy 3:13–16: Those who deceive will become worse. Evil people are obvious while imposters are not (v. 13). Henri Nouwen said, "The many disasters in our world, and all the tragedies that happen to people each day, can easily lead us to despair and convince us that we are the sad victims of circumstances. But Jesus looks at these events in a radically different way. He calls them opportunities to witness!"[6] For Timothy, he had been taught to know the difference and to live in the lifestyle of Christ, no matter what (vv. 14–15). The important thing is to

---

[3] Guzik, n.p.

[4] Oswald Chambers, "The Discipline of Difficulty," My Utmost for His Highest (website), August 2, https://utmost.org/classic/the-discipline-of-difficulty-classic/.

[5] Rich Mullins, "Lufkin, Texas Concert Transcript," Carpenter's Way Christian Church, July 19, 1997, http://www.kidbrothers.net/words/concert-transcripts/lufkin-texas-jul1997-full.html.

[6] Henri Nouwen, "Opportunities to Witness," Henri Nouwen Society, September 10, 2018, https://henrinouwen.org/meditations/opportunities-to-witness/.

abide and continue in those, and to never let them go. Timothy had been taught the Old Testament through his mother and grandmother. He knew the teachings of Christ. Those were the things he was to continue. That is the context for verse 16: "All Scripture is inspired by God and is profitable for teaching, for rebuking, for correcting, for training in righteousness, so that the man of God may be complete, equipped for every good work." "Inspired by" literally means "breathed out by God," and this is the only time it's used in the Bible (2 Peter 1:20–21). "All scripture" includes more than just the Old Testament. Paul changed his wording here because he recognized that what God uniquely brought forth from the apostles and prophets in Paul's time was also the God-breathed Word of God.

Closing

Remember that it is possible to believe in the inspiration of the Bible in principle but deny it in practice. Vast Bible knowledge and regular church attendance won't do much if your attitudes and actions are not Christlike.

The Daily Word

Do you ever feel unequipped for the path the Lord has called you to? Perhaps you wish someone would hold your hand and guide and help you along your way? Timothy must have felt this way as Paul warned him about the difficult times ahead: growth of deception, increasing lack of godliness, and certainty of persecution.

Paul reminded Timothy he was equipped for these difficult days. In the same way, *you are equipped.* You have all you need in the Word of God because *all Scripture is profitable for teaching, rebuking, correcting, and training in righteousness so that you may be complete and equipped for every good work.* Therefore, read Scripture every day. Seek the Lord for wisdom while studying God's Word. Discuss it with friends. As you press on to know the Lord, He will *equip* and *empower* you to be ready and will *give you everything required for the work He calls you to.* You don't need to fear hard or troubling times, because the Lord, your loving Shepherd, promises to never leave you. Today, spend time in the Word so you will be equipped and complete for the journey ahead.

All Scripture is inspired by God and is profitable for teaching, for rebuking, for correcting, for training in righteousness, so that the man of God may be complete, equipped for every good work. —2 Timothy 3:16–17

Further Scripture: 2 Timothy 3:12–14; Hebrews 13:20–21; 2 Peter 1:3

Questions

1. Do you think we are in the last days? What are some indicators? (2 Timothy 3:1–5)
2. What do you think it means to have a "form of godliness, but denying its power"? What power is being denied? (Luke 5:17; 24:49; Romans 15:19; 1 Corinthians 2:5; 4:20)
3. Why will the men Paul wrote about, who oppose the truth, not get very far? (2 Timothy 3:9)
4. According to 2 Timothy 3:12, what will all who desire to live a godly life in Christ Jesus face? Does this scare you or prepare you for what is to come?
5. What did Paul say in 2 Timothy 3:15 that the Holy Scriptures are able to do? In verses 16–17, what is stated as the source of all Scripture, and how is it profitable to us?
6. What did the Holy Spirit highlight to you in 2 Timothy 3 through the reading or the teaching?

WEEK 83

Lesson 83: 2 Timothy 4

Righteous Judge: A Well-Lived Life

Teaching Notes

Intro

As we close out our study of Paul's second letter to Timothy, I think Paul was anxious to make sure Timothy understood Paul's passion for the word of Christ. Paul wanted to make sure his baton would be picked up and carried by those who followed him. This letter contains Paul's last words, as well as his testimony of a life well lived. My prayer for you is that you will one day be able to look back at your life and know that you too have lived your life well for Christ.

Second Timothy holds a special place for the church. Four words (one from each chapter) sum up Paul's instructions for Timothy. In chapter 1, Paul encouraged Timothy to HOLD FAST to the message against the worldly culture that did not support his message. In chapter 2, Paul told Timothy to BE STRONG, because he had been given the message that Paul held dearer than anything else. In chapter 3, Paul told Timothy to BE AWARE of what is coming in the end times and how to prepare for it. In chapter 4, Paul told Timothy to GO ON with the calling he had received. Paul wanted Timothy to go on and do what he had been prepared to do.

Teaching

2 Timothy 4:1–5: Paul was given the responsibility for overseeing the organization of the church and carrying on the message of Christ. The apostle John will later receive the responsibility of the apocalyptic message of the end times. In verse 1, Paul charges his son in the faith with taking on the role Paul had been fulfilling. Read John 16:7–8. Jesus said that when He went away, the Holy Spirit would come and reprove (bring back to the center; redefine) sin, righteousness, and judgment. Let's break down verse 2 some, with John 16 as our background. Paul told Timothy to:

- *Preach* (publish and proclaim openly the word)
- *Be Ready in Season* (be ready to take the opportunity whenever it comes)

- *Out of Season* (even when it's not convenient)
- *Exhort* (*para-ka-leo*, the work of the Holy Spirit who comes alongside)
- *With All Long Suffering* (consistency and patience)
- *Doctrine* (instruction)

All of us who are born again are born of the Spirit. Holy Spirit is within us and working in us. He will reprove me of sin and judge the things in me according to the standard of righteousness. All Holy Spirit does is testifies of Christ. I have been reproved within, that will come forth to the world, because it is Christ that is in me. Back to verse 2, be consistent even when you do not feel like it. Be ready when it is convenient and when it is not convenient. When Holy Spirit is working in us, it will be easy to bring it to others, both in encouragement and caution. We will start naturally bringing people out of the judgment of sin and into the path of life. Paul tells Timothy to hold fast and walk it out in straightness.

Paul said there would come a day when people would not tolerate sound doctrine but rather go their own self-focused way after their own lusts (v. 3a). They will find teachers that teach new ideas and what the people want to hear (for their itchy ears) (vv. 3b–4). There is meant to be a right and a wrong, a black and a white, without gray. But they will prefer to turn away from the truth and accept stories of fiction instead.

Paul admonished Timothy:

- *Watch* (sober, calm, and collected) all things
- *Endure* afflictions (be willing to suffer)
- *Do* the work of the evangelist by speaking out the message (Matthew 28:18–20)
- *Make* full proof of his ministry and don't hold back. Keep going until it's over by being persuaded and persuasive (v. 5).

God's design is that everything He created will produce fruit. Fruit in ministry is found in those who can pick up the baton and take it the next stage of the race—this is discipleship.

2 Timothy 4:6–8: Paul shared he was ready to be offered (poured out as a drink offering, consumed) and that the time of his death/departure (in the day this meant loosing the moorings of the ship) was at hand (v. 6). Paul said he had fought a good fight (he had contended/argued for the truth), he had finished his course (he had accomplished his mission), and he had kept the faith (he had held carefully to the truth) (v. 7). I see tear stains on this part of his letter. This was so real for Paul. Paul said that because of this, he knew there was a crown of righteousness (stephanos crown—Revelation 4:10), which the Lord would give him when he reached heaven. Paul points out that he will not be the only one that receives that crown, but that all those who look for Christ's return will receive it as well (v. 8).

2 Timothy 4:9–15: Paul's final instructions begin in verse 9. He asks Timothy to do his best to come to him soon. Paul's time was short, and he wanted to see Timothy again for several reasons (v. 9). Paul said that Demas had already turned away from both Paul and Christ and left for Thessalonica. Also, Paul had sent Crescens to Galatia and Titus to Dalmatia (v. 10). Paul was alone with Luke, so he asked Timothy to bring John Mark with him as well. Paul looked to John Mark to help with his ministry (v. 11). Paul said he had also sent to Tychicus to Ephesus. Paul asked Timothy to bring the cloak he left in Troas with Carpus and his parchments (vv. 12–13). Paul said Alexander the coppersmith (1 Timothy 1:20) had also done evil to him and had not been true to the faith after all (vv. 14–15).

2 Timothy 4:16–22: Paul told Timothy he had faced his first defense hearing alone except for the Lord who strengthened him to preach the word so the Gentiles could hear (v. 16–17a). Through the strength of the Lord, Paul had been delivered out of the mouth of the lion (his imprisonment in Rome).

Paul prayed the Lord would deliver him from every evil work and preserve him for God's kingdom (v. 18). Then Paul sent greetings to Prisca, Aquila, and the household of Onesiphorus, and also gave Timothy an update on Erastus and Trophimus (vv. 19–20). There is no information in Scripture to who Eubulus, Pudens, Linus, and Claudia were (v. 21). In verse 21, Paul begs Timothy to come to him before winter. Paul concludes with the blessing, "The Lord be with your spirit. Grace be with you" (v. 22).

Closing

I'm sure Paul did not want to end his letter with "amen" because he knew he would one day see his son Timothy, whether on the earth or in God's kingdom to come.

The Daily Word

As Paul's time on earth neared the end, he never gave up and continued to proclaim the good news of Jesus so others would hear. Paul fought the good fight, he finished the race, and he kept the faith. Paul poured his life out as a drink offering for the sake of the gospel. Paul shared a promise from the Lord in his final words to his disciple, Timothy, *Even when everyone deserted me, the Lord stood with me, the Lord strengthened me, and the Lord rescued me.*

Following Christ may be lonely, scary, and tiring as you press on, hold on, and go on sharing the gospel while living your life on the narrow path. However, even when friends turn their backs, when evil and temptations come your way, even when hardships and heartaches arise, *the Lord will stand with you. The Lord will strengthen you. The Lord will rescue you.* Dear friend, it is worth the cost to live for the sake of Jesus Christ. So even when you look around and see no one standing near, *do not fear.* The Lord is standing near. He hasn't left your side, and He will bring you safely into His heavenly kingdom. Go on . . . fight the good fight, finish the race, keep your faith, and share the good news!

But the Lord stood with me and strengthened me, so that the proclamation might be fully made through me and all the Gentiles might hear. So I was rescued from the lion's mouth. The Lord will rescue me from every evil work and will bring me safely into His heavenly kingdom. To Him be the glory forever and ever! Amen. —2 Timothy 4:17–18

Further Scripture: Isaiah 41:10; Mark 16:15; 2 Timothy 4:6–7

Questions

1. In 2 Timothy 4:2, what things did Paul charge Timothy to do? In whose presence did he do this? What is meant by calling Christ Jesus the one who is "going to judge the living and the dead" (John 5:28–29; Acts 10:42; 2 Corinthians 5:10; 2 Timothy 4:1; 1 Peter 4:5)?
2. Paul warned Timothy that a time would come when people would not put up with sound teaching. What will they turn to in its place? Give an example of someone like this you have met or seen.
3. In 2 Timothy 4:5, Paul encouraged Timothy to endure hardship. Paul mentioned hardship, suffering, and persecution multiple times in this letter to Timothy (2 Timothy 1:8, 12; 2:3, 9; 3:11–12; 4:5). Why do you think he brought it up so many times?
4. When Paul was defending himself against the attack by Alexander the coppersmith, the Lord strengthened him so he was able to preach to the Gentiles. Have you looked for opportunities to share the gospel in the midst of adversity and attacks? If so, share an example with your group.
5. What did the Holy Spirit highlight to you in 2 Timothy 4 through the reading or the teaching?

WEEK 82

Lesson 84: Titus 1

Savior: God Our Savior

Teaching Notes

Intro

This is another letter from Paul to an individual, Titus, who was then in Crete, an island in the Mediterranean Sea. Titus was mentioned thirteen times in the New Testament. Paul wrote the letter while he was journeying through Macedonia between his imprisonments in Rome (AD 62–64). This was probably his fourth missionary journey but took place after Luke had ended the book of Acts. Therefore, Titus was written between 1 and 2 Timothy from either Corinth or Nicopolis.[1] According to Titus 3:13, the letter was delivered by Zenas the lawyer and Apollos.

Possibly Paul led Titus to faith either before or during his first missionary journey. When Paul was being taken to Rome for his first imprisonment, they briefly landed at Crete. Paul later returned to Crete after he was released from prison and took Titus with him to minister at Crete. Paul left Titus there to continue the ministry when he moved on. Paul later sent either Artemas or Tychicus to carry on the ministry there so Titus could join him in Nicopolis for the winter (Titus 3:12).[2] Titus is mentioned in 2 Corinthians where Paul called him "my brother" (2 Corinthians 2:13) and "my partner and coworker" (2 Corinthians 8:23). Paul always seemed to be looking for the gifts converts had, so he knew where they would fit best in ministry. Titus was aware of the false teachers in the church and even accompanied Paul and Barnabas to the Council of Jerusalem (Acts 15) to address the subject of false teachings.[3]

Paul, an apostolic leader, left both Timothy and Titus in places to continue ministries he had started. Although Paul left both areas, he continued to pour into both young men through his letters and his prayers. It is a wonderful model of ministry. Paul wrote to Titus in response to a letter he had received, from either Titus or someone else in Crete, sharing what was happening in Crete. MacArthur

[1] John MacArthur, *The MacArthur Bible Commentary* (Nashville: Thomas Nelson, 2005), 1817.

[2] MacArthur, 1817.

[3] MacArthur, 1817.

points out that Paul's letter did not include anything on doctrine because he was confident in Titus' "theological understanding and convictions."[4] Instead, Paul warned Titus about the false teachers in Crete. Sadly, many of the believers in Crete would have been young, immature believers, because the ministry there was so new. MacArthur describes the situation in Crete: "In order to gain a hearing for the gospel among such people, the believers' primary preparation for evangelism was to live among them with the unarguable testimony of righteous, loving, selfless, and godly lives (Titus 2:2–14) in marked contrast to the debauched lives of the false teachers (Titus 1:10–16)."[5] The work in Crete was especially difficult because the people there were "always liars, evil beasts, lazy gluttons" (Titus 1:12–13).

Acts 2:11 states people from Crete were at Pentecost and spoke out in the Holy Spirit. Maybe this is how the gospel of Christ first came to the Cretans. Paul must have known that the Holy Spirit had already reached Crete. The Holy Spirit had gone before Paul.

Teaching

Titus 1:1–4: In verses 1–2, Paul brought greetings and stated his calling was to build up the faith in godliness and truth in the eternal hope that God had promised. He could be certain of that calling because God cannot lie. In fact, the first recorded discipline that God took on the early church was for lying to Him, Ananias and Sapphira (Acts 5:3). In 1 Timothy 4:1–2, Paul said the later times will have those who depart from the faith, deceitful spirits and teachings of demons, "through the hypocrisy of liars." God does not—cannot—lie! Paul acknowledged he had been entrusted with God our *Savior*'s revealed message (v. 3). As New Testament believers, we don't typically acknowledge God as *Savior*, but that is the entire thread of the Old Testament. For that reason, the theme for Titus is *Savior.* God is *Savior*, who saved us through the work of His Son on the cross. Salvation is nothing that we do for ourselves. We have been justified (made right) through Christ. We are all sinners, and we are saved by Christ's death on the cross. The letter to Titus has a huge theme of God as *Savior*.

Titus 1:5–9: In verses 5–9 Paul gave the characteristics needed for elders. These include: (1) having faithful children; (2) being the steward of God; (3) not self-willed or arrogant; (4) not easily angered; (5) loving what is good; (6) righteous; (7) holy; (8) self-controlled; and (9) holding to the faithful message of Christ. This list is a little different from the list in 1 Timothy 3.

---

[4] MacArthur, 1817.

[5] MacArthur, 1818.

Titus 1:10–16: In verses 10–16, Paul warns about false teachers, including what they were like and why they taught falsely.

Closing

Paul closes the letter with this warning about false teachers: "They profess to know God, but they deny Him by their works. They are detestable, disobedient, and disqualified for any good work" (v. 16). We too must watch for false teachings and false teachers because we have been saved and made holy through God our *Savior.*

The Daily Word

Paul wrote to encourage Titus, who was serving on the island of Crete. Paul described the people of Crete as detestable, disobedient, and disqualified for any good work. They professed to know God, but they denied Him by their works. The Lord called Titus to rebuke them and encourage them to remain strong in their faith.

Ever feel like Titus? As you live your life for the Lord, do you feel surrounded by people who say they believe in God with their lips, but their actions and words display something different? If the Lord has led you to this place, *rest assured that the Lord will strengthen you with the wisdom needed to care for those around you.* Be a light as you live your faith authentically. Share about the Lord's grace and mercy in your own life. Open up about your struggles and temptations and testify about the power of the risen Savior. His power gives strength when your flesh is weak. His power gives hope when your spirits are down. His power provides for your needs when you have nothing. Today, pray for those who profess to know God but whose words and actions do not affirm the same. May the power of God in your life encourage others to live their lives for Him.

They profess to know God, but they deny Him by their works. They are detestable, disobedient, and disqualified for any good work. —Titus 1:16

Further Scripture: Isaiah 29:13; Mathew 15:8; Titus 1:5

Questions

1. Was Titus a Jew or a Gentile (Galatians 2:3)? Just as he did Timothy, Paul called Titus "my true son" in the faith (1 Timothy 1:2; Titus 1:4). What do you think is meant by this?

2. Why did Paul leave Titus in Crete? What qualifications was Titus looking for in appointing elders in every town?
3. How were the false teachers in Crete much like those Timothy had to deal with in Ephesus (1 Timothy 1:3–7)? How was Titus to respond to false teachers (Romans 16:17–18)?
4. How did Paul say that false teachers were corrupt or defiled (Matthew 15:15–20)? Have you seen anything in your lifetime that validates Titus 1:15–16?
5. What is the danger of saying you know God while not living in obedience?
6. What did the Holy Spirit highlight to you in Titus 1 through the reading or the teaching?

WEEK 82

Lesson 85: Titus 2

Savior: Sound Teaching and Christian Living

Teaching Notes

Intro

The letter to Titus is a fascinating letter about how to live out faith. Paul told Titus that he had been sent to Crete to make a difference in the lives of those Cretans who were known for their lies and evil ways. Demorest describes it as "a beautiful summary of everything contained in the Pastoral Epistles."[1]

Teaching

Titus 2:1–5: Paul told Titus to teach differently from those he described in chapter 1. While the false teachers taught legalism and fables, Titus was to teach sound doctrine in order to fulfill Jesus' Great Commission (Matthew 28:19–20). It is the height of hypocrisy to say we believe the truth of the Bible if we ignore how it tells us to live our lives. Oswald Chambers wrote, "Beware of harking back to what you were once when God wants you to be something you have never been."[2]

The Greco-Roman world in which Paul lived had two age categories—young and old.[3] That's very different from the way our culture divides people into myriad generational divisions (such as: Gen Z and Millennials). These two divisions were used to set forth responsibilities in groups already recognized. Paul told older men to be levelheaded and worthy of respect (v. 2). They were to be leaders/ examples to the younger people in the congregation. Paul said they must live with the maturity and wisdom that their years should give them. The older men should be sound in faith, love, endurance, and hope (1 Thessalonians 1:3). The word "endurance" means steadfast and active, not passive waiting. "Older men

[1] Gary Demarest, *The Communicator's Commentary: 1, 2 Thessalonians, 1, 2 Timothy, Titus* (Waco, TX: Word, 1984), 311.

[2] Oswald Chambers, "What Next," My Utmost for His Highest (website), June 8, https://utmost.org/classic/what-next-classic/.

[3] Demarest, 311.

are not to just patiently wait around until they pass on to the next world. They are to actively endure the challenges of life; even the challenges of old age."[4]

Older women were to be reverent in their behavior and teach what is good to encourage younger women in godliness in their homes (vv. 3–4). "In the same way" means there was no difference between what was expected of older men and women. The phrase "reverent in behavior" can be understood as priests carrying out their duties. The older women were to see their entire lives as worship to God (Romans 12:1). The word for slanderers is the same word used for devils. That means that when the older women—or anyone else for that matter—slander and gossip, they do the devil's work. Drinking too much wine was a common failing of older women in Roman and Greek cultures. Paul described it with the verb *doulo*, which meant "bondage" (RSV interpreted it as "slaves to drink") (v. 3). Note that Paul told Titus to teach older and younger men, older women, and slaves, but not young women. Titus was to equip and encourage the older women to teach the young women (v. 4). Paul told the older women to love their husbands and their children because God had given them a strategic position of influence and assistance to their husbands and children. They were to let love dominate their influence and assistance. Keep in mind the submission here is mutual, biblical submission (Ephesians 5:21–33). When Christians don't live in a biblical, godly manner, the Word of God may be slandered among those who do not know the Lord.

Note that the importance of a good wife and mother never changes. However, this context is different. In Crete, young women had no option about marriage and motherhood; the only employment for a young woman outside the home was as a prostitute.[5] Paul was not limiting a woman's place to being a slave to her husband but was rather addressing them where they were at that time. Demorest explains the people coming to Christ saw themselves as all part of one body:

> "For people raised in culture where women were regarded as inferior and treated like chattel—and slavery was normative—the Christian view introduced an entirely different way of living, of thinking. That this would change the outward forms of the community has been validated in history. But we must understand the tension created by the gospel in this and other areas of human relationships . . . early Christians wrestling with how to relate their new relationship of freedom in Christ to the oppressive structures of the world around them."[6]

---

[4] David Guzik, "Titus 2—Teach Them How to Live," Enduring Word, https://enduringword.com/bible-commentary/titus-2/.

[5] Demarest, 315.

[6] Demarest, 315–16.

Titus 2:6–8: Paul addressed younger men "in the same way," with the requirements for them (v. 6). It shows that the young men need to learn what the younger women, the older women, and the older men need to learn. Paul gave one command to be emphasized to younger men ("to be self-controlled in everything"), a challenge for some younger men. Further, Paul told Titus to be a good example (a role model) to the younger men through his good works, integrity, and dignity in teaching (v. 7). His guidance could not be taken seriously if he was not pursuing the Lord.

Titus 2:9–10: Paul said the slaves were to be submissive to their masters, well-pleasing, respectful, and honest, showing their faithfulness to the teaching of God. Although this passage historically has been used to justify Christians having slaves, that is contrary to Paul's intent. Paul's message was directed to slaves who were Christians living out the Christian lifestyle even while being despicably used as slaves. He presented freedom in Christ to the culture of the day when it was commonplace with both Greeks and Romans to own slaves. In the ancient world, Christians shocked the larger culture by mixing slaves and masters in the social setting of the church service. My sense is, Paul believed the change in following Christ would eventually overthrow slavery throughout the world. Demorest noted that "it is the prerogative of the slave to choose to submit—even to injustices—if by so doing the Gospel can be attractively adorned."[7]

Titus 2:11–14: These verses give the gospel in one paragraph. God brings salvation for all people. God doesn't have a gospel of grace for some and a gospel of law or self-justification for others (v. 11). God's grace pushes godlessness and worldly lusts into our pasts, and teaches us to renounce and avoid them (v. 12). We live in the interim between the two appearances of Christ—giving us the opportunity to live in anticipation and knowing that our days are numbered (v. 13). Of verse 14, Guzik wrote, "Every word of this description of Jesus' work is important."[8] Jesus gave (which was voluntary) Himself (everything He could give) for us (as a substitute for sinful man). In this sense, we can learn how dear and precious we are to Christ because of what He willingly did for us—a people of His own possession. We are His treasure above all other treasures. Paul spelled out that one thing will always characterize the special treasures of God—the eagerness (or zealousness) to be bright witnesses to the truth of God's love and saving grace.

---

[7] Demarest, 320.

[8] Guzik.

Titus 2:15: One day, the righteous, saving reign of God shall no longer be a matter of faith but of full sight (v. 15). And so the church of every age prays, "Amen! Come, Lord Jesus!" (Revelation 22:20).

Closing

Jesus is coming back, and we have a mission because of that. We are to be engaged in the ministry, not observers. What areas in your life would you want to see improved if you knew for sure that Jesus is coming back soon? Because of the grace of God, the followers of Jesus Christ are set on living a life that is energetic in goodness, and in their daily experience they live looking for His return (Titus 2:13). We get so confused and panicked by the arguments and events that we have forgotten that the *Savior* has purified for Himself a special people, expecting that we will eagerly live a life worthy of the call we have received, looking for the glorious appearing of our great God and *Savior*.

The Daily Word

Paul told Titus to continue to instruct, encourage, and rebuke with authority while remaining consistent to the sound teaching of the gospel of Jesus Christ. Paul reminded Titus, *it is only because of the grace of God, through His Son Jesus, that you and I are redeemed from all lawlessness and cleansed as God's people.* Because of the grace and mercy they received, it encouraged others to eagerly do good works for the world to see.

God calls you to speak this consistent gospel message, encourage others, and rebuke with authority from the truth of His Word. You have a responsibility to remain true to the call, to remain pure, to remain honest, and to take time to encourage young women and young men. As you live your life for Christ, open your eyes to see people around you. Share the truth consistent with sound teaching. Always encourage others. As the Spirit moves in your heart, ask the Lord for His timing to rebuke when necessary. Today, be eager to do this good work because of the love you first received from Jesus. May His great love motivate you as you go out in His name.

He gave Himself for us to redeem us from all lawlessness and to cleanse for Himself a people for His own possession, eager to do good works. Say these things, and encourage and rebuke with all authority. Let no one disregard you. —Titus 2:14–15

Further Scripture: Matthew 28:19–20; 2 Timothy 4:2; Titus 2:1

Questions

1. What did Paul admonish the older men and the older women to do? Do you see this happening in your church?
2. What did Paul ask Titus to encourage the young men in the church to do?
3. What were the three common sins slaves must avoid (Ephesians 6:5–8)? Is it possible to obey in action but not from the heart (Ephesians 6:6)? How does the term slave or bondservant apply to us as believers (1 Corinthians 7:22)?
4. What two appearances of Christ did Paul mention in Titus 2:11–13?
5. What instructions did Paul give on how to live a life after salvation? How do we accomplish living this way (John 14:16; 15:5)?
6. What did the Holy Spirit highlight to you in Titus 2 through the reading or the teaching?

WEEK 82

Lesson 86: Titus 3

Savior: Basic Church Instruction

Teaching Notes

Intro

Before we start on our Bible study, I want us to think about the background of this passage. First, Paul referred to Titus in this book with the same term of endearment that he used with Timothy—"mine own son" (1 Timothy 1:2; Titus 1:4 KJV).

Second, I want us to think about the island of Crete. As Kyle points out in Titus 1, there were believers, who had been a part of Pentecost, on Crete before Paul arrived there. Paul's work in the mission of the church came years after Pentecost. Also, the people on Crete had their own island culture. The people of Crete were called "lazy." Typically islands don't have a lot of industry but rather rely on tourism. For someone coming out of a faster-moving culture, the island culture would have seemed much slower and lazy. Because of shipping goods and transporting passengers by water, many people would have gone through Crete in their travels. The people traveling through could have helped promote the growing church in Crete, and took the Word from there on to other places.

All this just shows how incredible the letter to Titus is, because in three short chapters, Paul covered the work and organization of the church, as well as the full gospel message. This had to have been part of the whole divine strategy of building on the people going through Crete. Today, no one would go there in passing because they would fly over it on their journey. Yet God knows how to reach every generation!

Teaching

Titus 3:1: Paul begins the chapter with instructions for the ministry of the church. He told Titus that believers were to subject themselves before principalities and governmental powers and to obey the judges so they would be ready to do good work (v. 1). Don't be distracted by principalities and powers (Romans 8:38; Ephesians 1:21; 3:10; 6:12; Colossians 1:16; 2:10, 15). The word for rulers (*archae*), could refer to either human leaders or spiritual leaders. Obviously, here in Titus 3, these are human. Typically, in an island nation, you'll find a lot of people doing their own thing, and governmental authority is not a big deal. But Paul countered that, because God's way expects us to be subject to the people who are over us.

Titus 3:2: Paul told them to not speak ill of anyone but to be gentle and show meekness to all people. Paul's instructions meant believers are not to be obstinate. We should be those who contribute to the well-being of community. We should be hands to help those who are in need. We get along with people and use the "faith difference" as an opportunity to do good, not as a divider between us.

Titus 3:3: Paul knew what the Cretans had been called, and he responded to that by describing who he and other believers had been before Christ: foolish, disobedient, deceived, having diverse lusts and pleasures, living in malice, envy, hate, and hating one another. Paul's point is that when we realize where we have come from, surely we have hope for others.

Titus 3:4–7: Verse 3 was the before-Christ picture. Verses 4–7 give the after-Christ picture. We received the kindness and love of God our *Savior*, and because of His great mercy, He saves us through regeneration and the renewing of the Holy Spirit (vv. 4–5). God's mercy was abundantly given to us through Christ our *Savior*, justifying or making us right before God so we could be His heirs having eternal life (vv. 6–7).

Titus 3:8–11: Paul repeated that believers were to devote themselves to good works (v. 8). Paul said this is what believers should be known for because it is a good testimony and peaceable lifestyle. Paul said they were to avoid (turn away from) foolish questions (worthless debate) and genealogies, contentions (the talk of differences), and strivings or disputes about the law. These are unprofitable to the church and vain for the individual—they are useless and serve no godly purpose (v. 9). Paul then said to reject a divisive person (a heretic) after two warnings because that person is perverted, sinful, and self-condemned (vv. 10–11). Think of the impact the island culture could have on the church. Many islands have a subculture of voodoo or witchcraft or special beliefs that could easily have been pulled into the island church if they did not turn away the divisive heretic.

One definition of a heretic is: *one who takes truth and speaks it out of balance of what it is meant to do*. Truth out of balance is heresy. Quite simply, that means taking a truth from the gospel and adding requirements and expectations to it that the Bible did not give it. Sometimes we need to look past the words someone is saying to the heart of what they are saying.

Titus 3:12–15: Paul ended with final instructions to Titus. He told Titus he would send Artemas or Tychicus to take his place in Crete so he could join Paul in Nicopolis for the winter (v. 12). Paul then asked Titus to help Zenas and Apollos on their journey (give them financial support) so they would have everything they needed (v. 13). Paul also repeated to Titus that the people were to devote themselves to good works to meet urgent needs so they would be fruitful (v. 14). Finally, Paul sent Titus greetings from all those who were with him and asked Titus to give his greetings to the believers in Crete as well (v. 15).

Closing

I think the book of Titus is often overlooked or unappreciated. I have often overlooked it because I focused on Timothy. But now, I wonder what God's call on us is today. I wonder who is already in a strategic position that God will use to present His gospel.

"God, use us. You've already sent us, so give us an understanding of what You want us to do for You."

The Daily Word

Every believer has a story of Christ's love and redemption changing his or her life. *Your story of God's saving grace can encourage others on their journeys.* Paul encouraged Titus to live his life through the power of the Holy Spirit with kindness and gentleness. Paul not only poured this truth into Titus, he then challenged Titus to diligently pour into others, like Zenas and Apollos, on their own journeys. The Lord also calls you to share your journey with others.

Pray and ask the Lord for someone you can diligently pour into and help on their journey with Christ. They may have a different occupation from you, they may have a different calling, but one thing remains the same: You are *all* called to live for Jesus through the power of the Holy Spirit. God wants you to live in community and diligently help one another pursue Christ. Don't isolate yourself. Pray and ask the Lord to bring someone into your life to help. The Lord hears your prayers and will answer you. *Just start praying.* Remember, as you pursue Christ, He promises to provide help along the journey.

Diligently help Zenas the lawyer and Apollos on their journey, so that they will lack nothing. —Titus 3:13

Further Scripture: 2 Corinthians 5:17; Titus 3:3–5; James 1:4

Questions

1. As you read Titus 3:1–3 and 9–10, do you see anything that you need to work on for right living as a Christian? How can you begin to do this?
2. How do you see all three persons of the Trinity working together in Titus 3:4–6? Do you see and feel this in your life on a daily basis?
3. In Titus 3:5, what does the phrase, "through the washing of regeneration and renewal by the Holy Spirit" mean? Is it necessary to be baptized in order to be saved (Luke 23:39–43; Act 2:21; Ephesians 2:8–9)? Why do some verses in the Bible such as Mark 16:16 and Matthew 28:19 seem to contradict the above referenced verses? How do you explain this to an unbeliever or a newly saved Christian? Read James 2 to help you with this.
4. What did the Holy Spirit highlight to you in Titus 3 through the reading or the teaching?

WEEK 82

Lesson 87: Philemon

Master: Redemption and Restoration

Teaching Notes

Intro

So, this is our 537th lesson, and our 40th book of the Bible. Our goal in this two-year study is to encourage learners to identify where they see the Messiah in every book of the Bible. The book of Philemon is the shortest of Paul's letters; 25 verses, and it is only about three people. In this letter Paul was pleading with a friend on behalf of a third person. Our word for Philemon is *Master*, and it comes from Philemon 1, in which Paul referred to himself as a prisoner or "bondservant," and his *Master* was Christ. In Matthew 23:10, Jesus said; "And do not be called masters either, because you have one *Master*, the Messiah."

The book of Philemon is a story of redemption and forgiveness. Paul wrote the letter between AD 60–62, about the same time he wrote Colossians. Paul and Philemon met probably in Ephesus, and Paul led Philemon to Christ there (v. 19). Philemon was a wealthy man (the church met at his house) (v. 2) and a slave owner with at least one slave, Onesimus, whose name means "useful." Onesimus ran away from his master, Philemon, and made it all the way to Rome where he met Paul and was converted. Possibly Onesimus stole something from Philemon to help him pay for his expenses to Rome. Paul grew to love Onesimus and wanted Onesimus to stay with him in Rome, but Onesimus had broken Roman law by running away. Paul sent Onesimus back to Colossae with a letter for Philemon. Paul sent Tychicus as protection for Onesimus as well as to deliver Paul's letter to the church there.[1]

Wiersbe explains, "If a slave ran away, the master would register the name and description with the officials, and the slave would be on the 'wanted' list. Any free citizen who found a runaway slave could assume custody and even intercede with the owner. The slave was not automatically returned to the owner, nor was he automatically sentenced to death."[2] It is estimated that 60 million slaves were

[1] John MacArthur, *The MacArthur Bible Commentary* (Nashville: Thomas Nelson, 2005), 1826.

[2] Warren W. Wiersbe, *The Bible Exposition Commentary: Ephesians–Revelation* (Colorado Springs: David C. Cook, 2003), 270.

in the Roman Empire, and one could be bought for 500 denarii to 50,000 denarii, depending on the slave's qualifications and skills. Onesimus found freedom in the Lord—he became redeemed and forgiven. Paul knew Onesimus' past, and that Onesimus had been changed by Christ.[3] Wiersbe describes Paul's relationship with Onesimus as "the beloved friend . . . the beseeching intercessor . . . the burdened partner."[4] I think Paul sent Tychicus with Onesimus so he could vouch for the changes in Onesimus' life, just as people had to vouch for Paul after he met Christ on the road to Damascus.

Teaching

Philemon 1–7: Paul began with greetings to Philemon, Apphia, Archippus, and the congregation meeting in Philemon's home (vv. 1–3). *Nelson's Commentary* points out that in verses 4–7, Paul established "the basis for the plea in a commendation of Philemon."[5] Paul explained that he always thanked God for Philemon because of his love for the Lord and "for all the saints" (vv. 4–5). Paul then said he prayed Philemon's "faith may become effective" through good works that are the acknowledgement of what Christ has done in the believer's life (v. 6). Paul's statement meant he understood that Philemon's faith was strong and that he walked out that faith in his life.

Philemon 7–8: Remarkably, Paul acknowledges his own great joy and the encouragement he received through Philemon's love, even while still imprisoned (v. 7). In verses 7–8, Paul made his first appeal to Philemon: because of who Philemon was in Christ and the love he had shown to Paul, Paul could boldly appeal to him. Paul was building Philemon up by letting him know that he was of value to Paul and to the church in Colossae. Paul stressed he had the authority to command Philemon to do what he wanted him to do but that he would not do that. His appeal was for Philemon to do the right thing.

Philemon 9–11: Paul's second appeal was made on the basis of love (v. 9a). To strengthen his appeal, Paul played the sympathy card and pointed out that he was an elderly man (which meant he was 55 years old or older) and was in prison because of his faith (v. 9b).[6] Paul next appealed to Philemon for "my son, Onesimus" whom he fathered (led to Christ) even while he was in chains (v. 10)

[3] MacArthur, 1826.

[4] Wiersbe, 270–71.

[5] Earl D. Radmacher, Ronald B. Allen, and H. Wayne House, eds., *Nelson's New Illustrated Bible Commentary* (Nashville: Thomas Nelson, 1999), 1630.

[6] Thomas L. Constable, *Expository Notes of Dr. Thomas Constable: Philemon*, 13, https://planobiblechapel.org/tcon/notes/pdf/philemon.pdf.

(1 Corinthians 4:15). Paul's fourth appeal was that Onesimus had been useful to him, just as he would now be useful to Philemon (v. 11).

Philemon 12–16: Paul explains how Onesimus was valuable to him: he was a part of Paul now; and he was help to Paul while imprisoned (vv. 12–13). Paul then said he respected Philemon so much that he wouldn't have kept Onesimus with him without Philemon's permission (v. 14). Paul didn't want to force Philemon to do something but instead wanted Philemon to make the right decision as a believer of the Lord Jesus Christ. In verse 15, Paul suggests the separation of Philemon and Onesimus might have been the divine providence of God so that Onesimus would have the opportunity to become a believer and return to Philemon for eternity,[7] not as a slave but as a brother in Christ (v. 16).

Philemon 17–19: Therefore, Paul asks Philemon to accept Onesimus as he would accept Paul (v. 17). He then offered to repay anything Onesimus owed Philemon (v. 18). The word for this is "imputation," or "charge that to my account." Robert Gromacki says, "Paul's offer is a beautiful illustration of biblical forgiveness based on imputation (Romans 5:13; 2 Corinthians 5:21)."[8] Paul points out he wrote the letter himself with his own hand, making the letter a legal contract between them (v. 19a). Paul promised to pay Onesimus' debt, but also reminded Philemon that he owed a debt to Paul for his salvation (v. 19b).

Philemon 20–25: Paul asks Philemon to "refresh my heart in Christ" (v. 20). Paul then told Philemon that he was so confident Philemon would do the right thing, that he knew Philemon would do even more than he had asked him to do (v. 21). Meanwhile Paul asked Philemon to prepare the guest room for him because he hoped he would be able to visit (v. 22). Paul closes with more greetings: from Epaphras, a fellow prisoner who was well known in Colossae, and from Mark, Aristarchus, Demas, and Luke (vv. 23–24). He concludes with blessing Philemon with the grace of the Lord (v. 25).

Closing

Nelson's Commentary provides six "big lessons for a little letter" in Philemon:

1. In Christ there is always the opportunity for reconciliation and second chances.

---

[7] Wiersbe, 271.

[8] Robert G. Gromacki, *Stand Perfect in Wisdom: An Exposition of Colossians and Philemon* (Grand Rapids: Baker Book, 1984), 200–201.

2. God works to bring people to saving faith and restored relationships with others.
3. The gospel can work at any distance—from one city to another and one continent to another.
4. There is true value in older believers mentoring younger believers in Christ.
5. The fact Onesimus had to go so far away to hear about Jesus shows the "irony behind God's patience and providence."
6. "In Christ, people can change."[9]

The point is, will you submit your life to the *Master*?

The Daily Word

While in prison, Paul witnessed Onesimus, Philemon's runaway slave, give his life to Christ. Therefore, Paul wrote a letter to his friend and fellow believer, Philemon, requesting he grant freedom to Onesimus as a slave, since they were now brothers in Christ. Paul understood the big picture of God's grace, explaining *perhaps* God allowed Onesimus to go to prison, *so that* he'd receive the gospel and become a dearly loved brother in Christ.

If you trust God as your Master in life and live fully submitted to Him, then He promises to work all things together for good. Even if you end up in prison, even if you go through a health crisis, or even if you give in to the temptation to sin. Yes, these times bring difficulty and pain, but *perhaps* you go through them *so that* you can return, no longer a slave to the world, no longer a slave to sin, but as *a brother or sister in Christ.* Free from sin. Free from bondage. Free to dance in the grace and victory found in Jesus. *Perhaps this is why.* With Christ as your master, fully surrendered to Him, you can see all things work together for good. Today, ask yourselves: *What is my "perhaps this is why" moment?* God is a God of providence. Live surrendered to His will so you can find grace and victory in the midst of each situation.

For perhaps this is why he was separated from you for a brief time, so that you might get him back permanently, no longer as a slave, but more than a slave—as a dearly loved brother. He is especially so to me, but even more to you, both in the flesh and in the Lord. —Philemon 1:15–16

Further Scripture: Psalm 103:19; Romans 6:22; 8:28

[9] Radmacher et al., 1631.

Questions

1. Why did Paul write this letter to Philemon, and where was he when he wrote it?
2. According to the book of Philemon, what kind of person was Philemon? Who was Onesimus, and why was Paul asking him to be reconciled to Philemon at this time?
3. What would you say is the main theme of Philemon? How does this speak to you?
4. Have you ever had a dispute or a difference with a person who was not a believer and stopped associating with him because of it only to be reconciled with after he became a believer? Why do you think this is important?
5. What did the Holy Spirit highlight to you in Philemon through the reading or the teaching?

Contributing Authors

Dr. Kyle Lance Martin

Kyle Lance Martin is the founder of Time to Revive, a ministry based in Dallas, Texas, whose mission is to equip the saints for the return of Christ. His heart's desire, aside from loving his wife and four kids, is to engage people with the Word of God directly in their own environment. Kyle believes when people turn to the Messiah in humility and have a willingness to walk in the Holy Spirit, they can know and experience the calling of being a disciple of Jesus Christ. Kyle received his master of biblical studies from Dallas Theological Seminary and his doctor of ministry in outreach and discipleship from Gordon-Conwell Theological Seminary.

Pastor Gordon Henke

Gordon Henke is a pastor from northern Indiana, serving the church for 25 years. His passion is the studying of the Word. With confidence in the truth of the Word, he passionately helps people boldly share their faith.

Pastor Tom Schiefer

Tom Schiefer is the senior pastor of Nappanee First Brethren Church in Nappanee, Indiana. Prior to accepting a call to pastoral ministry, he was a band and choir director in Ohio. In the context of these two careers, he loves to orchestrate the Word of God, and the message it contains, into harmony with people's lives.

Pastor Fred Stayton

Fred Stayton is the lead pastor of Sonrise Church in Fort Wayne, Indiana, and has a passion for turning the hearts of fathers back to their children. Fred and his wife, Cheryl, have six children and one grandchild.

Ryan Schrag

Ryan Schrag is the national director for Time to Revive and has a heart to "equip the saints for the return of Christ" in the United States. Prior to joining full-time ministry, he was formerly the owner/operator of a lawn care business.

Wesley Morris

Wesley Morris is the Georgia state chairman for Time to Revive. A former construction worker turned pastor, he now trains and equips people to encounter Jesus and boldly share their faith.

Josh Edwards
Josh Edwards is the Minnesota state chairman for Time to Revive and leads worship both nationally and internationally. For the past 20 years he has been leading worship and speaking to the body of Christ about his heart's desire to see the church united, revived, and equipped to do the work of the ministry.

Shawn Carlson
Shawn Carlson is the executive director for Time to Revive. He has a strong desire to see people grow closer to Jesus through the study of God's Word and the carrying out of His mission.

Matt Reynolds
Matt Reynolds is the president of Spirit & Truth, a ministry aimed at equipping believers and churches to be more empowered by the Spirit, rooted in the truth, and mobilized for the mission. After serving as a local pastor for 13 years, Matt responded to a missionary calling to pursue Spirit-filled renewal in the church.

Larry Hopkins
Larry Hopkins is a businessman and entrepreneur in Dallas, Texas, who loves studying and discussing God's Word. He has a heart for revival, which stems from his love and desire for the Bible.

Pastor Kyle Felke
Kyle Felke is a former pastor in northern Indiana. He grew up in a home where both parents were teachers, which instilled in him a passion for teaching. This, combined with a love for Jesus, led him to pursue a biblical education and pastor a church in northern Indiana.

Contributing Authors

The Pentateuch
Kyle Lance Martin

The Gospels
Kyle Lance Martin
Josh Edwards
Ryan Schrag
Matt Reynolds

The Historical Books
Kyle Lance Martin
Wesley Morris
Josh Edwards
Pastor Gordon Henke
Pastor Tom Schiefer
Pastor Kyle Felke
Larry Hopkins

Acts
Kyle Lance Martin
Pastor Gordon Henke
Pastor Tom Schiefer
Wesley Morris
Shawn Carlson

The Wisdom Books
Kyle Lance Martin
Pastor Gordon Henke
Pastor Tom Schiefer
Wesley Morris
Ryan Schrag
Pastor Fred Stayton
Shawn Carlson
Josh Edwards

Paul's Letters
Kyle Lance Martin
Pastor Gordon Henke
Pastor Tom Schiefer
Wesley Morris
Shawn Carlson
Josh Edwards
Ryan Schrag

The Major Prophets
Kyle Lance Martin
Pastor Gordon Henke
Pastor Tom Schiefer
Pastor Fred Stayton
Ryan Schrag
Josh Edwards

General Letters
Kyle Lance Martin
Pastor Fred Stayton
Shawn Carlson

The Minor Prophets
Kyle Lance Martin
Josh Edwards

Revelation
Kyle Lance Martin
Pastor Gordon Henke
Pastor Tom Schiefer

www.ingramcontent.com/pod-product-compliance
Lightning Source LLC
LaVergne TN
LVHW010942100826
845153LV00002B/119
* 9 7 8 1 6 3 2 0 4 1 0 5 0 *